STUDIES ON
CANADIAN LITERATURE
Introductory and
Critical Essays

Edited by
Arnold E. Davidson

The Modern Language Association of America
New·York   1990

© 1990 by The Modern Language Association of America

For information about obtaining permission to reprint material from MLA book publications, send your request by mail (see address below), e-mail (permissions@mla.org), or fax (646 458-0030).

Library of Congress Cataloging-in-Publication Data
Studies on Canadian literature : introductory and critical essays /
    edited by Arnold E. Davidson.
        p.   cm.
    Includes bibliographical references and index.
    ISBN 0-87352-199-4 ISBN 0-87352-380-6 (pbk.)
        1. Canadian literature—History and criticism. 2. French-Canadian
    literature—History and criticism. I. Davidson, Arnold E., 1936–
    PR9184.6.S77   1990
    810.9′971—dc20   90-6529

A version of "Writing and Reading 'Otherwise': Québec Women Writers and the Exploration of Difference" is reprinted by permission of the author, Karen Gould, from *Writing in the Feminine: Feminism and Experimental Writing in Quebec,* © 1990 by Board of Trustees, Southern Illinois University.

2nd printing, 2004

Published by The Modern Language Association of America
26 Broadway, New York, NY 10004-1789
www.mla.org

CONTENTS

III

ACKNOWLEDGMENTS

THE EDITOR WISHES, first, to thank the contributors for their efforts. A collective venture such as this cannot work without an unusual degree of cooperation. I would like to thank, too, the Canadian Embassy in Washington, DC, for a Faculty Research Grant that helped defray the costs of manuscript preparation; the Canadian Studies Centre at Michigan State University as well as Kobe Jogakuin Daigaku (Kobe College, Japan) for support during the initial stages of editing this volume; and the Canadian Studies Center at Duke University for assistance during the final stages.

INTRODUCTION

VARIOUS SIGNS CAN signify the arrival of a national literature on the international stage. For some time now Canadians have been certain that the country has produced a distinctive literature. More recently, much of the rest of the world has also begun to take notice. Canadian studies (in its various aspects) is now taught in many countries, and many of those countries have their own academic associations to foster further Canadian studies. Books by Canadian authors are being read outside Canada in greater numbers than ever before. Early in 1989, to single out a notable (if not exactly representative) example, two of the top ten titles on the *New York Times Book Review*'s list of best-sellers were Canadian novels. O strange new world! Margaret Atwood and Robertson Davies up there with Danielle Steel, Sidney Sheldon, Tom Clancy, Jack Higgins, and Robin Cook. Indeed, on the listing to which I refer (26 Feb. 1989, p. 40), the only serious literary novels included among the top ten were *Cat's Eye* and *The Lyre of Orpheus*. The nearest United States equivalents, Anne Tyler's *Breathing Lessons* and Larry McMurtry's *Anything for Billy*, came eleventh and twelfth.

If I am perhaps making too much of something as transitory as one week's best-seller list, it is partly because for many years the predominant United States attitude to Canadian literature could be summed up in an old Hollywood adage (recounted by W. J. Keith in his introductory overview of English-Canadian literature in this volume): boy meets girl in New York and we have a story; boy meets girl in Winnipeg, and who cares? But now encounters in places as obscure as Manawaka, Manitoba, or Hanratty, Ontario, have generated a certain international notice, and significant literary action can take place even there and even if readers are not always sure just where "there" is.

As a Canadian who has taught Canadian literature in the United States for many years and who has, on two occasions, taught and lectured on that subject in Japan, I am well aware of the pitfalls facing anyone who sets out to introduce a new subject to the uninitiated while at the same time attempting to do justice to its complexities. Yet the distinctive essays collected in this volume describe not only why many Canadians care about books set, sometimes, in Winnipeg but also why those who continue to maintain smugly imperial attitudes toward the literature of the country north of the continental United States are overlooking a major contemporary literary phenomenon.

The essays in the present collection need only brief introduction, largely because each speaks for itself, in a distinctive and sometimes even delightfully idiosyncratic voice. My working editorial principle in assembling these pieces has been determinedly laissez-faire. By this I mean that, from its conception, when I first approached the Modern Language Association about the possibility of the volume, I envisioned an assemblage that, in its critical representation, would be almost as diverse and as multivocal as Canadian-Québec literature itself. The subtext of this collection (or, less grandiosely, the ruling assumption of its editor) is that any significant literature, as well as the critical discourse about it, resists simplistic categorization, so even those operative adjectives *Canadian* and *Québec* are necessarily deployed in diverse linguistic, political, and ideological senses.

Canadian critics will recognize immediately (and those not familiar with Canadian critical discourse are here referred to the essays by Barry Cameron and Barbara Godard) that the editorial position of the volume is, at least implicitly, a reaction to the thematic criticism that dominated Canadian literary studies in the late sixties and early seventies. While thematic criticism afforded many valuable insights (and inspired a number of essays in the present volume—including, to a certain extent, my own), in general it attempted to answer definitively one unwieldy question: What is intrinsically and distinctively *Canadian* about Canadian literature? This volume emphasizes that the answer to that question is no longer simple, if ever it was. The many styles, attitudes, ideologies, positions, perspectives, voices, tones, preferences, peeves, values, vendettas, hobbyhorses, obsessions, and mere likes and dislikes of English-Canadian as well as Québec or native or ethnic authors and critics—not to mention the different works in different genres produced by these authors—cannot be totalized, even in an introductory volume such as this, where the temptation to create a unifying narrative is always great.

Yet this volume *is* intended primarily for those who might possess considerable critical sophistication yet relatively little actual knowledge of Canadian-Québec literature or critical discourse. With this envisioned readership in mind, I asked the noted scholars who generously contributed to the book to remember that many in our audience may be well outside the usual circle of Canadian-Québec allusion, unfamiliar with historical developments, critical controversies, current social and political questions. To contextualize was the mandate. And to come up with a descriptive rather than an evocative title so that the reader could browse at will in the volume. Except for those very basic editorial guidelines, the individual contributors were free to write in their own styles, highlighting what they thought was important.

Narratives, as Jean-François Lyotard has emphasized, legitimize or delegitimize particular issues or concerns. The chief "narrative" set forth by this volume as a whole is conveyed by its overall structure: eight essays on Canadian writing in English; eight essays on Canadian writing in French; four essays that cross and conjoin that linguistic divide (Philip Stratford's comparatist approach; Robin McGrath and Penny Petrone's analysis of native literatures outside the dominating languages of either English or French; Lorna Irvine and Paula Gilbert Lewis's pedagogical modeling of both literatures; the novelist-poet-critic Robert Kroetsch's poststructuralist musings on postcolonialism and, of course, on post–thematic criticism). Annotated bibliographies (subdivided again, and not always discretely, into Québec and English-Canadian sections) conclude the volume by directing the reader to other discussions of the many subjects introduced or alluded to. The bibliographies following individual essays will also point the reader—specialist or new student of Canadian literature—to many further sources.

This volume is designed not to be read cover to cover, like a single-author monograph, but, rather, to be browsed through or to be consulted for specific information or overviews of specific aspects of Canadian literary studies. It might be assigned in a Canadian studies class or, even better (see Irvine and Lewis), in an American studies class. It could obviously be used in a comparative literature context or in courses of various critical and theoretical orientations, Canada providing a test case for numerous current literary concerns such as questions of periodization and canonization or considerations of ethnicity and gender or assessments of the intersections between political structures (such as cultural imperialism) and literary form.

In essence, Canada provides a North American experiment different from the one regarded as definitive ("manifest") by most residents of the United States. Yet just what this difference is remains difficult to define. The following essays implicitly or explicitly worry that question. But, more important, individually and collectively, the essays represent mappings of what will probably be, for most readers, a new literary territory. It is territory just across the border yet, as Kroetsch reminds us, "reading across a border" also has a way of changing the mapped place we know as home.

AED

W. J. Keith

THIRD WORLD AMERICA: SOME PRELIMINARY CONSIDERATIONS

> Canadian-American relations sounds like a dull subject, and it is, unless you've ever tried explaining them to an American.
> Margaret Atwood, *Second Words*

I

THE WELL-KNOWN TWAYNE series of critical studies is divided into three sections: American, British, and World. From a New York or Boston perspective, this may appear natural enough; from Toronto or Vancouver (and, I suspect, from Montréal), it seems bizarre. While there may be something attractive about seeing Canadian authors grouped with the great writers from non-English-speaking countries, their segregation from the two mainstreams of literature in English is troubling. Besides, "World" insistently suggests "Third World," though it is difficult to be sure whether this thought derives from an uneasy, even neurotic, sense of Canadian inferiority or from a shrewd assessment of subconsciously imperialistic attitudes of the United States. (One remembers the famous headline that is supposed to have appeared in a London newspaper at a peak of British imperial power: "Fog in English Channel: Continent Cut Off.")

For many years Canada has chafed under a sense of Third World status in cultural affairs, especially vis-à-vis our southern neighbor. Only recently have Canadian authors begun to appear with any regularity in the big anthologies of literature in English designed for freshman college teaching. Hitherto, we had seemed beyond the pale, and even now representation suggests merely token recognition, the grudging acknowledgment of a minority group's existence.[1] Still more recently, however, Canadians have begun to recognize the unexpected advantages in this equivocal status. Readers in other countries, we find with some surprise, are increasingly interested in a view of the world that is North American and yet different from that of the United States (see Kroetsch and Nischik; Stanzel and Zacharasiewicz). Moreover, there is evidence, of which the present book forms part, that Canadian literary achievements are even arousing attention on the other side of the famous undefended border.[2]

Before Americans can fully appreciate Canadian writing, however, they need to become conscious of the subtly different perspective out of which this writing emerges. Indeed, one fundamental problem built into the Canadian experience can be conveniently illustrated from my previous sentence. I referred there to "Americans," but what I meant, of course, was "citizens of the United States." Oddly, there is no proper noun or adjective available (if we except the ambiguous and somewhat derogatory "Yankee"). The usual distinction between "Canadian" and "American" (which, for convenience and for want of any other solution that is not hopelessly cumbersome, I shall continue to employ) is troubling on the northern side of the border, since Canadians are both at once. The general assumption that an American comes from the United States is properly offensive to most thinking Canadians.

Another of the facts of life that a Canadian has to accept is the awkward truth that Canadians need to acquire at least an elementary knowledge of the United States, whereas most Americans can spend their whole lives in blissful ignorance of Canada. Too often the word *Canada* appears to conjure up no more than an image of total and perpetual snow or the origin of distinctive brands of whisky and ginger ale. (In the 1960s, of course, Canada was also known as a convenient place to escape the Vietnam draft.) A persistent rumor circulates in Ontario that Americans regularly arrive at the border near Niagara Falls in midsummer with skis strapped to the tops of cars and show surprise at the absence of snow. This may be a myth, but the fact that such a myth can develop is itself significant. Indeed, Canadian myths about the States and American myths about Canada will need to be examined at various points throughout this article.

But first, a few personal anecdotes may be worth offering as representative examples of the frustrations that Canadians often experience in across-the-border situations. For some years I was editor of the *University of Toronto Quarterly* and received a considerable number of American submissions. I got used to the inclusion of return postage in United States stamps, though it seemed to suggest that, even in the minds of certain university professors, Canada was regarded as the fifty-first state. More disturbing was the regular receipt of articles referring to "our president" or "our House of Representatives" without any apparent awareness that such phrases would sound incongruous in a Canadian journal. Moreover, I am sorry to have to report (given the sponsorship of this volume) that, in the late 1960s, when the MLA was in a committed, active, and protesting mood, I was obliged to resign for political reasons. I objected to the imperialist implications of my being exhorted—and expected—to support resolutions that applied only to the United States and that were written by academics who seemed oblivious to the existence of any other "American" (let alone "North American") country with different attitudes and problems. As the Canadian writer Frederick Philip Grove remarked in a probing volume entitled *It Needs to Be Said*, "America is a continent, not a country" (8, 85).

As always, there is another side to the question. In discussing representation in freshman anthologies, I mentioned our minority-group status; but, of course, given our population (roughly one-half of the population of the United Kingdom and one-tenth that of the United States), we *are* a minority group. Moreover, until a few decades ago, if occasional interest were shown in Canadian literature, we had reason to be embarrassed by the thinness of the crop. Although some significant work had been produced earlier (part of it to be specified shortly), it is perhaps fair to state that a distinctive body of Canadian literature of quality did not show signs of growth until the 1920s. The reasons for this slow development are not wholly unrelated to Canada's geographical position in North America, and the most important of them is discussed in the following section.

II

The literary history of the North American continent looks different when Canadian materials are taken into consideration. For example, what may reasonably be described as the first American novel (a point that rarely gets included in United States literary histories) is in fact Canadian—or, to be more circumspect, semi-Canadian. Frances Brooke's *History of Emily Montague* (1769) belongs in its traditions, assumptions, and even its epistolary form to the English eighteenth-century novel, but much of its action takes place in Québec in those few years, between 1759 and 1775, when North America was predominantly under British control. Brooke came to the New World when her husband was appointed chaplain to the British garrison, and her somewhat conventional officer-class love story is enhanced by much North American local color as well as by some useful documentary material about social life in the new British possessions. From the viewpoint of North American literary history, the novel is a landmark.

But why, it may be asked, did not this early manifestation of literary activity form the basis for a rapidly evolving Canadian literature in the eighteenth century? A brief but not wholly inadequate answer would be, simply: the American Revolution. If we are to understand the full implications of this period of history, however, it is wise to avoid the standard stereotypes of progressives versus reactionaries. What looks to an American like a triumphant revolt against tyranny and empire sometimes looks to a Canadian uncomfortably like a civil war. Thomas Raddall has described this period in a somewhat romantic but historically accurate novel, *His Majesty's Yankees*. The title refers to the inhabitants of Halifax and Nova Scotia, half of whom were American in origin and in no way dyed-in-the-wool supporters of the British cause. Sympathy with the American aspirations was in fact widespread. But the people of Nova Scotia were caught in a transatlantic cross fire, subject to the assaults of both British press-gangs and American privateers. It was a period of split loyalties, complicated and confused motives, allegiances often decided by local conditions and short-term goals. Raddall shows how perilously thin were the ties that eventually held the Nova Scotians to the British side.

In addition, the successful secession of the original thirteen colonies saw the influx into eastern Canada of the so-called United Empire Loyalists, whose minority convictions (often not so much a patriotic love for British tradition as a rejection of precipitate and violent revolt) seemed unlikely to be tolerated within the land of the free. This influx was to have profound effects on the future development of what we know as Canada, starting with a Canadian suspicion of American violence that may perhaps be exaggerated but that (as the world now recognizes) is not wholly without foundation.

So begins the long history of Canadian-American relations, in which the Canadian component often displays a queer but not incomprehensible mixture of envy, suspicion, admiration, and distaste. Nowhere is this more evident than in an early examination of the phenomenon, T. C. Haliburton's tales of Sam Slick, especially *The Clockmaker* (1836–40). Like a number of other early representations, Sam Slick is an enterprising and irrepressible Yankee "character," but he gains a certain piquancy by being the invention of a Canadian—and of a congenital Tory at that. Slick spends his time traveling on commercial circuit in the Maritimes, satirizing native ("Bluenose") lack of initiative and continually praising the energy, sharpness, and intelligence of the Yankees. He is intended to represent a forcefulness to be emulated as well as a brashness and moral slipperiness to be rejected, although, as often happens with satiric figures, his ebullient high spirits tend to obscure the satiric edge. Moreover, the vitality of his speech (which added many colloquial phrases to the language) transcends the immediate circumstances for which Haliburton invented him. *The Clockmaker* and to a lesser extent the inevitable Sam Slick sequels represent both a specimen of, and a commentary on, early relations between the two North American communities.

But the independence of the United States created an urgency to establish a distinctive literature that was absent when Canada consisted of separate colonial provinces. Canada did not begin to come together as a nation until the confederation of Canada East (Québec), Canada West (Ontario), New Brunswick, and Nova Scotia in 1867, almost a century after American independence. Geographical, political, and economic factors all combined to stifle strong cultural development in the earlier decades. Pioneer settlements were scattered and communications poor. Few of the inhabitants had time for any leisured cultural activity; most had strong ties with America (it is estimated that, in the early years of the nineteenth century, some 80% of the population of southern Ontario was American in origin) or with Great Britain (where emigration to Canada increased dramatically at the end of the Napoleonic wars). Most Canadians were therefore content to rely on British and American books.

In any case, the smallness of their numbers was an almost insuperable economic barrier to independent Canadian publishing. Many Canadian writers, realizing that their own country was unable to support them, were attracted to fresher woods and larger markets. Of the so-called Confederation poets, both Charles G. D. Roberts and Bliss Carman lived for a considerable period in the United States and published most of their books there. Archibald Lampman and Duncan Campbell Scott, though remaining and originally publishing in Canada, eventually found a wider audience (both of magazine and book readers) south of the border. As Roberts remarked in a poem titled "The Poet Is Bidden to Manhattan Island,"

> Your poet's eyes *must* recognize
> The side on which your bread is buttered!   (74)

Most Canadian works in the nineteenth century either happened (like Haliburton's) to appeal to a wider audience than the one for which they were originally intended or were deliberately written for a foreign readership (British or American). Many of them were nonfiction accounts of conditions within the settlements, notably Catharine Parr Traill's *Backwoods of Canada*, her sister Susanna Moodie's *Roughing It in the Bush*, and the British traveler Anna Jameson's *Winter Studies and Summer Rambles*. Novelists occasionally tried to cash in on a market for lurid or romantic historical fiction. The best-known of these works is John Richardson's *Wacousta*, a melodramatic treatment of Pontiac's sacking of Fort Michilimackinac in 1763.[3] The same writer's *Canadian Brothers* similarly exploits the events that climaxed with Tecumseh and the War of 1812 (notice in both instances Canada's concern with American violence on its borders). William Kirby's *Golden Dog*, which combines melodrama, romance, and sentiment with a somewhat unexpected sense of atmospheric particularity, evokes New France in the years before 1759. By contrast, Canadian poetry in the early nineteenth century rarely ventured beyond a rather pallid version of English Romanticism. There was no serious attempt to produce a distinctively national poem; Earle Birney sums up the situation in a phrase from his poem "Can. Lit.": "no Whitman wanted" (1: 138).

Canadian confederation, originating partly as a response to American expansionist tendencies northward, was immediately caught up in the parallel expansion westward. Here we encounter once again the pervasive influence of popular myth. The American image of the West—or at least a vulgarized version of it—has spread across the world in the form of the Hollywood cowboy movie; the Canadian version sets the Mounties on center stage, though Hollywood's popularization of the Mounties through the movie *Rose-Marie* speaks volumes about the cultural-economic facts of Canadian-American relations. Basically, we may say that in the American myth the Indian always bites the dust, while in the Canadian equivalent the Mountie traditionally "always gets his man" (alive). Both versions are false but profoundly revealing. The Canadian myth focuses on law and order, the American on lawlessness (in each, of course, violence is the automatic preliminary assumption). A related Canadian myth maintains that the Canadians' treatment of the Indians has been more humane than the Americans' has. This view is not always easy to sustain. The story of the extinction of the Beothuck Indians of Newfoundland (told in historically accurate form in Peter Such's novel *Riverrun*) is no less contemptible than is the sequence of events that led to Custer's last stand. But it nonetheless should be noted that the Mounties' early appearance on the scene in the Canadian West prevented much of the bloody anarchy that raged south of the border. The distinction between Canadian redcoats and American blue-coats (or "longknives," as they were called) may involve no more than the lesser of two evils, yet the qualitative difference is undoubtedly important.

The temptation to take sides is great, but it so happens that one of the best studies treating the development of the two wests has been made by an American, Wallace Stegner, in *Wolf Willow*. It is fair to quote two passages:

> [T]he American attitude [toward the Indians] was more impatient and more violent than the Canadian, and the circumstances of the American West gave freer play to the instincts of self-reliant and often criminal men. No one who has studied western history can cling to the belief that the Nazis invented

genocide. Extermination was a doctrine accepted widely, both unofficially and officially, in the western United States after the Civil War. (73–74)

It became clear very soon that the Canadian side was safer than the American, that the Mounted Police had more authority and were generally more to be trusted and were easier to get on with than the blue-coated American cavalry, and much more to be trusted than the Montana sheriffs or marshals or posses. (98)

These differences in approach and attitude may be explained, at least in part, by differences of historical development within the two countries. Acknowledgement of such differences is more important than any glib post-factum assigning of praise and blame. Canadians need to be reminded that discrimination against citizens of Japanese origin during the Second World War was more pronounced in Canada—involving large-scale confiscation of property as well as relocation—than it was in the United States. (The Canadian experience is documented by Joy Kogawa in her novel *Obasan*.)

In the twentieth century, Canadian-American tensions have frequently formed the subject of Canadian literature, and the growing influence of the United States as a world power has had considerable political, economic, and emotional effects on the country that once believed that this might be "Canada's century." Sara Jeannette Duncan's *Imperialist*, set in the small town of Elgin (modeled on Brantford) in southern Ontario—"this little outpost of Empire" (21)—focuses on English-Canadian political relations but subtly indicates the social and economic realities of the close proximity to the States. The daughter of the leading family "had been taught to speak ... with what was known as an 'English accent'. The accent in general use in Elgin was borrowed—let us hope temporarily—from the other side of the line. It suffered local modifications and exaggerations, but it was clearly an American product" (49). The two-way pull, especially in the phrase between dashes, is quietly but palpably communicated. Similarly, when the hero returns from a visit to "the mother country," a female acquaintance welcomes him "in a rocking-chair, with her pretty feet in their American shoes well in evidence.... I must add that the 'rocker' was also American; and the hammock in which Stella reposed came from New York; and upon John Murchison's knee, with the local journal, lay a pink evening paper published in Buffalo" (128). *The Imperialist* cannot be understood unless the implications of these details are appreciated in all their historical and geographical complexity.

A related though less subtle unease is reflected by the humorist Stephen Leacock in two of his best-known books, *Sunshine Sketches of a Little Town* and *Arcadian Adventures with the Idle Rich*. In the former, Mariposa, Leacock's Canadian "little Town in the Sunshine" (153), is presented with

piquant criticism but also with affection and even love; in the latter, Plu-
toria, the wicked city, is set firmly in the United States and might even be
seen as presenting Sam Slick's compatriots no longer as an ambiguous
model but as an unequivocal threat. Americans may see this implication
as a churlish and petty manifestation of sour grapes—and perhaps it is.
But the Canadian experience, which survived in literary terms until the
recent past and is still evident in the sociopolitical sphere (note the continuing bitterness and uncertainty about the control of acid rain), needs
to be recognized as an alternative viewpoint.

Commercial pressures are also a recurring irritation. Morley Callaghan,
who began writing novels and short stories about North American life in
the late 1920s, based his settings on Toronto and Montréal but left the
cities unnamed, since a Canadian locale would have damaged his American
sales. A similar problem arose over the possible filming of Hugh Mac-
Lennan's *Barometer Rising*, a novel centered on a historical explosion in
Halifax harbor in 1917, the largest artificially produced disaster before
Hiroshima. The deal eventually fell through, despite the film company's
efforts to switch to a United States locale, because the historical facts
proved intransigent. But the message was clear: if you want to be read in
America, don't set your book in Canada. MacLennan wrote up the incident
in an article in *Scotchman's Return* entitled "A Boy Meets a Girl in Winnipeg
and Who Cares?" Rudy Wiebe had a similar experience in the early 1970s
when an American publisher advised him to write about American Jews
rather than the Canadian Mennonites who are his own people. Only recently
have such writers as Mavis Gallant and Alice Munro been able to publish
stories in the *New Yorker* without their Canadian settings seeming an obvious liability.

But the crucial text on this topic is clearly Margaret Atwood's *Surfacing*.
It is doubtful whether an American can ever fully comprehend the national
(not merely nationalistic) tensions underlying the novel. The unnamed
protagonist is traveling to her father's cabin in Québec wilderness country
to investigate reports of his disappearance and is accompanied by three
Americanized young Canadians. They pass additional evidence of American
infiltration: first, an underground defense installation (based on a complex
near North Bay, Ontario); then an advertisement display consisting of stuffed
moose and including "a little boy moose in short pants, a striped jersey
and a baseball cap, waving an American flag" (13). Later, at the cabin, an
American from Michigan offers to buy the property ("we've had our eye
on this piece for quite some time" [94]). On an expedition into the bush,
they encounter a boatload of Americans, who disturb the lake's peaceful-
ness with a souped-up power engine and are suspected by the protagonist

of pointlessly killing and mutilating a great blue heron. Atwood's satiric trap is sprung, however, when the two parties meet. Not only do the presumed Americans turn out to be Canadians, but they in turn had assumed the protagonist's group to be Americans. The effect is complex. One result is that the protagonist herself—who is engaged in illustrating, simplifying, and in the process vulgarizing a translation of Québec folktales—sees an uncomfortable parallel between English-Canadian domination of Québec and American domination of Canada. And behind all this unease lies the white treatment of native peoples and Canadian connivance in the betrayal of their own culture: "It doesn't matter what country they're from, . . . they're still Americans, they're what's in store for us, what we are turning into. They spread themselves like a virus" (129). This conclusion is no simplistic anti-Americanism; it represents, in terms of serious art, a profound and responsible investigation of the worldwide implications of the so-called American way of life.

III

It is important to acknowledge, however, that for all the justified stress on traditional values, Canada is no longer, and can never be again, the homogeneous dream of the early Loyalists. With its two official languages and its policy of offering education in English or French wherever numbers permit, Canada is a bilingual country, but it is also a multicultural country. Canada has traditionally seen itself as tolerant of minority cultures maintaining themselves within its boundaries and as opposed to the melting-pot philosophy of the States. This assumption has the makings of another national myth, and exceptions are not difficult to find. Obviously, pressure to assimilate is frequently felt in Canada; by the same token, various American groups have succeeded in preserving their distinctive practices and life-styles. But Canada has tried to draw a fine line between integration and full-scale assimilation, and by and large ethnic differences are reflected more prominently in Canadian than in American literature. This is not merely because some writers—notably the Czech Josef Skvorecky, the German Walter Bauer, and the Hungarian George Faludy—continued to write in their own languages after emigrating to Canada—a circumstance more conspicuous in the relatively small world of Canadian writing. (The 1984 winning of a Governor General's Award by Skvorecky for a novel written in Czech may be significant here.) Nor is it because many writers of other than English or French linguistic origin have risen to prominence (the Jewish contribution to Canadian literature has been especially spectacular). More important, ethnic difference and coexistence have become pervasive subjects within the national literature itself, and so they have both reflected and asserted the multicultural make-up of contemporary Canada.

Regional differences are also strong. Because Canada is a huge country encompassing an extraordinary variety of geographical terrain and because so many human settlements, even in an age of fast communications, remain isolated from one another, literary development still tends to occur within regional contexts. Thus the Maritimes, because of their longer history of European settlement, have maintained a cohesive traditionalist stance approximating a Canadian equivalent to the ethos of New England. Québec, distinguished by its language, was until recently affected for good or ill (current Québécois literary sentiment tends to stress the ill) by the cultural dominance of the Roman Catholic church. Both linguistic and religious differences have played a part in inhibiting literary relations between Québec and the rest of Canada, though the political unease of the last quarter century has led to earnest efforts to bridge the gap—a movement that may nurture increased literary interchange in the not-too-distant future. Yet the flavor of Québec literature—even when the medium is English—remains distinct.

Because of the presence of the national capital and the importance of Toronto as a publishing center, Ontario has often been regarded as representing the central Canadian experience. An objective reading of Canadian literature reveals this as yet another national myth, but the Ontario contribution has nonetheless been crucial. The way of life in Ontario's small towns—whether Duncan's Elgin, Leacock's Mariposa, Robertson Davies's Deptford, Alice Munro's Jubilee and Hanratty, or the poet Al Purdy's Roblin Mills—has provided (sometimes ironically as a result of their anti-artistic philistinism) a convenient microcosm for literary purposes. And Toronto, so often seen by outsiders as a brash and culturally aggressive metropolis, is both envied and hated as a presumed source for "American" tendencies.

The Prairie Provinces, though relatively sparse in population and containing many non-English-speaking groups, have made a conspicuous contribution to the Canadian novel and have perhaps saddled Canadian fiction with a reputation for dour realism. The writings of Frederick Philip Grove and Sinclair Ross are influential here, and the tradition culminates in Margaret Laurence's Manawaka series. Like all the best regional literature, these works transcend their regional origins. The dramatic history of prairie settlement, the juxtaposition of races (white and Amerindian), the ethnic variety of immigrant groups, the claustrophobic isolation of rural prairie communities—all encouraged fictional presentation. At the same time, a strand in prairie experience has fostered the imaginative and the mystical, and certain writers, notably Robert Kroetsch and Rudy Wiebe, have injected into prairie realism a healthy strain of the iconoclastic, the zany, the visionary, and the prophetic. This strain is also evident in British Columbia, where the terrain runs the gamut from the sublimely rugged to the lushly fertile. British Columbian writing, like that of California and the magic realism of South America, has widened the horizons of Canadian writing. It is not too much to say that recent developments have shifted Canada's center of literary activity from east to west.

IV

"An American who rejected the Revolution": ultimately, this may be the most satisfactory (or least unsatisfactory) definition of a Canadian, though citizens of the United States sometimes have difficulty believing that such an aberrant species can exist. But the persistence of Canada, an obstinate challenge to Manifest Destiny, indicates that an alternative North American experience is not only viable but even, to some, attractive. The existence of this volume testifies to the revising of old stereotypical notions. The traditional myths are being recognized as myths. In 1960, when Robertson Davies published a collection of linked essays about the art of reading, specifically designed for an American readership, he called it *A Voice from the Attic*, alluding to a line from "Poem on Canada," by Patrick Anderson, that described Canada as "America's attic." This image, an empty room for discarded lumber, is employed with a typically Canadian ironic deference, but it also contains a condescending superiority. In physical terms, the head is the attic of the body, the home of intellect—even, perhaps, of moral conscience. (A comparable image-myth occurs in the United States. I once saw a western movie in which a cowboy returned from the Calgary stampede with a Canadian wife instead of a thoroughbred horse; she was characterized as elegant and cultured—which meant that she brought with her a mechanical piano player and an exaggerated Oxford accent.) By 1968, relations were more strained, and Al Purdy's collection *The New Romans*, a thought-provoking nonfiction companion to *Surfacing*, documents an almost paranoid suspicion of Americans by Canadians. The future, one hopes, will replace extreme myths with informed realities—on both sides.

But experience has taught Canadians to be a cautious people. We are not yet used to the new interest being taken in us and feel the need to tread warily. Margaret Atwood had the first word, and it is appropriate that she should be given the last. With a poet's wit and economy she has summed up, straightforwardly and dramatically, a crucial difference in Canadian and American perspectives: "South of you you have Mexico, and south of us we have you" (*Second Words* 392).

NOTES

¹The *Classroom Guide* to *The Norton Introduction to Literature* (ed. Bain, Beaty, and Hunter), for instance, contains a section entitled "Poems by Black Poets: A List," followed by a shorter section entitled "Poems by Canadian Poets: A List" (167–68). No other groups are segregated in this way. The editors doubtless believed that they were being both "liberal" and helpful. Had they imagined themselves into a black or a Canadian viewpoint, they might have had second thoughts. The example is innocent, but all the more revealing for that reason.

²For other discussions of Canadian-American literary and cultural relations, see Carrington; Harrison; Hinz; Atwood, "Canadian-American Relations: Surviving the Eighties" (*Second Words* 371–92); and Northrop Frye, "Sharing the Continent" (*Divisions on a Ground* 57–70).

³Interestingly enough, the only full text of *Wacousta* is the first edition (London, 1832). All North American editions have been abridged and derive mainly from an 1833 United States version that seriously distorts the meaning by omitting anti-American material (see Cronk). A complete scholarly edition has now been published by the Center for Editing Early Canadian texts at Carleton University.

WORKS CITED

Anderson, Patrick. "Cold Colloquy." [From "Poem on Canada."] *The New Oxford Book of Canadian Verse in English.* Ed. Margaret Atwood. Toronto: Oxford UP, 1982. 170.

Atwood, Margaret. *Second Words: Selected Critical Prose.* Toronto: Anansi, 1982.

———. *Surfacing.* 1972. Don Mills, ON: Paperjacks, 1973.

Bain, Carl E., Jerome Beaty, and J. Paul Hunter, eds. *The Norton Introduction to Literature: Classroom Guide.* 4th ed. New York: Norton, 1986.

Birney, Earle. *Collected Poems.* 2 vols. Toronto: McClelland, 1975.

Brooke, Frances. *The History of Emily Montague.* London, 1769.

Carrington, Ildikó de Papp, ed. *Canadian-American Literary Relations.* Spec. issue of *Essays on Canadian Writing* 22 (1981): 1–168.

Cronk, Douglas. "The Americanization of *Wacousta*." *Recovering Canada's First Novelist: Proceedings from the John Richardson Conference.* Ed. Catherine Sheldrick Ross. Erin, ON: Porcupine's Quill, 1984. 33–48.

Davies, Robertson. *A Voice from the Attic.* New York: Knopf, 1960.

Duncan, Sara Jeannette. *The Imperialist.* 1904. New Canadian Library. Toronto: McClelland, 1971.

Frye, Northrop. *Divisions on a Ground: Essays on Canadian Culture.* Toronto: Anansi, 1982.

Grove, Frederick Philip. *It Needs to Be Said.* Toronto: Macmillan, 1929.

Haliburton, Thomas Chandler. *The Clockmaker.* 1st ser. Halifax, 1836. 2nd and 3rd ser. London, 1838, 1840.

Harrison, Dick, ed. *Crossing Frontiers: Papers in American and Canadian Literature.* Edmonton: U of Alberta P, 1979.

Hinz, Evelyn J., ed. *Beyond Nationalism: The Canadian Literary Scene in Global Perspective.* Spec. issue of *Mosaic* 14.2 (1981): 1–188.

Jameson, Anna. *Winter Studies and Summer Rambles.* 3 vols. London, 1838.

Kirby, William. *The Golden Dog (Le chien d'or).* Montréal, 1877.

Kogawa, Joy. *Obasan.* Toronto: Lester and Orpen Dennys, 1981.

Kroetsch, Robert, and Reingard M. Nischik, eds. *Gaining Ground: European Critics on Canadian Literature.* Edmonton: NeWest, 1985.

Leacock, Stephen. *Arcadian Adventures with the Idle Rich.* 1914. New Canadian Library. Toronto: McClelland, 1969.

———. *Sunshine Sketches of a Little Town.* 1912. New Canadian Library. Toronto: McClelland, 1960.

MacLennan, Hugh. *Barometer Rising.* Toronto: Collins, 1941.

———. *Scotchman's Return.* Toronto: Macmillan, 1960.

Moodie, Susanna. *Roughing It in the Bush.* 2 vols. London, 1852.

Purdy, Al, ed. *The New Romans: Candid Canadian Opinions of the U.S.* Edmonton: Hurtig, 1968.

Raddall, Thomas. *His Majesty's Yankees.* Garden City: Doubleday, 1942.

Richardson, John. *The Canadian Brothers.* 2 vols. Montréal, 1840.

———. *Wacousta.* 3 vols. London, 1832.

Roberts, Charles G. D. *Selected Poetry and Critical Prose.* Ed. W. J. Keith. Toronto: U of Toronto P, 1974.

Stanzel, Franz K., and Waldemar Zacharasiewicz, eds. *Encounters and Explorations: Canadian Writers and European Critics.* Würzburg: Königshausen, 1986.

Stegner, Wallace. *Wolf Willow: A Writing, a Story, and a Memoir of the Last Plains Frontier.* 1962. New York: Viking, 1971.

Such, Peter. *Riverrun.* Toronto: Clarke, 1973.

Traill, Catharine Parr. *The Backwoods of Canada.* London, 1836.

Linda Hutcheon

THE CANADIAN POSTMODERN: FICTION IN ENGLISH SINCE 1960

I

THE 1960S ARE generally accepted as the years that saw the burgeoning of Canadian fiction. The provocations were diverse: nationalist sentiment, governmental support for publishers and writers, and the general feeling that, in cultural terms, Canada had finally ceased to be what Earle Birney called a "high-school land / deadset in adolescence." Despite the continued strong presence of traditional realist fiction by Hugh MacLennan, Morley Callaghan, Robertson Davies, W. O. Mitchell, and others, something new began to appear in the seventies and eighties: postmodernism had arrived in Canada. But the form it took was distinctly Canadian. To make clear this distinctiveness, I should first define what I mean by this overused—and underdefined—term. From the usage of the term in describing literature, film, architecture, painting, video, and photography, postmodernism seems to designate cultural practices that are fundamentally self-reflexive, in other words, art that is self-consciously artifice, art that is textually aware of its production and reception as a cultural artifact and that is as related to the past of other art as to the present reality of society. This description, however, could also apply to modernist art, with its belief in aesthetic autonomy and self-sufficiency. The continuity is real and important, but the distinction between the two is that, in postmodernism, textual self-reflexivity is paradoxically made the means to a new and overt engagement with the social and the historical, which has the effect of challenging our traditional humanist beliefs about the function of art in society.

For example, both Sheila Watson's *Double Hook* and Margaret Laurence's

Diviners are metafictional works, aware of their processes of creating order through myth and art. Despite what some would call postmodern techniques (fragmentation and parody), both reveal more a modernist search for order in the face of moral and social chaos than a postmodern urge to render both problematic and provisional any such desire for order (or "truth") through imagination. What to many American critics is archetypically postmodern—the extreme self-referential textuality of surfiction (Federman)—is yet another form of this (late) modernism, the logical extreme of its aesthetic and aestheticist tenets and its ultimate faith in the human imagination. While clearly derived from these modernist roots, postmodernism is a more paradoxical and problematic beast: it both inscribes and subverts the powers and conventions of art; it uses and abuses them in an attempt to challenge both modernist artistic autonomy and the conventional notion of realist transparent reference.

Walter Pache has argued that Canadian postmodern writers have mostly responded to American forms of metafictive self-consciousness (65), but in Canada there is very little of the formalism of surfiction. Stanley Fogel claims that metafiction is "almost completely absent" from Canadian literature (8). While this statement is partly the consequence of his polemical focus on the received canon of "Can lit," it is typical of a common view of Canada's lagging behind the United States in matters of culture. According to Fogel, Canadian fiction lacks the formal experimentation and ideological engagement associated with metafiction (15, 18) because Canadian writers are unencumbered by the ideological baggage carried by American novelists. But surely it is more a matter of Canadian writers just having different ideological baggage, baggage that includes not a revolution and a civil war in its history but a more conservative cultural past as a colony. The Canadian experience may indeed make for more deference to authority (22–25) and to a more overt need to sustain a distinct cultural identity than can be found in the United States—or Britain. In other words, Canada has never been in sync with America in terms of cultural history, so it is perhaps unwise to look for exact parallels, even within contemporary postmodernism.

Canada's particular moment of cultural history today has produced a form of fiction that uses and abuses, installs and undercuts, prevailing values and conventions in order to provoke a questioning of all that "goes without saying" in culture. Postmodern writers are always "agents provocateurs"—taking potshots at the culture in which they know they are unavoidably implicated but which they still wish to submit to a critique. This almost inevitably puts them in a marginal or "ex-centric" position with regard to the dominant culture because the paradox of underlining and undermining cultural "universals," of revealing the writers' grounding in the particular, implicitly challenges any notions of centrality in or centralization of culture. Since the margin might also describe Canada's perceived international position, perhaps the postmodern ex-centric could even be seen as part of the nation's identity. In postmodernism, though, the center and the periphery do not just change places. Nor is the margin conceived as only a place of transgression; the periphery is the frontier, the place of possibility.

Margins also challenge the idea of borders as limits. Marshall McLuhan once called Canada a borderline case, and certainly it is a vast nation with little sense of firm geographical center (except in terms of the American border) or ethnic unity (the multicultural mosaic is not a melting pot). In fact, Canada might be said to have quite a firm suspicion of centralizing tendencies, be they national, political, or cultural. In literature, there is an analogous suspicion of genre borders. In Robert Kroetsch's words, "modern literature closed the boundaries; what is needed is a breaking across these boundaries, a post-modern literature" (van Herk, "Biocritical Essay" xxxiv). The margin or the border is the postmodern space par excellence, the place where new possibilities exist. It is also, however, the place where the center is both paradoxically acknowledged and challenged, whether the center is seen by Canadians as elsewhere (Britain, the United States) or as localized in Ontario. Canada can in some ways be defined as a nation whose articulation of its national identity has sprung from regionalist impulses: the ex-centric forces of Québec, the Maritimes, the West. In a sense, of course, its history is one of defining itself *against* centers, first British (and French) and then American.

Canadian writers, then, are perhaps primed for the paradoxes of the postmodern by their split sense of identity, both regional and national, and by their history. They may feel the link between those postmodernist contradictions and what Robert Kroetsch calls "the total ambiguity that is so essentially Canadian, be it in terms of two solitudes, the bush garden, Jungian opposites" (Kroetsch and Bessai 208). The postmodern irony that refuses resolution of contraries—except in the most provisional of terms—would appear to be a useful cultural framework in which to discuss, for instance, the obsessive dualities in the work of Margaret Atwood (body-mind; male-female; culture-nature; reason-instinct; time-space; prose narrative–lyric poetry) or the echoing doubling of (and within) the characters and plots of Kroetsch's novels. Perhaps postmodern is the best way to describe the genre paradoxes of the work of Michael Ondaatje (biography? fiction? poetry?) or Alice Munro (short story collection? novel?). And certainly Canadian fiction is full of examples of the postmodern internalized challenge to the boundaries of specifically "high art" genres: we find comic books and movies (Cohen's *Beautiful Losers*), murder mysteries (Findley's *Telling of Lies*), and sports tales (Kinsella's *Shoeless Joe*).

II

In "Progressions toward Sainthood: There Is Nothing to Do but Die," Aritha van Herk offers a fictional dialogue between Jeanne d'Arc and Louis Riel on many topics, including the cultural representations of the ex-centric by both "date-compilers" (50) and creative writers (George Bernard Shaw and Rudy Wiebe). Though separated by time and gender, the woman and the Canadian find they have much in common. (This affinity will not surprise historians of Canadian literature, who have long noticed the strong female presence within the Can lit canon: from Moodie and Traill through Ostenso and Wilson to Laurence, Gallant, Atwood, Thomas, Munro, and so on.) Women and Canadian writers seem to share a necessary, self-defining challenge to the dominant (male; British and American) traditions. What Stan Fogel calls Margaret Atwood's obsession with "character formation and the difficulty of maintaining ontological security" (116) is true of much feminist fiction, and the reason is obvious—and it is not that women writers are more conservative and traditionally realist. The reason, I think, is that one can only assume and challenge selfhood (character formation) or subjectivity when one has attained it. Subjectivity in the Western humanist tradition has been defined in terms of rationality (the Cartesian cogito), individuality, and power—in other words, those domains traditionally denied women in return for the female realms of intuition, familial collectivity, and submission. I exaggerate only slightly in my rhetoric here: the last twenty years of feminist research have argued convincingly for the historical existence of these two differently en-gendered subjectivities.

If women have not yet been allowed access to (male-defined) subjectivity, then it is very difficult for them to contest it, as the (male) poststructuralist philosophers have been doing lately. Feminist writing may thus appear more conservative, but, in fact, it is just different. Women must define their subjectivity before they can question it; they must first assert the selfhood they have been denied by the dominant culture. Their doubled inscribing and then challenging of the subject have been major influences on postmodernism's resolutely paradoxical nature. There is an analogy here with the situation of the Canadian writer, female or male. Why do Canadians still feel the need to publish books with titles like *A Passion for Identity* (Mandel and Taras)? What Fogel sees as important to postmodernism in the United States—its deconstruction of national myths and identity—is only possible within Canada once those myths and identity have been defined. Like women writers in general, Canadian novelists must return to their history (as do Wiebe, Bowering, Kogawa, and many others) in order to discover, before they can contest, their national myths. First, however, they must deconstruct British social and literary myths in order to redefine their colonial history: myths such as the glory of war (Findley's *Wars*) or imperialistic exploration (Bowering's *Burning Water*). Through generic parody, they have contested the canonical myths and forms of European (and American) literature: the picaresque (van Herk's *No Fixed Address*), the *Künstlerroman* (Munro's *Lives of Girls and Women*), the Grail legend (Thomas's *Mrs. Blood*).

A number of critics lately (Howells; Irvine) have noted the relation between the national search for a Canadian cultural identity and the feminist seeking for a distinctive female identity in terms of the paradoxical (and postmodern) recognition and contesting of colonial positions with respect to the power of dominating cultures. They have pointed to shared themes of powerlessness, victimization, and alienation, as well as to a certain ambivalence or ambiguity. Lorna Irvine believes that the female voice "politically and culturally personifies Canada" (11). On a national level, the realm of male aggression is said to be analogous with the United States, while Britain represents the stifling force of tradition. As Mavis Gallant put it, "The father in Canada seemed no more than an apostle transmitting a paternal message from the Father in England—the Father of us all" (269). Different from Québec women writers, however, with their more overtly radical challenges, Canadian women writing in English (along with many of their male counterparts) use a disguised form of subversion (Irvine 25) that implicitly questions prevailing authority. In so doing, they also contest the related humanist notions of originality and uniqueness, tied in with (male) notions of individuality.

III

Often these writers use parody to effect this challenge: they inscribe the (male; British or American) canonical texts of our culture, both "high" and popular, and then invert their status and power. For example, many critics have asserted the importance of biblical structures in Canadian literature, but novels such as Timothy Findley's *Not Wanted on the Voyage* parody these in typically postmodern ways, exploiting and undermining their undeniable cultural authority. Many of Kroetsch's novels, such as *Badlands*, assert the male myths of the quest (of Odysseus, Orpheus, Conrad's Marlow, the knight errant) in order to show male (and female) cultural roles as fictions or constructs. Both the male will to knowledge (and power) and the undermining of it are parodically presented through Kroetsch's conjunction of male story and female first-person narration (see Neuman and Wilson 97). Atwood's novel *The Handmaid's Tale* uses a parody of Yevgeny Zamyatin's *We* and Nathaniel Hawthorne's *Scarlet Letter* to achieve similar ideological and political ends. Parody, then, becomes a major form of critique, allowing a writer to speak to her or his culture from within it but without being totally co-opted by it. The irony and distance implied by parody permit separation at the same time as its structure of textual superimposition demands recognition of complicity.

By recalling the texts of the past—the texts of literature or even of history—postmodern parody also questions whether there can ever be a definitive inscription of subjectivity. Novels like Rudy Wiebe's *Temptations of Big Bear* and *Scorched-Wood People* all renarrate and reconceptualize the past, both literary and historical, and thereby reformulate the possibilities of subjectivity. Cohen's early novel *Beautiful Losers* desacralizes the male, European, Jesuit inscription of the selfhood of the female, early Canadian Indian saint Catherine Tekakwitha. As Lorna Irvine has also shown, Audrey Thomas, in *Blown Figures*, parodies the form and imagery of the Greek epic and *Heart of Darkness*, feminizing their maleness, transcoding their death, war, and violence into terms of life, reproduction, and love (63–65). Similarly, Kroetsch "Canadianizes" the American western genre and the Greek epic in *The Studhorse Man*.

All this play with the texts of the past does not, however, result in sterile narcissism. What renders this obviously echoing form specifically postmodern is the paradoxical fact that it is precisely this intertextuality that brings about a direct confrontation with the issue of the relation of art to the world outside it, to the world of those social, cultural, and ultimately ideological systems by which we all live our lives. If, as many have claimed, language is the "absolute precondition for nearly all our social life" (Kress and Hodge 1) and is inextricably bound to thought, then language and self-consciousness about language cannot but be social phenomena, rather than solipsistic navel gazing. Feminists have taught us much about the effects of language on our social concepts, and novels like Atwood's *Life before Man* or Thomas's *Intertidal Life* further study the past of language through etymological wordplay, in order to analyze the literal history of women's inscription into language and reveal the gendered bias encoded in the very words we so unself-consciously use daily.

Atwood does not just "use language in a largely referential way, providing verisimilitude that is a staple of realist fiction and that authenticates the world and the word's relationship to it" (Fogel 102), though she does do this; she also subverts the authority of that word-world relation in a most postmodern—that is, contradictory—way. Like Kroetsch, Wiebe, George Bowering, Jack Hodgins, and others, Atwood uses and abuses the conventions of both language and narrative in her fiction in an attempt to make us question any naive critical notions we might have about modernist formalism (art as inherently autonomous) and about realist transparency (art as simply a mirror of the social). Postmodern art situates itself squarely in the context of its own reception and creation as social and political actualities, as acts rooted in a particular society with inevitable political intentions and consequences. For many Canadian novelists, the act of making fictions is an unavoidably ideological act, a process of creating meaning in a social context. Along with the novels of Salman Rushdie, Gabriel García Márquez, Umberto Eco, and E. L. Doctorow, to name but a few, much Canadian fiction presents itself as investigating the relation between art and what we choose to call reality, between artistic discourse and the structures of social and cultural power.

IV

The sixties saw inscribed into history previously absented ex-centrics: those defined by differences in class, gender, race, ethnic group, and sexual preference. And the years since have seen their inscription into fiction in forms that vary from the historicity of the native people and Métis (in Wiebe's work) to the metaphoricity of the freaks in Paul Quarrington's *Home Game*. The sixties, for all their silliness and presentism, were years of challenges to authority that left their mark on postmodernism in Canada, as elsewhere. It was also the time of an upsurge in Canadian nationalist politics and of the rise of the women's movement. Not surprisingly, the fiction of the writers formed ideologically and intellectually in these years is often engaged fiction, dealing with issues ranging from national identity to gender politics. It has been pointed out (Davey 21; Kroetsch in Neuman and Wilson 35) that challenges to authority can lead as easily to anarchy as to decentralization of power, but the postmodernism that grew from these early roots has turned out to be more constructively contestatory. One example is Dave Godfrey's novel *The New Ancestors*, which can be seen as both inscribing the humanist individualist view of character and challenging it with a Marxist analysis of the historical, political, and social forces that condition that individual subjectivity. The contradiction remains; the novel does not resolve it (see Deer 93–133). Similarly, the African words remain in African; the glossary is omitted. Any tendency to resolve difference into unity or to absorb the margin into the center is frustrated.

Margaret Atwood has called writers "eye-witnesses, I-witnesses." This juxtaposition suggests why she, as a novelist with a distinct moral and political point of view, is attracted to Amnesty International: "all it does is tell stories. It makes *the story* known. Such stories have a moral force, a moral authority which is undeniable." In her *Bodily Harm* or even *Life before Man*, the moral is the political, "having to do with power: who's got it, who wants it, how it operates" (*Second Words* 203, 350, 353). As a Canadian and a woman, she protests any tendency toward easy passivity and naïveté; she refuses to allow either Canadians or women to deny their complicity in the power structures that may subject them.

Although much of the impulse behind the postmodern came from the sixties, those years also come under severe criticism from postmodernism, which both exploits and contests the values that gave it birth. In that decade, the buzzword of culture was the natural, the authentic. What postmodernism has done is show how the natural is, in fact, the constructed, how the social is the made. And the "natural" is never free from an intimate relation with power. Trenchant critiques of ideological naïveté in novels like *Intertidal Life* are reminiscent of those Brechtian attacks that Roland Barthes launched in *Mythologies* against everything seen as "given" in culture. He argued that these assumptions are anything but eternal, universal, and unchangeable values; rather, they constitute myth or ideology, the unspoken (and therefore more powerful) system of belief specific to a particular place and time. What any society deems truth is really, therefore, socially, culturally, economically, and historically determined.

Perhaps it is not surprising, then, that the art of a period adopting such a multiply conditioned notion of truth might be a very self-conscious art, that its fiction might be metafiction, that its writers might also be critics. In Canada, the theoretical and the literary have had an especially close connection because of the presence of a great number of these writer-theorists: Robert Kroetsch, Frank Davey, George Bowering, Stephen Scobie, Dennis Lee, and, to some extent, Margaret Atwood. Through these and others, the impact of poststructuralist philosophy, linguistics, semiotics, reader-response theory, and Marxist and feminist critiques has been simultaneously felt by Canadian criticism and literature.

V

One common and particularly theoretically self-consicous form of fiction seems paradigmatic of the paradoxes that characterize the postmodern. I call it historiographic metafiction—fiction that is intensely self-reflexive but also clearly grounded in historical, social, and political realities: Findley's *Famous Last Words*, with its evocation of the duke and duchess of Windsor and the political climate of Europe before and during the Second World War, or Chris Scott's *Antichthon*, with its account of the trial and death of Giordano Bruno, a frighteningly modern portrayal of the consequences of differing belief in an age of ideological conformity. These works are not quite historical novels in the traditional sense, for they are meta-fictive in their attention to the acts of writing, reading, and interpreting. Thus, they are self-consciously fictive but also concerned with the acts and consequences of reading and writing stories, both historical and fictional. In other words, the aesthetic and the social, the present and the past, are not separable discourses in these novels. They represent a post-modern reflexivity that moves outward to the discourses of the world beyond their borders—the discourses of history, biography, philosophy, religion, theory.

Historiographic metafiction is not a modernist denial of the literary import of historical fact in the name of aesthetic autonomy; nor is it a realist use of that fact to authenticate the fictional world (see Scobie). Instead it is a critical counterpointing of the texts of both history and art, conducted in such a way that it does not deny the existence or significance of either. Recent theorists of historiography have similarly challenged the traditional causal, linear nature of narrative history. No longer is history accepted as how things actually happened, with the historian in the neutral role of recorder. Hayden White, Michel Foucault, Louis O. Mink, and many others have studied the implications of seeing history as construction, as something having been made by the historian through a process of selecting, ordering, and narrating. It is perhaps not odd, then, that when fiction writers like Rudy Wiebe come to deal with historical personages such as Louis Riel, they should do so equally self-consciously.

Indeed, *The Scorched-Wood People* and *The Temptations of Big Bear* are models of postmodernist historiographic metafiction in yet another way. If the view of history as ordered and neatly closed-off narrative is now under attack, then, logically, so too should be the traditional presentation of historical events and characters in fiction. Jean-François Lyotard has defined the "postmodern condition" as one characterized by a distrust of totalizing metanarratives, of the grand narrative systems that once made sense of things for us. Canadian novels have contributed to the incredulity felt about everything from the state (Kogawa's *Obasan*) to religion (Scott's *Antichthon*). In a similar vein, novels today seem to find it hard not to display their distrust of certain literary conventions that were once taken for granted, such as coherent narrative point of view. Wiebe, in telling the story of Big Bear, gives us multiple perspectives on his protagonist's actions and intentions and then leaves us to make up our own minds. The loose ends are not tied up neatly—even when official versions of history have claimed that they are (or, at least, were).

By overtly presenting his novels as novels, while offering a variety of historical perspectives, Wiebe makes the past present in a distinctly post-modernist way. He has described the difficulties of writing about historical events: "Though the acts themselves seem quite clear, some written reports of the acts contradict each other" (Wiebe and Mandel 152). Part of this problem Wiebe incorporates into the form of his novel by contrasting the imperialist ideology of the British who wrote those reports with the oral Indian tradition whose version of events did not survive quite as readily: the written British documents have a hollow and sterile ring when placed beside the metaphorical and rhetorical intensity of Big Bear's speech. The formal irony of the confrontation of the two languages, two worlds, and two histories is paradoxically created in one language, by a white—if ex-centric (Mennonite)—Canadian.

Like Michel Foucault, Robert Kroetsch argues that we might want to move from a notion of history (which both see as unavoidably totalizing) to one of archaeology, which Kroetsch claims "allows the fragmentary nature of the story, against the coerced unity of traditional history" ("On Being" 76). As contemporary theorists of historiography have also taught, we can no longer accept that the givens or the "facts" of history are eternally fixed and natural, and it is the self-conscious pointing to the mechanisms of historical (as well as literary) fiction making in postmodern novels that helps teach us this. Historical fact is the systematized, con-structed version of brute event; it is given meaning by its writers and readers. The past is not coherent, continuous, or unified—until we make it so. This implied complicity of readers and writers depends on a rec-ognition of the complex discursive situation of literature: the producer, the receiver, the text, and the entire historical, social, political, and literary context out of which the text is produced and received. We seem to be coming out of a resolutely formalist stage of our critical history. With the obvious presence of much metafiction and of reader-response theory, we have been made aware of that complicitous and active role of the reader in granting meaning to texts. As Geoff Hancock puts it, "Your own memory, imagination, and wits are part of the narrative strategy" (introduction 5). In postmodern metafiction, we are lured into a world of imagination, only to be greeted by the world of history and thus to be forced to rethink the ontological and epistemological categories by which we normally distin-guish fiction from reality.

VI

The kind of general problematizing that results from these clashing con-tradictions might well suggest a self-consciousness and skepticism about basic values and beliefs in literature (and life), but that same problematizing has also given new impetus to many fields of art and theory. Jacques Derrida's subversive questioning of the categories of Western metaphysics has opened up new areas of study that no longer take for granted such basics as the definition of *Man* as a rational being, in control of everything. Thanks to the work of Michel Foucault and a battalion of feminist writers, we are facing a new situation: exit Man, enter Humankind, including Woman. The monolithic (and male) concept of humanist Man has given way to a more diversified concept of experience based on difference. In postmodernist literature this has meant a turning to those modes that can accentuate difference in the face of a mass culture that tends to homogenize and obliterate the ex-centric. In Canadian writing, two of these new modes to appear have been those of ethnicity and feminism. While not all the work done in these areas has been postmodernly paradoxical, some clearly has. Metafictional novels like Susan Swan's *Biggest Modern Woman of the World* are serious and self-conscious investigations into what it means to be a woman and a Canadian—in artistic and political terms. Both theory and fiction, in Canada as elsewhere, are responding to common social provocations, such as immigration patterns or the rise of feminism. And they are doing so very self-consciously in order to help us recognize that contemporary cultural practices are *events* in which we participate as active agents.

Another consequence of the postmodern valuing of the different is perhaps more particularly Canadian. With a motto like "a mari usque ad mare" to contrast with "e pluribus unum," Canada is a nation that has resisted the more American model of unification, whether geographical, demographic, or ideological. The postmodern has recoded the Canadian valuing of regionalism in literature (see New), for instance, into a concern for the different, the local, the particular, in opposition to the uniform, the universal, the centralized: the West of Aritha van Herk; the Maritimes of David Adams Richards; the West Coast of Jack Hodgins; the southern Ontario of Matt Cohen. Northrop Frye, Robert Kroetsch ("For Play"), and others have addressed the importance of the Canadian cultural disparity and of local tradition. The discrete and the occasional have always been valued in Canadian literature's regionalist emphasis, in contrast with the more American or British monolithic sense of cultural hegemony. To render the particular concrete, to celebrate ex-centricity: this is the Canadian postmodern.

This kind of writing is also self-consciously process, not product. It is not fixed, closed, eternal, and universal. Instead of this unfixing of certainties being a threat, to a postmodern culture it can be liberating and stimulating. Perhaps the loss of faith in system, order, coherence, and wholeness can suggest new models based on the once suspect: contingency, multiplicity, fragmentation, discontinuity (Davey). There is still, however, considerable debate among writers, theorists, and readers about the value and even the meaning of these various postmodernist possibilities. For example, there are those like Kroetsch who are happy to call themselves postmodern, arguing further that the national discontinuities of Canada have made it ripe for the discontinuities of postmodernism (Neuman and Wilson 112). In contrast, there are novelists, like Matt Cohen, who argue that postmodernism lives only as a theory and not as a reality in fiction (69). I think the numbers are against him here: there are many postmodern novels in Canada. George Bowering sees, at long last, the demise of the realist novel in Canada ("Modernism" 8). But the numbers are against him too: realist novels—and responses to them—abound in Canada. In fact, what is striking and particular about Canadian postmodernist fiction is that the challenge to the conventions of realism has come from within those conventions themselves. Unlike the more radical American surfiction or the Québécois linguistic experimentation, English Canadian novels have self-consciously exploited realism for all its power, even while parodying or subverting its conventions. This is yet another of the paradoxes that define the postmodern.

Gerald Graff once argued that postmodernism "begins at a point beyond realism" (311), but realism, like mimesis, is a convention and thus *"constitutively* a social and historical phenomenon" (Foley 42). In a polemical article entitled "What Was Canadian Literature? Taking Stock of the Canlit Industry," T. D. MacLulich worries about the appearance of technically innovative fiction in Canada. He feels it denigrates "the straightforward possibilities of fiction" by which art mirrors culture (25). But have there ever been such "straightforward possibilities"? Or have there only been critics who deny the conventionality and complexity of realist representation? Postmodern fiction has not lost all desire to "examine specific social conditions and particular backgrounds—whether ethnic, religious, regional" (MacLulich 25); it merely does the examining in a different way, challenging the notion that realism is the only convention able to undertake such an examination.

Ever since the birth of the English novel in the eighteenth century, the twin impulses of realism and self-reflexivity have vied for control of the genre. Postmodernism tries at once to incorporate and to question both impulses. The realist novel is not dead in Canada; it is the specific and defining base on which postmodern challenges operate. As Kroetsch says of García Márquez, "He nips at the heels of realism and makes the old cow dance" (Hancock, "Interview" 38). Munro's and Hodgins's very different kinds of "magic realism" (see Wilson) are one manifestation; another is historiographic metafiction's internalized subversion. Much of the fiction of Bowering and Findley use and abuse the conventions of the realist novel, forcing us to rethink conventions, this time as conventions and also as ideological strategies. They render problematic those things we used to

think we could take for granted when reading novels: narrative unity, reliable point of view, coherent character presentation. The once transparent
has now been made opaque. Postmodernism in Canada has forced a
rethinking—but not a denial—of realism, challenging it and taking it seriously.

Realist fiction has often used historical narrative as its model. As we
have seen, however, that too is no longer unquestioned and unquestionable.
Like fiction, history is viewed through frames, and those frames bring only
certain preselected things into the foreground. Public history and private
biography function the same way. Michael Ondaatje's tale of the New Or-
leans jazz musician Buddy Bolden (*Coming through Slaughter*) contests
not only the borders between poetry and prose but also the boundaries
between biography and fiction. In *Running in the Family*, he adds the further
complication of autobiography and its conventions. One of the paradoxes
of postmodernism has been that textual self-reflexivity has led to a general
questioning of the meaning and value of making firm distinctions between
different forms of discourse. The borders between the novel and what has
traditionally been considered the nonfictional are constantly being crossed
today in biographical fictions like Joseph Skvorecky's *Dvorak in Love* or
Heather Robertson's *Willie*. In the end, though, genres are defined by readers. The limits of textualized life and textual art are tested, not only by
fictionalizing historians, but by their readers. And, of course, historians
and biographers are themselves readers: they find and interpret the documents or the texts of the past. So too do postmodern novelists.

VII

It is easy to see that postmodernism in its broadest sense is a name we
have conveniently given to our culture's narcissistic obsession with its own
workings—both past and present. In academic and popular circles today,
books abound that offer us new social models, new frameworks of knowledge, new analyses of strategies of power. This phenomenon may well
betray our loss of faith in what were once the certainties of liberal humanist
culture. But that loss need not be debilitating. In postmodern literature,
as in architecture, it can mean a new vitality, a new willingness to dialogue
with history on new terms. It can mark a move away from an interest in
fixed products and structures to a concern for open cultural process, for
culture as event. It can mean a general turning from the expectation of
sure and single meaning to a recognition of the value of difference and
multiplicity, a turning from passive trust in system to an acceptance of
responsibility for the fact that art and theory are both actively signifying
practices—in other words, that it is *we* who both make sense of and make
our culture.

WORKS CITED

Atwood, Margaret. *Bodily Harm.* Toronto: McClelland, 1981.

———. *The Handmaid's Tale.* Toronto: McClelland, 1985.

———. *Life before Man.* Toronto: McClelland, 1979.

———. *Second Words: Selected Critical Prose.* Toronto: Anansi, 1982.

Barthes, Roland. *Mythologies.* Trans. Annette Lavers. London: Granada, 1973.

Birney, Earle. "Canada: Case History." *The Blasted Pine: An Anthology of Satire, Invective and Disrespectful Verse Chiefly by Canadian Writers.* Ed. F. R. Scott and A. J. M. Smith. Toronto: Macmillan, 1967. 3.

Bowering, George. *Burning Water.* Don Mills, ON: General, 1980.

———. "Modernism Could Not Last Forever." *Canadian Fiction Magazine* 32–33 (1979–80): 4–9.

Cohen, Leonard. *Beautiful Losers.* New York: Viking, 1966.

Cohen, Matt. "Notes on Realism in Modern English-Canadian Fiction." *Canadian Writers in 1984: Twenty-Fifth Anniversary Issue of* Canadian Literature. Ed. W. H. New. Vancouver: U of British Columbia P, 1984. 65–71.

Davey, Frank. *From There to Here: A Guide to English-Canadian Literature since 1960.* Vol. 2 of *Our Nature—Our Voices.* Erin, ON: Porcépic, 1974.

Deer, Glen. "Rhetoric, Ideology, and Authority: Narrative Strategies in Six Innovative Canadian Novels." Diss. York U, 1987.

Federman, Raymond. *Surfiction: Fiction Now . . . and Tomorrow.* Chicago: Swallow, 1975.

Findley, Timothy. *Famous Last Words.* Toronto: Clarke, 1981.

———. *Not Wanted on the Voyage.* New York: Viking, 1984.

———. *The Telling of Lies: A Mystery.* New York: Viking, 1986.

———. *The Wars.* Toronto: Clarke, 1977.

Fogel, Stanley. *A Tale of Two Countries: Contemporary Fiction in Canada and the United States.* Toronto: ECW, 1984.

Foley, Barbara. *Telling the Truth: The Theory and Practice of Documentary Fiction.* Ithaca: Cornell UP, 1986.

Foucault, Michel. *The Archaeology of Knowledge and the Discourse on Language.* Trans. A. M. Sheridan Smith. New York: Pantheon, 1972.

Frye, Northrop. *The Bush Garden: Essays on the Canadian Imagination.* Toronto: Anansi, 1971.

Gallant, Mavis. *Home Truths: Selected Canadian Stories.* Toronto: Macmillan, 1981.

Godfrey, Dave. *The New Ancestors.* 1970. Toronto: New, 1972.

Graff, Gerald. "Babbitt at the Abyss: The Social Context of Postmodern American Fiction." *TriQuarterly* 3.3 (1975): 305–37.

Hancock, Geoff. "An Interview with Robert Kroetsch." *Canadian Fiction Magazine* · 24–25 (1977): 33–52.

————. Introduction. *Metavisions.* Ed. Hancock. Montréal: Quadrant, 1983. 5–10.

Hodgins, Jack. *The Invention of the World.* Toronto: Macmillan, 1977.

Howells, Coral Ann. *Private and Fictional Words: Canadian Women Novelists of the 1970s and 1980s.* London: Methuen, 1987.

Irvine, Lorna. *Sub/version: Canadian Fictions by Women.* Toronto: ECW, 1986.

Kinsella, W. P. *Shoeless Joe.* New York: Houghton, 1982.

Kogawa, Joy. *Obasan.* Toronto: Lester and Orpen Dennys, 1981.

Kress, Gunther, and Robert Hodge. *Language as Ideology.* London: Routledge, 1979.

Kroetsch, Robert. *Badlands.* Don Mills, ON: Paperjacks, 1975.

————. "For Play and Entrance: The Contemporary Canadian Long Poem." *Dandelion* 8 (1981): 61–85.

————. "On Being an Alberta Writer." *Robert Kroetsch: Essays.* Spec. issue of *Open Letter* 5th ser. 4 (1983): 69–80.

————. *The Studhorse Man.* Toronto: Macmillan, 1969.

Kroetsch, Robert, and Diane Bessai. "Death Is a Happy Ending: A Dialogue in Thirteen Parts." *Figures in a Ground: Canadian Essays on Modern Literature Collected in Honour of Sheila Watson.* Ed. Diane Bessai and David Jackel. Saskatoon: Western Producer Prairie Books, 1978. 206–15.

Laurence, Margaret. *The Diviners.* Toronto: McClelland, 1974.

Lyotard, Jean-François. *The Postmodern Condition: A Report on Knowledge.* Trans. Geoff Bennington and Brian Massumi. Minneapolis: U of Minnesota P, 1984.

MacLulich, T. D. "What Was Canadian Literature? Taking Stock of the Canlit Industry." *ECW* 30 (1984–85): 17–34.

Mandel, Eli, and David Taras, eds. *A Passion for Identity: An Introduction to Canadian Studies.* New York: Methuen, 1987.

McLuhan, Marshall. "Canada: The Border Line Case." *The Canadian Imagination: Dimensions of a Literary Culture.* Ed. David Staines. Cambridge: Harvard UP, 1977. 226–48.

Mink, Louis O. "Narrative Form as a Cognitive Instrument." *The Writing of History: Literary Form and Historical Understanding.* Ed. Robert H. Canary and Henry Kozicki. Madison: U of Wisconsin P, 1978. 129–49.

Munro, Alice. *Lives of Girls and Women.* New York: McGraw, 1972.

Neuman, Shirley, and Robert Wilson. *Labyrinths of Voice: Conversations with Robert Kroetsch.* Western Canadian Literary Documents 3. Edmonton: NeWest, 1982.

New, W. H. "Beyond Nationalism: On Regionalism." *World Literature Written in English* 23.1 (1984): 12–18.

Ondaatje, Michael. *Coming through Slaughter.* Toronto: Anansi, 1976.

————. *Running in the Family.* Toronto: McClelland, 1982.

Pache, Walter. " 'The Fiction Makes Us Real': Aspects of Postmodernism in Canada." *Gaining Ground: European Critics on Canadian Literature.* Ed. Robert Kroetsch and Reingard M. Nischik. Edmonton: NeWest, 1985. 64–78.

Quarrington, Paul. *Home Game.* Toronto: Doubleday, 1983.

Richards, David Adams. *Lives of Short Duration.* Ottawa: Oberon, 1981.

Robertson, Heather. *Willie: A Romance.* Don Mills, ON: General, 1983.

Scobie, Stephen. "Amelia: Or, Who Do You Think You Are? Documentary and Identity in Canadian Literature." *Canadian Writers in 1984: Twenty-Fifth Anniversary Issue of* Canadian Literature. Ed. W. H. New. Vancouver: U of British Columbia P, 1984. 264–85.

Scott, Chris. *Antichthon.* Montréal: Quadrant, 1982.

Skvorecky, Joseph. *Dvorak in Love: A Light-Hearted Dream.* Trans. Paul Wilson. Toronto: Lester and Orpen Dennys, 1986.

Swan, Susan. *The Biggest Modern Woman of the World.* Toronto: Lester and Orpen Dennys, 1983.

Thomas, Audrey. *Blown Figures.* Vancouver: Talonbooks, 1974.

———. *Intertidal Life.* Toronto: Stoddart, 1984.

———. *Mrs. Blood.* Vancouver: Talonbooks, 1970.

van Herk, Aritha. "Biocritical Essay." *The Robert Kroetsch Papers: An Archival Inventory.* Calgary: U of Calgary P, 1985. ix–xxxix.

———. *No Fixed Address: An Amorous Journey.* Toronto: McClelland, 1986.

———. "Progressions toward Sainthood: There Is Nothing to Do but Die." *Border Crossings* 5.3 (1986): 47–50.

Watson, Sheila. *The Double Hook.* Toronto: McClelland, 1959.

White, Hayden. *Metahistory: The Historical Imagination in Nineteenth-Century Europe.* Baltimore: Johns Hopkins UP, 1967.

Wiebe, Rudy. *The Scorched-Wood People.* Toronto: McClelland, 1977.

———. *The Temptations of Big Bear.* Toronto: McClelland, 1973.

Wiebe, Rudy, and Eli Mandel. "Where the Voice Comes From." *A Voice in the Land: Essays by and about Rudy Wiebe.* Ed. W. J. Keith. Edmonton: NeWest, 1981. 150–55.

Wilson, Robert Rawdon. "On the Boundary of the Magic and the Real: Notes on Inter-American Fiction." *Compass* 6 (1979): 37–53.

W. H. New

TENSE / PRESENT / NARRATIVE: REFLECTIONS ON ENGLISH-LANGUAGE SHORT FICTION IN CANADA

"Once upon a Time Far Away . . ."

BEFORE THIS STORY can be told, "far away" has to be explained. What I'm suggesting is not original, but it is worth reiterating, here. Fiction narrates; fiction also narrates in context. Hence not only will the subjects of a story vary with a story maker's knowledge of the world; so also will the strategies of storytelling vary with the story maker's understanding of what a story consists of, where a story lies. It lies, of course, both in place and in method. It lies in a cast of speech and in a cast of expectation. The cast of characters came later.

The earliest of English-language stories about Canada are therefore not narratives in Canada at all, or even narrative in any conventional sense. They're the absences off the edge of European maps, terra incognita translated into sixteenth-century ornaments of the fanciful and savage, the wild and bizarre. It was an image that was hard to live up to in empirical reality but not hard to reconfirm by story. When European travelers and explorers subsequently set eye and foot on the land that was new to them, they were conditioned by the tale telling that had preceded them. They were prepared to accept exaggerations as truth, they were susceptible to anecdote, even willing to perpetrate further exaggerations in the name of truth. *Vast, strange, untamed, barren*: these were their words. The land was adjectival, beyond the reach of familiar nouns. And they read the land not as here, where they were, but as there, a place apart—apart, most especially, from themselves.

That they nonetheless attempted to name it, claiming personal possession of the far- and farther-away, announces something of the way in which they resolved their (dis)connection with place and with other people. Their actions spoke of rewriting territory in terms of received notions of space; their stories spoke of rewriting the unknown in the familiar terms of received history.

They accomplished this rewriting in at least two ways: one, by adopting an apparently objective narrative strategy that recorded the newfound wilderness; the other, by neglecting the physical wilderness entirely and focusing instead on "histories" of court intrigue and Oriental romance, which located dramas of manners and circumstance elsewhere. These strategies appear to be different, yet the notion of "elsewhere" is germane to them both. The second form is the easiest to see in these terms. Such nineteenth-century writers as Susanna Moodie, Harriet V. Cheney, Rosanna Leprohon, and numerous others wrote with an eye on what was presumed to be the sophisticated taste of the United States or England (frequently, as with Moodie, an England left behind by an immigrant educated in the literary conventions of some previous decade). Setting, vocabulary, style: all the elements of their storytelling emphasized the precedence of writing over speaking, of convention over experience. Their tales of high society or moral adventure largely followed a historical format: events were set in motion and resolved over time most conventionally with the reintegration of a central character into European norms, or with the tragic but instructive death of a character who transgressed the rules of accepted and acceptable order.

While such tales demonstrate an interest in adventure—that is, in departures from the status quo—their focus was more generally on the moral necessity of deferring to social convention than on the viability of individual resistance to it. Sentimental paradigms were commonplace. They usually appeared as didactic lessons, inserted within a larger narrative frame and designed to corroborate it. Occasionally—especially among women writers in the later years of the nineteenth century and more recently—such contained narratives operated at an oblique angle to the frame, in some sense challenging its authority; but for the earliest of the tale writers these potential ironies of form were less consequential than were the ironies that derived from personal decision. Moodie, for example, who followed her husband to Canada and to a life in the bush for which she was ill-suited, did so because she perceived it her duty to follow him and to reassert the system of authority that sanctioned such actions. She was aware of the ironies attendant on anyone who tried to live as a lady in the bush; but it was nevertheless the order of a gentlemanly code that sustained her and the orderly power of expression that she most esteemed in literary method.

She followed convention: used adjectives such as *sublime* and *noble* to characterize behavior (rather than words that would concretely represent the empirical world) because that was the vocabulary valued at one time by authority. When revising her periodical sketches into book form in *Roughing It in the Bush*, she repeatedly replaced specific terminology with the language of decorum. And when she used dialect, she was diminishing the speaker, asserting yet again the validity of hierarchy, of received convention, even in territory where such conventions were not native but imposed.

It is here that the overlap between the romantic society tales and the ostensibly objective records becomes apparent. Moodie's sketches were theoretically from life; but when she intentionally wrote "fiction," she chose not to record life but to imitate received models. "Life" may well have been lived close at hand to the wilderness; but "literature" was a category she held apart, attaching it to the codes of civilization whose justification was ethical hierarchy, whose intention was political control, and whose medium was language. Language thus separated from experience, devising order more in terms of design than in systems of process. And for all their apparently documentary character, the "objective" journals in effect did the same.

For they were not objective, of course. From Jacques Cartier in the sixteenth century to Alexander Mackenzie and others at the end of the eighteenth, the journals of the explorer-travelers were as designed as Moodie's tales were to appeal to the expectations of a culture located elsewhere. Canada itself may have been the ostensible subject of such enterprises, but Canada, the object of study, was also an object in the way of actual navigation between Europe and Asia: it was not what was expected. One kind of problem for the explorers, the "new land" represented another kind of problem for the publishers of exploration narratives. For the explorers, it presented empirical difficulties but also opportunities for misinterpretation; for the publishers it presented problems of comprehension and acceptance. Hence the explorers claimed a territory they deemed largely barren and inhospitable *by naming it*—after their saints, patrons, and friends—and so building it semantically into the frame of reference they brought with them. For the publishers, transforming the wilderness into readable terms meant accepting as "sublime" or "picturesque" what they could not deal with in any other way. But by rewriting reality, they opened up possibilities for more pronounced equations between the distant and the fanciful. Some explorers perpetrated deliberate hoaxes (Baron Lahontan invented imaginary dialogues with noble Indians, and others claimed falsely to have visited distant places and seen monstrosities or wonders); others naively accepted tall tales as truths. (The wilderness, being "uncivilized," was by definition at the time the potential home only for the savage, the satanic, and the grotesque, so that the use of the very word *wilderness* automatically invited a set of fanciful associations.) All commentators embroidered their observations into narrative. "Documentary truth" was framed, for example, by the tripartite rhetoric of moral exemplum and by the first-person constructions of chronicle: that is, it was fictionalized by the familiar patterns of European discourse.

Publishers often employed English writers to rework the explorer-travelers' manuscripts—as William Combe edited Alexander Mackenzie's accounts of his travels to the Arctic and the West Coast, for instance—with the result that the published narratives further entered European literary frames of narrative. Methodologically, the revised versions recurrently depart from the field-note form of the manuscripts; they emphasize oddity, impute motivations and consequences that are not in the original, and modify the particular vocabulary of observation into a received vocabulary of prospect and scene. As for narrative events, these turned into the same sorts of formal adventures that conventional polite fictions framed as illustrations of moral truths.

When Samuel Hearne, for example, wrote of a massacre of Esquimaux by marauding Indians in *A Journey from Prince of Wales's Fort* (published posthumously in 1795), he cast himself as the ineffectual but sympathetic narrator-observer and designed the Esquimaux as the hapless, pathetic, but inevitable victims of wilderness. The Indians he depicted as the agents of savagery: little more, little less. What they did was in accord with the European determination of wilderness behavior. "Godless," the wilderness was without perceptible plan, and, while it was therefore beyond reason that civilized human beings should inhabit it, it was not beyond verbal control. But named, framed, it became "there," the world that was different from "here." It is the romance-adventure paradigm at work once more, the same paradigm that allowed Combe's Mackenzie to be read in England as a fillip to the imagination, a travel tale; and it is the same pattern that (in its inverse form) led the early Canadian tale writers to equate romance-adventure with aesthetic quality.

For readers as for the writers, the wilderness unadorned was more problematic. How could one write of the uninhabitable wilderness and yet live in it? How could one allow the wilderness to be inhabitable without implicitly denying the existing hierarchies of order? This dilemma was both logical and (in literary terms) tactical. Ostensibly documentary forms rewrote reality; clearly fictional tale forms took the writer and reader away from the empirical world. If writers chose to give up neither their place nor their vocabulary, they ran the danger of simply sounding parodic. A different and more fulfilling answer for Canadian writers lay in accepting the obliquity of the language they possessed, its inexact adaptation to non-European territory, and designing instead the implied stories of a culture in place.

"Here, in This Wilderness, . . ."

I have been arguing, directly, that conventional European expectations of Canada semantically defined the kinds of story that the idea of Canada could communicate; I have been arguing more indirectly that neither the conventional forms of romantic tale nor the narrative paradigms of presumed documentary could provide an adequate base for anglophone Canadian short fiction. Ratifying "here" required writers to do something else, to reconcile themselves with the mobility of the new world rather than to reposition the new world in the presumed stasis of the old. At the same time, writers recurrently chose to maintain received distinctions among levels of usage rather than sever all connections with the inherited tongue. There were several kinds of result, of which four demonstrate a range of nineteenth-century trends. All have to do with the sketch form and with its growing precedence in anglophone Canada as the preferred form for storytelling (it took precedence over the forms of tale and history, for example, whereas the folktale continued to exert its paradigmatic precedence in francophone Canada at the same time). The four examples in question are works by Thomas Chandler Haliburton, Sara Jeannette Duncan, Charles G. D. Roberts, and Stephen Leacock.

With Haliburton in the 1830s (as with his Maritime predecessors), there emerged a skill with vernacular anecdote that seems at first to belie everything I have just said about conventional form. Especially in his first stories of Sam, a garrulous, itinerant Yankee clock peddler in Nova Scotia, collected as *The Clockmaker*, Haliburton displays a remarkable inventiveness with speech sound and idiom (phrases such as "conniption fit" and "a nod is as good as a wink to a blind horse" are attributed to Haliburton). Yet the important feature to notice is that he accords the inventive energies of language to his Yankee character, a man with a shrewd talent for selling and an equally shrewd eye (though always biased in favor of Yankee nationalism) for political pettifoggery. Sam's anecdotes are placed within the context of the narrative sketch, which turns the anecdotes to another purpose: one involving political reform *in Canada* and shaped to Haliburton's command. Moreover, the narrator (one Squire Poker, in the early sketches an English judge) is a man of formal idiom and controlled cadence, and it is these rhythms that shape the way the reader both perceives Sam and estimates him. The judge does not wish to emulate Sam, but he does learn to like him and to admire his energy. Hence Sam and the judge at once become filters through which to study Nova Scotia. Conservative Haliburton did not endorse the republican model for his society. But he was aware of the dangers of cultural apathy. In the *Clockmaker* series, the native Nova Scotian (or "Bluenoser") has no identifiable voice. The political message Haliburton indirectly conveys (by means of formal arrangement) involves less the desirability of a separate speech than the necessity for separate action, but the two are related. The real "story" here lies not in Sam's anecdotes but in the implied response to them.

The sketch form in Canada, that is, was already by 1840 more than merely a descriptive impression or a periodical feuilleton. And it was not intrinsically static. Inherent in it was the dynamism of indirect story, frequently conveyed through the subjective eyes of an ostensibly objective recorder —the subjectivity of documentary now used as the matrix of narrative. The recorder, moreover, often used irony as the means by which to direct the reader-listener to the "narrative" dimension—that is, the alternative reading of the surface text.

Such a practice is clearly apparent by the time Leacock and Duncan were writing. In the reportorial sketches Sara Jeannette Duncan wrote for Toronto and Montréal newspapers in the 1880s and 1890s, for example, are glimpses of covert story. On the surface, a prose passage such as "Winnipeg: The Veritable West" seems to be merely an amused glimpse of a provincial society in love with its own image; and "A Visit to a Carmelite Convent" seems a travel essay, an account of a short conversation with a cloistered nun, and little more. Yet neither the glimpse of place nor the glimpse of person stops at that. Both sketches are constructed with the listening reader in mind. The irony of the voice narrating the Winnipeg sketch cuts through the most obvious social pretensions to expose the pretentious suppositions of the first-person observer-traveler herself. The irony of the Carmelite sketch is a means by which to question, through implied character, the motivations that have led to sequestration in the first instance and that underlie the claims of satisfaction in the silent cloister. Voicelessness is a thematic issue as well as a textual one. Insistently, Duncan claims the power, the necessity, of voice—especially of a voice for women. The ironies provide her with a way of speaking through—but also past—the current social norms.

For Leacock, too, in the many books he wrote in the early years of the twentieth century—most notably *Sunshine Sketches of a Little Town*— irony was a function of voice, a claim on indirect understanding. While for Duncan, however, the irony conservatively served reform, in Leacock it served the author's desire for social security in an age of increasing upheaval. His claim on fixity—on an ordered system that would act as a safeguard against social naïveté, that would, for example, resist any change in women's roles—results often in parodic satires of human foible. More often still, it resulted in topical entertainments, limited by their time to the very degree that they failed to acquire perspective toward themselves or to use voice to "narrate" the alternatives to the overt topic, the status quo.

With the works of Roberts—the "animal stories" of *Kindred of the Wild* and many other volumes—the sketch took yet another form. Like other nature writers of the time, Roberts presumed to express the thought processes that directed animal behavior, by this means asserting some connection between human beings and natural law. Yet his message was mixed. The assertions about nature textually combine a "scientific" objectivism in descriptive method with a sentimentalizing subtext, apparent in image and idiom. In "Prisoners of the Pitcher-Plant," for example, the objectivity of botanical terminology is undercut by the subjectivity of childhood similes and adjectival diminutives. Such an effect, however, was less apparent or at least less objectionable or obtrusive to the readers of Roberts's day. For them, the force of the "scientific" surface was convincing. In historical terms, the nature "story" at the time therefore won precedence over Duncan's ironies—that is, it became the more popular, influential literary *form*—especially insofar as it was taken also to represent the character of real Canadian experience. Roberts, it was understood, made clear the "wilderness sensibility" that lay at the heart of a moral civilization (the morality implied by the persistence of the sentimental subtext). Hence for Roberts's contemporaries, the sentimentality was even functional. It was Duncan, nevertheless, who gained the more discerning audience by the latter half of the twentieth century, not simply for her insights into human behavior or simply because irony later became a privileged form of discourse, but also because she evolved a technique for expressing the narrative complexities of a people who lived with uncertainty.

"People Lived and Died Alone Together . . ."

Separate but not apart. Individuals but still joined to a community. By other standards, perhaps, "fragments," but no longer just fragments of a coherent "elsewhere." Others' standards no longer constituted the sole authority either for the colonists or their art, and just as they found a new context for themselves within the emerging society in Canada, so they also began to redesign the forms by which they expressed themselves. The legitimacy of the society and the acceptability of the art depended, however, on observers' recognizing them. Literary recognition called on the interpretative sensitivities of the reader.

By the early 1900s, as Leacock's *Sunshine Sketches* demonstrates, it had become a commonplace venture to publish in a single volume a collection of sketches, which (taken separately) read as entire units but which (taken together) constituted a different kind of unit. Such a larger unit was often cumulative in effect—less a construction in sequential plotting or recurrent character than a "narrative" told by recurrent design. (This essay itself, in some measure, follows such a pattern, making a continuous narrative out of its headings, though such a narrative develops by means of its periodic reconstruction of the previous semantic constructions rather than by the simple extension of a single syntactic pattern.) Using form to reinterpret form, using sequence as a process of revisioning a previous understanding, using recurrence and pattern (rather than, necessarily, recurrent characters or an ongoing plot) as measures of narrative progress: these features marked the kinds of nonlinear sequence that were coming into play. Writers saw such works as coherent units. *Sunshine Sketches of a Little Town*, like many another example, was not titled with the phrase "and other stories" in tow: such titles (Norman Duncan's *Soul of the Street*, Duncan Campbell Scott's *In the Village of Viger*, Jessie Georgina Sime's *Sister Woman*) do not suggest the disparateness of collection that is inherent in the "and other stories" format. But a simple unitariness was not the intent of such books either; read attentively, they invite the reader to appreciate a plurality of perspectives without equating plurality with random arrangement. In arrangement, in fact, and in juxtaposition, lie some of the devices of technique that allow such works to focus on the processes of changing perspective and to see such processes (rather than fixed beginnings or fixed conclusions) as the stuff of fiction.

There were antecedents, of course. The miscellany was one, and such collections as Charles Dickens's Christmas sketches, Washington Irving's sketches and tales, and Ivan Turgenev's (variously translated) *Huntsman's Sketches* had their impact on some Canadian readers. Behind them—if reaching back so far can still suggest direct influence—lay Johnson, Addison, perhaps even Cervantes and Chaucer. Serial fiction was commonplace. One recurrent publishing experiment in the nineteenth century was to assemble a variety of fictional forms inside one loose frame. Haliburton's *Old Judge*, for example—using the literary device by which a company of travelers tell one another a variety of stories or (stranded by weather conditions) even retell stories once told them—brings together such forms as the ghost story, the morality tale, the transformation tale, the landscape sketch, the historical essay, the sentimental romance, the anecdote, the legend. Variety was one criterion of literary value that was being appealed to, the same criterion that led Moodie to interrupt the autobiographical sketches of the book edition of *Roughing It in the Bush* with verses and earnest moral lessons.

By the 1890s in Canada, such miscellanies were coming to take shape as carefully designed units. Duncan Campbell Scott's *In the Village of Viger* provides a model. It is not the variety that constitutes the structuring principle here (though, indeed, the stories in this book do follow a range of patterns, from pathetic tale to sketch and mystery) but the arrangement. By means of the arrangement, Scott constructs a narrative about social change that is only dimly apparent in each story separately. The implied narrative, in other words, is embodied in the formal structure.

On the surface Scott's individual stories tell of a May–December romance, a young man gone mad, a happy marriage, an accidental murder, and other such incidents. They are vignettes, scarcely ever extended by plot; more characteristically they proceed by image and fragmentary recorded dialogue. In "The Bobolink," for example, the central image is that of a caged bird, which a blind girl frees. In this most consciously sentimental story of the whole sequence, the image is, however, ironic. The blind girl does not regain her sight on freeing the bird; the bird offers no thanks; the girl feels no joy on having performed her action. It is not fairy tale. The very lack of correspondence is the more effective measure of "truth." Scott emphasizes such discontinuity by placing "The Bobolink" next to the most sardonic story in the volume, "No. 68 Rue Alfred de Musset," which tells of a manipulative young woman's machinations to use everyone around her—her brother especially, whom she has incarcerated—in order to advance herself in the world. She entices another young man into marriage, moreover, achieving the freedom to which she aspires only by the deliberate entrapment of others. (The social issue, of whether she acts this way by natural amorality or because social inequities dictate the forms of freedom to which women have access, remains unresolved.) Such stories as "The Bobolink" and "No. 68" can be read for their paradigmatic variation or for the way in which they reiterate thematic motifs. But they also fit into the larger scheme of the book as a whole. Scott designs the book as a set of two parallel cycles of stories: the first ends in the illusory freedoms that attend sentimentality, the second with the insecure support of knowledge. The variation in the paradigm requires the reader to shift from one apprehension of the society portrayed to another. However attractive they might be (the book's structure suggests), nostalgic versions of social behavior are ill-equipped to contend with contemporary life; yet knowledge is a problematic substitute. Its comforts, too, are potentially illusory. But at the end of the book, knowledge is the only measure by which the villagers can deal with the irrepressibility of change.

For, of course, *In the Village of Viger* also portrays a village by means of fragmentary moments from the lives of the villagers. The village, moreover, is a Québec village, on the edge of an expanding city, a village in which the church and other institutions are of less direct consequence than personalities and social relationships are. Hence Scott's portraits also have a social function, in that they report on a culture in flux, shifting—partly through the increase in urbanization, partly by the abandonment of fixed values—to embrace a motive culture it does not altogether understand. Interpreting this change opens a variety of possibilities. For one thing, values do not thereby disappear, but in an age of change old values require a kind of nurture they had not previously seemed to need; nevertheless, such faith in knowledge (however problematic) may also suggest Scott's own presumptive commitment to a cultural mainstream in Canada, a commitment devoted to empirical reason and an idea of beauty shaped by reason, presumptive because it implicitly sees alternative cultural systems within Canada as deviations from an inevitable norm.

Yet by the time of Georgina Sime's *Sister Woman*, it was clear that normative presumptions were misleading; the war had disrupted lives, and the interrupted short-story sequence came to be used as another portrayal of fracture: asserting an alternative speech and (therefore) an alternative social possibility. Again, Sime uses the vignette form, but here she does so specifically to tell incidents that reveal the hidden (i.e., the suppressed character of) female lives. She sketches the woman who chooses a life of deliberate servitude over a life of marriage, the single mother, the divorcée, the woman whose lover dies, the woman who suffers a stillbirth. This set of vignettes is contained within a loose frame, wherein a man asks a woman what it is that "women really want"; the vignettes constitute her answer. I can tell you only by stories, she replies, choosing an indirect narrative medium of explanation rather than the more familiar argumentative ones, because she knows that the man will interpret familiar patterns of discourse only in his own terms. The fractured narrative, that is, is a way of opening up social discourse, of combating received limits on discourse and of leaving results or endings inconclusive. At the same time, as the metaphors of village in Scott and sisterhood in Sime suggest, the fracture does not concurrently imply a loss of community.

"At Least, So I'm Told . . ."

Numerous short narratives at the turn of the century asserted a community only in establishment terms, as is apparent in the works of Gilbert Parker. Parker's *Pierre and His People*, for example, undertook to portray life in the Northern Woods, but the result is romance—life as distanced from local reality, which was southern-based and urban, yet as shaped by the conventions of local reality, as were the earlier tales of foreign court and Oriental intrigue. In particular, life was distanced from local norms by the rhetorical handling of speech. Dialect records of other people's speech—

stories told by others, recorded and hence distanced by a narrator using received standard speech patterns—implicitly consigned "heard lives" to a lower category of cultural accomplishment, even in the act of making stories from them. Certain vernacular speech patterns were accorded "charm" or "quaintness" (French, Scots, Irish); other "dialects" (stereotyped black diction, for example) were deemed comic. Critical practice allowed for the record of such voices in a context; but critical respect was reserved for the received standards of grammatical accuracy, periodicity, balanced pattern, "elegant" phrasing, and narrative closure. The dynamism of speech representation was resisted. Hence the role of the speechmaker was characteristically held apart from that of the storyteller, reinforcing the difference between received anglophone traditions and the contrary forms of folktale, linear narrative, and Indian myth.

Such traditions persisted over several decades, despite the increasing number of alternative fictional forms being practiced and the solidification of the sketch (or, by this time, the narrative vignette) as the form that would ratify the ordinary rhythms and vernacular pronunciation of Canadian speech. When Raymond Knister brought out his benchmark anthology *Canadian Short Stories*, he described it as a historical survey, a collection of representative examples. He focused on two periods. The first was the 1890s, a time when tales of region (Parker's Northern Woods, Norman Duncan's Newfoundland, E. W. Thomson's Scots Maritimes, and in this context Scott's Québec and Roberts's animal wilderness) were being marketed to an urban community eager for both its wilderness image (which it equated with manliness, health, and adventure) and for sophistication (which, when claimed, could allow the violence or the presumed primitivism or even the impropriety of wilderness to be consigned, safely, to the past). The other period was the 1920s, a decade when a technically more impressionistic fiction—as evidenced by the work of Morley Callaghan, Thomas Murtha, or Knister himself—was emerging to challenge the earlier conventions. The force of the cultural appeal of the earlier works shows, however, in the way the book was critically received. It was praised for establishing a Canadian tradition, and, in the words of B. K. Sandwell, the influential editor of *Saturday Night*, it was important for preserving the work of "those four princes of the last days of the century," that is, Roberts, Scott, Parker, and Thomson, whom Sandwell preferred to the "accomplished and earnest youngsters" Murtha and Callaghan. What Sandwell was honoring in fiction, in other words, was a version of tradition that the contemporary writers were already passing by and a way of using language to control alternatives, whereas it was the alternatives that were reclaiming the sketch's obliquity of form. Sandwell was also reinforcing the sense that story came from elsewhere, that other people had stories to tell, and that

Canadian fiction might suitably record them. The new writers, by contrast, were claiming voice as their own.

Sandwell had difficulty with the new writers' technique partly, it must be assumed, because he had difficulty with the premises underlying it. Elsewhere, for instance, he approved the work of Leslie Gordon Barnard, perhaps because it presumed to examine the difficulties of modern life in the familiar patterns of received discourse. Mazo de la Roche and, later, Thomas Raddall would similarly employ conventional story forms and win a popular audience. Sandwell was astute enough to recognize what it was, technically, that Callaghan and other writers of the 1920s were doing; he just had difficulty seeing why it needed to be done, and he therefore misread its effect:

> they are writing dialect, not merely when their characters are talking but when they are thinking, and not merely when the characters are thinking but when the author is thinking to himself. It is as if it were necessary for the author to impersonate an individual of the class with which he is dealing.

Callaghan and Knister were, however, not *impersonating* character, or espousing "futility" as Sandwell also suggested, or "revolting against everything that passed for style in the good old days" just for the sake of revolt. They were simply using the techniques of indirect discourse, following the lead set by the American writer Sherwood Anderson, using the cadences of speech to evoke attitudinal dilemmas in contemporary society rather than using speech as a device to ornament a stable class system and social state.

"I Said—"

Local speech became ratified both in story and by it—and became a new formal paradigm, asserting the empirical validity of the first-person voice, which subsequent generations would (as inevitably as they did previous changes) choose once more to subvert. An early section of Morley Callaghan's "Ancient Lineage," a 1928 story collected first in his *Native Argosy* and later in *Morley Callaghan's Stories,* illustrates how this technique works. It begins with a young man heading to a small Ontario town to interview an aging woman about her presumed family line; he arrives with confidence intact, his condescension toward woman, family, and small town all reinforced by his age, class, and university training in history. The story's sentences are the agency not only of establishing this impression but also of indicating the likelihood of some sort of comeuppance. Upon his arrival, the man hurried along the platform and jumped down on the sloping cinder path to the sidewalk.

Trees were on the lawns alongside the walk, branches drooping low, leaves scraping occasionally against the young man's straw hat. He saw a cluster of lights, bluish-white in the dusk across a river, many lights for a small town. He crossed the lift-lock bridge and turned on to the main street. A hotel was at the corner. (158)

Setting functions as image. The repetitive emphasis—down, slope, droop, cross, bridge, turn, and corner—suggests a point of imminent change. The rhythms, moreover (rhythms of associational as well as sequential observation), are those of unthinking security: that is, the story initially establishes the voice of a presumptive faith in the empirical limits of reality and, by analogy, in the certainties of genealogical history, which he has come to town to investigate. By the end of the story, neither border proves secure. The rhythms of the prose change, and through the altered rhythms the reader becomes aware that the young man's sexuality has begun to interfere with his presumed objectivity. It is a story about power. The reader is also reminded of the sexuality implicit in lineage: reminded (though the young man appears to remain ignorant of the signs) that the process of inheritance is a process of connection and change, not one solely of retrieving "fact" and establishing "pattern."

Between the 1930s and the 1960s, writers experimented further with vernacular cadence and the rhythms of indirect form. Callaghan published in the international avant-garde magazines of the 1920s—*Transition, This Quarter.* Knister briefly helped edit the *Midland.* Others such as Sinclair Ross, Joyce Marshall, and Henry Kreisel contributed to established journals such as *Queen's Quarterly.* Mavis Gallant began to publish regularly in the *New Yorker.* Left-wing magazines such as *New Frontier* arose in the 1930s to publish a range of writers, from Abraham Klein to Dyson Carter. And in 1956 Robert Weaver began *Tamarack Review* as a way of encouraging short forms of art (story, essay, lyric) to continue to develop. Among the books that subsequently appeared are Ross's *Lamp at Noon and Other Stories,* Knister's *First Day of Spring: Stories and Other Prose,* Marshall's *Private Place,* Kreisel's *Almost Meeting and Other Stories,* and George Elliott's *Kissing Man.*

Perhaps even more influential on short fiction than were his editorial efforts in small magazines and anthologies were Robert Weaver's efforts to introduce short fiction forms to radio. As a program designer for the Canadian Broadcasting Corporation, Weaver encouraged short-fiction writers to write for the new medium, with a listening audience in mind. As

Mavis Gallant observed, the challenge of listening was also a training in compositional technique:

> There is something relentless about a story being read aloud. Lack of rhythm, vagueness and faulty characterization are glaringly obvious because you can't skip and you can't reread. ("On the Air")

The blend of literary form and aural medium also heightened the importance of the speaking voice as an indicator of narrative nuance.

Some of the most effective of contemporary story writers—among them Gallant, Alice Munro, Margaret Laurence, Hugh Hood, Alden Nowlan, and Clark Blaise—have used first-person technique in ways that indicate their close awareness of aural idiom and rhythm. Though by no means their only strategy (Blaise's "Eyes" is a tour de force in second-person technique, for example), each of these writers uses first-person forms of speech both to provide and to transcend the illusory documentary character of realism. Like the early journals, first-person and autobiographical modes suggest the precedence of empirical record and the validity of the eye; and yet the stories of these writers question that validity at the same time, for they question the very division that separates eye from other. Hugh Hood makes the point. Along with Blaise, John Metcalf, Ray Smith, and Raymond Fraser, Hood was a member of the Montréal Story-Teller (a story "performance group" of the 1970s), and he understands the force of voice; it is the medium of implied meaning. Further, he traces the character of his own work to the sketch form and to Catholic parable (hence he acknowledges Callaghan, Leacock, and Turgenev as literary forebears, although not as models). He constructs sentences, uses style itself, to shape literary response: in style substantive communication takes place. As in his personal, cyclical evocation of Montréal life and history, *Around the Mountain*, or his studied meditations on ritual, *None Genuine without This Signature*, Hood designs careful formal patterns (iterative, triune) by which to suggest the effective borders between the shades of personal understanding and the shapes of contextual meaning.

Perhaps most directly, the several volumes of American-born Clark Blaise—among them *A North American Education* and *Resident Alien*—challenge the limits of autobiographical form. Characteristically shaped as broken sequences (stories that overlap in some formal measure, resisting both the linear sequentiality of plot and the random connections of anthological arrangement), Blaise's collections are preoccupied with the stylistic (hence attitudinal) challenges of representing experience. Experience is social; experience is also personal and verbal, open to arrangement by historical force and personal decision, both of which in turn are, for the writer, phenomena of language. Hence *Resident Alien*, for example, interleaves subjective autobiography with "autobiographical" fictional form, crossing generic borders as it tells "about" the occupational (in both its meanings: territorial or "resident" as well as vocational) hazards of moving from one set of social apprehensions to another.

For Munro and Nowlan there are further solutions to the challenges of representing and re-creating borderline sensibilities. Both used interrupted sequential form. Nowlan's *Various Persons Named Kevin O'Brien* is in some respects the most conventional example: it assembles a series of stories in chronological sequence, though by the fractured continuity between stories it asserts that the identities of the single protagonist are necessarily made multiple by time. An instructive comparison is provided by Malcolm Lowry's *Hear Us O Lord from Heaven Thy Dwelling-Place*. In this book, Lowry (who had earlier, in letters to James Stern and others, theorized about the literary function of the interrupted sequence [*Selected Letters*]) assembles a series of stories that appear separate not only in time and place but also in character. What joins them are the recurrent formal paradigms: the circle out and back, for example, adumbrated in "The Bravest Boat" and reiterated in the macrocosm of the text as a whole (a text that is in turn potentially a microcosm in other texts, and so on). Sometimes the result is comic; at others it dislocates. The formal recurrence provides a mechanism by which to examine (or at least to recognize) the book's multiple characters (or at least identities) as cumulative variants of one another. The result is a sense of self (perhaps textual, perhaps authorial) that redefines the character of coherence.

While Lowry's work thus moves in the direction of espousing the subjective autonomy of a text, for other writers empirical validity still rests in the "fact" of the process of seeing, as distinct from the "fact" of the thing seen or, especially, from the "fact" of another person seen and presumed therefore to be understood or explained by prose. Hugh Hood explains, "My own motives are mysterious to me. I can't extricate them one from another. And about your motives I know nothing. But I can see you" ("End" 156). With some writers—notably Hood himself, Gallant, Munro—literary realism is a surface illusion. The fluid uncertainties of perception and understanding, which here underlie the ostensible certainties of empirical document, consequently become a covert implied text. Such structures reiterate the idea that narrative exists at some remove from appearance, but they no longer suggest that narrative simultaneously exists at some remove from the self. The narratives in Gallant's *From the Fifteenth District*, for example—the title story, or "The Latehomecomer," or "The Moslem Wife"—communicate at once a world of empirical assertion and the several worlds of subjective interpretation that obliquely undermine the declarative realities of the first, even though they also sometimes defer to it. "The Latehomecomer" tells of a German prisoner of war, released later than he should have been after the war is over, who returns to a home that he does not recognize and that recognizes him only in its own (evasive, recollective, reconstructive) terms. While such an environment shapes how it sees him (and so remembers history), the story nevertheless belongs to the ex-soldier, whose real life (however enclosed) is not invalidated by external forces. The handling of tone and syntax tells otherwise. Again, style becomes meaning; the progress of changes in verbal aspect communicates a set of relationships that reshapes the ostensible narratives of surface belief. So with Gallant's title story, a trio of ghostly testaments that protests the way memory and documentary record have distorted for the sake of living reputations the character of the lives of the departed. Acerbic, sardonic, witty, this story distinguishes between image and likelihood; it gives a voice to those whose real voice seems to have been muted by history.

In the work of Alice Munro, Margaret Laurence, and many other writers—Sandra Birdsell, Jane Rule, Audrey Thomas, Margaret Atwood—it is the voice of women that is reclaimed from marginality. In the stories of Bharati Mukherjee, Basil Johnston, Neil Bissoondath, Austin Clarke, Gertrude Story, Mordecai Richler, W. D. Valgardson, Rohinton Mistry, and several others, it is the voice of ethnic minorities in an anglophone, particularly an anglo-Protestant, culture. In the stories of David Adams Richards and Dave Godfrey, it is the voice of a people made inarticulate by class and region. Munro's work lucidly illustrates how the literary forms of paradox and oxymoron can be made into effective weapons against cultural staleness; Laurence's stories show the difference between a literature of observation and a literature of voice. The contrast between Laurence's first story collection, *The Tomorrow-Tamer and Other Stories*, and her second, *A Bird in the House*, highlights the degree to which narrative can variously portray the otherness of others or use the fact of otherness to suggest the retrieval of self.

The stories in *The Tomorrow-Tamer* are all set in Africa; they are characteristically in third-person form; they acknowledge the force of an oral culture (now largely lost to African characters here), but they document this culture by the conventional paradigms of European written language. The ironies of form are instructive but not always evidently deliberate. In *A Bird in the House*, set in Laurence's native Manitoba, the stories are arranged as an interrupted first-person sequence, in which the several age-differentiated voices of the narrator, Vanessa MacLeod, interact with the voices of other, primarily female, characters and also with the male, written-language forms of the culture Vanessa has inherited, the forms of a culture that she (and through her, Margaret Laurence) wants to preserve in memory and ritual but to transcend in life and social attitude.

For Munro, too, place and past are the source of story; and again there is a strong temptation to read as realist social record the consequent narratives—*Something I've Been Meaning to Tell You*, for example, or *Who Do You Think You Are?* (called *The Beggar Maid* in editions outside Canada), or the "Chaddeleys and Flemings" sequence in *The Moons of Jupiter*. Once more, however, form works to counter normative expectations. In the early "The Office" (*Dance of the Happy Shades*), a woman seeking a place where she can write is hounded out of her rented room by a man determined to interpret her aspirations in his own way; the further irony of the form— the realist memoir turning into narrative fable—derives from the reader's realization that this story author has found she can tell only the man's story. The later "Chaddeleys and Flemings," which balances an anecdotal recollection of family with a documentary record of family, ultimately contrasts a matrilineal with a patrilineal heritage—claiming both, rejecting neither, but determining methodologically that "heritage" and "model" are separate notions and that a narrative "I," while never free from the constraints of social precedent and verbal code, need never be limited by a single narrative line. There comes to be an aesthetic of discontinuities. Opposites suggest likenesses. Parallel patterns invite the reader to recognize divergences. Oxymorons hint at the knots of multiple understanding that shape the shapes of both personal trauma and personal opportunity. In the shape of text itself, in other words, the realities of the fictions of life inhere.

"And the Little Dog Laughed."

Perhaps, however, the little dog is no longer the familiar figure of European fairy tale; perhaps it's Coyote, the trickster. Perhaps the European models no longer easily apply.

In recent Canadian fiction, neither realism nor modified forms of realism constitutes the only observable mode of narrative discourse. Trickster figures are common; non sequiturs and verbal fragments abound. Fracture de-signs the new whole; carnival designs the new norm. Fantasy and magic realism predominate in the works of Ray Smith (*Cape Breton Is the Thought Control Center of Canada*), Andreas Schroeder (*The Late Man*), J. Michael Yates (*The Abstract Beast*), Virgil Burnett, Brian Fawcett, Stephen Guppy, and many others. Jack Hodgins exaggerates cultural idiosyncrasies, for satiric effect, in *Spit Delaney's Island* and *The Barclay Family Theatre*. The "theater" of fiction emphasizes its antimimetic, subversive character. Audrey Thomas, in *Ladies and Escorts*, and Margaret Atwood, in *Bluebeard's Egg*, retell fairy tales in order to subvert the male biases that the fairy tales in their conventional forms encoded. Leon Rooke, in several volumes, including *The Birth Control King of the Upper Volta*, pursues the patterns of conventional fictions (detective story, adventure, romance) in order to acquire, through parody, an authorial, textual freedom from the previously trained (and therefore, in these terms, limiting) expectations of the conventional reader. George Bowering (who takes Sheila Watson rather than the realist writers as his literary mentor) pursues a similar strategy in *A Short Sad Book*, in order to challenge the documentary, explorer-model presumptions of traditional Canadian cultural analysis. And there are many other examples of the rewriting of reality. David Arnason, for example, makes language play, so that the old traditions can be reanimated. In his story "Girl and Wolf" he rewrites the European fairy tale "Little Red Riding Hood" in such a way as to invite readers to recognize all literary paradigms as verbal games. But at the same time the old tale in modern dress and contemporary idiom becomes a history of adolescence, a serious ploy, a narrative about the language of sex and the language of power. Such fantasies and parodies, however seemingly bizarre, still connect with the empirical world, for inasmuch as they lodge themselves in the subjective but narrative territory of the verbal imagination, they implicitly ask for the participation of the reader (still an empirical other) in the syntax and rhythms of discovery. Not necessarily of the discovery of meaning. "Conclusions" might even be anathema. But participation *in the text*, in the story, and therefore in speech. Heteroglossia: the polyphony of voices reconstructing history, speaking story, in the end, *here*.

WORKS CITED

Arnason, David. "Girl and Wolf." *The Circus Performers' Bar.* Vancouver: Talonbooks, 1984. 131–35.

Atwood, Margaret. *Bluebeard's Egg.* Toronto: McClelland, 1983.

Blaise, Clark. "Eyes." *A North American Education.* Toronto: Doubleday, 1973. 16–24.

——. *Resident Alien.* Markham, ON: Penguin, 1986.

Bowering, George. *A Short Sad Book.* Vancouver: Talonbooks, 1977.

Callaghan, Morley. "Ancient Lineage." *A Native Argosy.* Toronto: Macmillan; New York: Scribner's, 1929. Rpt. in *Morley Callaghan's Stories.* Toronto: Macmillan, 1959. 158–63.

Duncan, Norman. *The Soul of the Street: Correlated Stories of the New York Syrian Quarter.* New York: McClure, 1903.

Duncan, Sara Jeannette. "A Visit to a Carmelite Convent." *Week* (Toronto) 10 Nov. 1887. Rpt. in *The Prose of Life*. Ed. Carole Gerson and Kathy Mezei. Downsview, ON: ECW, 1981. 191–96.

———. "Winnipeg: The Veritable West." *Montreal Star* 6 Oct. 1888. Rpt. in *Selected Journalism*. By Duncan. Ed. T. E. Tausky. Ottawa: Tecumseh, 1978. 79–81.

Elliott, George. *The Kissing Man*. Toronto: Macmillan, 1962.

Gallant, Mavis. *From the Fifteenth District*. Toronto: Macmillan, 1979.

———. "On the Air." *Standard Review* (Montréal) 21 Feb. 1948: 4.

Haliburton, Thomas Chandler. *The Clockmaker*. Halifax: Howe, 1836. Rpt. Toronto: McClelland, 1958 [from the 1871 edition].

———. *The Old Judge*. London: Coburn, 1849. Rpt. Ottawa: Tecumseh, 1978 [from the 1860 edition].

Hearne, Samuel. *A Journey from Prince of Wales's Fort in Hudson's Bay to the Northern Ocean*. London: Strahan, 1795. Ed. Richard Glover. Toronto: Macmillan, 1958.

Hodgins, Jack. *The Barclay Family Theatre*. Toronto: Macmillan, 1981.

———. *Spit Delaney's Island*. Toronto: Macmillan, 1976.

Hood, Hugh. *Around the Mountain: Scenes from Montreal Life*. Toronto: Martin, 1967.

———. "The End of Emma." *Canadian Literature* 100 (Spring 1984): 148–56.

———. *None Genuine without This Signature*. Downsview, ON: ECW, 1980.

Knister, Raymond. *The First Day of Spring: Stories and Other Prose*. Ed. Peter Stevens. Toronto: U of Toronto P, 1976.

———, ed. *Canadian Short Stories*. Toronto: Macmillan, 1928.

Kreisel, Henry. *The Almost Meeting and Other Stories*. Edmonton: NeWest, 1981.

Lahontan, Louis Armand de Lom d'Arce, Baron de. *Nouveaux voyages*. Trans. as *New Voyages to North-America*. 1703. Rpt. with introd. by Reuben Gold Thwaites. Chicago: McClurg, 1905. Ed. Stephen Leacock as *Lahontan's Voyages*. Ottawa: Graphic, 1932.

Laurence, Margaret. *A Bird in the House*. Toronto: McClelland; New York: Knopf, 1970.

———. *The Tomorrow-Tamer and Other Stories*. Toronto: McClelland, 1963.

Leacock, Stephen. *Sunshine Sketches of a Little Town*. London: Lane, 1912.

Lowry, Malcolm. *Hear Us O Lord from Heaven Thy Dwelling-Place*. Philadephia: Lippincott, 1961.

———. *Selected Letters of Malcolm Lowry*. Ed. Harvey Breit and Margerie Bonner Lowry. Philadelphia: Lippincott, 1965.

Marshall, Joyce. *A Private Place*. Ottawa: Oberon, 1975.

Moodie, Susanna. *Roughing It in the Bush*. London: Bentley, 1852. Ed. Carl Ballstadt. Ottawa: Carleton UP, 1988.

Munro, Alice. *Dance of the Happy Shades*. Toronto: Ryerson, 1968.

———. *The Moons of Jupiter.* Toronto: Macmillan, 1982.

———. *Something I've Been Meaning to Tell You.* Toronto: McGraw-Hill Ryerson; New York: McGraw, 1974.

———. *Who Do You Think You Are?* Toronto: McGraw-Hill Ryerson, 1978. Published in the US as *The Beggar Maid.* New York: Knopf, 1979.

New, W. H. *Dreams of Speech and Violence: The Art of the Short Story in Canada and New Zealand.* Toronto: U of Toronto P, 1987.

Nowlan, Alden. *Various Persons Named Kevin O'Brien.* Toronto: Clarke, 1973.

Parker, Gilbert. *Pierre and His People.* London: Methuen, 1892.

Roberts, Charles G. D. *Kindred of the Wild.* Boston: Page, 1902.

———. "Prisoners of the Pitcher-Plant." *The Haunters of the Silences.* Toronto: Copp Clark, 1907. 84–91.

Rooke, Leon. *The Birth Control King of the Upper Volta.* Downsview, ON: ECW, 1982.

Ross, Sinclair. *The Lamp at Noon and Other Stories.* Toronto: McClelland, 1969.

Sandwell, B. K. "The Short Story in Canada." *Saturday Night* 25 Aug. 1928: 7.

Schroeder, Andreas. *The Late Man.* Port Clements, BC: Sono Nis, 1972.

Scott, Duncan Campbell. *In the Village of Viger.* Boston: Copeland, 1896. Rpt. as *In the Village of Viger and Other Stories.* Toronto: McClelland, 1973.

Sime, Jessie Georgina. *Sister Woman.* London: Richards, 1919.

Smith, Ray. *Cape Breton Is the Thought Control Center of Canada.* Toronto: Anansi, 1969.

Struthers, J. R., ed. *The Montreal Story Tellers: Memoirs, Photographs, Critical Essays.* Montréal: Véhicule, 1985.

Thomas, Audrey. *Ladies and Escorts.* Ottawa: Oberon, 1977.

Yates, J. Michael. *The Abstract Beast.* Port Clements, BC: Sono Nis, 1972.

Shirley Neuman

AFTER MODERNISM: ENGLISH-CANADIAN POETRY SINCE 1960

> It is quite apparent that the American example will become more and more attractive to Canadian writers; that we are approaching a period when we will have "schools" and "movements" whose origin will be American. And perhaps it is safe to say that such a period is the inevitable half-way house from which Canadian poetry will pass towards an identity of its own.
>
> John Sutherland

> I don't see much Modernism in our literature.... We came into contemporary writing with relative ease because we didn't have an Eliot or a Pound to deal with.... I think that has been because we had little contact with Modernism but also because we have ... basically an open, discontinuous system of communication. A great deal of what happens in Canada, including our literature, has to do with our having always to deal with gaps and spaces. Our national discontinuities made us ripe for Postmodernism.
>
> Robert Kroetsch

BETWEEN THE PRESCIENCE of John Sutherland's observation and the retrospection of Robert Kroetsch's, the poetry that concerns me in this essay gets written. Sutherland's was a prophecy already fulfilled by the 1950s as a group of Montréal poets—Louis Dudek, Raymond Souster, and Irving Layton among them—took the colloquial speech rhythms of William Carlos Williams and Charles Olson for their own. In 1961, the Montréal poets became a (quickly renounced) example for a group of young writers in Vancouver. These writers, who included George Bowering, Frank Davey, and Fred Wah, adopted aspects of the poetics of Olson, Creeley, and Duncan and began editing the mimeographed magazine they irreverently named with the anagram *TISH*. By that time, Black Mountain poetics had become far more influential in Canada than it would ever be in the United States.

Robert Kroetsch's speculation from *Labyrinths of Voice* (Neuman and Wilson) proves more problematic. It elides issues that critics less intent on constructing a master narrative of recent Canadian literary history will want to take up: since Canadian poets have always read their Anglo-American colleagues and predecessors, in what sense can they be said not to have to "deal with" Pound, Eliot, and modernism? Which modernism are we talking about? Eliot's? Pound's? H. D.'s? Stein's? Williams's? Stevens's? *Were* these modernisms absent from Canadian letters? Is postmodernism not continuous with modernism rather than opposed to it, and do we not find modernism's traces in postmodernist writing, particularly when that writing had its impetus in Canada from Black Mountain poetics, which had its impetus from Pound...? Does *postmodernism* in fact describe Canadian poetry of the last twenty-five years or does it inscribe a new set of inclusions and exclusions in a shifting canon? What does the use of *postmodernism* in reference to Canadian poetry tell us about the interests at work in its invocation, in view of the term's apparent inclusion, in a master narrative, of George Bowering, Fred Wah, Daphne Marlatt, bpNichol, Michael Ondaatje, Robert Kroetsch himself, sometimes Eli Mandel, sometimes Phyllis Webb, and Lola Lemire Tostevin but its apparent exclusion of Irving Layton, Margaret Avison, Al Purdy, Wilfred Watson, P. K. Page, D. G. Jones, and Dorothy Livesay?

Despite such questions, Kroetsch's assertion has received uncritical welcome. That welcome attests to its double-edged narrative appeal. One side of its labrys represses the post-Eliot literary history described by John Sutherland in which the "new poetry" in Canada in the 1940s remained colonial because "predominantly English in tone," still mostly written by "a cultured English group who are out of touch with a people who long ago began adjusting themselves to life on this continent" (16). To represent Canadian poetry as having leaped from the pinnacle of a nature-and-nationalism verse, across the abyss of modernism, to land surefooted on an opposite plateau of postmodernism is at least in part a narrative of postcolonial resistance to colonial debates and tropes that dominated dis-

cussion of Canadian literature from the 1930s through the 1970s. There
was the decades-long debate, for example, about whether literature should
be "regional" or "cosmopolitan" and whether it could be both; and there
were tropes such as Northrop Frye's "garrison mentality" (830) and Margaret Atwood's *Survival*. On the other side of the labrys, Kroetsch's assertion disseminates a narrative by which a group of poets unfledged in 1960
and now central (as writers, publishers, and critics) in the production and
reception of Canadian poetry become precursors in a brave new postcolonial literature. This is a narrative of resistance *within* Canada embraced
by a generation of poets who first admired but soon wished to supersede
those who, writing since the 1940s, remained powerful and productive. And
it is a narrative by poets most of whom began their literary careers on the
prairies or West Coast asserting themselves against the literary hegemony
of Montréal and Toronto. The trajectory of that double resistance is inscribed in *TISH*. Where George Bowering in *TISH* 6 "agree[s] with most of
the description Layton issues about the nature of poetry" and labels him
"a good poet," although condemning his "extrapoetical ranting" ("Quarter's
Worth"), by *TISH* 9 he complains in an obvious allusion to Layton among
others about "Eastern poets who are satisfied to heap the page with images
of blood & narcissistic sexuality & hope they can pass it off as passion"
("Eyes" 11). Frank Davey's editorial in *TISH* 11 fulminates against the mis-
understanding of Black Mountain and beat poetry disseminated by "certain
Toronto magazine editors" (1), and in his response to a letter from Denise
Levertov in the same issue he represents himself as "continually annoyed
by eastern Canadians with an over-abundance of form, myth, and image,
and no testimony." By *TISH* 13 Davey demands that editors "suppress [the]
future ravings ... of Layton, ... once quite a promising poet," whose work
is now "unreasoned, clumsy, archaic, dull and clichéed," as well as flawed
by "a marked and skulking avoidance of real literary issues" ("Brief Review"). Between the beginnings of *TISH* and Davey's rough rhetoric in issue
13, the editors enact the prelude to the double edge of Kroetsch's literary-
historical narrative. As Sheila Watson would later put it in an allusion to
"Laurentian Man," one of Wilfred Watson's satires of Layton (*Poems* 47–
49; first published in 1959 in another West Coast literary journal, *Prism*),
"an ironic tension could exist between Pacific and Laurentian man" (Bowering, *West Window* 9; preface). Like many such narratives, the one developed in the wake of *TISH* and recently disseminated by Kroetsch constructs
a story of itself as origin and end by "reading history backwards," as Eli
Mandel, quoting Juliet Mitchell, has it (*Family Romance* xii). Doing so, it
occludes recognition both of the complexity of its own genealogy and of
the continuing activities of family members not central to its own version
of the family romance.

The Narrative's Exclusions: Layton, Avison, Purdy

The 1958 to 1963 winners of the Governor General's Awards for poetry can roughly signal the context against which the *TISH* generation of poets defined itself: James Reaney for *A Suit of Nettles* in 1959; Irving Layton for *A Red Carpet for the Sun* in 1960; Margaret Avison for *Winter Sun* in 1961; Robert Finch for *Acis in Oxford* in 1962; finally, Reaney, again, for *Twelve Letters to a Small Town*. Reaney's first award was for a set of satiric pastoral eclogues; the second for an autobiographically reminiscent collection of prose poems and dialogues cast as a libretto. Like Finch, he drew heavily on mythic and archetypal traditions. However, despite the overwhelming influence of Northrop Frye's archetypal theory of modes on Canadian criticism of the period, poetry such as Finch's and Reaney's had little influence in the 1960s and after.

Polemical, egotistic, and anti-intellectual, Layton in *A Red Carpet for the Sun* celebrated a bawdy and avowedly proletarian poet-as-chastiser-and-prophet, satirized his (he thought) phlegmatic Canadian audience, spoke out of a specific history of marginalization as the son of Jewish immigrants and out of an unfocused socialism, and asserted his sexual and intellectual mastery of one woman after another in aggressively unpolished verse that relied on devices as trivial as frequent "rhymes" on the word *bum*. Presenting himself as an irrational, outraged, and besieged one-man literary and sexual revolution, Layton throughout his career nonetheless looked backward at least as often as forward: his quarrel was with the intellectualism of poets such as Eliot and particularly with their display of learnedness and their formal preoccupations. In this he carried on a struggle begun by the poets in *New Provinces* to put their own earlier modernism behind them and to be "post-Eliot" (Gnarowski, introduction to *New Provinces* xi, quoting F. R. Scott to E. J. Pratt, 11 Jan. 1934). John Sutherland accurately represented Layton's particular place as central to "the new social poetry of the forties" written in the wake of W. H. Auden, Stephen Spender, Dylan Thomas, and George Barker (13), to which Layton added and vulgarized the poetic diction of William Carlos Williams; it was a place Layton never left. If, however, Layton's proletarianism, his bawdiness, and his colloquialism ranked him with the "new" poets of his generation, his social preoccupations frequently remained those of certain of the modernists: he writes out of a humanist tradition that decries "this singular business of human evil," that seeks a stay against that moment when "the Poet, as a type, [will] join the Priest, the Warrior, the Hero, and the Saint as melancholy museum pieces for the titillation of a universal babbitry," that finds "a modern tragedy [in] the depersonalization of men and women" and fears "[m]odern women . . . cast in the role of furies striving to castrate the male;

their efforts aided by all the malignant forces of a technological civilization that has rendered the male's creative role of revelation superfluous" (*Red Carpet*; foreword). Whatever Layton's struggles against the modernists, his charges against the world are precisely theirs: they echo those of Yeats, Eliot, Pound, and Wyndham Lewis.

If to the West Coast poets Layton at first appeared as an example to be reckoned with (he had, after all, embraced the colloquialism of Williams, and Williams had embraced him in his introduction to Layton's *Improved Binoculars*), then as a force to be reckoned against, Margaret Avison for quite different reasons was first welcomed, then no longer discussed. Her obvious attractiveness included her commitment to language and music in poetry: she handles in concrete language and with technical virtuosity a range of prosodic forms from sprung rhythm and free verse to quatrains, rondeaux, sonnets, and sardonic couplets. Moreover, her poetic credo at first glance seems akin to the phenomenological poetics being developed out of Olson's *Maximus* poems: "The optic heart must venture: a jail-break / And re-creation" (*Winter Sun* 17; "Snow"). But hers is also a formal and formalist verse, and her poetics of the "optic heart," which posits the harmony of image, emotion, spiritual journey, and writing, proves more metaphysical than proprioceptive, and shows Avison herself to be more modernist than potentially postmodernist. Although invited with six United States Black Mountain and beat poets as a speaker at the 1963 Vancouver Poetry Conference, where she impressed George Bowering as "a spirit" who "gives herself & the gift is great" (*West Window* 54), she was written out of Dave Dawson's account of the conference in *TISH* 21, an account that concentrated on the male American poets (right down to Duncan's orange socks). Avison was also written out of further discussions of the new poetics.

Other poets' work about whom we now hear comparatively little has affinities with that of Layton or Avison. Al Purdy, for example, masters a colloquial and anecdotal voice, weds it to controlled prosody as Layton never could, and conjoins it to wryly lyrical insights. At home with a wide range of learning and poetic styles, Purdy can hazard a contrast such as that between Kiangs, Onagers, and "the last Quagga screaming in African highlands" and the Cariboo horses "arriving here at chilly noon / in the gasoline smell of the / dust and waiting 15 minutes / at the grocer's" (8), a contrast that depends on its controlled free-verse diminuendo. Purdy took what served him from William Carlos Williams and the Black Mountain poets, yet, perhaps because he never developed the same phenomenological poetics or the same degree of self-reflexivity about poetry and about literary intertextuality as did the group of mainly West Coast poets beginning from the same sources, he too has been increasingly marginalized by the narrative of postmodernism in Canada.

The Narrative's Undecidabilities: Page, Jones, Birney, Livesay, Watson

Still other poets belong to "a generation caught between generations: post(modern)/modern." The phrase is again Robert Kroetsch's, spoken this time with an ear to gradations in order to describe Eli Mandel and D. G. Jones ("For Play" 103). In Mandel's transition from learned and formalist rhetoric to the recognition—in long poems such as *Out of Place* and *Life Sentence*—that language mediates rather than reproduces experience, critical emphasis has fallen on his later postmodernist work. But the premodern-to-postmodern narrative leap has dealt less generously with a group of poets who belong, broadly speaking, to the tradition of Margaret Avison, poets such as P. K. Page and D. G. Jones who use polished and sometimes traditional verse forms and learned allusions to convey personal epiphanies. Always prosodically precise, P. K. Page's poetry has increasingly reached for the sacred. Generally cited for her poems of the 1940s on social themes such as "The Stenographers" and "Typists" (22–24), she turned from this work to poems that move from a strong visual image to an epiphanic recognition. The image of children gopher-hunting, for example, expands to "we two, dots upon that endless plain, Leviathan became / and filled and broke / the glass air like twin figures, vast, in stone" (61; "And We Two"). Or she finds the satirized "terrible tourists with their empty eyes" also "somehow beautiful": "Classic in their anxiety they call / all sculptured immemorial stone / into their passive eyes, as rivers / draw ruined columns to their placid glass" (66; "The Permanent Tourists"). Page's later belief in Sufism, with its doctrine of an Absolute Being who is Absolute Beauty and therefore apprehensible through the phenomenal world, intensifies the import of these optically sharp moments: "A dream through binoculars / seen sharp and clear" yields the metaphoric and epiphanic insight, "A single leaf can block a mountainside; / all Ararat be conjured by a leaf" (97, 100; "Cry Ararat!").

While D. G. Jones does not embrace a doctrine of the sacred such as Avison's Christianity or Page's Sufism, epiphanic moments tending to consecration of the natural world do figure largely in his work, which is concerned not with "knowledge, no, but a constant / reintegration" into the "disaggregate world" (69, 94; "Diamond Sutra," "Soon, Yes"). This reintegration is achieved in poetry through precision of perception and language. Poststructuralist undecidability occasionally surfaces in his work but as a kind of tour de force refutation rather than as a question of poetics: in "A Little Mise en Abîme" (100), for example, the deconstruction of a series of unstable puns and homonyms begins *matter/mater (ma)* and reverses di-

rection to end up at identity (*am*). Jones's more usual epiphanies are
phenomenal, and his metaphors often become literal, no more so than in
his most praised sequence, "Kate, These Flowers ... (The Lampman Poems),"
where acrostics spell the plants whose features make literal the emotions
of the lovers: "GrassEs in snow" (sec. 10), for example, begins "Gone, love's
body, like a field / reclaimed by winter / ... flesh itself / surrendered to the
uniform / Euclidean space" (53).

Two other poets seldom alluded to in the trend to a master narrative
for postmodernist poetry, both writing since the 1920s and both living in
Vancouver in the 1960s, found new stimulus in the poetic revisionism going
on around *TISH* and around the visits of Duncan, Denise Levertov, Creeley,
and Olson. Earle Birney in his *Collected Poems* extensively rewrote even
his 1920s work in the direction of the new poetics, and during the last two
decades of his career he experimented radically with verse forms, typog-
raphy, and concrete poetry in ways consistent with the emergence at the
end of the 1960s of sound-poetry groups such as *The Four Horsemen* and
Re/Sounding. Dorothy Livesay in her earliest work had been imagist, while
in poems such as "Depression Suite" and "Catalonia" (86–91, 98–101) she
documented more strongly than did any of her contemporaries the socialist
themes of the 1930s; yet the 1960s and her exposure to the Vancouver
poetry scene ("Now that the poetry's bursting out / all over the place," she
wrote in "The Incendiary" [262]) turned her from social documentary to
a poetics in which concrete images and taut lines chronicled the subjective
experience of the woman in her body and in her society. Late in life, she
would break into fiercely erotic and self-assertive love poetry that, with
the exception of a special issue of *Room of One's Own* (1979), has been
unjustly neglected by Canadian feminist critics, who theorize feminism
largely within a poststructuralist context.

Livesay and Birney prove difficult to locate in a narrative of postmodernist poetry because they adapt the language practices of the 1960s poetic
revisionism without entirely adopting its sense of language's relation to
the world. If we try, as Robert Kroetsch seems to, for a perfect fit of postmodernism and contemporary Canadian poetry, what looks like postmodernism but in fact comes from sources other than Black Mountain poetics
or poststructuralist theory proves a particular problem as we stumble
against the work of one anomalous poet after another. Consider Margaret
Atwood, who apart from *The Journals of Susanna Moodie* does not figure
in Kroetsch's narrative; but she is another essay. Or take the very different
poet Wilfred Watson.

Watson's first collection, *Friday's Child*, used intense imagery in a rhetoric that, while undeniably skillful, remained under the sway of W. B. Yeats
and Dylan Thomas. During the 1960s, departing from the ideas of Marshall

McLuhan and of Bertolt Brecht and Antonin Artaud and working closely with all aspects of rehearsal, he created some of the most experimental theater in Canada. His plays had their effect on his poetry: in the early 1960s he wrote his way through his fascination with Yeats's late poems (and through Yeats's fascination with Blake) by dramatizing a woman's voice in the "Bawl of Wool" sequence (*Poems* 63–140). Speaking through "Jenny Blake" enabled Watson to adopt a freer metric and a more colloquial style and, by satirizing the culture from a woman's persona, to rid himself of the monologically didactic voice of the Poet. Returning constantly to Greek and Renaissance drama and to the Christian mass for dramatic structures, Watson gradually evolved a contrapuntal choric technique for the most savage and anguished political poetry written in Canada during these years. By the late 1960s, in the work collected as "pièces je constate," he provided counterpoint in a poem such as "good friday, 1970" by means of a chorus interrupting the poem's narrative to remind the reader that "THE INVADERS OF VIETNAM ARE PRISONERS" (*Poems* 170), while in poems such as the following "Lines 1967" his contrapuntal voices made his satiric point by analogy:

> they flew across our borders at the speed of light.
> **HANOI IS HERE**
> dropping images which fell alike on women children and infants
> **HANOI IS HERE**
> we had only a few poems to defend ourselves with
> **HANOI IS HERE**
> and no strong men like Thoreau, Whitman or Lincoln
> **HANOI IS HERE** . . .
> they raked our streets with plays.
> they sent in lowflying jets armed with recordings.
> they blew us to bits just as we were saying
> they seemed such nice people.
> **HANOI IS HERE.** (*Poems* 172)

Moving increasingly toward performance, Watson would in his later poetry devise a number grid system of notation by which he could count syllables, words, and even phrases and, by stacking them, precisely coordinate the simultaneous speaking of two or more contrapuntal voices. The resulting poetry, he maintained, consisted neither in its visual form on the page nor in its auditory form in performance but in "its *transformations* from its visual to its auditory forms" (*Mass* xiv), with its potential for repeated transformations producing its vitality.

The poets I have been discussing each share something with the poetics of those now termed postmodern. Yet even though they often foreground language in its relation to the world as the essential problem or material of poetry, privilege the colloquial, invent notations for the music of the poem, draw on eclectic materials, and use discontinuous or interrupted forms, their poetics still retains something of the metaphysical in their responses to the traditions and contexts in which they found themselves. The sum of their poetics, while hardly modernist, does call into question the notion that Canadian poetry leaped over modernism into postmodernism. It does not, however, equal the sum of postmodernism.

The Narrative's Inclusions: TISH and After

In editorials, reviews, and essays, *TISH* outlined a postmodern poetics derived from Charles Olson, Robert Duncan, and Robert Creeley. It called on poets to speak in the idioms and rhythms of oral language, to take the breath as the measure of the line, and to use language as material substance and subject of poetry. Living and writing in the materiality of language, some Canadian poets regarded as the most significant aspect of their poetics a phenomenological relation between language and the "real" that, like Olson, they termed proprioceptive. Wah explained in a self-introductory manifesto in *TISH* 1:

> The origin of the poem is an action (interaction, reaction) between the poet and the actual living forces in our environment (objects, human behavior, facts and events). There is ... percussive and reverberating energy released from a cathexis of the poet on contemporary reality—a merging of himself with his natural surroundings, aiming at establishing a connection between language and reality. And this alliance, this new equilibrium set up, is the energy of musical release which is the poem ... as an energy preserving object. It must preserve the instants of the poet's own dance with his environment.... (Editor's statement)

Although this initial formulation is derivative of Olson's *Maximus Poems* and adaptive of Pound's definition of *logopoeia* as the "dance of the intellect among words" (25), it states the fundamental assumption, however arrived at, however phrased, underlying the divergent texts of Canadian postmodern poetry.

In a poetics in which the writer establishes "a connection between language and reality" through the poet's own perceiving consciousness, the notion, as Robert Creeley put it in a *TISH* 13 editorial, that "art is local ... to a place and to a person" became particularly important. For once in Canada, *place* referred not to nation or region but rather to phenomenological "stance," an idea elliptically conjoined to poetic form by Frank

Davey: "the margin is LOCUS (of the poet) is REALITY (to the poet). The margin is the indicator of the poet's location/stance/locus (for reception) in the universe" ("Problem" 11). Fred Wah elaborated on this explanation, defining the poet's stance as the "relationship that he sets up between himself and his environment" (or the "real") and the poet's locus as "the location of the poet, the position in which he is standing," a position that is "the medium between (the overlapping place of) the poet's STANCE and the poem, on the page or voiced. It includes both realities ..." ("Margins" 5).

Before such enunciations, the distinction between modernism and postmodernism breaks down or holds up at all only if we confine *modernism* to a symbolist-derived aesthetics running from Mallarmé through Eliot to Wallace Stevens. As Marjorie Perloff shows us in her reading of Harold Bloom's criticism, such a definition of modernism reifies the lyric "as expression of a moment of absolute insight, of emotion crystallized into a timeless pattern" (*Dance* 181) at the expense of fragmented, discontinuous, narrative, and encyclopedic forms. T. S. Eliot's definition of poetry as "escape from emotion," "escape from personality" (21), Perloff points out, continues to reify Romantic "stress ... on subjectivity," for it still figures a poet "confronted by Self" (*Dance* 179–80). But if we distinguish between "modernisms," if we grant what Perloff terms "the other tradition" (*Poetics* viii), then the Black Mountain poets' own assertion of continuity with Pound's emphasis on the musical phrase and with Williams's emphasis on speech idiom and rhythm, as well as the attentiveness writers such as George Bowering and bpNichol paid to Gertrude Stein's insistence that what writing is takes shape from the process of writing, directed by the word qua word, makes perfect sense: Canadian postmodernist poetry, like that in the United States, has its impetus in and is continuous with this "other tradition." (And, despite the reductiveness of the statement with which Robert Kroetsch conflates the modernisms of Pound and Eliot to separate them from postmodernism, he knows this very well, for he coedited for many years *Boundary 2: A Journal of Postmodern Literature*, each issue of which prints Pound's phrase "Le Paradis n'est pas artificiel / but is jagged.")

The emphasis on the materiality of proprioceptive language especially informs the entire oeuvre of Daphne Marlatt and Fred Wah. Marlatt summarizes this poetics in *What Matters*:

> *perceive* (apprehend, seize what exists:
>
> the bodies of words: their physical reality (sound)
> their meanings   history & derivatives
>   association, ways of linking ...

poetics then consists of attention to extension (implication unfolded
no more the notion of filling up a form—but the *act*, out in the open

care with words means/words mean with their interactions   (23)

In her early work, Marlatt uses that poetics to describe her immediate
world in works such as *Our Lives* with

> language making connections as i felt our lives were ... from one to one, to
> the family & house, to the society I walked & dreamed & talked myself inside
> & out of. Trying to be free to follow the line to the edge of the page, & finding
> out what happens after you fall off the edge, continuing.   (39–40)

"Continuing" is what happens in *Steveston*, Marlatt's long poem about a
Japanese fishing and cannery community on the mouth of the Fraser River.
"Imagine a town," she instructs herself (13); "multiplicity simply there: the
physical matter of / the place (what matters) meaning" (23). Outside the
community, as she seeks to apprehend it from within, her perception includes an awareness that the town's own perception of her affects her
interactions with it; she preserves the energy not only of her apprehending
but of the interaction it generates. In the poem, the Fraser River embodies
something of this interactive process; it gives rhythm to Steveston's lives
and *Steveston*'s lines: "This is the story of a town," Marlatt (never) ends,

> these are the people, whose
> history locates inside of dream, in site of (in situ) down by the riverbank a
> torrent pouring past its sloughs & back channels ...
> by reaches of the sea our lives respond to, irresistibly drawn, these
> precarious floats, boats equipt with the latest machinery ...
> ... always continuing to return, always
> these lovely & perilous bodies drifting in spawn, swarm on out to sea.   (86)

In Fred Wah's *Pictograms from the Interior of B.C.* the pictograms (Wah's
letter pictures) face reproductions of pictographs (Indian rock paintings),
but the pictograms neither explicate nor illustrate the pictographs. Instead,
they interact with them. The poem comes into being neither in the words
nor in the drawings but in the interaction between the two in which the
reader participates. In *Breathin' My Name with a Sigh* the very title makes
material in language the poet's grief at his father's death by uttering their
name, "Wah," through the intake ("breathin'") and outrush ("sigh") of
breath. Language and perception become phenomenologically one and
continue as the poet listens to the breath that materializes his name, his
signature, going on:

> the build up
> how I listen to myself make it
> "hold on"
> so that the day remains open
> the next collision in the light
> and catch up to the breath
> breathing somewhere
> > > the air
>
> as it comes out ahead of me
> wah^h, wah^h

Such poetry necessarily remains open-ended, since, as long as the perceiving and interacting consciousness of the writer goes on, so, presumably, can the poem. "The poem as long as a life. The lifelost poem" (Kroetsch, "Continuing Poem" 81), the *Life Sentence* (Mandel), the "biotext" (Bowering, *Errata*), the long poem, in short, proves a ubiquitous (non)genre in Canadian postmodernism. Understood phenomenologically as a poem of process, it finds its apotheosis in *The Martyrology*, which bpNichol repeatedly pronounced ended and which continued to continue. For Nichol "sacredness" resides neither in world nor in language itself but in "the *activity* of language" ("Talking" 234; my emphasis) which connects the two:

> in vocation
> i am
> a singer
>
> every letter
> invokes a spell
> ing is
> the power
> letters have
> over me
>
> word shaping
>
> addition of the I
> (*Book 3*; "Coda: Mid-Initial Sequence")

The poet, an "i ambient / eye / ear" (*Book 6*; "After Bird," sec. 7), looks "for the place the puns flesh out," where "the body of speech / is re vealed the veil / drops away" (*Book 6*; "Inchoate Road," sec. 8) and the poem "re veal[s]" the "realating of realationship's shape / between the letter & the letter / word and worlds / . . . which is the day to day life of writing" (*Book 5*; chain 9).

Such work makes quickly apparent the postmodern attributes of recent

Canadian long poems: self-reflexivity; playfulness; open-endedness; an acknowledgment of the impossibilities of origin; strategies of deferral and
discontinuity; metonymy; formal, rhetorical, and generic eclecticism; intertextuality; a conception of language as inescapably mediating our knowledge or perception of the real; and a repudiation of holistic notions of the
self. Many of those attributes structure an unequaled 1965 sequence, Phyllis
Webb's "Naked Poems" (*Vision Tree*). It includes a "Non Linear" suite, a
"Suite of Lies," and "Some Final Questions" cast as questions and answers
and ending with a single question of many and no possible meanings, "*Oh?*"
(108). Using language that is minimal, "naked," each poem makes anguish
and loss felt not through stated sentiment or description but through gaps,
discontinuities, repetitions, what Webb calls its "total music":

> In a suite like this where the image is not realized in terms of metaphor,...
> the *thing* is named—like the room, the plum colour, the curtains and the
> gold colour. These ... have a kind of image-like impact as they build up ...
> a linking effect and are part of what I'd call the total music of the
> poem. ("Polishing" 48)

That she too depended on Williams to arrive at this poetic she makes clear
when, speaking of "the physics of the poem, Energy/Mass," she alludes to
the "The Red Wheelbarrow": "So much depends upon: the wit of the syntax,
the rhythm and speed of the fall, the drop ..." ("On the Line" 66–67).

Such poetry shares with all postmodernism a destabilization of the notion
of presence that has underpinned more traditional poetics. Webb gives the
"I" of "Naked Poems" so little "self," for example, that readers generally
fail to notice that the poem inscribes the desire not only of the poet for
the poem but of the bereaved woman for the departed woman; that is, the
process of inscribing that desire signifies more than its object. In a work
as different from "Naked Poems" as Michael Ondaatje's *The Collected Works
of Billy the Kid*, disjunctures in the self multiply: between the accepted
literary sense of "collected works" and the "works" Billy's left (gun) hand
effected; between the documentary and the poetic Billy; between the view-
points of Billy, Angela D., Sally Chisum, Pat Garrett; between interviews,
biographies, poems, and comic books; between written discourses and
photographs; between languages and photographs and the blank frame that
opens the book; between Billy's life (ended) and the poet's writing (going
on): "It is now early morning, was a bad night. The hotel room seems
large.... I smell the smoke still in my shirt" (105). We can construct no
self or persona out of the gaps, ambiguities, and contradictions of these
poems; at many moments we cannot even be sure whether we are reading
about Billy or the poet (or both). Writing and written from a stance that

throughout *The Geographical History of America* Gertrude Stein called "entity" rather than "identity," the "I" written and writing itself in such poems is "adrift between the signifier & the signified / sliding thru the years / myself as definition changing" (Nichol, *Book 5*; chain 3). The archaeological metaphor in a title such as *Field Notes* for Kroetsch's "continuing poem" signals the shards of discourse and narrative (excerpts from the real world, as another title has it) that make up the poem. Lines in the first person cancel each other by beginning alternately with "and" and "but" ("The Sad Phoenician" and "The Silent Poet Sequence"); a column of realist description opposes a column of surrealist dream imagery (*Field Notes*: "The Criminal Intensities of Love as Paradise"); the "poem" and "the story of the poem" interpenetrate in "Mile Zero," "the story of the poem / become / the poem of the story / become" (*Advice* 41). "Double or noting," Kroetsch teases us seriously in a poem about having encountered his *doppelgänger*-with-a-difference: "The notation / keeps it moving" (*Advice* 120, 127; "The Frankfurt *Hauptbahnhof*"). But that "it" has no clear antecedent; "it" refers to a poem and a self in flux in the margins of these differing discourses.

Such an open-ended, discontinuous, and paradoxical notion of self as "definition changing" through the very act of writing inevitably calls into play the many (generic) discourses of the apprehending and changing self or selves in (changing) place(s). An early work by George Bowering, *Rocky Mountain Foot*, effects such a discursive collage. Its proprioceptive lyrics share each page with excerpts from other poems, newspaper reports, histories, guidebooks, and the "Back to the Bible Hour"—a weekly Sunday broadcast by Alberta's Premier Manning—all enacting perceptions of Alberta and cumulatively seeming to confirm that "*nobody / belongs anywhere, // even the / Rocky Mountains // are still / moving*" (125). Journals and poems differ from and double each other in Eli Mandel's *Life Sentence*. The discourses of letters, ledgers, seed catalogs, tombstones, airline tickets, railway schedules, country and western music, hockey broadcasts, journals, and translations create an intertextuality of word and world in Kroetsch's poetry. The writer's own (other) work can become part of an *intra*textuality: later books of *The Martyrology* reassess the earlier books' mythology of saints and once "translate" passages from the earlier books into the style of the Language Poetry movement (*Book 5*; chain 4). Phyllis Webb's chameleon "I" in *Water and Light* both plays off several literary Daniels in the "I Daniel" sequence and makes her own earlier "Naked Poems" part of the new text's "now" by numerous allusions to the "star fish / fish star" inversion that serves as epigraph to "Naked Poems" and that, of course, calls up Ishtar. Such inter- or intratextuality inscribes the apprehending consciousness as continuous with and different from itself and others. Interpreted as an intersection of the cultural and the personal, intertextuality gives us Robert Kroetsch's "Delphi: A Commentary" (*Advice*) in which the poet's "commentary" typographically surrounds on up to three sides quotations from James Frazer's commentary on Pausanias's commentary on Delphi. George Bowering's *Kerrisdale Elegies* most radically materializes the intersection of the cultural and the personal by recognizably "translating" line for line Rilke's *Duino Elegies*. But his "translation" is not from German into English but from Rilke's consciousness as inscribed in *Duino Elegies* into the consciousness, the "now" of George Bowering, middle-aged (postmodern) poet living in Vancouver's Kerrisdale in the 1980s. More important than freeing the writer from Rilkean poetics, such intertextuality makes material in language his (differing) interaction from his own (differing) locus.

An/other: The Feminist Postmodernism of Marlatt and Tostevin

Theorists of proprioceptive poetics did not consider that the consciousness apprehending the world was gendered ("the poet, he" is omnipresent in *TISH*); nonetheless their emphasis on the poet's stance did make a space within which Daphne Marlatt could write into the body of language the language of a child-carrying, child-bearing, child-nurturing body in *Rings*. It was a rare moment in Canadian poetry, where feminist themes such as Livesay's and Atwood's have been far more common than have attempts to develop specifically feminist poetics, and it was a moment that Marlatt would try for again in *How Hug a Stone*. There the poet stands between her son and her mother, apprehending through etymology and genealogy her changing and plural place as daughter/mother in what Marlatt conceives of as the mater/iality of language and body.

However, despite Marlatt's work within a proprioceptive context, feminist poetics did not significantly intersect with postmodernist poetics in Canada until the early 1980s. French poststructuralist theory proves crucial in bringing about this conjunction. It has only recently been accessible to non-French speakers through translations but also through the increased contact between anglophone and francophone feminist writers in Canada brought about by the 1983 Women and Words/Les femmes et les mots conference in Vancouver (of which Marlatt was an organizer) and by translations into English of the work of Nicole Brossard, Louky Bersianik, Denise Boucher, and Jovette Marchessault. Central to the development of a postmodernist feminist poetics in English Canada are Daphne Marlatt (who also works with Brossard on mutual translations) and Lola Lemire Tostevin, a francophone living in body and in language in English Canada. Both make space for feminism within postmodernist poetics by appeal to Julia Kristeva's distinction between *phéno-texte*, the "logical" language of communication, discursive analysis, and semantics, and *géno-texte*, the rhythmical, "pre-syntactic, postlexical field" (Marlatt, *Touch* 48) of the child who has not learned to speak, of the poet's "music." Asking how a *phéno-texte* "tied to male experiencing" (47) can convey a woman's experience of her body, Marlatt proposes a feminist poetics "on that double edge where [a woman] has always lived," between *phéno-texte* and *géno-texte*,

> between the spoken and the unspeakable, sense and non-sense. only now she writes it, risking nonsense, chaotic language leafings, unspeakable breaches of usage, intuitive leaps, inside language she leaps for joy, shoving out the walls of taboo and propriety, kicking syntax, discovering life in old roots. (48–49)

Lola Lemire Tostevin is one of the few poets who provides a material basis for Kroetsch's assertion that "national discontinuities made us ripe for Postmodernism." In *Color of Her Speech* she began to forge a poetic of the "double edge" out of linguistic duality:

> 4 words french
> 1 word English
>
> slow seepage
> slow seepage
>
> . . . . . .
>
> 1 word french
> 4 words English
>
> *'tu déparles'*
> my mother says
>
> *je déparle*
>   yes
> I unspeak

The book doubly inscribes this (un) speaking: it

> unconceals
>
>   implicates
>
> between two ...
>   between
>
> the way I speak
> the way I spoke

as an anglophone, as a francophone, as a woman, as patriarchal Woman. The concept of a *géno-texte* gives her a "different tongue to penetrate" in *Gyno-Text* (afterword). Like Marlatt's *Rings*, this poem inscribes the experience of carrying and birthing a child, but where Marlatt's lines are long, continuing, Tostevin writes a taut, minimalist line. The body of language and the language of the body move to birth: "mute / skeleton / moves / to / muscle / string / pulled / taut / from / A / to / Zone." In the next and last poem, three successive moments—the moment before birth, the moment of birth (of the child, of the poem, of language), and the moment after birth of mutual relief (of mother-poet, of child-poem, for old metaphors are being written in a corporeal language only women can literally speak)—are recorded in the mother tongue: "*vagin / vagir / enfin*".

By the time she writes *Double Standards*, Tostevin has arrived at a double and deconstructive gesture by which "rereading reverses to resist" the discourses of patriarchy in order to arrive at a female textual erotics

                                                   as the re of
            desire reverses   into the erotic sequence of a sentence
            into the consequential climax of the writer over and over

            (once more?)   ("Re")

In recent books both Marlatt and Tostevin write the language of female sexual-textual eroticism for the first time in English-Canadian poetry since "Naked Poems." Marlatt's *Touch to My Tongue* achieves the "double edge" by interrupting its nonetheless continuing syntax with parentheses and etymologies that reinvent female and feminist "life in old roots." Tostevin's *'sophie* inscribes the double edge of the pleasures of the mind (the *sophie*, knowledge, of philosophy) and the pleasures of love (the *philo*, love, missing from the title). Her *'sophie*, whose exclusion from both pleasures in Western culture is indicated by the reduction of her signature to an apostrophe at the head of many of the poems, uses the double edge of language to deconstruct postmodernist philosophical discourse and to make material in language a woman's (erotic) desire.

Were some new forecaster, perhaps a woman this time, to appear on the Canadian critical scene, she might well observe that Sutherland's prophecy of "an American example" to Canadian poets was more than fulfilled, that those same poets have through that example arrived at a postmodernist poetics having a "postcolonial identity of its own" precisely because it is concerned with language and not with nationalist and colonialist thematics. She surely would contest Kroetsch's assertion that Canadians bypassed modernism, but she might hope that both she and Kroetsch would land safely on the plateau of postmodernism. She might observe too that our "national discontinuities" have been most obviously productive of a new feminist poetics. She might hazard with Lola Tostevin that it is quite apparent that the postpatriarchal "muse has learned to write," that she can say "I love you now that I am no longer / spoken for" ('*sophie*, "Song of Songs," sec. 8). Canadian poetry may be on the way to a Song of Songs of her own.

WORKS CITED

Atwood, Margaret. *The Journals of Susanna Moodie.* Toronto: Oxford UP, 1970.

———. *Survival: A Thematic Guide to Canadian Literature.* Toronto: Anansi, 1972.

Avison, Margaret. *Winter Sun.* Toronto: U of Toronto P, 1960.

Birney, Earle. *The Collected Poems of Earle Birney.* 2 vols. Toronto: McClelland, 1975.

Bowering, George. *Errata.* Red Deer, AB: Red Deer College P, 1988.

———. "The Eyes Are Open, the Eyes Are Shut." *TISH* 9 (May 1962): 11–12.

———. *Kerrisdale Elegies.* Toronto: Coach House, 1984.

———. "A Quarter's Worth of Poetry." *TISH* 6 (Feb. 1962): 12.

———. *Rocky Mountain Foot: A Lyric, a Memoir.* Toronto: McClelland, 1968.

———. *West Window: The Selected Poetry of George Bowering.* Toronto: General, 1982.

Creeley, Robert. "Why Bother?" *TISH* 13 (Sept. 1962): 2.

Davey, Frank. Editorial: "Acorn and the Montreal Squirrel." *TISH* 11 (July 1962): 1–2.

———. "Brief Review." *TISH* 13 (Sept. 1962): 14.

———. Letter to Denise Levertov. *TISH* 11 (July 1962): 4.

———. "The Problem of Margins." *TISH* 3 (Nov. 1961): 11–12.

Eliot, T. S. *Selected Essays.* London: Faber, 1952.

Finch, Robert. *Acis in Oxford and Other Poems.* Toronto: U of Toronto P, 1959.

Frye, Northrop. "Conclusion." *Literary History of Canada: Canadian Literature in English.* Ed. Carl F. Klinck. Toronto: U of Toronto P, 1973. 821–49.

Gnarowski, Michael. Introduction. *New Provinces: Poems of Several Authors.* 1936. Toronto: U of Toronto P, 1976.

Jones, D. G. *A Throw of Particles: The New and Selected Poetry of D. G. Jones.* Toronto: General, 1983.

Kroetsch, Robert. *Advice to My Friends.* Toronto: Stoddart, 1985.

———. "The Continuing Poem." Kroetsch, *Essays* 81–82.

———. *Excerpts from the Real World.* Lantzville, BC: Oolichan, 1986.

———. *Field Notes.* Don Mills, ON: General, 1981.

————. "For Play and Entrance: The Contemporary Canadian Long Poem." Kroetsch, *Essays* 91–110.

————. *Robert Kroetsch: Essays.* Ed. Frank Davey and bpNichol. Spec. issue of *Open Letter* 5th ser. 4 (1983).

Layton, Irving. *The Improved Binoculars.* Introd. William Carlos Williams. Highlands, NJ: Williams, 1956.

————. *A Red Carpet for the Sun.* Toronto: McClelland, 1959.

Livesay, Dorothy. *Collected Poems: The Two Seasons of Dorothy Livesay.* Toronto: McGraw-Hill Ryerson, 1972.

Mandel, Eli. *The Family Romance.* Winnipeg: Turnstone, 1986.

————. *Life Sentence.* Toronto: Porcépic, 1981.

————. *Out of Place.* Erin, ON: Porcépic, 1977.

Marlatt, Daphne. *How Hug a Stone.* Winnipeg: Turnstone, 1983.

————. *Our Lives.* Lantzville, BC: Oolichan, 1980.

————. *Rings.* Vancouver: Georgia Strait Writing Supp. 3, 1971.

————. *Touch to My Tongue.* Edmonton: Longspoon, 1984.

————. *What Matters: Writing 1968–70.* Toronto: Coach House, 1980.

Marlatt, Daphne, and Robert Minden, photographer. *Steveston.* 1974. 2nd rev. ed. Edmonton: Longspoon, 1984.

Neuman, Shirley, and Robert Wilson. *Labyrinths of Voice: Conversations with Robert Kroetsch.* Western Canadian Literary Documents 3. Edmonton: NeWest, 1982.

Nichol, bp. *The Martyrology.* Toronto: Coach House. *Books 1 and 2.* 1972. Rev. ed. 1977. *Books 3 and 4.* 1976. *Book 5.* 1982. *Book 6.* 1987.

————. "Talking about the Sacred in Writing." *Tracing the Paths: Reading ≠ Writing* The Martyrology. Ed. Roy Miki. Vancouver: Talonbooks, 1988. 233–36.

Olson, Charles. *The Maximus Poems.* 1960, 1968, 1975. Ed. George F. Butterick. Berkeley: U of California P, 1983.

Ondaatje, Michael. *The Collected Works of Billy the Kid: The Left-Handed Poems.* Toronto: Anansi, 1970.

Page, P. K. *The Glass Air: Selected Poems.* Toronto: Oxford UP, 1985.

Perloff, Marjorie. *The Dance of the Intellect: Studies in the Poetry of the Pound Tradition.* Cambridge: Cambridge UP, 1985.

————. *The Poetics of Indeterminacy: Rimbaud to Cage.* Princeton: Princeton UP, 1981.

Pound, Ezra. "How to Read." 1919. *Literary Essays of Ezra Pound.* Ed. T. S. Eliot. London: Faber, 1954. 15–40.

Purdy, Alfred. *The Cariboo Horses.* Toronto: McClelland, 1965.

Reaney, James. *A Suit of Nettles.* Toronto: Macmillan, 1958.

————. *Twelve Letters to a Small Town.* Toronto: Ryerson, 1962.

Stein, Gertrude. *The Geographical History of America: Or, The Relation of Human Nature to the Human Mind.* New York: Random, 1936.

Sutherland, John. "The Old and the New." Introd. *Other Canadians: An Anthology of the New Poetry in Canada 1940–1946.* Ed. Sutherland. Montréal: First Statement, 1947. 5–20.

Tostevin, Lola Lemire. *Color of Her Speech.* Toronto: Coach House, 1982.

———. *Double Standards.* Edmonton: Longspoon, 1985.

———. *Gyno-Text.* Toronto: Underwhich, 1983.

———. *'sophie.* Toronto: Coach House, 1988.

Wah, Fred. *Breathin' My Name with a Sigh.* Vancouver: Talonbooks, 1981. N. pag.

———. Editor's statement. *TISH* 1 (Sept. 1961): 9.

———. "Margins into Lines: A Relationship." *TISH* 4 (Dec. 1961): 5–6.

———. *Pictograms from the Interior of B.C.* Vancouver: Talonbooks, 1975.

Watson, Wilfred. *Friday's Child.* London: Faber, 1955.

———. *Mass on Cowback.* Edmonton: Longspoon, 1982.

———. *Poems Collected/Unpublished/New.* Edmonton: Longspoon; NeWest, 1986.

Webb, Phyllis. "Polishing Up the View" and "On the Line." *Talking.* Dunvegan, ON: Quadrant, 1982. 46–50, 66–71.

———. *The Vision Tree: Selected Poems.* Ed. Sharon Thesen. Vancouver: Talonbooks, 1982.

———. *Water and Light: Ghazals and Anti Ghazals.* Toronto: Coach House, 1984.

Arnold E. Davidson

THE REINVENTION OF THE WEST IN CANADIAN FICTION

FOR ALMOST ALL North Americans—Canadians as well as Americans—the term *western* immediately evokes a certain narrative structure that John G. Cawelti, in *The Six-Gun Mystique*, has cogently analyzed in terms of a frontier conflict between advancing civilization and retreating savagery (the civilization defining, of course, the savagery). This structure dramatizes, for those on the safe side of the dividing line, the opposition between, on the one hand, the need for a stable social order with an enforced morality and, on the other, the appeal of individual freedom and irresponsibility pursued to the point of lawlessness and moral chaos. Despite the temptation of the latter, the issue is regularly resolved in favor of the former through the actions of a hero who makes the right judgments and who, as "a man with a gun" (57), makes those judgments stick. As Cawelti points out, the ambivalent moral stand of the traditional American western is reified by the ambivalent hero, who employs violence to counteract violence. Like the frontier, this protagonist, too, is poised between a feared and a desired freedom, an essential and resented order. His action suspends his indecision. Small wonder the imperatives of heroism, in the American frontier mythos, are seldom resisted.

Not all fictions set in the West fully exhibit this western formula. Thus John R. Milton, in *The Novel of the American West*, distinguishes between "the western of the lowercase *w* [with] its popular appeal to mass audiences" and "a higher form of literature" (the "Western" in the uppercase mode) that "strives to become significant in both theme and form" (40). As this critic acknowledges, however, "the legendary cowboy . . . has in the past seventy-five years ridden through an amazing number of bad novels" and only "a few good ones" (16). But I would suggest that even the few "good ones"—novels such as A. B. Guthrie, Jr.'s *Way West*, Frederick Manfred's *Lord Grizzly*, Walter Van Tilburg Clark's *Ox-Bow Incident*, or Frank Water's *Man Who Killed the Deer* (all works that Milton assesses in some detail) —are still closer to the formula western than are their Canadian counterparts, and partly because that cowboy still rides through them.

The very way in which Milton's capitalized "Western" critically examines what the other "subliterary genre" (40) merely conveniently assumes, still conjoins the two forms as explorations of the essential mythos of the West. For example, in *The Ox-Bow Incident* the three lynched "outlaws" are not guilty of the rustling and murder for which they are put to death, a state of affairs never envisioned in standard westerns, in which lynchings abound but the mob somehow always gets the right man. So what is normally a paradigm of rough-and-ready frontier justice turns out to be the real crime. As such and as one of the conscience-stricken actual killers subsequently attests, it could have and should have been prevented—prevented, indeed, by the very code that underwrote it. Or as Milton notes, "what characterizes *The Ox-Bow Incident*" as serious literature "is the lack of the strong will and the fast gun" (203). Yet that absence, along with its consequence, serves to validate much the same ethos affirmed by the presence of the hero and his trusty Colt .45 in more standard westerns (Milton's smallcase category). With both forms we are, then, very much on the frontier and a quintessentially American frontier at that. Furthermore, as Dick Harrison observes in "Fictions of the American and Canadian Wests," "even [the highly praised western] satiric writers such as Thomas Berger in *Little Big Man* and Ken Kesey in *One Flew over the Cuckoo's Nest* are ultimately less concerned with criticizing frontier values than with lamenting their passing" (97).

Canadian writers, however, have not produced authentic all-Canadian-content versions of American westerns because a key ingredient is missing. As Harrison emphasizes in *Unnamed Country*, the first Canadian settlers, like the early settlers of the United States, encountered great difficulties, but they viewed their experience differently. "They had the sense of a plain patrolled by the North West Mounted Police, surveyed for settlement, with a railroad stretching out to cross it. They were not on the edge of anything; they were surrounded by something, and they took it to be the civilized order they had always known" (73). The land was all surveyed and neatly divided before it was occupied by families who moved west mostly on the new railroad instead of by wagon train. Consequently, as Rosemary Sullivan has aptly observed, "nineteenth- and early twentieth-century Western Canadian literature is different from traditional Western American literature because there never has been a [Canadian] frontier literature" (152). There was no frontier literature because there was no frontier, and that lack freed the novel to a different task—"to create," in the words of Rudy Wiebe (qtd. in Sullivan 154), "a past, a lived history, a vital mythology."

Essentially and, admittedly, to simplify a much more complex matter, American writers of the West, in an ambivalent praising of the frontier and its attendant freedom, produced a pervasive form of entertainment (i.e., pulp magazine stories and novels, movies, radio, and then television programs) convention-bound almost to a moribund degree. Canada, too, has been barraged with the products of this industry. But for both historical and cultural reasons, the American myth of Manifest Destiny, with its accompanying metaphors of mastery, did not inform many Canadian fictions of the West. To start with, Canada had a different western history, one largely lacking in wagon trains or Indian wars. It is a history that does not accommodate the construct of the frontier as originally formulated in the United States in the fiction of James Fenimore Cooper and then massively popularized by Zane Grey and others in the early decades of the twentieth century.

Neither is the frontier a main feature of what we might call the Canadian literary imagination, as Robert Kroetsch points out in one of his early interviews, significantly titled "The American Experience and the Canadian Voice": "In the United States, the Freudian metaphor has swept the boards, the superego versus the id kind of thing. The id is the good guy trying to free himself . . . youth or the frontiersman, the man in the ten-gallon hat." Canadians, in contrast, are "more Jungian"; they are "fascinated with problems of equilibrium," whereas "Americans are interested in expansion." "This difference," Kroetsch concludes, "has to have an effect on our literature, on our language" (49).

That "effect," I think, can be seen especially in recent Canadian western writing. Inundated by fictional cavalry and Indians, cowboys and rustlers, shootouts and stampedes—inundated despite a history different from the American experience, in which such elements are at least loosely grounded—Canadians can feel a certain anxiety of influence. A number of contemporary authors have responded with fictions setting forth mythologies of the Canadian West conceived in a new vein best characterized as the conscious deconstruction of alternative mythologies, the mythologies of earlier Canadian prairie fiction as well as the obsessive mythology of Manifest Destiny perpetrated by the American western. As authors dispense with, in literature, the frontier they never in fact had, they free themselves, their fiction, and their readers into a play of textuality and intertextuality. That play, moreover, serves to subvert the standard western dialectics of power, the established relationships between the pioneer and the prairie, the cowboy and the Indian, the masculine and the feminine. The result, on the largest level, is the reinvention of the West and the western, the creation of a literary landscape in which both author and reader are invited to work out new possibilities of being.

For example, in the conclusion of George Bowering's *Caprice*, all the old western verities can be blatantly reversed. When the eponymous *heroine*, after avenging the death of a *brother*, rides off alone, *she* leaves her lover behind. *He* cannot come with her, because he is a teacher and "the school year" has "just begun." As she insists, his "place is already made" (265), hardly the usual western version of "a man's gotta do what a man's gotta do!" She rides off, moreover, "into the sunrise," not the sunset (that cheaply elegiac objective correlative for the passing of a whole way of life) and she rides eastward, "eastward through the west that was becoming nearly as narrow as her trail" (266). In those last words of the novel, the western itself circles back to the east that ever defined it, and what was cast as limitless panorama and possibility self-deconstructs to trail, to the delimiting text of the western that has always been both larger and smaller than the landscape it would contain.

Such questioning of the western by the western is now a well-established Canadian literary tradition. Abstracting from three excellent studies of Canadian novels set in the West (Edward McCourt's *Canadian West in Fiction*, Laurence Ricou's *Vertical Man/Horizontal World*, and, most important, Harrison's *Unnamed Country*), we can note how, in this fiction, one mythos has succeeded another. As Harrison, especially, emphasizes, early Canadian writers developed a uniquely Canadian myth of the West, a myth of a garden to be cultivated in the name of empire. Such authors as Ralph Connor or Nellie McClung evolved that mythic Canadian West from a strong sense of self and an even stronger identification with the empire, whose comforting presence they felt—or strove to envision. But their literary West was achieved more through expectation than observation, and the garden myth foundered on the inescapable fact that even the most sustained effort of creative imagination could not put much bloom on a forty-degree-below-zero prairie blizzard. So, starting in the 1920s, Canadian writers replaced this early fiction of the Canadian West with grimly realistic novels—most notably Frederick Philip Grove's *Settlers of the Marsh*, Martha Ostenso's *Wild Geese*, and Robert J. C. Stead's *Grain*— that documented the limitations of prairie life instead of extolling its promise.

The stark realism of the late 1920s and early 1930s, with its dark portrayals of drought and Depression, found fullest expression in the prairie patriarch striving to impress his will on all around him in a futile effort to achieve the garden of his imagination. His failures to dominate either his family or the land and his consequent dispossession in the text despite his self-proclaimed central role anticipated his virtual exclusion from subsequent texts. Saddled with this fictional father, his author sons and daughters soon had an easy Oedipal revenge and simply wrote him out of existence. Stand-ins were occasionally provided—for example, the kindly hired hand in W. O. Mitchell's *Jake and the Kid*. But even better, the dis-placement of the father could itself become a ground of origin and being, leaving the protagonist as well as the author and the reader all true orphan heirs to their previous prairie placelessness. Realistic portrayals that tended to tragedy thereby gave way to mythic visions tinged with comedy, but the myth now was a myth of lost origins and a consequent reconstruction of imagined history and/or genealogy whereby past, present, place, and protagonist might all be conjoined.

The third mythos is thus in opposition to the first as well as to the second. The garden myth was, as noted, a simple, straightforward hope for the future, a vision of what the garden might be when it had become the garden it should be. Contemporary mythic fiction is more complex and subtly paradoxical. It gives us mythic portrayals of the need for myth, and the myth most needed is a mythic picture of the past. Furthermore, the search for the missing myth is regularly mocked and parodied in the very works that also portray that same search as essential. And there is still another structuring polarity to this new mythic fiction. In "Unhiding the Hidden," Kroetsch observes that he once "considered it the task of the Canadian writer to give names to his experience, to be the namer," but "now suspect[s] that on the contrary, it is his task to un-name" (43). More and more this author, and others too, have insisted on unnaming, on the need to free experience from the constraining term or label. Words must take us beyond the import of those words, just as myth must provide us with an imaginative pattern that gives to the facts of experience a depth and dimension that those facts do not necessarily possess in themselves.

The garden myth as a myth was far too limiting and served mostly to reduce western Canada to Toronto's (and England's) back forty—the wheat fields out there that help support the rest of us back here. At least as constraining, and as colonial, was the far more pervasive North American myth of the frontier West that well might have reduced western Canada to Ponderosa North—an extension of Hollywood instead of empire. But in this case too, the facts of the land helped to refute the myth whereby the land might have been falsely imaged out of its own authentic existence.

The best contemporary Canadian western writers undo the preexisting models that I have just discussed in order to achieve their different mythic models that are mostly an amorphous and thus unlimiting search for a model. For example, *The Double Hook*, by Sheila Watson, begins with the father missing and then disposes of the mother too. That mother's matricidal son, a reverse Oedipus, frees himself into life but his sister into death (everything is doubled in this novel), while Coyote, as a kind of sphinx conjoining attributes of the Christian God and the Indian trickster, presides over the action. Margaret Laurence, in *The Diviners*, interweaves her dislocations of linear plot to emphasize both the simultaneity of past and present experience and the way in which each is a construct of the other. Or Jack Hodgins re-creates, in *The Invention of the World*, the history of Vancouver Island so that it becomes the re-created history of Ireland to become, in turn, the re-created history—the invention—of the world. Or still more to the point, Robert Kroetsch, in such novels as *The Studhorse Man, Gone Indian*, and *Badlands*, plays with the very constructs out of which his novels are formulated to highlight their fictionality, the fact that they are the invention of themselves and their world.

Badlands—to look in some detail at one of these novels—begins with Anna Dawe retracing, some fifty years later, her father's 1916 expedition after dinosaur bones down the Red Deer River and through the Alberta Badlands. She would recover the father missing in her life by uncovering his story, and in that story, too, there is a significant absence. Its potential hero early went AWOL. "In the western yarn those men were trying to tell each other," Anna observes, "he was the only one with the ability to become a hero, the wisdom not to. Home was a word he understood, and heroes cannot afford that understanding" (45). "He" is Claude McBride, and even his name has the right heroic ring—like Kit Carson or John Wayne, as direct and forceful as the thunk of an axe. But how can this auspiciously named character desert the task at hand and how can the novel get along without him?

Very well, it seems, for Kroetsch's western is working with a new mythology, one that dispenses with the older central figure and his potential for heroic selfhood. McBride is replaced, on the first expedition, by Anna Yellowbird, a fifteen-year-old Indian girl, a child-widow whose husband has gone off to be killed in World War I. Because she has her own mythologies, because a shaman has told her that a hunchback will lead her to the spirit of her husband, she joins the bone-hunting venture and becomes its guide. She becomes, too, the lover of its leader as well as of most of his crew. The expedition, headed by William Dawe (who intends to immortalize himself by discovering a hitherto unknown dinosaur of his very own), is also replaced by a subsequent expedition—his daughter in search of her origins and looking for the place where her father had gone wrong.

The mythmaking of *Badlands* is not, then, any myth of the "Old West": 1916 was rather late for the "Old West." It was rather late, too, for Dawe's idiosyncratic exercise at discovering a much older West. Paleontological pioneering, as much as any other, was largely over and done. The important action was earlier or elsewhere. Moreover, by 1916, standard western myths

of heroic bravery and armed valor were being deconstructed with a vengeance in the trenches of Europe. Dawe would avoid the lesson of the
European trenches, but he still proceeds to discover, through dynamite
and death, the dinosaur to which he gives his name but that does not in
return redeem his life, as his subsequent suicide attests.

He is superseded by his daughter and her search, which itself devolves
into different searches—first for her father but then for herself, her country,
her fiction, her myth. In the course of this searching, she finds Anna Yellowbird, now a drunken old woman also devoid of myth and ready to go
looking. Together they retrace the route of Dawe's expedition and then
reverse that course to follow the river to its source in the mountains. There
the quest devolves to carnival, to a comic repudiation of everything male.
The "field notes" (partly faked) the daughter has kept for ten years since
her father's death as well as the photographs the other Anna has saved for
over fifty years are scattered into the mountain lake.

In that deprivileging of both the patriarchal principle and the written
word, Anna Dawe achieves, to quote from another Kroetsch novel (*Gone
Indian* 152), "a complex of possibilities rather than a concluded self." The
father's excavations, his search for a definitive paleontology and a place
in the history of that search, give way to a different archaeology, an archaeology of the open site content with fragments, glimpses. Thus Dawe
"come[s] to the end of words" (269) in one way and his daughter in another.
But it is that second way that informs this text that is itself a kind of
archaeological open site, as is emphasized by the texts of other searches
—Homer's *Odyssey*, Joyce's *Ulysses*, Twain's *Huckleberry Finn*, Conrad's
"Heart of Darkness," Faulkner's *Absalom! Absalom!*, Watson's *Double Hook*,
Atwood's *Surfacing*—embedded in the text of *Badlands*.

Kroetsch's redefinition of traditional mythic values and structures con-
troverts the six-gun mystique with its attendant assumption of Manifest
Destiny on two different levels. First, manifest to whom? The vacillating
narrative stance of *Badlands* undermines the authority of all the voices
whereby the text is rendered. Second, whose destiny? By confuting the
standard mythic teleologies, particularly the final ascendancy of the—by
definition, male—hero, the novel raises ontological questions about the
validity of any pursuit of the signs and symbols of transcendence, whether
the bodies of recently vanquished enemies or the bones of long-dead dinosaurs. Destiny is hardly manifest. On the contrary, it is a concept as
dead end (and particularly so in a postmodernist context) as William Dawe's
tedious field notes or the skeleton he found that cost him his surrogate
son.

To mark the difference of this deprivileging, let us look now at Walter
Prescott Webb's *Great Frontier* and more specifically at a brief story (not

a novel itself but the paradigm of one) that Webb presents to illustrate the ostensible workings of the American frontier. In his chapter "The Emergence of the Individual" and in a section itself significantly titled "Jim Brown Knows the Way," Webb asks us to imagine five men setting out on a journey into the forest and on to hostile Indian country: four who "have risen to high position in their respective occupations" and who "represent civilization at its best" and a fifth who has "not so distinguished himself" (36). The first four are a general, a banker, a professor, and a preacher, while the fifth is, of course, Jim Brown, who, not surprisingly, turns out to be the natural leader of the expedition. He can read the lay of the land, find game, tan leather to make them all new clothes when the civilized garb of the four "tenderfoot" travelers soon wears out; he can also bring down the Indian leader when the white men are, predictably, attacked.

This whole narrative is, for that matter, so predictable that it does not at all serve, as Webb intends, to illustrate "how natural political democracy . . . in the truest sense of the word" comes into being on the frontier through the agency of men, like Jim Brown, who had already freed themselves from "civilization's stamp of human inequalities" (45, 39). As even the rhetorical overkill of "democracy . . . in the truest sense of the word" attests, we are, all along, well into the realm of received myth. Thus Jim Brown can be quite unimpressed by the general's medals, the banker's moneybelt, the professor's discoveries and inventions, or the preacher's fine sentiments and avowed reluctance to take life—and the story valorizes all Mr. Brown's views. The general "wear[s] his uniform and medals on this expedition" (36) and the uniform soon wears out. The stuffed moneybelt that the banker embarks with comes back just as stuffed. Or the professor who "has studied so hard that he has ruined his digestion" (37) of course recovers it with campfire cooking. On his first night out, "Professor Fairchilds forgot his stomach and took a second helping" (41).

All four come to be substantially better men by virtue of their wilderness excursion, so much so that one wonders how they could have been so incompetent in the first place. A general (European, admittedly) setting off for weeks in the wilderness in his full dress uniform? Or a banker who knows so little of the financial institutions of his country that he anticipates stores in the Mississippi Valley of 1800? Or did he plan to buy Ohio from the Indians and pay them cash on the barrelhead? And why would a competent Jim Brown stay with such a crew, especially when they at first call him "Boy" and treat him as the general servant? None of them, for that matter, has any reason for their wilderness excursion other than the fact that the story requires it. All of them are nothing but the literary clichés that the story also requires.

The very way in which this fantasy can be elevated into ostensible example illustrates how deeply the myth of "the great frontier" and the supposed workings of that frontier are ingrained in American thought and literature. Moreover, this myth, even in Webb's idealized redaction, has its distinctly pernicious aspects. The largest change recorded in the story is that of the Reverend Henderson Fowler, who learns first to hunt and then to hunt Indians; who feels, with his first human kill, a "sense of exaltation ... he had never known before" and who realizes that (the last words of the story) "in the new theology of the forest, the Sixth Commandment does not apply to Indians" (44). How convenient that the forest allows an elision of religion and genocide in the name of nature.

Webb's frontier fantasy sets forth a metaphysics of Indian killing as much as a politics of natural democracy. Standing mostly outside both that politics and that metaphysics, the Canadian author can look critically at this American construct—can, as we see in *Badlands*, consign its natural hero to the more natural business of attending to his family and farm instead of playing cowboy and Indians in the wild. I would also here note that in western Canadian fiction the Indian tends more to be an envisioned alternative to white life than an implacable threat. Thus, in Mitchell's *Vanishing Point*, the protagonist, a teacher at an Indian school, sets out to civilize his prize pupil, Virginia Rider, but she ends up "Indianizing" him. Or in Kroetsch's *Gone Indian*, Jeremy Sadness, an American graduate student, goes to Canada to discover (comically, of course) his real life as a fake Indian.

But only, it must be noted, as a fake Indian. Critics such as Terry Goldie and Jane Tompkins have emphasized that any concept of "Indian" is always, in white discourse, a construct that serves white interests. Furthermore, as Tompkins points out, "an Indian account of what transpired when the European settlers arrived here [wherever "here" is] would look nothing like our own," and "their (potential, unwritten) history of the conflict could bear only a marginal resemblance to Eurocentric views" (109). Yet it is precisely that "potential" and hitherto largely "unwritten" Indian history of western Canada that Rudy Wiebe assays in his major novel *The Temptations of Big Bear*.

Wiebe is well aware of the contradictions at the heart of his enterprise. Indeed, what we well might term the two temptations of Rudy Wiebe, temptations out of which his best fiction comes, are, first, the desire to learn Cree and, second, the desire not to. The temptation to learn Cree stands in, of course, for another and admittedly impossible authorial desire, to enter not just into the fictional life of created characters but into a whole different culture. One might then shed the burden of being white and participate fully in the Indian's radically different and perhaps more authentic mode of being. The countering temptation to remain caught in one's own experience and language, easy and mundane as that objective is, acknowledges the romanticism at the heart of any desire to escape. It is a recognition of the limits of the self, of the world, but a recognition partly transcended by the other desire that it denies. In short, the two temptations are inextricably linked, and the resonance between the two sounds persistently in the fictions of this complex and comprehensive artist.

Sustained by that first resonance relationship is another, related one, the interconnections, for Wiebe, between history and story. History is what we already have, our accepted version of what we did and of who, consequently, we are. It is a collective language of a collective self reified by repetition, by the particular stories we choose to retell to one another—stories, for the most part, already chosen for us. Thus the potential of story, for Wiebe, is always larger than the particulars of history, since history selects some of the possible stories that can go into that history and supresses others. Wiebe himself, in an interview with Shirley Neuman (230), sums up this relationship in terms that also implicitly premise his fictional agenda: "I doubt the *official* given history ... there is another side to the story and maybe that's the more interesting side. Maybe even truer."

Wiebe seeks to recover something of that "more interesting" and "maybe even truer" other side. To do so, he casts history into a kind of alembic to see if a certain applied creative pressure might not force it to yield up the very story that it has programmatically concealed—to make it, in a sense, talk Cree. Thus in *The Temptations of Big Bear* and, similarly, in *The Scorched-Wood People*, Wiebe casts the expected antagonist (Big Bear in the former, Louis Riel in the latter) as the protagonist. The result is a deconstruction and reconstruction of the standard western novel. An expected epic of victory (How the West Was Won) gives way to an epic of loss—what the Indians lost, what the Métis lost, and what the prevailing whites lost, too, through those two other losses. Both novels thereby contradict established teleologies of western fiction and western history. Both are also odd historical fictions in that they effectively deny (fictionalize?) the very history out of which they are meticulously made. And if, as W. J. Keith observes, "it is impossible to forget completely [in reading *The Temptations of Big Bear*] that Wiebe is a white striving to reproduce the Indian viewpoint" (80), it is also impossible not to notice that the object of that struggle is to portray Big Bear, in Wiebe's own words, as "an incredibly great man" (Keith 63).

The dialectic, in Canadian fiction, between white and Indian is different from the more pervasive (in terms of mass entertainment) American dialectic. So, too, as already suggested by *Caprice* and *Badlands*, is the dialectic between male and female. Contemporary Canadian westerns ex-

hibit a distinct deprivileging of traditional masculine narrative authority
along with a concomitant claiming of female narrative authority, or at least
a partial recognition of female claims. In *The Invention of the World*, for
example, the brutal and self-serving rule of the "Father" (one of Donal
Keneally's preferred titles as the leader of an Irish village he transports to
Vancouver Island) is replaced by the more benign rule of the mother when
Maggie Kyle comes into possession of what was Keneally's Revelations
Colony of Truth and thereby also inherits and cares for some of the maimed
survivors of that "Truth." Or, to return to *Badlands*, Anna Dawe's search
to recover her lost biological father is superseded by a reunion with her
previously lost figurative mother, the woman after whom she was named.
The two Annas do have the final words in the story, words that roundly
renounce the heritage of Dawe. "And I took that last field book with the
last pompous sentence he ever wrote, the only poem he ever wrote, a love
poem to me, his only daughter, and I threw it into the lake where it too
might drown" (269–70). Freed from Dawe's paper rule, the two women
"walked through the night, stumbling [their] way by the light of the stars"
and "did not mention dinosaurs or men or their discipline or their courage
or their goddamned honour." Singing together, they "walked all the way
out" from the mountain lake and "did not look back, not once, ever" (270)
to that lake, to the papers scattered in the lake, or to the drowned man
whose notes and pictures have now been sent after him.

   Yet even the retrospective cast of this final claim gives it, as Robert
Lecker has argued, the lie. The whole book, too, enacts versions of that
concluding contradiction: a looking back at not looking back, an accounting
of a discounting, telling the story of not telling the story. In short, throughout *Badlands* the reader is ever on slippery ground, and, characteristically,
the feminist poetics partly affirmed by the conclusion is also pervasively
undermined. Thus the song that the two women sing is that "awful" one
"about rolling over in the clover" (270), which is, all at the same time, old-
fashioned, classically sexist, and oddly revolutionary in that at least sometimes the woman is on top.

   For a more firmly grounded feminist poetics in an equally idiosyncratic
Canadian western we can turn briefly to Aritha van Herk's *Tent Peg*. In this
novel a young woman graduate student who "wanted to head for nowhere
and look at everything in [her] narrow world from a detached distance"
(23) must pass as a male to sign on as the cook for a Yukon geological
exploring expedition. Her ruse is soon uncovered and everyone, especially
the protagonist, must come to terms with the resulting tensions. The traditional ploy of the journey to the new land eliciting a new sense of self
is here given a distinctly feminist cast, and then the novel, as a sort of

"Surfacing West," is crossed back with the traditional western when a soupçon of "Shoot-out at the O. K. Corral" is thrown in at the end.

The gun play with which this text, in part, concludes emerges almost inevitably from its form and structure. The work is broken into brief disparate sections—for the most part the passing comments of the nine men on the expedition—that document the attempts of those men to claim both the female and the narration. The logic to the conjunction of these sundry claims is the way they all cancel each other out, leaving the protagonist standing quite alone and still very much her own woman. That independent stance proves too much for the most pathologically macho of all the men. He would enforce, through rape, his own demeaning definition, but she nails him instead and with his own gun at that.

She knees him in the groin, grabs his prized magnum revolver away, and by threatening to "blow [his] balls off" (221) demonstrates that she really does not need to. His abject cowering proves that, in the symbolic sense, he hasn't "got any." (And is that perhaps why so many conventional western heroes are so given to their guns?) Yet the admittedly melodramatic nature of this resolution does not obscure its meaning. The pistol passing from his hand to hers is a shifting signifier that validates the biblical implication of the novel's title and its protagonist's name or, more accurately, her initials, which have, throughout the novel, served as her name. As she early notes, "I knew that if I put down my name, J. L., and left the sex, F for female, box unchecked, they would assume I was a man. Only one gender has initials, the rest of us are misses and mistresses with neither the dignity of anonymity nor the prestige of assumption. All men are equal" (23). Of course J. L., as those readers not versed in the Bible are finally told near the novel's end, refers to Ja-el, the Hebrew heroine who killed Sisera with a tent peg. That *The Tent Peg* serves as a contemporary fable for the empowerment of women is also early indicated by the dedication to "all my women friends who carry tent pegs of their own" (n.p.). No wonder the protagonist was at one point reading "Freud [because] I sometimes feel I must refresh my dislikes" (23). The novel nails him, too.

J. L. is partly sustained by her memories of her one close friend, Deborah, and by recalling conversations the two have had about their problems with men. In Anne Cameron's *Journey* both the friendship of women and the problems with men are taken one significant step further. Even more than van Herk, Cameron early asserts her intention to reverse, to revolutionize even, the western. Her dedication is, in part, "for all the little girls who always wanted to be and never could grow up to be cowboys" (n.p.). One of the epigraphs reads:

> I see by your outfit that you are a cowboy
> I see by his outfit that he's a cowboy true,
> I see by their outfits that they are all cowboys,
> If I get an outfit can I be cowboy, too.
>   (as sung by those of us tied for
>   too long to trees and stereotypes)   (n.p.)

Equally germane and appended to the dedication and epigraphs is a kind of genealogy for the novel, in which Cameron notes how integral to childhood the Saturday western movies were and how the boys "could identify with the heroes" whereas the girls "had Dale Evans" who herself had "no guns" and "the slower horse, [and] who rode behind Roy just in time to catch the mud flying from his gallant steed's hooves." Because of the iconography of the movie western, the author caught a certain amount of "mud" too: "And so, because I had long hair, worn in pigtails, and the stereotype did not allow me a six-gun, a rifle, or a knife, I spent many hours tied to trees, the captive Indian. Perhaps that was the beginning of this story" (n.p.).

In that "beginning" we can read the "end" of this story, which is to untell the more standard story of how the West was won/one. Foregrounding other stories typically suppressed in the dominant discourse of the western, *The Journey* requires the reader to recognize how much those other stories have been there all along and how their recognized presence undermines the ethos that would exclude them. For example, give one of the Chinese coolies working on the railroad a tale of his own and a chance to tell it and the heroic task of creating a nation by traversing it with steel rails also becomes (as it no doubt was) an extended exercise in brutal exploitation. Or, similarly, let the typical dance hall encounter be described by the woman participant whose present prostitution is part of her larger story, not simply a pleasant interlude subsumed into his:

> "I'm not very experienced at this," she lied again, "and I know you probably are."
> "Not too," he contradicted, beginning to feel less awkward and stupid. "Not too much."   (22)

In those lies—his and hers—we see the much bigger lie of the myth of male mastery. It is in this sense especially that the novel provides more than the obvious reversals inherent in a lesbian western.

Such characteristically Canadian demythifying and remythifying of standard western mythic teleologies are first fully observed in Howard O'Hagan's *Tay John*, a novel that establishes many of the resonances that distinguish the contemporary Canadian mythic western from the different myths of the American western. To start with, the first mythic givens in *Tay John* are not western myths of self-assertion, of progress and profit, of heroic selfhood. Far from it; those precise myths are themselves mocked in the novel through the misadventures of Alf Dobble, who aspires to establish a tourist kingdom in the Rockies and fails disastrously. What we have first is Indian myth but Indian myth arrayed, to borrow a title from Joseph Conrad, under western eyes. And a curiously western Indian myth too: an Indian people await a great leader who will take them on a western journey to a promised land. The interplay of different and conflicting myths continues when Tay John, the blond-haired Indian born from his dead mother's grave, renounces the role of Indian leader to enter the white world, where he just as resolutely insists on his placelessness. Tay John is not at all the lone, celibate, male hero whose actions preserve the world in which the womenfolk may be (but should never act). Instead, he interacts with the women in his world—perhaps too much—yet in that interaction male and female as much as white and Indian become inverted mirrors for one another and not simplistic polarities symbolizing such opposites as action versus passivity or the lure of adventure versus the comforts of home. Thus in the first scenes of *Tay John*, Red Rorty, who came to the Indians to preach, remains to rape an Indian woman but is, as punishment, then killed by other Indian women—an immediate rebalancing of racial and gender stereotypes as well as the undoing of Rorty's mission in the wilderness. And in the final scene of the novel, Tay John, who found his proper mate in a dark-haired, dark-skinned white woman, apparently pulls that woman, pregnant and dead, on a toboggan through a winter wasteland of falling snow and back into the earth from which he came. The irresolution of the novel—on the face of it, Tay John has simply disappeared from the world—is a complex balancing of birth and death, beginning and ending, story and silence.

That last term effectively sets forth yet another feature of the Canadian mythic western. In the standard western, omniscient narration ("Meanwhile, back at the ranch ...") is the outward expression of ontological certitude. Destiny will be, must be, manifest. In the Canadian western, omniscience is regularly replaced by a chorus of uncertain voices, and manifest truth gives way to provisional hypothesis. To simplify a number of different complex authorial strategies, I would finally suggest that this depotentizing of narrative on the part of the different Canadian authors emphasizes the Canadian western's attention to silence. If the American Dream is a dream of destinations—the buzz and business of the future— the Canadian Dream is, in Kroetsch's evocative phrase, "a dream of origins" ("Uncovering Our Dream World" 29). Those origins are silence, the silence of the prairie, the mountain, the coastal island, the land new to its white transgressors but ancient in Indian time, and, beyond that, timeless. One passage in *Tay John* perfectly sums up this re-vision of other quests— whether Western, in the broadest sense (going back to Homer), or western, in the local sense (going back to James Fenimore Cooper):

> Every story—the rough-edged chronicle of a personal destiny—having its source in a past we cannot see, and its reverberations in a future still unlived—man, the child of darkness, walking for a few short moments in unaccustomed light—every story only waits, like a mountain in an untravelled land, for someone to come close, to gaze upon its contours, lay a name upon it, and relate it to the known world. Indeed, to tell a story is to leave most of it untold.... You have the feeling that you have not reached the story itself, but have merely assaulted the surrounding solitude. (166–67)

Jack Denham (O'Hagan's Conradian narrator), musing on his own mistelling of his story of Tay John, comes close to telling (i.e., not telling) the story of the contemporary Canadian western too. From O'Hagan to Kroetsch and Cameron, these narratives are not prophecy, not truth, but not exactly mere fictions either; they are mostly metafictions—fictions about the making of fiction and metafictions made with a fundamental awareness that the rest is silence.

WORKS CITED

Bowering, George. *Caprice.* Markham: Penguin, 1987.

Cameron, Anne. *The Journey.* San Francisco: Spinsters/Aunt Lute, 1986.

Cawelti, John G. *The Six-Gun Mystique.* Bowling Green: Bowling Green U Popular P, 1975.

Goldie, Terry. *Fear and Temptation: The Image of the Indigene in Canadian, Australian, and New Zealand Literatures.* Kingston: McGill-Queen's UP, 1989.

Grove, Frederick Philip. *Settlers of the Marsh.* 1925. Toronto: McClelland, 1966.

Harrison, Dick. "Fictions of the American and Canadian Wests." *Prairie Forum* 8.1 (1983): 89–97.

———. *Unnamed Country: The Struggle for a Canadian Prairie Fiction.* Edmonton: U of Alberta P, 1977.

Hodgins, Jack. *The Invention of the World.* Toronto: Macmillan, 1977.

Keith, W. J. *Epic Fiction: The Art of Rudy Wiebe.* Edmonton: U of Alberta P, 1981.

Kroetsch, Robert. "The American Experience and the Canadian Voice." *Journal of Canadian Fiction* 1.3 (1972): 48–52.

———. *Badlands.* 1975. Don Mills, ON: Paperjacks, 1976.

———. *Gone Indian.* Toronto: New, 1973.

———. *The Studhorse Man.* Toronto: Macmillan, 1969.

———. "Uncovering Our Dream World: An Interview with Robert Kroetsch." *Essays in Canadian Writing* 18–19 (1980): 21–32.

———. "Unhiding the Hidden: Recent Canadian Fiction." *Journal of Canadian Fiction* 3.3 (1974): 43–45.

Laurence, Margaret. *The Diviners.* Toronto: McClelland, 1974.

Lecker, Robert. *Robert Kroetsch.* Boston: Twayne, 1986.

McCourt, Edward. *The Canadian West in Fiction.* Rev. ed. Toronto: Ryerson, 1970.

Milton, John R. *The Novel of the American West.* Lincoln: U of Nebraska P, 1980.

Mitchell, W. O. *Jake and the Kid.* Toronto: Macmillan, 1961.

———. *The Vanishing Point.* Toronto: Macmillan, 1973.

Neuman, Shirley. "Unearthing Language: An Interview with Rudy Wiebe and Robert Kroetsch." *A Voice in the Land: Essays by and about Rudy Wiebe.* Ed. W. J. Keith. Edmonton: NeWest, 1981. 226–47.

O'Hagan, Howard. *Tay John.* 1939. Toronto: McClelland, 1974.

Ostenso, Martha. *Wild Geese.* 1925. Toronto: McClelland, 1961.

Ricou, Laurence. *Verticle Man/Horizontal World: Man and Landscape in Canadian Prairie Fiction.* Vancouver: U of British Columbia P, 1973.

Stead, Robert J. C. *Grain.* 1926. Toronto: McClelland, 1963.

Sullivan, Rosemary. "Summing Up." *Crossing Frontiers: Papers in American and Canadian Western Literature.* Ed. Dick Harrison. Edmonton: U of Alberta P, 1979. 144–57.

Tompkins, Jane. " 'Indians': Textualism, Morality, and the Problem of History." *Critical Inquiry* 13 (1986): 101–19.

van Herk, Aritha. *The Tent Peg.* Toronto: McClelland, 1981.

Watson, Sheila. *The Double Hook.* 1959. Toronto: McClelland, 1966.

Webb, Walter Prescott. *The Great Frontier.* 1964. Lincoln: U of Nebraska P, 1986.

Wiebe, Rudy. *The Scorched-Wood People.* Toronto: McClelland, 1977.

———. *The Temptations of Big Bear.* Toronto: McClelland, 1973.

Annette Kolodny

MARGARET ATWOOD AND THE POLITICS OF NARRATIVE

I

MORE THAN TWENTY years before its publication, Margaret Atwood's novel *Life before Man* (1979) had been anticipated by Kenneth Burke. The prologue to the 1954 edition of Burke's *Permanence and Change* outlined "a kind of melodrama" played out on a stage clearly demarcated as foreground and background:

> In the foreground ... there was to be a series of realistic incidents, dealing with typical human situations, such as family quarrels, scenes at a business office, [or] lovers during courtship.... In the background, like a set of comments on this action, there was to be a primeval forest filled with mythically prehistoric monsters, marauding and fighting in silent pantomime.
>
> These two realms were to have no overt connection with each other. The monsters in the "prehistoric" background would pay no attention to the everyday persons of the foreground; and these everyday persons would have no awareness of the background. But the pantomime of the background would be in effect a "mythic" or "symbolic" way of commenting upon the realistic action of the foreground. (li–liii)

If the exhibits of the Royal Ontario Museum have replaced Burke's primeval forest in Atwood's novel, the relationship between background and foreground is otherwise in place. Against a backdrop in which reconstructions of long-extinct creatures "rear their gigantic heads and cavernous eye-sockets" (81), Atwood's human characters play out analogous scenarios of territoriality and survival.

For Burke, the conceit attained full meaning only when background and foreground collided. "Gradually, . . . with increasing frequency," wrote Burke, "there were to be fleeting moments when the two realms seemed in more direct communication. And the play was to end with a sudden breaking of the frame, whereat the monsters of the background would swarm forward, to take over the entire stage" (lii). For Atwood, by contrast, narrative integrity depended on the two realms remaining separate. Lesje, a museum paleontologist, might on occasion daydream her way into Jurassic swamps and try to imagine *"what it would be like if suddenly the dinosaurs came to life,"* but in the end she finds "she can't do it. . . . In the foreground, pushing in whether she wants it to or not, is what [a co-worker] would call her life" (310, 311). By collapsing the background into the foreground, Burke moved his "modernized morality play" (li) from allegory to romance. In *Life before Man*, Atwood purposefully rejected the narrative strategies of romance—strategies she had employed successfully in the past—and composed her first true novel.

The distinction derives from Nathaniel Hawthorne, with whose work Atwood became familiar in the early 1960s at Harvard, while attending Perry Miller's lectures on American Romanticism. Articulating the distinction for the first time in his preface to *The House of the Seven Gables* (1851), Hawthorne declared that the novel aims "at a very minute fidelity, not merely to the possible, but to the probable and ordinary," while the romance may swerve from the probable in order to give the writer's imagination freer play (1). Taking up the argument a year later, in his preface to *The Blithedale Romance* (1852), Hawthorne again declared that, unlike the novelist, the romancer "is allowed a license with regard to every-day Probability." What the romancer wanted to create, he explained, was "a theatre, a little removed from the highway of ordinary travel, where the creatures of his brain may play their phantasmagorical antics" (2, 1). In effect, Hawthorne was describing Burke's final "breaking of the frame": the imagined theater stage on which the allegorical and symbolic intermingle with, even swarm forward to take over, the ordinary.

Measured by Hawthorne's narrative categories, Atwood was essentially a romancer until *Life before Man*. In *The Edible Woman, Surfacing*, and *Lady Oracle*, she allowed her characters their "phantasmagorical antics," inventing worlds in which the marvelous and the mundane easily intermingle. In the comic romance *The Edible Woman*, for example, the monsters have already taken over the stage. Images from prepackaged consumer goods so invade daily perception that the grittiness of reality all but disappears and people's expectations become delusory. Advertisements for girdles promise purchasers that "they were getting their own youth and slenderness back in the package," while beer commercials depict hunting and fishing scenes in which the fish have "no slime, no teeth, no smell," and "the hunter who had killed a deer stood posed and urbane, no twigs in his hair, his hands bloodless" (93, 150). When the central character, Marian McAlpin, momentarily breaks through the packaging to the reality it would mask, she is unprepared. Cellophaned and neatly labeled super-market meat is intended to conceal the fact that what is being sold is "part of a real cow that once moved and ate and was killed" (151). When Marian realizes that this, in fact, is what is on the plate before her, she becomes increasingly unable to eat. In true romance fashion, however, she shows no signs of wasting away, no evidence of malnutrition. After all, Marian continues to consume in the one way her society most approves: she goes to a beauty parlor for a new hairdo and buys a red dress for her fiancé's party.

If *The Edible Woman* amusingly examines the impossibility of living authentically amid the self-induced delusions of consumer society, *Surfacing* is a serious romance about escaping inauthenticity. The monsters who invade the stage here, though, are sources of healing and refuge. For, in *Surfacing*, it is the magical and the numinous that swarm forward to initiate the narrator's transformation, and, in this narrative, the breaking of the frame results in the woman's assumption of "the power for what I must do now" (91). What she must do is give up the false myth of personal powerlessness that she has so carefully constructed for herself over the years. "This above all," she asserts at the end, "to refuse to be a victim. Unless I can do that I can do nothing. I have to recant, give up the old belief that I am powerless and because of it nothing I can do will ever hurt anyone" (222).

Encountering the dry spare prose in which the narrator tells her story, the reader does not expect a romance. But as in a gothic romance (to which Atwood would turn next, in *Lady Oracle*), the reader of *Surfacing* must work at untangling the real from the unreal. What proves unreal is the narrator's account of her wedding, her failed marriage, and a child given over to the husband she had divorced. It is this version of events, she claims, that has left her "inoculated, exempt" (105) from further emotional entanglements. When she enters a numinous wilderness, however, the fabricated past unravels to reveal only a collage of random memories pieced together so as to camouflage what she cannot accept: "that mutilation, ruin I'd made, I needed a different version" (169). There had been no wedding, we learn, only a tawdry affair with an older man, her college art professor. And there had never been any child, only a back-alley abortion, urged on her by her married lover. For this unwilling complicity in the taking of a life, she believes herself a destroyer, "a killer" (170). And so she has ever after clung to a belief in her own powerlessness and fabricated "a different version" to live with. "If it hurts invent a different pain" (15).

Having taken to heart Hawthorne's advice to "make a very moderate use of the privileges" of romance (*Seven Gables* 1), Atwood grounds the transition from mundane to numinous in physiological plausibility. The narrator's first visionary experience in the lake—when she sees something "drifting towards me from the furthest level where there was no life" (167)—follows upon a third dive. She is dizzy, weak, and suffering from the symptoms of oxygen deprivation, which, among other things, can cause hallucinations. Days later, after she has abandoned her parents' cabin in order to live like an animal in the woods, the narrator feels herself merging with the natural world: "I lean against a tree, I am a tree leaning." She is hungry—in itself an explanation for hallucinatory experience—but she has also just eaten wild mushrooms. "They taste musty," she admits, "I'm not sure of them" (212).

In the narrator's view, she has entered one of "the sacred places" and been granted "true vision" (171). The text itself never determines whether oxygen deprivation, exhaustion, hunger, mushrooms, or the powers of ancient Indian gods account for her altered perceptions. What is certain is that, whatever the plausible physiological explanation, this woman slips the confines of everyday rationality to momentarily immerse herself in the ground of being: "I am not an animal or a tree, I am the thing in which the trees and animals move and grow, I am a place" (213). That the narrator now experiences herself as a source of life—rather than death—signifies the process as healing, whatever its origin. When she feels "separate again," moreover, the narrator for the first time sees the human symbol of the generativity that she seeks both to know and to become. There, "standing in front of the cabin,... her hair ... long, down to her shoulders in the style of thirty years ago, before I was born," she sees her mother (213).

Another renewal marks the end of *Lady Oracle*—but in this case, the monsters that invade the stage are the conventions of romance's most highly stylized form, the gothic. The heroine, Joan Foster, composes popular "costume gothics" aimed at female readers and, as well, lives out the genre's fantasies of escape and transformation. As a slim, attractive adult, Joan conceals a former life: her unhappy childhood, when she was chronically overweight. She also conceals her secret identity as Louisa K. Delacourt—the name under which she publishes books like *Love, My Ransom*. In a brief excursion into the occult, she experiments with automatic writing and ends up composing a best-selling volume of poetry, entitled *Lady Oracle*. When the success of *Lady Oracle* causes her to become prey to a blackmailer who threatens to expose her alternate identity as Louisa Delacourt, Joan fakes an accidental drowning and escapes to Italy—under yet another assumed name. In each of her successive incarnations, Joan Foster eagerly identifies with "the pure quintessential need of my readers for escape, a thing I myself understood only too well" (34).

Plainly, Joan Foster's life is a catalog of the gothic conventions she employs in her writing. The transition from fat child to stunning young woman represents the magical transformation. She flirts briefly with the supernatural in her experiment with automatic writing. And, like every gothic heroine, she is fatally attracted to a lover who "liked creating images of virtue violated" (29). If this interpenetration of one world by another proved a source of knowledge and healing for the narrator of *Surfacing*, for Joan Foster it is otherwise. "Why did every one of my fantasies turn into a trap?" she cries (334). The answer is that this is a romance about the dangers of romance.

As the chapters progress, Joan's different lives become indistinguishable from those of the characters she is inventing for *Stalked by Love*, the working title of the costume gothic she is currently composing. In Italy—stalked by a strange man whom she cannot identify and isn't even certain exists—Joan (like the Surfacer) momentarily slips the bonds of everyday rationality and enters the garden of her gothic imaginings. The punning statement *"Suddenly she found herself in the central plot"* (341) refers both to Redmond's garden and to the story line. Here, then, in the penultimate chapter, the merging of the frames is complete.

The problem is that, like all Joan's fantasies, the fabled garden maze of *Stalked by Love* is a trap. Offering rescue is the menacingly handsome Redmond, the ambiguous male protagonist of *Stalked by Love*, who in turn takes on the appearance of all the men in Joan Foster's life, from her father to her husband. "'*Let me rescue you*,'" appeals Redmond, and then—sounding like one of Joan's former lovers—"'*we will dance together forever, always.*' . . . *Once she had wanted these words, she had waited all her life for someone to say them*" (343). But this time the appeal fails. The familiar plot has unraveled, and Joan realizes that her belief in miraculous rescues and timely escapes is the real danger. Breaking the pattern, she opens her eyes, accepts the potential threat of the present moment, and prepares for a man who may actually be following her.

The man at the door turns out to be a reporter who has tracked her from Canada. Uncharacteristically for her, Joan tells him the truth about herself, and "the odd thing is that I didn't tell any lies" (345). "I suppose I could still have gotten out of it. I could have said I had amnesia or something. . . . Or I could have escaped" (344). That she does neither signals the cessation of gothic fantasies in both her life and her work. She will not give up writing, she affirms, but "I won't write any more Costume Gothics . . . I think they were bad for me" (345).

In Joan's statement, Atwood was announcing her own intention to take up a different narrative design. Having explored the major conventions of romance—from the comic in *The Edible Woman* to the serious in *Surfacing*—she ended up parodying the form in *Lady Oracle*. The ruthlessness of the parody (for all its comedic effect) suggests a certain impatience on Atwood's part with the romance's propensity for fantasies of escape, rescue, and transformation. In fact, in the fictions to follow, Atwood resolutely rejected these as narrative strategies, replacing romance's interpenetrating frames with a Sartrean "no exit." If she had not altogether exhausted the possibilities of romance, Atwood was nonetheless embarked on a new project for which romance would not serve. The practice piece for that project was *Life before Man*, "a novel novel," Atwood told an interviewer. "It stays very firmly within the boundaries of realism" (*Black Warrior Review* 89).

The foreground action of *Life before Man* takes place before two different background frames, each imaged in the buildings between which Nate jogs on a Sunday afternoon in 1976. "Behind him are the Parliament Buildings," squat pinkish reminders "that he once thought he would go into politics" (48). "Ahead of him" are the gray buildings of the Royal Ontario Museum, where Nate's wife, Elizabeth, and his mistress, Lesje, are members of the professional staff and where Elizabeth's lover, Chris, had worked until his suicide. Against the novel's images of political statecraft, Nate, Elizabeth, and Lesje negotiate their own terms for power and territory. Against museum exhibits in which prehistoric form and movement are simulated out of bone fragments and fossil remains, these three middle-class Torontonians piece together lives from the fragments of childhood traumas and out of the shards of broken marriages and failed affairs. What secures *Life before Man* its status as a novel is that neither politics nor prehistory threatens to invade reality—as in *The Edible Woman*; nor do they provide alternate realities for healing or escape—as in *Surfacing* or *Lady Oracle*. The frames remain firmly fixed *as frames*. In that capacity, they provide a variety of commentaries—ironic, symbolic, sometimes even prophetic.

Nonetheless, *Life before Man* is very much a transitional text, replete with reminders of the romance narratives that preceded it. Elizabeth's former lover, Chris, for example, appears cut from the same mold as Redmond, the dangerous seducer of Joan Foster's *Stalked by Love*. As Elizabeth remembers him, "Chris had been a dangerous country, swarming with ambushes and guerilas, the centre of a whirlpool, a demon lover" (213). For Nate, Lesje is another romance icon: the unattainable, otherworldly exotic. "Holding Lesje," Nate muses, "would be like holding some strange plant, smooth, thin, with sudden orange flowers. *Exotics*, the florists called them" (71). And Lesje, a paleontologist by both vocation and avocation, is first introduced as "wandering in prehistory. Under a sun more orange than her own has ever been, in the middle of a swampy plain lush with thick-stalked plants and oversized ferns," Lesje likes to imagine herself "watching through binoculars, blissful, uninvolved," as "a group of bony-plated stegosaurs" graze and "a flock of medium-sized pterosaurs glides from one giant tree-fern to another" (18).

The purpose of flirting with—but never employing—the romance possibilities is to expose them for what they are. The demon lover turns banal in his dependency and ultimately pathetic in his desperate suicidal vengeance. Nate's initial response to Lesje as an otherworldly exotic is a throwback to adolescence, and Nate quickly identifies the "image, place[s] it in time: a Saturday matinée of *She*, seen when he was an impressionable twelve and masturbating nightly" (71). Nor can Lesje's Jurassic swamps offer solace or escape. In the end, although she still hungers to imagine "*what it would be like if suddenly the dinosaurs came to life*," she finds "she can't do it. . . . In the foreground, pushing in whether she wants it to or not, is what Marianne would call her life" (310, 311). *Life before Man* thus goes beyond *Lady Oracle* in rejecting the generic conventions of romance, aiming instead at Hawthorne's "minute fidelity, not merely to the possible, but to the probable."

The probable, it turns out, proves wholly adequate to the transformations these characters seek. For, no less than the romances, *Life before Man* also recounts change and transformation. Elizabeth survives both her lover's death and Nate's leaving, realizing that, despite all, she has managed to build "a dwelling over the abyss" (302). Nate emerges from the passivity of his marriage to Elizabeth and makes a commitment to Lesje. Lesje, in her turn, gives up her daydreams of prehistoric Jurassic swamps and makes a commitment to the future by throwing away her contraceptive pills. If none of these entail the mystery of the Surfacer's metamorphosis into wilderness creature or the eerie psychodrama of Joan Foster's entry into the garden of her gothic imaginings, that is precisely the narrative point. In the novel, as in life, people must learn to negotiate within the confines of being "worn, ordinary; mortal" (309). Atwood the romancer had turned realist.

Her audience, by habit, remained loyal to the romancer. A number of critics had difficulty with *Life before Man*, and, as Atwood herself acknowledged in an interview, "they didn't know quite what to do with that one because it didn't have the things in it that they were looking for" (*Black Warrior Review* 89). To ensure against further misunderstandings, Atwood anchored even the most bizarre elements in her subsequent novels to demonstrable realities. The police station's pornography collection in *Bodily Harm* replicated sequences in the Canadian Film Board documentary

This Is Not a Love Story (a film in which Atwood reads a poem). In interviews and public readings, Atwood left no doubt that that novel's St. Antoine had both a geographic and a political counterpart in a West Indies island she had been fond of frequenting. And review copies of *The Handmaid's Tale* arrived from the publisher with selections from a CBC interview in which Atwood declared that every event in the novel was now happening or had already happened somewhere in the world. "I clipped articles out of newspapers," she told the interviewer. "I now have a large clipping file of stories supporting the contentions of the book" (CBC Interview 1).

This new emphasis on a realistic base underpinning the fiction was crucial because the shift in narrative strategy was intended to enable a shift in thematic focus. After *Life before Man*, Atwood turned away from her previous concentration on the power politics of intimate relations and looked, instead, at the abuse of power in the public arena. It was not an entirely new focus for her, to be sure. In a series of poems that would be published in *True Stories*, she had written, "power / like this is not abstract" (50). But the examination of this kind of power was new to her fiction. The moral dimension of that change, she knew, would be lost if readers believed they were taking in only fictive inventions, the phantasmagoria of a romancer's perfervid imagination. Ironically, therefore, even as contemporaries like Ariel Dorfman and J. M. Coetzee turn to romance fantasies to cope with political horrors that defy rational understanding, Atwood reverted to what Hawthorne called the "minute fidelity" of the novel in order to render the dread palpable.

II

The narrative structure of *Bodily Harm* follows a pattern familiar in Atwood's fiction. As the action of the plot unfolds, memory and association trigger flashback sequences. Thus, revelations from earlier years help the reader understand the central character's actions and responses in the present. In this case, what we learn through flashback is that Rennie Wilford spent her childhood in the narrow and repressive town of Griswold, Ontario, finally escaping to Toronto as a university student. After college she supported herself as a freelance journalist specializing in "lifestyles." In college she had taken on controversial issues, writing a piece "on blockbusting as practiced by city developers and another on the lack of good day-care centers for single mothers." When she graduated, "it was no longer 1970," editors were not interested in social issues, and Rennie put away the "ambitions, she now thinks of as illusions" (62).

What intrudes upon Rennie's carefully constructed complacency is the appearance of a cancer requiring a partial mastectomy. The operation so traumatizes her that she withdraws sexually from her live-in lover, Jake, and he moves out. At the same time, Rennie develops a crush on her surgeon, Dr. Daniel Luoma, but that too ends badly. Then one afternoon she returns to her apartment to discover that an intruder has entered and left a coiled rope on her bed. Unable to cope with what seems an increasingly threatened existence in Toronto, Rennie attempts an escape. She persuades the editor of *Visor* magazine to let her do a travel piece and ends up with an assignment "off the beaten track": a Caribbean island she "had never heard of" (22).

Rennie's experiences on St. Antoine and its neighbor, Ste. Agathe, are the novel's present and constitute the unfolding of the plot. Essentially, the plot is about recovery. Rennie recovers her capacity for sexual pleasure in a brief affair with a small-time local drug runner named Paul. She recovers her capacity for compassion in her relationship with Lora (whose life story also winds its way through the narrative). And through Dr. Minnow—a local politician who is assassinated—Rennie recovers the outrage at injustice that had once fueled her journalism. The irony is that Rennie comes back to life when she is, in fact, most vulnerable: jailed in wretched conditions, uncertain that she will ever be let out, hearing the cries of the tortured all around her, and thinking about "her own lack of power ... what could be done to her" (241). Under these circumstances, her cancer scar "seems of minor interest, even to her. . . . She may be dying, true, but if so, she's doing it slowly, relatively speaking. Other people are doing it faster: At night there are screams" (251).

The catalyst for these transformations is Rennie's belief in the possibility of being "away ... invisible ... safe" (41). But because St. Antoine is so far off the regular tourist path and because she arrives on the eve of the first election since the British gave up colonial rule, her very presence arouses suspicion. Rather than becoming invisible, she is watched wherever she goes. Finally, when the corrupt local government attempts to thwart the election results, Rennie is suspected of being a foreign agent. In a place where corruption and unbridled power mean that "nothing is inconceivable" (121), Rennie learns that there is no such thing as safety. Once and for all, she abandons the notion that "she's a tourist. She's exempt" (182).

Rennie first attracts curiosity when she tours the island in the company of Dr. Minnow, a man she met on the plane from Barbados. Rennie expects to be shown the local attractions, but Minnow has a different itinerary. He takes her to a squalid encampment where the victims of a previous year's hurricane huddle, without adequate food or shelter—even though the "sweet Canadians" have given the government ample funds with which " 'to rebuild their houses. . . . Only it has not yet happened, you understand' " (114).

Minnow's tour highlights the island's poverty and the corruption of the present regime. What Minnow also reveals in the course of the afternoon is that he is the major opposition candidate in the upcoming election, and he wants Rennie to cover that event. " 'Look with your eyes open and you will see the truth of the matter,' " Minnow pleads. " 'Since you are a reporter, it is your duty to report.' " But "Rennie reacts badly to the word *duty*. Duty was big in Griswold" (121).

Politics is "not my thing," protests Rennie, "I do lifestyles." Minnow takes the word literally and agrees that this, too, is what *he* is after. " 'It is our duty to be concerned with lifestyles,' " he says. " 'What the people eat, what they wear, this is what I want you to write about' " (123). Only later, when Minnow appears to have won the election and is shot by the new CIA agent on the island, does Rennie understand the urgency behind his pleading. "Now she knows why he wanted her to write about this place: so there would be less chance of this happening, to him" (222).

In the aftermath of Minnow's assassination, some of his followers attempt to overthrow the present government. The tiny insurrection is brutally put down, and Rennie, having been seen in Minnow's company, is jailed as a subversive. Rennie's cellmate is Lora, another white woman who had drifted to the island and become involved with "Prince," the second opposition candidate.

The two are unlikely companions. In contrast to Rennie's stolidly middle-class upbringing, Lora is the child of poverty and abuse. Where Rennie is university-educated, Lora has had to become streetwise. In fact, as Rennie is slow to realize, some of the privileges they enjoy in jail—Lora's supply of cigarettes, a comb, a package of chewing gum—result from Lora's sexual favors to their guards during the daily latrine run. For Rennie, silently repeating the wisdom of Griswold, "it isn't decent." To the hardened Lora, it is simply a survival tactic. It's " 'not any different from having some guy stick his finger in your ear' " (252).

Not that Lora is doing it for cigarettes or chewing gum. The guards have promised to arrange for her to see Prince, whom they claim is also incarcerated. As the days go by, Lora becomes increasingly impatient: the guards keep promising, but they never deliver. When Lora cries over her dilemma, Rennie finds herself "embarrassed. She looks down at her hands, which ought to contain comfort. Compassion. She ought to go over to Lora and put her arms around her and pat her on the back, but she can't" (253). Finally, a new guard blurts out that Prince was never imprisoned, having earlier been "caught in the crossfire" (257). Lora realizes that he, too, has been assassinated and that she has been used. Her rage and grief explode, provoking the two guards, and Rennie watches, helpless, as Lora's body endures their relentless beating. At last, against her will, Rennie is doing what Minnow had asked: " 'Look with your eyes open' " (121). "She doesn't want to see, she has to see, why isn't someone covering her eyes?" (158).

Unlike *Life before Man, Bodily Harm* is tenaciously novelistic, refusing even a flirtation with romance elements. Rennie may have once found it "soothing to think of Daniel," her kindly but deeply conventional surgeon, but she knew all along that this was only "a fantasy" (210). The intended escape to "somewhere warm and very far away" (21) has embroiled her in Third World political upheavals. And her lover, Paul, never rescues her from jail. When she is released, she knows, it is sheer luck—it might easily have been otherwise. Indeed, what Rennie learns on St. Antoine is that "she will never be rescued" (266). There is no rescue from the realities on which this novel insists.

Moreover, where *Life before Man* still utilized framing backgrounds as symbolic commentary, in *Bodily Harm* the symbolic commentary is itself a product of the foreground. Rennie's cancer, which precipitates her journey to the Caribbean, is not only a plot device. It is also a metaphor for a malignant world. The disease really to be feared, Rennie comes to realize, is the capacity to take pleasure from another's pain. When the police arrest her at her hotel, she recognizes on the hotel manager's face "a look of pure enjoyment. *Malignant*" (232). In prison she watches a guard with a bayonet menacing a group of bound prisoners. The guard "walks slowly around to the back of the line with it, strolling, hips rolling, taking his time, luxuriating. He's not doing this just because he's been ordered to," thinks Rennie. "He's doing it because he enjoys it. *Malignant*" (255). In the end, what will save her sanity is what she had once most feared: massive involvement. Only now the term has a different meaning.

If there are neither romance elements nor background frames in *Bodily Harm*, there is what the novel calls "a subground, something that can't be seen but is nevertheless there" (23). That subground is Griswold, where Rennie "learned three things well: how to be quiet, what not to say, and how to look at things without touching them" (54). As such, Griswold does not offer commentary but it does help to define the absences, or lacunae, in Rennie's personality. First and foremost, as Rennie remembers it, Griswold was a place without compassion. "In Griswold everyone gets what they deserve. In Griswold everyone deserves the worst" (23). Second, the old Victorian house of Rennie's childhood is a place of emotional withholdings, remarkably without touching or intimacy.

One of Rennie's most vivid memories is of her aging grandmother complaining that she has lost her hands: the hands "I had before, the ones I touch things with" (57). Repeatedly during such episodes, Rennie had been unable to respond to her grandmother's anxiety. She "cannot bear to be touched by those groping hands," and so "she puts her own hands behind her and backs away" (262).

By the time she first arrives on St. Antoine, Rennie's emotional withdrawal has become so complete that her grandmother's delusion is now her own nightmare. On her second night on the island, Rennie dreams she's "rummaging through her slips, scarves, sweaters. . . . It's her hands she's looking for, she knows she left them here somewhere, folded neatly in a drawer, like gloves" (106). But as she stays on St. Antoine, Rennie's hands again become capable of touch—first with Paul and then, more important, with Lora.

Rennie had never responded well to the living Lora, but after witnessing the beating, she is unable to ignore Lora's dying body. Bruised beyond recognition, Lora's face makes Rennie want to throw up and turn away, as though from a stranger. But "she can't do it . . . it's the face of Lora after all, there's no such thing as a faceless stranger." Rennie reaches out, finds the use of her hands, and takes hold of Lora's cold hand with both of her own. By the sheer act of will, Rennie attempts "to pull her through" (263). It "is the hardest thing she's ever done": "She holds the hand, perfectly still, with all her strength. Surely, if she can only try hard enough, something will move and live again, something will get born" (264). What gets born is a new Rennie. Upon her release, Rennie is aware that she has been changed irrevocably. For the first time, "she's paying attention, that's all" (266). "What she sees has not altered; only the way she sees it" (264–65). On the flight back to Canada, Rennie feels "the shape of a hand in hers, both of hers, there but not there, like the afterglow of a match that's gone out" (264).

Ironically, the time on St. Antoine has made her what before she's been in name only: "A reporter. She will pick her time; then she will report" (265). The Canadian official who passes on a request from the local government that she not write about what happened to her, we know, has no influence. Rennie has become what they accused her of: "a subversive. She was not once but she is now" (265). The feel of Lora's hand in hers—"it will always be there now"—is the pledge that Rennie will eventually bear witness to what she has seen.

As has been characteristic of all of Atwood's longer fictions, then, the central character of *Bodily Harm* also undergoes a major transformation. As with *Life before Man*, however, the transformation takes place without the alternate realities, interpenetrating worlds, or colliding frames of romance. What distinguishes *Bodily Harm* from *Life before Man* is that the unsparing brutality of the later novel makes the reader long for precisely such illusions—even as it renders them at once immoral and inaccessible. Rennie's craving for exemption, her impulse toward escape and invisibility, are inherently romantic. But it is these very conventions that must be denied if *Bodily Harm* is to have its intended narrative force. For the message of *Bodily Harm* is the message of a novel: "She will never be rescued.... She is not exempt" (266).

III

In contrast to Rennie, who learns to " 'look with [her] eyes open' " (121), the narrator of *The Handmaid's Tale* pays the price of living "as usual, by ignoring. Ignoring isn't the same as ignorance, you have to work at it" (66). Atwood's 1985 long fiction is thus a cautionary tale, illustrating the consequences of refusing the lessons of *Bodily Harm*. At the same time, *The Handmaid's Tale* represents the agony of telling that Rennie only contemplates. Where *Bodily Harm* asserts the moral imperative for bearing witness, *The Handmaid's Tale* elaborates the pain of that process. "I don't want to be telling this story," Offred repeats. "It hurts me to tell it over, over again" (279).

The time frame of the narrative is the not-too-distant future when everything that we would recognize as familiar has been relegated to "the other time, the time before" (55). The United States has undergone a coup d'état. The president has been shot, Congress "machine-gunned," and the Constitution "suspended" (183). Taking control is a well-armed, highly organized right-wing fundamentalist faction whose politics combine sociobiological justifications for literal interpetations of the Bible with an appeal to a return to "traditional values" (17). The new regime declares a state of emergency and establishes a police state named the Republic of Gilead.

The driving motive behind all this is racist anxiety at the declining Caucasian birthrate. Rather than direct its animus at the environmental causes of sterility—"nuclear plant accidents,... leakages from chemical and biological-warfare stockpiles and toxic-waste disposal sites,... the uncontrolled use of chemical insecticides, herbicides, and other sprays" (317)—Gilead points its finger at the erosion of family values and the liberation of women from the home. Gilead's solution is a white supremacist ideology and a skewed reinstitution of the patriarchal family. Blacks are deported to "homelands"; Jews are given the choice of conversion or immigration to Israel; and homosexuals are executed as "gender traitors."

The white women remaining in Gilead are prohibited gainful employment and the right to hold property or money in their own name; they are no longer permitted to read or write. The only exception to this last stricture are the Aunts, a small group of relatively privileged older women who police the rest. Those resisting the new order are declared Unwomen and are banished to the Colonies—forced labor camps or toxic cleanup sites, where the life expectancy is two to three years.

Males in Gilead are organized by a rigid hierarchy of class and power, each man's status announced by the female services to which he has access. Low-status males are presumably celibate until they gain sufficient status to be assigned Econowives, women who must both reproduce and take care of all household chores. Econowives wear dresses striped in blue, green, and red, indicating their multiple functions. Upper-echelon males enjoy Wives, always dressed in blue; household servants, called Marthas, dressed in dull green; and Handmaids, attired in red.

The sole function of the Handmaids is breeding. Assigned to the childless households of high-status males and their wives, the Handmaids engage in a formal copulation Ceremony—once monthly, when they are ovulating. The Ceremony replicates the scene of Rachel and Bilhah in Genesis 30 and thus claims biblical precedent. The Ceremony notwithstanding, the odds are against successful reproduction because most of Gilead's adult males are sterile. And even when impregnation does take place, "the chances are one in four" (122) that the fetus will miscarry or the infant prove deformed. When a Handmaid produces a healthy infant, she nurses it for a brief period but then turns it over to its legal parents and moves on to her next posting. Unless terminated by a successful pregnancy, each posting lasts two years. The reward for successful reproduction is the promise that the Handmaid will never be sent off to the Colonies. Should she fail to produce a healthy child after three postings, her fate is sealed. Because Gilead does not recognize male sterility but only female infertility, the Handmaid who does not conceive is declared an Unwoman and banished.

For almost a year, watching with her as the seasons change, we live inside the head of one such Handmaid, known to us only as Offred. Like all Handmaids, her name denotes her possession by the high-status male in whose home she is currently posted (that is, she is the property *of* Fred). Because women are not persons so much as functions in Gilead, her given name, like her individual identity in the time before, is what the regime is bent on obliterating. Struggling to retain some vestige of her former personality, Offred hoards her memories. "The night," she says, "is my time out. Where should I go?" Alone in a sparsely furnished room at the top of the stairs, the "somewhere good" she chooses on one occasion is a college reminiscence (47). At other times, she remembers scenes from her childhood or from her marriage.

Offred's willed excursions into the "distant past" (94)—along with her nightmares—flesh out the narrative. In these sequences, we learn something of her personal history—her prickly relationship with her ardently feminist mother, her marriage to Luke, the birth of their daughter, and her tendency to take "too much for granted; I trusted fate, back then" (37). We also get her fragments of knowledge about the coup and the changes gradually instituted in the months following. Women were let go from their jobs, denied employment, and—with the regime in command of all the computer data banks—their money and property were transferred to the control of husbands or male relatives. "There were marches, of course," Offred recalls, "a lot of women and some men." But "when it was known that the police, or the army, or whoever they were, would open fire almost as soon as any of the marches even started, the marches stopped." For her part, the narrator attempted withdrawal into domesticity, "doing more housework, more baking." Too often, though, she found herself crying "without warning" (189). When Luke remained insistently reassuring, she realized—to her horror—that "he doesn't mind this. . . . He doesn't mind it at all. Maybe he even likes it. We are not each other's any more. Instead, I am his" (191).

Only when their marriage is decreed invalid—because of Luke's prior marriage and divorce—does Luke attempt escape. But their forged documents are detected at the Canadian border, and a desperate run into the woods is quickly thwarted. Luke is shot, the narrator captured, and their five-year-old daughter taken away. In the worst of her nightmares, Offred can still "see her, . . . holding out her arms to me, being carried away" (85). Except for a small Polaroid photograph purloined by Serena Joy, Offred never sees her daughter again; nor does she know what became of Luke, whether he is alive or dead.

Following the capture at the border, her memory lapses. "There must have been needles, pills, something like that. I couldn't have lost that much time without help" (49). When the narrator regains full consciousness, she is at the Leah and Rachel Centre, formerly a high school, now converted for the training of Handmaids. Here—in a flashback sequence—the novel opens. The present time of the plot, however, covers the period from Offred's arrival at the home of the Commander and his wife, Serena Joy, through her final escape from Gilead in a black van. Thus, in what is by now a familiar pattern in Atwood's longer fictions, the events of the present are set against an interweaving of the past, with the past requiring the reader's active reconstruction.

If the narrative structure is familiar, the narrative voice is not. Offred's is the most anguished voice in Atwood's fictions to date, and the most self-conscious. She struggles with the process of telling, trying out different versions, inventing—then recanting—scenarios that might show her in a better light, and agonizing over missed opportunities in a past she can never recover. "I wish this story were different" is her repeated refrain. The anguish is heightened by Offred's uncertainty that she has an audience.

Everything she has suffered and her attempt to bear witness to that suffering, after all, are rendered meaningless without a recipient who will honor her survival by learning its lessons. Offred therefore has no choice but to take a leap of faith and will her audience into being. "By telling you anything at all I'm at least believing in you, I believe you're there, I believe you into being.... I tell, therefore you are" (279). But willing the audience's existence is not enough. She must also ensure that her audience will interpret her story as she intends.

Her narrative is not to be taken in the spirit of George Orwell's *Nineteen Eighty-Four*—that is, as a fable about totalitarian control. Offred thinks she has another lesson to teach. "Maybe none of this is about control," she muses. "Maybe it isn't really about who can own whom, who can do what to whom and get away with it, even as far as death. Maybe it isn't about who can sit and who has to kneel or stand or lie down, legs spread open" (144–45). Instead, she speculates, her story is "about who can do what to whom and be forgiven for it" (145). The speculation arrests attention. First and foremost, it suggests that Offred might consider forgiving the Commander, an architect of the regime that now enslaves her. Second, it underscores the travesty of Christianity that this repressive monotheocracy represents, by reminding us of the absence of anything like charity or forgiveness in Gilead. And, finally, in the face of a totalitarian police state that has seemingly appropriated all power to itself, Offred proposes that power takes many forms. "Remember," she enjoins, "forgiveness too is a power. To beg for it is a power, and to withhold or bestow it is a power, perhaps the greatest" (144).

In the narrative as we have it, we never hear the Commander beg for forgiveness. Even so, we know that he has at least dimly understood that the Handmaids suffer and, because of this, he has embarked on an awkward effort to make Offred's situation endurable: he begins a clandestine friendship of sorts with her. Late at night in his study, he invites her to play Scrabble with him, provides forbidden reading material, and supplies a bottle of contraband hand lotion. On one occasion, he even sneaks her into Jezebel's, Gilead's underground version of a Playboy Club and whorehouse for the male elite. For all that, Offred never tells us that she bestows the single power she can still claim as her own. Having seen this sympathetic side of her Commander, she admits that "he was no longer a thing to me." But it is, at best, a "realization" that "complicates" (170), not one that leads ineluctably to forgiveness.

Offred worries the point because she wants her audience to understand what it would mean if this *were* "about who can do what to whom and be forgiven for it." For all his attempts at amelioration, her Commander wields power on behalf of a regime that outlaws love, charity, intimacy, and forgiveness, ruling by terror and intimidation. To forgive such brutality would imply unthinkable power—not to the bestower but to the recipient—because it confers ultimate impunity. Rennie's nightmare on St. Antoine, where "nothing is inconceivable" (121), pales in comparison to Offred's hint at a moral constellation in which nothing is unforgivable. "If you happen to be a man, sometime in the future, and you've made it this far," Offred appeals, "please remember: you will never be subjected to the temptation of feeling you must forgive, a man, as a woman. It's difficult to resist, believe me" (144). But resist she does.

The "man, sometime in the future" who takes charge of Offred's narrative turns out to be the exegete Offred had tried to guard against. In "Historical Notes," which follows as an appendix, Professor James Darcy Pieixoto, Director of the Twentieth and Twenty-First Century Archives at Cambridge University, England, addresses an academic conference in the nation of Nunavit (a nation carved out of what was once northern Canada by the native peoples). The date is 25 June 2195. Gilead no longer exists, but in its wake the map of North America has been radically redrawn. Pieixoto's subject is the provenance of the *Tale* and the problems he has had, as a historian, in authenticating it. The narrative we have just read, it turns out, is Pieixoto's (and his collaborator, Professor Knotly Wade's) arrangement and transcription of some thirty tape cassettes "unearthed on the site of what was once the city of Bangor," Maine. The cassettes are "of the type that became obsolete sometime in the eighties or nineties with the advent of the compact disc." Offred is presumed to have made the tapes while hiding out at a "way-station" en route to Canada on "The Underground Femaleroad" that operated secretly in Gilead (313).

Pieixoto opens his remarks with a series of sexist puns. He then details the discovery and transcription of the tapes, briefly digressing to what he terms "an editorial aside" before launching into his main subject. The editorial aside is a caution against "passing moral judgement upon the Gileadeans" (314). His main subject is the attempt to "establish an identity for the narrator" (315) or for any of the personages mentioned by Offred. Bringing his remarks to a close, Pieixoto registers disappointment at the "gaps" (322) in information within the narrative and reiterates his contention that voices from the past are "imbued with the obscurity of the matrix out of which they come" (324).

The reader who has been moved by Offred's rendering of the dailiness of suffering in Gilead is unprepared for this kind of discourse. Because of the subject matter of the Handmaid's testament, what jolt us in Pieixoto's remarks are both his delight in salacious puns—especially those "having to do with the archaic vulgar signification of the word *tail*" (313)—and his "editorial aside" against "passing moral judgement." Pieixoto subscribes to the relativist argument that all "such judgements are of necessity culture-specific" (314). As a congress of historians, he states, "our job is not to censure but to understand" (315).

The implied objectivity of this stance has the effect of repressing moral valuation because it flattens the uniqueness of Offred and her telling into a domesticating matrix. She has been consigned safely to history. Her document is merely additional evidence for fleshing out a context that no longer exists. As Pieixoto puts it, "Our author ... was one of many, and must be seen within the broad outlines of the moment in history of which she was a part" (317). As a result, what Pieixoto means by *understanding* comes dangerously close to what Offred would have named forgiveness. By telling his audience that "Gileadean society was under a good deal of pressure, demographic and otherwise" (315), Pieixoto has not so much explained as *explained away* racist and sexist policies that led to a virtual reign of terror. This refusal to judge or censure thus makes of historical discourse—at least as Pieixoto practices it—a discourse of exoneration.

The "Historical Notes" was an inspired device. Pieixoto's analysis of the history and ideological underpinnings of Gilead, along with his pursuit of the identity of Offred's Commander, provides Atwood a mechanism for offering information to which her first-person narrator could not have had access. At best, Offred had managed "to see the world in gasps" (40). At the same time, the "Notes" section provides Atwood with a mechanism for posing profound questions about what should constitute the narrative of history. The progress from the romantic to the increasingly realistic had brought Atwood to the view that "life can never be truthfully represented as having the kind of formal coherency met with in the conventional, well-made fabulistic story" (White ix). She therefore put forward two opposed narrative possibilities: Offred's halting reconstruction of her own "limping and mutilated story" (279) followed by Pieixoto's orderly excavation of identifiable personages, relationships, and motivations that might be derived from it. The two stand opposed not because of content—both are incomplete attempts at accurate reconstruction—but because the single response demanded by the primary document is the same response that its interpreter categorically refuses.

Offred bears witness that lessons may be learned, judgments made, future atrocities avoided. Her recollections are an admonition. "There were stories in the newspapers, of course," that gave clues to a right-wing takeover in the offing, Offred remembers, but most people "lived, as usual, by ignoring" (66). Pieixoto records past social and cultural practices *for their own sake*. Among "his extensive publications" is an article entitled "Sumptuary Laws through the Ages" (312). Pieixoto does not read the Handmaid's tale as *we* have been reading it: that is, as a call to critical awareness of the praxis current in one's own society. Thus Pieixoto is able to congratulate his era for being "happily more free" of the adverse demographic and environmental factors to which Gilead reacted (315), but he is oblivious to the Gileadean echoes in his own sexist jokes. As Pieixoto would construct it, in other words, history is not a narrative that asserts moral awareness or hones a critical perception of the present.

The point in all this goes beyond George Santayana's observation that "those who neglect the study of the past are condemned to repeat it." As Hayden White has commented, "It is not so much the study of the past itself that assures against its repetition as it is how one studies it, to what aim, interest, or purpose. Nothing is better suited to lead to a repetition of the past than a study of it that is either reverential or convincingly objective in the way that conventional historical studies tend to be" (82). By engaging the reader first in an empathetic identification with Offred, Atwood has ensured that Pieixoto's putative objectivity will not be ours. In so doing, Atwood places us in the peculiar position of rejecting one kind of formal historical narrative—Pieixoto's—about a past—Offred's—that has not yet occurred but might be our future. The result is that we, as readers, are doubly inscribed in this text as the *writers* of history. On the one hand, our objections to Pieixoto's conference paper force us to consider how we would want historians to construct their narratives. On the other hand, jolted by Offred's narrative to reexamine current praxis, we realize that our action—or inaction—in the present is already writing the future that is Offred's past.

Because *The Handmaid's Tale* is a dystopia set in an invented future, there is some temptation to regard it as a romance fantasy. Atwood herself, however, insisted that she had projected only "a slight twist on the society we now have." In the widely publicized CBC interview, she explained: "There isn't anything in the book that isn't based on something that hasn't already happened in history or in another country or for which the materials are not already available" (1). Futuristic though it is, then, in its "fidelity, not merely to the possible, but to the probable," *The Handmaid's Tale* adheres to Hawthorne's definition of a novel.

Unlike a romance, moreover, *The Handmaid's Tale* functions without interpenetrating alternate realities that could invite fantasies of rescue or escape. The best that Offred can manage is "time out" through memory. But even this is never a sure refuge. If she lingers too long in the past, she calls forth scenes painful to endure. And, finally, the past is not even surely there. "I ought to have . . . paid more attention, to the details," she agonizes. She didn't, though, so now Luke, too, is "fading. Day by day, night by night he recedes" (281).

That said, there is a way in which *The Handmaid's Tale* might be read as romance. Offred's "time out" is the time we live. Ours is the world she attempts to conserve in memory. When we find fault with Pieixoto's commentary, we become the appropriately responsive audience whom Offred has willed into existence. In effect, *we* are the alternate possibility brooding over Gilead, ours the realm of potential interpenetration. *We* are the romance element that this novel everywhere invokes. Atwood has come full circle. She has offered her readers a return to romance—*if*, that is, we are willing to take on the obligations of history. We can both *re*write Pieixoto's narrative and *un*write Offred's if only we attend to the warnings in her tale and guard against the Gileadean impulses in the contemporary United States. To recognize these obligations is to recognize that we are Offred's ultimate fantasy of escape. To do otherwise is to measure Offred's future suffering in the magnitude of our present complacency. The generic choice is ours. Whether *The Handmaid's Tale* proves prophetic novel or cautionary romance depends on how seriously we take our political responsibility as readers who inevitably write history.

WORKS CITED

Atwood, Margaret. "An Interview with Margaret Atwood." From an interview with the Canadian Broadcasting Corporation. New York: Houghton, n.d. 1-4.

———. "An Interview with Margaret Atwood." With Elizabeth Meese. *Black Warrior Review* 12.1 (1985): 88–108.

———. *Bodily Harm.* New York: Simon, 1982.

———. *The Edible Woman.* Toronto: McClelland, 1969.

———. *The Handmaid's Tale.* Toronto: McClelland, 1985.

———. *Lady Oracle.* New York: Simon, 1976.

———. *Life before Man.* New York: Simon, 1979.

———. *Surfacing.* New York: Fawcett, 1972.

———. *True Stories.* Toronto: Oxford UP, 1981.

Burke, Kenneth. *Permanence and Change: An Anatomy of Purpose.* 1935. 3rd ed. 1954. Berkeley: U of California P, 1984.

Hawthorne, Nathaniel. Preface. *Blithedale Romance.* 1852. Centenary Edition. Columbus: Ohio State UP, 1964.

———. Preface. *The House of the Seven Gables.* 1851. Centenary Edition. Columbus: Ohio State UP, 1965.

White, Hayden. *The Content of the Form: Narrative Discourse and Historical Representation.* Baltimore: Johns Hopkins UP, 1987.

Terry Goldie

SEMIOTIC CONTROL: NATIVE PEOPLES IN CANADIAN LITERATURE IN ENGLISH

IF THE IMAGE of native peoples in Canadian literature is analyzed in semiotic terms, the signifier, the literary image, does not lead back to the implied signified, the racial group usually termed Indian or Amerindian, but rather to other images.[1] This phenomenon could be seen as simply another version of Jacques Derrida's analysis of semiosis, which might be termed the Quaker Oats box view of the sign. The person on the box is holding a box with a picture of the same person holding a box with a picture of the same person holding a box ... The root image cannot exist, for there must always be another image on the box being held, no matter how small. In the same way, each signifier can refer only to another signifier. Any implied signified is unreachable.

But the signifier can be quite precise in itself. John Berger's *Ways of Seeing* states as follows of the visual image:

> An image is a sight which has been recreated or reproduced. It is an appearance, or a set of appearances, which has been detached from the place and time in which it first made its appearance and preserved—for a few moments or a few centuries. (9–10)

A literary representation might seem less absolute, but the indigene in literature is similarly a reified preservation, an extreme example of the law noted by Edward Said in *Orientalism*: "In any instance of at least written language, there is no such thing as a delivered presence, but a *re-presence*, or a representation" (21). Each representation of the indigene is a signifier for which there is no signified except the image. The referent has little purpose in the equation. In the context of the indigene, the unbreachable alterity between signifier and signified is never what many have claimed, an abstruse philosophical concept with nihilist tendencies, but an important aspect of the "subjugated knowledges" to which Michel Foucault refers in *Power/Knowledge* (81). The valorization of the image is defined by a process in which the signified is signifier, in which representation is Image.

Yet there is a significant hidden connection between text and reality. In *Orientalism* Said suggests that what is important in Western representations of Eastern culture is not the approximation of presence that seems to be the intention but rather the conformity of the works to an ideology called orientalism. Said studies not the reality the works seem to represent, the truths they claim to depict, but the reality of the texts and their ideology, and of the ideology of the authors and their culture. In the case of Canadian native peoples, creative literature is but one of the more visible reflections of a process that permeates our culture, even those aspects of it that seem most removed from native peoples. For instance, I am 'writing' this line on a computer purchased from Beothuck Data Systems, named for the now-extinct indigenes of Newfoundland.

The reality of the ideology is shaped by the reality of invasion and oppression. Eric R. Wolf comments on the creation of "race":

> Racial designations, such as "Indian" or "Negro," are the outcome of the subjugation of populations in the course of European mercantile expansion. The term *Indian* stands for the conquered populations of the New World, in disregard of any cultural or physical differences among native Americans. (380)

But the details and even the major events of the conquest are not significant factors in the image of the native. History awarded semiotic control to the invaders. Since then the image of native peoples has functioned as a constant source of semiotic reproduction, in which each textual image refers to those offered before. The image of "them" has been "ours."

This analysis attempts to reveal the semiotic limitations of various texts, particularly of those that have been said to provide "positive" or "realistic" views of native peoples. I seek Pierre Macherey's "ideological horizon" (132), the concealed but omnipresent ideology controlling the text. Yet in identifying that horizon, in deconstructing that center of control, I must recognize that I cannot avoid asserting my own center, as a white Canadian male of a certain age. Like any other critic I must recognize that, in Yeats's words, "The centre cannot hold."

The shape of the signifying process as it applies to native peoples is formed by a certain semiotic field; the images function within its bound-

aries. A few associations suggest the area: war dance, war whoop, toma-
hawk, and dusky. The native is a semiotic pawn on a chessboard controlled
by the white signmaker; yet the individual signmaker, the individual player,
can move these pawns only within certain prescribed areas. To extend the
analogy, the textual play between white and native is a replica of the black
and white squares. The basic dualism, however, is not good and evil, although it is often argued to be so, as in Abdul R. JanMohamed's "Economy
of Manichean Allegory": "The dominant model of power—and interest—
relations in all colonial societies is the manichean opposition between the
putative superiority of the European and the supposed inferiority of the
native" (63). In some early and many contemporary texts the opposition
is, rather, between the "putative superiority" of the indigene and the "supposed inferiority" of the white. A white teacher in Philip Kreiner's *People
like Us in a Place like This* explores the northern barrens with his Indian
friend, Elijah Sealhunter: "I feel pulled out of myself. And what I like best
about being out there by the bay is that I know it's not my place to be out
there. I know that if Elijah wasn't there, and I was, I would die" (31). The
white alien is given life by the prophet–natural hunter. As with Said's
Oriental Other, positive and negative images are swings of the pendulum:

> Many of the earliest Oriental amateurs began by welcoming the Orient as a
> salutary *dérangement* of their European habits of mind and spirit. The Orient
> was overvalued for its pantheism, its spirituality, its stability, its longevity,
> its primitivism, and so forth.... Yet almost without exception such over-
> esteem was followed by a counter-response: the Orient suddenly appeared
> lamentably underhumanized, antidemocratic, backward, barbaric, and so
> forth. (150)

Said's "overvalued" is present in the short passage from Kreiner, but even
there the "counter-response" is always implied.

The complications extend beyond racial opposition, as noted by Sander
Gilman:

> Because there is no real line between self and the Other, an imaginary line
> must be drawn; and so that the illusion of an absolute difference between
> self and Other is never troubled, this line is as dynamic in its ability to alter
> itself as is the self. This can be observed in the shifting relationship of
> antithetical stereotypes that parallel the existence of "bad" and "good" rep-
> resentations of self and Other. But the line between "good" and "bad" re-
> sponds to stresses occurring within the psyche. Thus paradigm shifts in our
> mental representations of the world can and do occur. We can move from
> fearing to glorifying the Other. We can move from loving to hating. (18)

The problem is not the negative or positive aura associated with the image but rather the image itself. As the passage from Kreiner suggests, the Other is of interest only to the extent that it comments on the self, a judgment that could correctly be applied to the present study, concerned primarily not with native peoples but with the image of the native, a white image.

This image is usually defined, as it is in Kreiner, in association with nature. The explorers attempted to make their signifying process represent real experience, to create the "informational" text defined by Mary Pratt: "[T]he invisible eye/I strives to make those informational orders natural, to find them there uncommanded, rather than assert them as the products/producers of European knowledges or disciplines" (125).

Thus, to define the Indian as "natural" seems to be "natural" in Samuel Hearne's *Journey from Prince of Wales's Fort*, but it continues to be so in contemporary fiction—for instance, W. O. Mitchell's *Since Daisy Creek*. The field, that uniform chessboard, has remained, particularly in the few basic moves that the indigenous pawn has been allowed to make.

At least since Frantz Fanon's *Black Skin White Masks* it has been a commonplace to use "Other" and "Not-self" for the white view of blacks and for the resulting black view of themselves, an assertion of a white self as subject in discourse that leaves the black Other as object. The terms are similarly applicable to the Indian and Inuk but with an important shift. They are Other and Not-self but also must become self. Gayatri Spivak, in "Three Women's Texts," examines the value of the colonized to the colonizer: "The project of imperialism has always already historically refracted what might have been the absolute Other into a domesticated Other that consolidated the imperialist self" (253). Any imperialist discourse valorizes the colonized according to its own needs for reflection.

But in Spivak's area of study, the Indian subcontinent, the imperialist discourse remains admittedly nonindigenous. India is valorized by imperialist dynamics but it "belongs" to the white realm only as part of the empire. Canadians have long had a clear agenda to erase this separation of belonging. The white Canadian looks at the Inuk. The Inuk is Other and therefore alien. But the Inuk is indigenous and therefore cannot be alien. So the Canadian must be alien! But how can the Canadian be alien within Canada? There are only two possible answers. The white culture might reject the indigene, by stating that the country really began with the arrival of the whites, an approach no longer popular but significant in the nineteenth and early twentieth centuries. Or else the white culture can attempt to incorporate the Other, in superficial gestures such as naming a firm Mohawk Motors, or in sensitive and sophisticated creative endeavors such as the novels of Rudy Wiebe.

The importance of the alien within cannot be overstated. In their need to become "native," to belong in their land, whites in Canada have required a process I have termed "indigenization," the impossible necessity of becoming indigenous. For many writers, the only chance seemed to be through the humans who are truly indigenous, the Indians and Inuit. As J. J. Healy notes in the Australian context:

> The Aborigine was part of the tension of an indigenous consciousness. Not the contemporary Aborigine, not even a plausible historical one, but the sort of creature that *might* persuade a white Australian to look in the direction of the surviving race. (173)

Many Canadians have reacted strongly to other such "creatures" and to their own need to become indigenous. Of course, the majority of writers have paid little if any attention to native peoples. But the process of indigenization is complex, and each nineteenth-century reference to the white Canadian as "native" is a comment on indigenization, regardless of the absence of Indians or Inuit in those references. As Macherey states, "an ideology is made of what it does not mention; it exists because there are things which must not be spoken of" (132). In other words, absence is also negative presence, which might be opposed by the "positive absence" of a name like Beothuck Data or of texts such as Isabella Valancy Crawford's "Malcolm's Katie," written in 1884. The Indian is neither subject nor overt object of the poem, but natural phenomena are often represented through overtly "Indian" metaphors, an apparent attempt to "indigenize" the text.

Said notes a number of what he terms "standard commodities" associated with the Orient. Two commodities that appear to be standard in the economy created by the semiotic field of the Indian and Inuk in Canadian literature are sex and violence. They are poles of attraction and repulsion, temptation by the sensual maiden and fear of the fiendish warrior. Often the two poles are found in the same work; in John Richardson's *Wacousta*, the warrior constantly attacks, but the maiden helps the white to avoid that attack. They are emotional signs, semiotic embodiments of primal responses. Could one create a more appropriate signifier for fear than the treacherous redskin? He incorporates the terror of an impassioned, uncontrolled spirit of evil. He is strangely joined by the Indian maiden, who tempts the being chained by civilization toward the liberation of free and open sexuality, not untamed evil but unrestrained joy. Following the pattern noted in Gilman's *Difference and Pathology*, "the 'bad' Other becomes the negative stereotype; the 'good' Other becomes the positive stereotype. The former is that which we fear to become; the latter, that which we fear we cannot achieve" (20). Added to this construction is the alien's fear of the warrior as hostile wilderness—this new, threatening land—and the arrivant's attraction to the maiden as restorative pastoral—this new, available land. The absent Indian and Crawford's Indianized poem might also be seen in this context. The general sign of fear leads to an indigenization that excludes the indigene. Temptation promises an indigenization through inclusion.

An intriguing yet unanswerable question is whether the depiction of the Indian leads to an emphasis on sex and violence or whether desire for the frissons of sex and violence suggests the Indian. For instance, through the first part of Joseph Howe's "Acadia" (written in the 1830s), the image of the Indian approximates the noble savage but includes a stridently gory scene of the massacre of a pioneer family, in which the Indian appears as demonic savage par excellence. The interest seems more in violence than in the Indian. Or the motivation to include the Indian might be generic, the epic shape of "Acadia." The poem presents a vision of the founding of a nation, and the Indian must fit. Thus before the arrival of the whites, the noble Indian provides an extended history for the greatness of Nova Scotia. After the whites take over, Indian treachery becomes a justification to direct the readers' empathy to the invaders rather than to those recently presented as an indigenous aristocracy. Similarly, in contemporary confessional lyrics, the sexuality of the Indian becomes a means of exploring personal and societal guilt, as in Al Pittman's "Shanadithit."

A mixture of values is present in that part of Hearne's narrative known as "The Coppermine Massacre." With himself, or his first-person persona, as physical focus, Hearne's apparently factual account presents the sexual and the violent indigenes in the same passage but with a clear split in gender and also in race. The delicate native maiden (the usual sexual focus in literature of the eighteenth, nineteenth, and much of the twentieth century) who comes toward him is the Inuit woman. This image of sexual attraction meets the repulsive violence of the demonic male, the Indians. Until well into the twentieth century the male native was almost always violence, never sex. A major change occurs, however, in novels such as Margaret Laurence's *Diviners* and Susan Musgrave's *Charcoal Burners*, in which a native male embodies a sexual attraction that the white female uses to liberate herself.

A third important commodity is orality, the associations raised by the indigene's speaking, nonwriting, state. The writers' sense of native peoples as having completely different systems of understanding, different epistemes, is based on an often undefined belief that cultures without writing operate within a different dimension of consciousness. In earlier works, white writers often deemed this a symptom of inferiority or, as in Ralph Connor's *Patrol of the Sundance Trail*, a sign of the demonic orator. Both the good and the bad sides of orality are usually presented as aspects of the natural. In Duncan Campbell Scott's poem "The Height of Land," for example, a "long Ojibwa cadence" rises from the land (55).

The philosophical base of the positive representations of natural orality found throughout twentieth-century literature is found in Walter Ong's *Orality and Literacy*:

> The fact that oral peoples commonly and in all likelihood universally consider words to have magical potency is clearly tied in, at least unconsciously, with their sense of the word as necessarily spoken, sounded, and hence power-driven. (32)

The orality of the native is seen to provide a connection to the inner world of humanity, unlike the alienating distance of the literary. In a self-reflexive denigration typical of much contemporary literature, texts such as *Spirit Wrestler*, James Houston's portrait of the Inuit, express ambivalence about the validity of writing through an elevation of the indigene's orality, represented as Said's "delivered presence."

The Indian narrator is often an important element of orality, especially in recent fiction. The representation of the text as the product of an Indian voice creates a "presence" by appearing to change the Indian from object to subject. W. P. Kinsella's Indian stories, such as those in *Dance Me Outside*, are all "told" by Silas Ermineskin. As in many other representations of minority cultures, humor arises from misperceptions of the majority culture: Silas interprets a white expression for pregnancy, "one in the oven," as a "kid in the stove" (84). Houston's historical novel *Eagle Song* uses a more sophisticated narration: "Hunters must be, oh, so careful later not to let women hear what happens on the whaling grounds, so, listener, remember, tell women nothing of these words you hear from me" (137). The narrator establishes an oral context with a clear ethnographic definition.

Representations of native language extend orality in a different direction. Perhaps the most superficial instance of this occurs in naming. At one level the conflict might be between true and false, between an Indian name that symbolizes Indian culture and an imposed white name that produces a false identity. A more significant element is asserted in A. M. Klein's poem "Indian Reservation," which states that references to nature put "fur on their names to make all live things kin" (295). It is as if a different semiotic field appears, not the field in which the writer places the indigene, but the field in which the indigene places the white and, presumably, himself or herself. There is thus a continuum, from early texts that use a few native words heavily glossed, to *Eagle Song*, in which Nootka terms are defined only by context. A simple record of indigene language might be considered more limited in its representation of the indigenous consciousness than a text in which the indigene is narrator, but its apparent absolute adherence to the indigenous semiosis could suggest that an even greater bridge has been touched if not crossed. Unlike the indigenous narrator, the white reader—and perhaps author—can barely penetrate the meaning. The narrator of Rudy Wiebe's *My Lovely Enemy* laments his inability to gloss this text:

> I don't speak Cree, I should do this properly but I don't, in the oral tradition remembering the past date by date is no Indian tradition, how can a white man find any fact beyond the story memory of a language he doesn't talk unless he tries to trace say one name of one person through all the white documents he can find, letters, diaries, notes, travel books, white gossip in the unlikeliest places you can dig from the nineteenth century? (43–44)

Yet the attempt at penetration seems essential. There is a realization that the indigenous language must be incorporated in order to connect with the power that the indigene represents.

The inclusion of Indian "speech" seems to constitute a prime example of Mikhail Bakhtin's "Discourse in the Novel":

> These distinctive links and interrelationships between utterances and languages, this movement of the theme through different languages and speech types, its dispersion into the rivulets and droplets of social heteroglossia, its dialogization—this is the basic distinguishing feature of the stylistics of the novel. (*Dialogic* 263)

Bakhtin sees dialogization as creating an important tension in fiction: "Every utterance participates in the 'unitary language' (in its centripetal forces and tendencies) and at the same time partakes of social and historical heteroglossia (the centrifugal, stratifying forces)" (272).

This suggests a positive view of the process, in which the "self" of the white text includes the Indian "Other" within its vision while at the same time representing the "social and historical" vision of the Other. Bakhtin goes so far as to call it *"another's speech in another's language"* (324). In opposition I would suggest that the image of the Indian is an example of the negative confluence of the centripetal and centrifugal Other. It is centripetal because always subject to the system of white texts. The Indian voice found in Canadian fiction "lives" only in that fiction. It is centrifugal because that Indian always reaches out to a semiotic field that has defined the image before its inclusion in the fluctuations of the individual text. The novel of the 1980s re-presents the extant image. The process is "stratifying" in a particularly pernicious sense.

There are many variants to the power of the oral Indian, such as taciturnity as the obverse of the orator's inflated diction. W. D. Lighthall provides a delightful combination of the two in *The Master of Life*: "Thou sayest 'Ugh!'" (127). The potential of this cliché is explored more extensively in *Wacousta*, which employs "the low and guttural 'ugh!'" "an assentient and expressive 'ugh!'" and an "almost inaudible 'ugh!'" within the space of three pages. These are said to indicate "astonishment," "approbation," and "eagerness," respectively (113–15). Many contemporary texts emphasize the power of silence. Mel Dagg writes in "Sunday Evening on Axe Flats": "She wraps herself in layers of silence, travelling outside herself, waiting" (*Same Truck* 44). In Sid Stephen's "She Says Goodbye to Mr. Cormack" silence surpasses even time for the last Beothuck woman:

> her tongue
> is even now becoming stone,
> dense with silence
> and hard with meaning.   (n.p.)

Through the hardening comes the fluidity, the ability to overcome the restraints of linear, logical, white interpretation. Orality becomes the land, becomes presence, and mystically becomes the silent invocation of the consciousness, the vision, of Other.

Orality thus leads to a fourth commodity, mysticism, in which the native becomes a sign of oracular power, either malevolent, in most nineteenth-century texts, or beneficent, in most contemporary ones. Just as many early texts suggest orality to be inferior, so indigenous beliefs constitute so many absurd superstitions. If such beliefs did represent a different dimension of consciousness, it was not worth achieving, and certainly not equal to white doctrine. Egerton Ryerson Young's *Winter Adventures of Three Boys in the Great Lone Land* refers to the Indian's transformation from the "degradation and superstition of a cruel paganism into the blessedness and enjoyment of a genuine Christianity and an abiding civilization" (79).

For other texts, however, particularly in the twentieth century, an alien space is attractive. In Wiebe's *Temptations of Big Bear*, probably still the most resonant fictional representation of the native in Canadian literature, the mystical sensitivity of the hero validates the Christian overtones of the title, in opposition to the white culture and representatives of the Christian church. In Fred Bodsworth's *Sparrow's Fall*, the Christian hymn of the title, with its claim that God protects each creature of nature, interferes with the natural order of the north, in which the Indian, Jacob, must kill to survive. But when Jacob finds himself far from home, his belief system works as he leaves a propitiatory caribou skull: "In this strange land there would be other spirits he didn't know, and they would be pleased at this respect for them that Jacob was showing" (151). In an interesting semiotic variant, the inadequacies of the author's culture, which offers little "true" knowledge through its own popular beliefs (in which the distancing Quaker Oats box leaves divine power beyond reach), is met by an indigenous belief system (usually quite asystemic) that offers a Presence to exceed even the presence of orality.

Spivak has commented on the "soul-making" agenda of imperialist missionaries (Address). They intended to take indigenous peoples who teetered between the absolute material and the false antiphenomenal and make new creations who would possess the reality of the Christian noumenal. But in many of the texts in this study, what the white needs is not to instill spirit in the Other but to gain it from the Other. Through the indigene the white character gains soul and the potential of becoming rooted in the land. An appropriate pun is that only by going native can the European arrivant become native. Often in such narratives the Otherness of the indigene is first heightened, as in the use of an indigenous semiotic field. A similar process is the defamiliarization of common aspects of white culture. When Indians are presented as having an intricately metaphorical "iron horse" view of a train, for instance, it makes the Indians doubly Other. They are Other because the white perceives them as such and also because their own perception is so clearly that of Other.

Often, however, as in the Beothuck poems of Sid Stephen and Al Pittman, or in Margaret Atwood's novel *Surfacing*, the Other is not living Indians but art or even just memories of tribes long obliterated—Indian presence but no present Indians. This temporal split is a fifth commodity in the semiotic field of the indigene, the prehistoric. Historicity, in which the text makes an overt or covert statement on the chronology of the culture, shapes the indigene into a historical artifact, a remnant of a golden age that seems to have little connection to contemporary life. Golden age assumptions underly the choice of genre in the various nineteenth-century heroic tragedies with native heroes, such as Charles Mair's *Tecumseh* (published in 1886). Robert Kroetsch's novel *Badlands* makes a specific comment on the prehistoric when the archaeologists find the Indian girl among the dinosaur bones: "her cabin of bones, her fossil tipi" (144).

Johannes Fabian's *Time and the Other* states of anthropology: "It promoted a scheme in terms of which not only past cultures, but all living societies were irrevocably placed on a temporal slope, a stream of time —some upstream, others downstream" (17). When native peoples, perceived to be of the "early," remain in Canadian society, which is of the "late," degradation is shown to be inevitable. A corollary of the temporal split between the golden age and contemporary decadence is a tendency to see native culture as either true, pure, and static or else not really of that culture. Wayland Drew's *Wabeno Feast* eulogizes the past Indian but begins and ends with a contemporary Indian drunk. The only other Indian in "time present" is a prostitute.

Through the commodities the white acquires Indian—"acquires," not "becomes." To "become Indian" is an absurdity or even madness, as Kroetsch's *Gone Indian* suggests. "Go native" is necessary, "gone native" is not. Some psychologists might diagnose even acquisition as a rejection of self for not-self. The typical narrative pattern must modify such a theory, however. The indigene is acquired; the white is not abandoned. Usually the connection is made through some form of sexual contact—in earlier works, a white male with a native female; in recent works, often the reverse. But in the majority of works of both types, the contact is followed by the death of the indigene. In *The Diviners*, Jules, a Métis sex object, acts as a "shaman," but removes himself after he has mystically transformed Morag, and then dies. He leaves part of himself in the form of their daughter, Pique, who might be seen as the fruition of native-white contact but could also be viewed as one more step in a deracinating chain. As much less of an Indian, although often lamenting that fact, she is another aspect of historicity. Her father is the dying Indian, a central figure in the semiosis associated with the golden age.

A variety of factors are involved in incorporating the native for the page, but still more are added when the genre requires that the native be corporeally present, in the theater. There must be presence in the theater, although the presence is that of the actors and not of the author. If the pawn is played by a white actor in disguise, signifying processes are at work, similar to those in the novel. If a native actor is used, the cross-cultural leap in which the white author creates the lines and the context for the indigene's speech might seem a beneficial erasing of boundaries, but it might also be considered a means of hiding some necessary distinctions. In the original 1967 production of George Ryga's *Ecstasy of Rita Joe*, the late Canadian actor Dan George, best known for his appearance in the film *Little Big Man*, began his rise to fame. His presence validated a noble savage stereotype of an order seldom seen in contemporary white culture. A novel can only attempt the Bakhtinian illusion of representing "another's voice." The dramatic text makes it possible for another's voice to speak the Other as described by the white self. Dan George's role as signifier of "reality" just made the limits of the image more acceptable. As long as the semiotic field exists, as long as the shapes of the standard commodities change but the commodities remain the same, the chess match can vary but there is still a definable limit to the board. The necessities of indigenization can compel white players to participate in the game, but they cannot liberate the pawn.

The chessboard analogy might in the end seem a diminution of the issue. It emphasizes the distance between the sign, the image of the native in Canadian literature, and the referent, the native peoples of Canada, but it perhaps deemphasizes the contradictions of the chessboard of Canadian political reality. If, as Derrida claims, there is nothing outside the text, then the image of the native is the clearest textualization of the erasure of native sovereignty in Canada. At a time when native self-government is a major issue in Canadian politics, a recognition of the manipulations of white indigenization in literature might be a stimulus to the reinstatement of the indigenous.

NOTE

[1]This paper provides a sketch of a theoretical approach used in my book *Fear and Temptation* and thus examples are kept to a minimum. The comments refer specifically to Canadian literature in English, but the majority of the assertions are applicable to a number of analogous literatures, most obviously Canadian in French and United States but also Australian and New Zealand and various South American literatures. To look beyond the "Indian" context, South African literature also fits, with J. M. Coetzee's *Waiting for the Barbarians* a perfect example of the valorization of the semiotic field of the indigene. For a general comparison, the ideological framework of Robert F. Berkhofer's *White Man's Indian* is different from the present study, but the conclusions are similar.

WORKS CITED

Atwood, Margaret. *Surfacing.* Toronto: McClelland, 1972.

Bakhtin, Mikhail. *The Dialogic Imagination: Four Essays.* Trans. Caryl Emerson and Michael Holquist. Ed. Holquist. Austin: U of Texas P, 1981.

Berger, John. *Ways of Seeing.* London: BBC, 1972.

Berkhofer, Robert F. *The White Man's Indian: Images of the American Indian from Columbus to the Present.* New York: Vintage, 1979.

Bodsworth, Fred. *The Sparrow's Fall.* Toronto: Doubleday, 1967.

Coetzee, J. M. *Waiting for the Barbarians.* Markham, ON: Penguin, 1982.

Connor, Ralph [Charles W. Gordon]. *The Patrol of the Sundance Trail.* Toronto: Westminster, 1914.

Crawford, Isabella Valancy. *The Collected Poems.* 1905. Toronto: U of Toronto P, 1972.

Dagg, Mel. *Same Truck Different Driver.* Calgary: Westlands, 1982.

Derrida, Jacques. *Of Grammatology.* Trans. Gayatri Chakravorty Spivak. Baltimore: Johns Hopkins UP, 1976.

Drew, Wayland. *The Wabeno Feast.* Toronto: Anansi, 1973.

Fabian, Johannes. *Time and the Other: How Anthropology Makes Its Object.* New York: Columbia UP, 1983.

Fanon, Frantz. *Black Skin White Masks.* Trans. Charles Lam Markmann. St. Albans, Eng.: Paladin, 1970.

Foucault, Michel. *Power/Knowledge: Selected Interviews and Other Writings 1972– 1977.* Trans. Colin Gordon et al. Ed. Gordon. New York: Pantheon, 1980.

Gilman, Sander. *Difference and Pathology: Stereotypes of Sexuality, Race and Madness.* Ithaca: Cornell UP, 1985.

Goldie, Terry. *Fear and Temptation: The Image of the Indigene in Canadian, Australian and New Zealand Literatures.* Montréal: McGill-Queen's UP, 1989.

Healy, J. J. *Literature and the Aborigine in Australia 1770–1975.* St. Lucia: U of Queensland P, 1978.

Hearne, Samuel. *A Journey from Prince of Wales's Fort in Hudson's Bay to the Northern Ocean Undertaken by Order of the Hudson's Bay Company for the Discovery of Copper Mines, a North West Passage &c. in the Years 1769, 1770, 1771, & 1772.* 1795. Edmonton: Hurtig, 1971.

Houston, James. *Eagle Song: An Indian Saga Based on True Events.* New York: Harcourt, 1983.

———. *Spirit Wrestler.* Toronto: McClelland, 1980.

Howe, Joseph. *Poems and Essays.* 1874. Toronto: U of Toronto P, 1973.

JanMohamed, Abdul R. "The Economy of Manichean Allegory: The Function of Racial Difference in Colonialist Literature." *Critical Inquiry* 12.1 (1985): 59–87.

Kinsella, W. P. *Dance Me Outside.* Ottawa: Oberon, 1977.

Klein, A. M. *Collected Poems.* Ed. Miriam Waddington. Toronto: McGraw Ryerson, 1974.

Kreiner, Philip. *People like Us in a Place like This.* Ottawa: Oberon, 1983.

Kroetsch, Robert. *Badlands.* Don Mills, ON: New, 1975.

———. *Gone Indian.* Toronto: New, 1973.

Laurence, Margaret. *The Diviners.* Toronto: McClelland, 1974.

Lighthall, W. D. *The Master of Life: A Romance of the Five Nations and of Prehistoric Montreal.* Toronto: Musson, 1908.

Macherey, Pierre. *A Theory of Literary Production.* Trans. Geoffrey Wall. London: Routledge, 1978.

Mair, Charles. *Dreamland and Other Poems; Tecumseh: A Drama.* 1901. Toronto: U of Toronto P, 1974.

Mitchell, W. O. *Since Daisy Creek.* Toronto: Macmillan, 1984.

Musgrave, Susan. *The Charcoal Burners.* Toronto: McClelland, 1980.

Ong, Walter. *Orality and Literacy: The Technologizing of the Word.* London: Methuen, 1982.

Pittman, Al. *Through One More Window.* Portugal Cove: Breakwater Books, 1974.

Pratt, Mary Louise. "Scratches on the Face of the Country; or, What Mr. Barrow Saw in the Land of the Bushmen." *Critical Inquiry* 12.1 (1985): 119–43.

Richardson, John. *Wacousta.* 1832. Toronto: McClelland, 1967.

Ryga, George. *The Ecstasy of Rita Joe.* Vancouver: Talonplays, 1970.

Said, Edward. *Orientalism.* London: Routledge, 1978.

Scott, Duncan Campbell. *Selected Poems.* Toronto: Ryerson, 1951.

Spivak, Gayatri Chakravorty. Address. University of Queensland, Brisbane, Australia, 1 Aug. 1984.

———. "Three Women's Texts and a Critique of Imperialism." *Critical Inquiry* 12.1 (1985): 243–61.

Stephen, Sid. *Beothuck Poems.* Ottawa: Oberon, 1976.

Wiebe, Rudy. *My Lovely Enemy.* Toronto: McClelland, 1983.

———. *The Temptations of Big Bear.* Toronto: McClelland, 1973.

Wolf, Eric R. *Europe and the People without History.* Berkeley: U of California P, 1982.

Young, Egerton Ryerson. *Winter Adventures of Three Boys in the Great Lone Land.* New York: Eaton, 1899.

Barry Cameron

ENGLISH CRITICAL DISCOURSE IN/ON CANADA

> Insofar as literary history is storymaking—and I think it
> is very radically storymaking—what we do is tell a
> story that makes us heroes; we tell a story that gives
> us a point of origin.
>
> Robert Kroetsch

THERE IS MUCH of interest in the history of Canadian criticism that precedes
our contemporary moment, but the full institutionalization of Canadian
literature as a recognizable and relatively autonomous discourse did not
take place until the mid- to late 1960s, when it became thoroughly inscribed
in both the agenda of Canadian publishers and the curriculum of Canadian
university departments of literature.[1] In this essay, while recognizing the
impossibility of comprehensiveness, the inevitable failure of all efforts at
totalization, I concentrate on the process of institutionalization in which
the production of critical texts has richly matched the profusion of literary
texts.

My site of exploration, to appropriate terms from Raymond Williams's
well-known discussion of cultural formations, is somewhere on the border
of corporate or dominant critical discourse—the main body of Canadian
criticism, situated generally in an expressive-realist concept of language
—and an emergent post-Saussurean critical discourse, located in a productive, differential theory of language.[2] Residual criticism in Canada, to
complete Williams's paradigm, might be characterized by the descriptive-
historical mode represented, in the mid-1980s, by David Stouck's *Major
Canadian Authors.*

One of the ways we might try to distinguish between traditions in Canadian critical discourse is to invoke the empowering generic distinction made by the formalist-structuralist tradition of critical discourse: the difference between "poetics" and "criticism." Allowing us to grasp simultaneously the discreteness and variety of literary texts, poetics in a strict sense is concerned not with a given set of texts but with "literary discourse itself as the generative principle of an infinite number of texts."[3] In modified versions, however, poetics does in fact interest itself in the resemblances between given texts, seeking to disengage their common characteristics (in systems in which these texts participate, in patterns that they might manifest, and in the ways in which the system allows meaning to be generated). It is nevertheless important to remember that poetics is a "theoretical discipline nourished and fertilized by empirical research but not constituted by it" (Ducrot and Todorov 79), for in significant contrast to this tenet Canadian poetics tends to constitute itself solely through empiricism. Criticism in this dialectic, as distinct from poetics, is concerned primarily with what is supposedly unique and particular to a given text, describing a particular work and designating its meaning. From this heuristic point of view, then, Canadian criticism since the late 1960s may be characterized as one governed by a (modified) poetics concerned with establishing a general grammar of Canadian literature as a whole and discovering certain kinds of patterns in Canadian literary texts.

The best known, as well as influential and controversial, of these poetics are D. G. Jones's *Butterfly on Rock*, Margaret Atwood's *Survival*, Laurence Ricou's *Vertical Man/Horizontal World*, and John Moss's *Patterns of Isolation in English Canadian Fiction* and *Sex and Violence in the Canadian Novel*. Treating Canadian literature or a segment thereof as a system whose rules and patterns must be elucidated, all of these studies provide taxonomies based on either theme or image analysis. They cut across a variety of texts, frequently effacing the material dynamics that inhere in a single text in favor of only one kind of intertextual trace. Unlike structuralist taxonomies, however—which rest on the *forms* of literary content and are based on a homology of differences—these Canadian poetics, for the most part, privilege the *substance* of literary content, although Atwood does set up a typology of forms of victimhood as a centering device for her treatment of thematic substance. This sort of systemic ordering also differs from structuralist poetics by grounding itself in empiricism or subjective, existential phenomenology. The former presupposes the classic subject-object structure of knowledge, viewing texts positivistically as verifiable data; the latter emphasizes intentionality and consciousness, positing, like empiricism, texts as apodictically perceived.

Whether they treat plot and character typologies or catalog images, all these studies rest on suppositions—sometimes unacknowledged—about "Canada." They view the literary text less as part of a larger, specifically literary system—say, the genre of the work or even the literary production of a given period—than as part of the production of an entire culture with an assumed unity; they view this literary system, in turn, implicitly as a subsystem of a more general system of cultural productions/discourses. Literary history, in these terms, becomes in a sense "Canadian studies," and through an analysis of "Canadian" symbols, images, and myths, literature is thus able for these critics to function potentially as a means of national identification and a possible force for national unity. Such studies thus manifest, as Eli Mandel has suggested ("Strange Loops" 37), a cultural Freudianism in that they attempt to tell Canadians "who they are" in their analogies between literature and personality, nation and person. But, in their espousal at times of an environmental determinism that assumes that literature arises causally out of or reflects geographical place—the sense that the land itself determines the nature of the representations of lived experience on that land—they also try to tell Canadians, as Ricou does, "where they are."[4]

Jones and Atwood have been especially influential because they attempt to fulfill a demand, insistent since 1967 (the year of Expo) for a literary tradition, which more often than not is really a desire "for an origin that will authorize a beginning" (Bhabha 96).[5] They have also been considered important because they implicitly attempt to repudiate the sort of colonial criticism (such as Northrop Frye's in his "Conclusion" to the first edition of the *Literary History of Canada* [1965] and in his "Preface to an Uncollected Anthology," reprinted in *The Bush Garden*) that would see the Canadian writer as an unfinished European or American writer or the sort of cultural imperialism—first British, then American—that would seek to create a Canadian elite to cherish the literary bourgeois values of the ruling classes of the imperialist country.[6] Despite significant ideological differences, this desire to discover indigenous traditions and thereby repudiate Canada's colonial status is one that Jones and Atwood share with the critical practice of Robin Mathews. How, in other words, does a colonial literature achieve independence except by discovering, "inventing," constructing a tradition, whether grounded in specific historical experience or otherwise? The tradition, not the language as such, so the argument goes, distinguishes the literature. (Witness, for example, the distinctive American tradition of literature written in a language shared by the British.) But how problematic, too, is the effort to construct a literary tradition in Canada, a country both linguistically and geographically fragmented that consequently has great difficulty identifying itself either differentially or positively. From a linguistic-literary point of view, nation is identical with the area in which the language is used. But what happens if the area contains more than one language and those languages are at once one's own and those of other, quite different and powerful cultures? What does "place" and "who" become in these circumstances?

Because Canada has been formed more strategically than culturally, it lacks a genuine sense of authoritarian culture: a sense of *"belonging to* or *in a* place," in Edward Said's terms, "being *at home in a place*" (8). Culture is, Said argues, an environment, a process, and "the assertively achieved and *won* hegemony of an identifiable set of ideas" (10). In Canada no such set of ideas has won over all the other competing ideas—at least not yet. Canada has territorial integrity, true, but it lacks a common language that would symbolize social identity and solidify it as a culturally based nation-state.[7] Canada is thus, it could be argued, without one of the most important preconditions of even political identity. As a result, it probably will never have the absolute moment of the nation-state in which the hegemony of a national class reflects itself in the linguistic coherence essential to the nation's integrative, centralizing state apparatuses (see Eagleton 55). To invoke cultural Freudianism again, it could in fact be said that Canada is a country suffering from desire—as the French psychoanalyst Jacques Lacan has discussed it, the experience of lack: unfixed, unsatisfied, without autonomy and unity, perpetually in contradiction. Canadians may have a common destiny, even a common history, but do they "naturally" belong together and share common interests? Yet it could also be argued that because Canada is still being constructed culturally, it is advantageously in process and thereby perpetually open to change in an optimistic sense.

In any case, these studies recognize Canada's lack of consciousness about national identity, a consciousness that would render intelligible and justify Canadians' living together, and they attempt to raise that consciousness. They are in effect concerned with discovering, inventing, an identity —a self and a country. Hence the powerful concern these studies and much other Canadian criticism in the same tradition manifest with authenticity, voice, place, social realism, and the emphasis on content-based typologies and so-called indigenous themes.

Frye, of course, has been both a direct example and an inspiration (some would say insidiously so) for the general thematic and cultural thrust of Canadian criticism that tries to answer "Who am I?" and "Where is here?" (*Bush Garden* 220), and certainly his anatomizing and taxonomical habits have provided at least an indirect model for poeticians like Jones, Atwood, and Moss. There is little evidence of the direct influence of Frye's seminal *Anatomy of Criticism* (1957), however. But the essays in *Divisions on a Ground*, which includes Frye's "Conclusion" to the 1976 *Literary History of Canada*, and especially in *The Bush Garden* have been central if con-

troversial documents, particularly in their advocacy of environmental determinism: the land as a hostile or indifferent wilderness or the north as
symbol, concepts Frye calls "the riddle of unconsciousness" (*Bush Garden*
243), an encounter with which produces "a garrison mentality" (225) that
takes several different shapes in Canadian literature. Environmental determinism of course is really a social construction of the landscape, a
semiotic coding of nature in terms of culture, though hardly anyone in
Canadian criticism, including Frye, speaks of this mediating structuration.
Instead, landscape is treated as a given.

Several other studies, although less concerned with poetics in the sense
in which I have used it, are also written in the thematic-environmental
tradition that begins effectively with Frye. Among them is W. H. New's
collection of essays *Articulating West*. Although New exhibits considerable
concern for nonthematic properties in a wide range of Canadian texts, he
himself—in the introductory essay in *Articulating West* and in the chapter
"Canadian Home Ground" in *Among Worlds*—situates his work in this
thematic-environmental tradition by positing landscape as the generative
principle of language and literature in Canada, a metaphor not unlike the
poetician's basic critical gesture and its less ambitious form in Ronald
Sutherland's *Second Image* and *New Hero* and Clément Moisan's *Poetry of
Frontiers*. New uses "West" in the figurative sense of exploration, openness,
discovery: "To speak the language of 'West' is not to be merely regional
in bias, . . . but to articulate the tension between order and disorder, myth
and reality, that underlies Canadian writing" (*Articulating West* xi). But,
unlike so many others, New recognizes a mediating structuration or semiotics in this process: "What these writers are also doing is creating a
rhetoric of landscape" (xii), " 'sentencing' their landscape" (xiv). The binary
opposition that New establishes here is picked up and developed, as we
shall see, in significant ways by Mandel, Harrison, and Kroetsch.

The reaction to this tradition of what has generally been labeled thematic
or nationalist criticism—which should in some cases be more properly
described, as I have suggested, as a type of poetics grounded in cultural
criteria—has been intense and widespread, beginning substantially with
Frank Davey's major attack on thematologists in his 1974 paper "Surviving
the Paraphrase" (published in *Canadian Literature* in 1976 and subsequently in his collection of essays of the same name), delivered at the
inaugural meeting of the Association of Canadian and Quebec Literatures
at York University. Reacting to the legitimacy of cultural poetics as critical
practice and valuing "literariness" above other criteria, Davey deplores the
dominant emphasis on theme in Canadian criticism to the mid-1970s at
the expense of language, form, and individual works. Such cultural-nationalist
critical practice, he argues, stems from a desire to avoid evaluation, a
stance derived from Frye, and to forestall treating Canadian literature as

serious literature. Extra- or antiliterary and reductionist in nature, such critical practice is no more than a paraphrase of the literature and culture in terms of themes that turn out to be not national but international. Such practice privileges metalingual representation in terms of content invariants over texture, the stylistic particularities of a work. Davey thus proposes a series of alternative critical practices: literary histories of technique, linguistic and genre studies, phenomenological criticism, and regionalist orientations.

Shortly after the publication of Davey's paper, there appeared, as Russell Brown has noted, what seemed like "a direct response to his call for new critical methods" (154): a special issue of *Studies in Canadian Literature* entitled significantly *Minus Canadian: Penultimate Essays on Literature*, edited by Barry Cameron and Michael Dixon. Cameron and Dixon had actually been working independently of Davey since 1973 on a collection they hoped would represent "a concerted effort to expand the scope of Canadian criticism" (137–38), but the overall effect of the special issue, which includes, incidentally, an essay by Davey himself, was, as Brown points out, a reinforcing extension of the thrust of Davey's essay—as their polemical introduction, "Mandatory Subversive Manifesto," makes clear.

Reacting to what might be called the vulgar sociology of Frye, Jones, Atwood, and Moss, which stereotypes Canadian consciousness, Cameron and Dixon argue that the ultimate goal of Canadian criticism should be "the consistent practice of a critical craft that is equivalent and responsive, in range and discipline, to the literature it treats" (138), and consequently —given the "thematic variety, formal abundance, and technical inventiveness" of Canadian literature (137)—that that literature deserves treatment as part of the relatively autonomous world of literary discourse. Stressing the importance of formal comparative contexts as an evaluative strategy, they assert that the choice of criteria and approach should be appropriate to the work under analysis. Although they emphasize formal values and mistakenly assume, like Davey, that form is ideologically innocent because they want to know what *Canadian* means as a literary term, their stance does not preclude either thematic or structuralist critical practice as such.

Brown's major review article, "Critic, Culture, Text," takes the movement toward a less content-based critical practice one step further in its specific advocacy of the potential available in structuralist criticism in which theme can be treated as cultural coding, a structural feature of the text, and genre as a horizon of expectations. However, Brown undermines an otherwise intelligent assessment of the role of Davey, Moss, Cameron and Dixon, Mandel, and Warren Tallman by placing Dennis Lee's *Savage Fields* within a structuralist discourse when the book should properly be situated within a tradition of phenomenology informed by Heidegger and Merleau-Ponty.

What seems to have disturbed most critics of the poeticians or thematolgists, then, is that the traits they isolate emphasize theme and image in a peculiarly nationalist ideological configuration at the expense of discursive and generic conventions, what the formalists call "literariness" or "poeticity." Resistance stems, too, from a repudiation of poetics itself: the credibility of the model or generative principle and the indeterminacy of the taxonomies provided. What is the relationship of the taxonomies to literary discourse? What is their relationship to reading practices? Are the categories ones on which the experience of literature is based, or are they merely arbitrary divisions invoked for purposes of rhetorical classification? These are the kinds of questions raised by such systemic critical practice in Canadian criticism, as they frequently are with respect to any systemic cultural practice.

There are other implications in the debate about thematic criticism that index significant trends in Canadian criticism, including not only the premature foreclosure of so much thematic criticism—what Jonathan Culler would call "the unseemly rush from work to world" (*Structuralist Poetics* 130)—but also assumptions about the nature of language, literature, and the writer's and reader's relationship to the text that characterize what I have called "corporate" Canadian criticism. Several corporate critics, thematologists or otherwise, delight in realist fiction that manifestly denies its own material and historical construction. Such criticism, which Belsey has characterized as "expressive-realist," sees the literary text not as a construct produced from available signifying systems of language but as a "natural" reflection of the world (historical and geographical) it supposedly delineates, and it takes that world as inherently more real than its representations. There is no questioning of a taken-for-granted conception of reality here and certainly no self-reflexivity in the critical act itself.

Those who hold such a representationist theory of language and literature, thematologist or not—that is, a predominantly mimetic view of the relation between the text and an assumed preconstituted reality—tend to base their critical practice in the classic subject-object structure of knowledge, in the divorce between language and experience, central to empiricist epistemology. Hermeneutic in thrust and perhaps a result of the hegemony of thematic poetics, such criticism posits knowledge as (mis)recognition of given objects—some supposed prediscursive history or geography—not knowledge as the production of meaning. The referent, itself a construct, is exalted over the sign, both the signifier and the signified; knowledge of the object becomes part of the object itself. Mimetic adequacy, in other words, provides the normative knowledge of the text in which the "image" is measured against the "essential" or "original" in order to establish its degree of representativeness and hence its authenticity or correctness. In emphatic nationalist-thematic versions of mimetic criticism, the exaltation of character is a frequent ideological strategy: character as a sign of the Canadian sociolect, a Canadian stereotype, an ideal image in relation to which the text is judged but that some antithematologists, given the decentered condition of Canada, would see as a normative fallacy. Such a reflexive or expressive principle of language and literature characterizes corporate Canadian criticism as a form of recognition, neither a discourse nor a practice, and it tends to privilege criticism itself as a mode of knowledge over other forms of discourse. It thus structures the critic as an arbiter of taste and the reader as a consumer by suppressing the active process of making or producing available to the reader in favor of the more passive activity of simply responding to the text.[8]

Emergent critical practice, which I have characterized as post-Saussurean, is represented most notably by such critics as Shirley Neuman, Linda Hutcheon, Heather Murray, Terry Goldie, E. D. Blodgett, Barbara Godard, and Barry Cameron, a number of whom are represented in *Future Indicative* (ed. Moss), a collection of papers given at a University of Ottawa Conference on Theory. The volume brings together a significant and representative sampling of the range of post-Saussurean critical practice in Canadian criticism, although it is by no means inclusive. The post-Saussureans would object to the assumption of the expressive-realists that language is a transparent medium of communication and that literature provides simply a window on the world. This naturalization of the sign suppresses the fact that the "real" can be constructed (created and organized) only in language, in a particular social formation, and at a particular time. Post-Saussurean linguistic theory, a theory of language as a system of differences, in fact severely problematizes if not shuts out questions about how accurately language represents the world. To ask whether something is authentic or true and how we know whether it is so may be irrelevant. Language precedes geography and experience, historical or otherwise, in the sense that they are not cognitively available to us until we construct them in language. They are available to us only in the guise of signifiers. Consequently, "to find a guarantee of meaning in the world or in experience is to ignore the fact that our experience of the world is itself articulated in language" (Belsey 54). In a realist problematic, place in the geographical sense is substituted for culture, and this—some would call it the referential fallacy—leads to an environmental determinism in the thematologists. Environment itself, however, the post-Saussureans would say, is a construct produced by language.

It would seem fair to say, then, that the emergence of post-Saussurean critical practice in Canada—whose structuralist and poststructuralist phases, as Goddard and Kroetsch have pointed out, arrived at the same time, with the result that the first did not have time to be absorbed before being displaced by the second—indicates a gradual movement away from an object-oriented criticism, away from interpretive or hermeneutic criticism exclusively, toward a recognition of criticism's own status as text. Such a self-reflexive concern about methodology and theory has hitherto been treated as a trivializing activity. Until the emergence of post-Saussurean criticism, however, existential or subjective phenomenology, which should be distinguished from dialectical phenomenology, was the dominant alternative to empiricist criticism in Canadian literature. Among its most notable practitioners in varying degrees of emphasis, although not always self-consciously so, are Davey, George Bowering, Robert Lecker, Mandel, and Tallman.

In his major studies of Earle Birney, Raymond Souster and Louis Dudek, and Margaret Atwood, as well as in *Surviving the Paraphrase* and his series of essays on writers since 1960 who mark the transition from modernism to postmodernism, *From There to Here*, Davey exhibits a New Critical concern with technique and form that sees literature essentialistically as privileged discourse and the text as apodictically present. That concern, however, is situated in an existential phenomenology mediated by United States (post)modernist poetics and especially by Charles Olson's consciousness-exalting proprioceptive self, of which Tallman speaks so often in his collection of essays, *Godawful Streets of Man*. Heidegger and Merleau-Ponty are layered in Davey's critical writing, as we might expect, since they address matters important to other phenomenologically oriented critics: human existence as a space of openness to the world as well as a disclosure of the world, the self-motivation and self-mirroring of language, the disclosure of presence ("letting something be seen") through language (unconcealment), and pre-Socratic letting-be or Heraclitian authenticity.

Davey and Tallman are attracted to a common range of binary oppositions in which they give precedence to one term, the first, over the other: process and stasis, the open and the closed, fragmentation and wholeness, discontinuity and coherence, temporality and spatiality, speech and silence, region and center, West and East (in New's terms), international and national, individual and corporate being, postmodernism and humanism, postmodernism and modernism, self as subject (life as process, a temporality of action and decision) and self as object, and proprioception and perception. Similar binary oppositions emerge in Mandel's *Criticism*, in which he argues for the desirability of a phenomenological savage criticism, at once subjective and unsystematic, that would experience the unmediated raw reality of the object-text—"to become one with the work of literature"—by favoring perception and "the meaning of the perceived moment" (71) over abstraction/structure/pattern and by eschewing interpretation, explanation, and evaluation.

Since phenomena are those things that show themselves to conscious-ness, criticism as language for a phenomenologist articulates the object-text as a phenomenon: a letting-be-seen of that which shows itself. There is no in-itself outside a perceiving consciousness: the object-text becomes visible through my perceptive critical act, and if the text appears to mean or to speak in such and such a way, it is for me, in relation to myself, that it appears so. All awareness is from a particular perspective. I am the center in relation to which one text appears as such and another as different.

A phenomenology of reading, then, stresses not only the text but also, and with equal force, the actions involved in responding to the text. In Davey and Bowering, however, the rhetorical strategies generate an ap-parent emphasis on the text, while in Mandel, Tallman, Lecker, and Lee, emphasis more often falls on response—on a recounting, as Culler would say, of the adventures of the critics' own subjectivity, of their developing responses ("reflections," "impressions") to the succession of words on the page (*On Deconstruction* 64–83). That is why such criticism is so epi-deictic—so highly performative and self-reflexively rhetorical—and why the object of criticism as an "intentional object" is really the structure of the critic's experience. The point is obvious in, say, Lecker's discussion of reading Clark Blaise or his dilation on a single story of Hugh Hood's in *On the Line*, Lee's response in *Savage Fields* to Leonard Cohen's *Beautiful Losers*, and Tallman's "impressions" of Mordecai Richler's various texts.

Bowering, Tallman, and Lecker are much less concerned than Davey, Mandel, and Lee with cultural grounding in their discussions of literary texts, though there is a strain of environmental determinism in Tallman's treatment of Canadian writers that could be construed as a concern with culture. Davey reads form analogically in political or ideological terms in *From There to Here*. Such an approach leads him, by way of Marshall McLuhan's influence, to identify regionalism with postmodernism and mi-croelectronic technology, on the one hand, and centrism with modernism and mechanical technology, on the other. In contrast, Lee, with the Ca-nadian philosopher George Grant, sees all technology as a homogenizing international (read "American") colonizing force. Both Grant and Lee te-naciously oppose bourgeois society, the priorities of liberal-democratic industrial capitalism, but in the absence of a genuine revolutionary critique in Canada, it is radical conservatism that fills the void.

A concern with regional consciousness is one of the modes of criticism that Davey proposes as an alternative to thematic criticism in "Surviving the Paraphrase": distinctive attitudes to language and form, specific kinds of images, and "language and imagery that in some ways correlate with the geographic features of the region" (*Surviving* 10). This last point, which

Milton Wilson would call "the geographical fallacy" (198), derives from Tallman's far western environmental determinism. It is a view that Mandel in his preoccupation with western regionalism ultimately rejects in his lifelong struggle to come to terms with Frye, one of the major proponents of environmentalism, alternately accepting and rejecting Frye's positions on nationalism, internationalism, and regionalism. Mandel comes to see that the national context is political and the regional context is cultural —that region, as both Sutherland and New imply, is a function of the nation but that, perhaps, the nation itself is an American region. Region is not a place, a community, or a political entity as such but a cultural boundary, a set of social relations, a language, a version of discontinuity and process in poetry, as it is for Davey, or a version of voice identified stylistically with oral and folkloristic tradition and formally with myth, as it is for Kroetsch. Regional cultures are established not by geography but by literary conventions, and such regionalism is, of course, a power move decentering in its effect, a way to undermine uniformity and centrism by paradoxically aligning itself with literary movements beyond the nation—ultimately continentalist, however, and not really internationalist, some would argue.

It is this alignment that Robin Mathews would resist. So too would Patricia Marchak, as her essay in *In Our Own House* makes clear, because such connections would be centripetal for her, reinforcing American power. It is "only through denying Central Canadian pretensions of unifying literary style" that the regions can "contribute to a culture strong enough to resist American dominance and to establish a culture of national unity" (Marchak 176). Again region is a function of nation.

Lee is also concerned with the problem of Canadian discourse and authenticity in his well-known paper "Cadence, Country, Silence" and in *Savage Fields*, which is in Lee's opinion "only incidentally a work of literary criticism" (11)—only in the narrow sense in which a New Critic might define literary, however, for this is an important Canadian critical text. The book explores in overt phenomenological terms the interaction of earth and world (Heidegger's terms adopted and modified by Lee) in Michael Ondaatje's *Collected Works of Billy the Kid* and Cohen's *Beautiful Losers*. The savage strife between these two overlapping force fields, these two modes of being—the cosmology of "savage fields"—is a model, Lee argues, that makes "the terrible era of modernity intelligible" (11).

As Blodgett points out in "Authenticity and Absence," an essay in a special section of *Descant* devoted to Lee, ontology and the metaphysics of presence, to use Jacques Derrida's locution, dominate the structure of Lee's thought. He wants to believe that language creates reality, that it articulates the world, that it is both what it names and that which calls the named into being. As for Heidegger, Lee wants to believe that to be is to be in language and that to be in language is to be shown to be, language and world having the same ontological features, but his fear is that there is no ontological structure of words. We cannot think earth in earth's terms, for we can speak of earth "only in terms of world's knowledge of it, because to speak at all is to assert our world-nature" (*Savage Fields* 114).

Lee's concern with authenticity is also apparent in "Cadence, Country, Silence." In this work he struggles to come to terms with living in Canada as a poet in a borrowed language by arguing that the impasse of writing in such language—its texture, weight, and connotations from abroad— must become its own subject, for "to be authentic, the voice of being alive here and now must include the inauthenticity of our lives here and now" (49). As in *Savage Fields*, liberalism and empiricism are repudiated, but to speak of our inauthenticity is a way to break out of the silence imposed on us by our dissent from liberalism. Such a step allows us to recognize that our condition under liberalism is only a muted one, not a silent one. Finally, in "Polyphony, Enacting a Meditation"—a later discussion of ca- dence, the press of meaning, of being—Lee argues that the polyphonic voice of meditation is necessary, an argument that may be aligned with a Lacanian understanding of textuality and perhaps a Bahktinian notion of polyglossia.[9]

There is much in subjective or existential phenomenology that struc- turalism and poststructuralism would quibble with, of course. As anyone working in post-Saussurean thought knows thoroughly, if language is a social institution that both precedes and exceeds us as individuals and if meaning is the product of the rules and conventions of different signifying systems—most notably language—there is no functional place for private meanings or intentions in this process. We do not have discretion over what our words will mean, and, so long as we speak a common language, we do not decide on the "meaning" of what we enunciate. Some forms of structuralism, however, beg the issue of consciousness, and positivism or empiricism is no viable alternative because it presupposes, as Lee notes, a separation of subject from object and thinks of the subject not in terms of a membership in a community but as a private subject in terms of purposes and attitudes that originate with the individual rather than with a language community. Dialectical phenomenology attempts to resolve this problem because it "treats consciousness not as originating with the in- dividual and mediating the individual's relation to society, nor as an epi- phenomenon of external social forces" (Bologh xii). Rather, it treats consciousness as an ongoing social and historical process.

As in subjective phenomenology, meaning in dialectical phenomenology is grounded in or internal to the relation of subject and object, critic/reader and text. It is internal neither to the object-text nor to the subject/reader/

critic. But, unlike subjective phenomenology, the object-text takes on meaning—its salience to a knower derives—from a signifying practice, an interpretive/reading strategy within which the knower/critic/reader, his- toricized and socialized, stands. Dialectical phenomenology, eschewing liberalism and psychologism, thus fuses certain features of phenomenology and structuralism, and it is evident in the critical practice of Dick Harrison and Robert Kroetsch.

Harrison's project in *Unnamed Country* locates itself firmly in a cultural formation in its concern with the contradictions that arise when non- indigenous semiotic systems, whether homologically structured or not, are used to read the western prairie. It is Canada's only archetypal region because it was the first area in Canada to be settled by Canadians them- selves: European or eastern Canadian culture—the named, the known, the mythic—confronting the geophysical prairie—the unnamed, the unknown, the historical. Such a confrontation is not unique, but it is a more acute situation on the prairie, ultimately resulting in a condition of alienation from the plains.

For writers as for settlers, the prairie was unnamed and therefore un- known, lacking the fictions, the literary and linguistic traditions, to make it real. As Kroetsch has put it in *Creation*, "In a sense, we haven't got an identity until someone tells our story. The fiction makes us real" (63). If to be, in Heideggerian terms, is to be in language and to be in language is to be shown to be, how can one authentically have being, given this con- tradictory situation, especially if language is "always already" the grounds for any inquiry? This is the question such writers as Rudy Wiebe and Kroetsch, like Dennis Lee, try to answer. They wish, in terms of both literary form and culture, to unname, demythologize, reconstruct the prairie and history more authentically. Wiebe says that "human understanding is tied to language, whose primal expression is *naming*" (4), and he speaks of the absence of indigenous memory, words, and myth that would help us un- derstand the prairie. Echoing Kroetsch's essay "Unhiding the Hidden" (*Es- says*), Wiebe writes of the necessity to reveal the hidden in imposed languages that must be read as palimpsests: beneath the politically motivated signifier, Regina is another signifier, "where the bones lie." Canadians must learn to read beneath the foreign myths carelessly attached to the Canadian West—American and British Ontario—to discover the concealed buried otherness of experience that is their own. And, Kroetsch believes, Cana- dians do this first by unhiding the hidden British or American experience in the Canadian word in order to remythologize it.

Kroetsch is, of course, a major Canadian novelist, but he is also, as Shirley Neuman and Robert Wilson tell us in *Labyrinths of Voice*, a "*magister labyrinthorum*, an author who continually re/reads his own writing in the context of his current thinking" (xi). But even when he is not dealing with his own writing, his criticism is always provocative because it is fully charged with a knowledge of both postmodern literary practice and post-Saussurean critical thought, as his *Essays*, which constitutes one of the two special issues of *Open Letter* devoted to Kroetsch, and *Labyrinths of Voice* testify. Godard has said, "the history of Kroetsch's publications is ... the unfolding history of the 'new new criticism' of Canadian literature" ("Other Fictions" 9). Kroetsch embraces phenomenology, structuralism, and post-structuralism: Heidegger, Barthes, Foucault, Kristeva, Derrida, and Bakhtin are all important theorists in his critical ground.

Davey, in his introduction to *Essays*, stresses Kroetsch's McLuhan-like phenomenological orientation—"Perception not only takes precedent over argument, but often replaces argument" (7). However, that perception, whose meaning can be produced only through language, is situated in a consciousness conceived as an ongoing social and historical process, changing but particular purposive activities. Both text and writer/reader/critic are always on the move, shifting ground, but always within the Canadian problematic. Many of the essays in their discontinuity and fracturing are reminiscent of Barthes's strategy, in *S/Z*, of starring the text. In Kroetsch, however, we get only a few stars, not the galaxy Barthes provides. *Labyrinths of Voice* is also an innovative and highly effective mode of critical discourse involving Neuman and Wilson in conversation with Kroetsch, the presence of three speakers rupturing the conventions of the interview. But woven into this ongoing conversation—itself an instance of Heideggerian phenomenology—is a myriad of stimulating quotations from other (usually) critical discourses that interact with the three voices in a variety of ways. The result is a rich plurality of signification and discursivity as the text traverses four broad *topoi*: influence, game, myth, and narration. Yet the main interest of the book is that Kroetsch the novelist, the "author," is one of the participants in this tapestry.

Much Canadian criticism takes if not "reality" then the author as a point of departure for interpretation, as the numerous critical series that ground their various texts in an author abundantly testify. Most of the special issues of Canadian critical and literary journals have focused on authors as well, and much of the work being done outside of Canada is frequently author-focused. While feminist criticism tends to be less author-oriented than other forms of critical practice, it too spends considerable time on single writers, almost exclusively women writers. There has not been as much work in, say, feminist readings of major male writers. Feminist work is also being done in the United States and Britain on Canadian women writers (see, for instance, Irvine; Howells). Such work parallels but is not as powerful as the feminist criticism emerging in Canada itself, including the pieces gathered in the publication of the Women and Words Conference of 1983 (Dybikowski et al.), the special issue of the *Canadian Journal of Political and Social Theory* (Kroker and Kroker), and especially the sophisticated essays in *A Mazing Space*, edited by Shirley Neuman and Smaro Kamboureli, and *Gynocritics/La Gynocritique*, edited by Barbara Godard. This last also contains a detailed bibliography of feminist criticism in Canada and Quebec. It is in the area of feminist critical practice that the real strengths of the emergent post-Saussurean criticism displays itself most notably.

One ideological effect of this emphasis on author-centered studies, compounded by the fact that many Canadian critics are also writers, is to reinforce the rhetorical and political power of the author function. The author's role is expressly to resolve the discontinuities or contradictions of discourse into a harmonious totality, a function premised on the concept of the originating subject for the stability of meaning and the homogeneity of experience, as if it were prior to its representations in language. Even the one notable book-length attempt at a European structuralist poetics, *Margaret Atwood: Language, Text and System* (Grace and Weir), takes not discourse but the individual subject as the source of the structures. System is not seen as a differential semiotic process but hermeneutically as a thematic or "organized network of obsessions" grounded in the writer as a phenomenological subject. But, as post-Saussureans have been telling us for at least two decades, "to posit an individual subject as an authority for a single meaning is to ignore the degree to which subjectivity itself is a discursive construct." To seek a guarantee of meaning in the world or in experience as social realists would do "is to ignore the fact that our experience of the world is itself articulated in language" (Belsey 54). The emphasis on author function as well as the predominance of thematic-cultural critical practice that focuses on character and image analysis may be a factor in the almost complete absence—except for the work of the contributing editors of *Open Letter*—of major studies that treat Canadian texts in terms of the relative material autonomy of literature— say, poetry in terms of verse forms, meter, and modes of representation. It is this sort of semiotic study of conventions and genres now needed in Canadian criticism.

Phenomenological criticism, in either its subjective or its dialectical modes, has been a major force in Canadian critical practice since the 1970s, overtaking and displacing systemic criticism. There is little doubt, however, that post-Saussurean criticism is rapidly becoming a critical force to reckon with, despite the walls that many in Canadian criticism would erect to keep the chaos out.

NOTES

[1]Some would argue that the initial step in the process of institutionalization was the founding, in 1959, of the journal *Canadian Literature*, the rhetorical and ideological effect of which was to proclaim that there was indeed such a thing as Canadian literature.

[2]See "Literature in Society" and *Marxism and Literature*. In the latter, Williams uses the term "dominant" instead of "corporate" to describe a common core of meanings, values, and practices in any society. Such a core never includes even all the significant practices; hence the need for the concepts of residual and emergent practices.

[3]Poststructuralism would be deeply troubled by the illusion of an Imaginary (in a Lacanian sense) originary center potentially implied by this notion of poetics.

[4]See, too, Henry Kreisel, "The Prairie" and Edward A. McCourt, *The Canadian West in Fiction*. These pioneering studies in Canadian western regionalist literature have affected subsequent studies of the subject—in particular, Ricou, Dick Harrison, Mandel, and W. H. New.

[5]Bhabha's discussion of the problematics of recognition, mimetic adequacy, and normative fallacies—on which I draw later in the essay—are informed by the work of Paul Hirst and Pierre Macherey, and many of his arguments about ideology complement those of Catherine Belsey, who is also indebted to Hirst and Macherey. On the Canadian desire for beginnings, see Robert Kroetsch, "Canada Is a Poem" (*Essays* 33–35).

[6]See Susan Crean and Marcel Rioux, *Two Nations* 57–58.

[7]"Economist Abraham Rotstein has described English Canada's brand of nationalism as 'mappism,' a kind of exaggerated identification of the nation with its territory" (Crean and Rioux 11).

[8]This sort of argument is made frequently in British Marxist literary criticism (see Bhabha; Belsey), as it is by such theorists as Roland Barthes.

[9]In *The Dialogic Imagination* Mikhail Bakhtin distinguishes between monoglossia—the unified, centralized, authoritative language—characterized by hegemony, and polyglossia, characterized by dispersal and differentiation.

WORKS CITED

Atwood, Margaret. *Survival: A Thematic Guide to Canadian Literature*. Toronto: Anansi, 1972.

Bakhtin, Mikhail M. *The Dialogic Imagination: Four Essays*. Ed. Michael Holquist. Trans. Caryl Emerson and Holquist. Austin: U of Texas P, 1981.

Barthes, Roland. *S/Z*. Trans. Richard Miller. New York: Hill, 1974.

Belsey, Catherine. *Critical Practice*. New Accents. London: Methuen, 1980.

Bhabha, Homi. "Representation and the Colonial Text: A Critical Exploration of

Some Forms of Mimeticism." *The Theory of Reading.* Ed. Frank Gloversmith. Sussex: Harvester, 1984. 93–122.

Blaise, Clark. *A North American Education.* New York: Doubleday, 1973.

Blodgett, E. D. "Authenticity and Absence: Reflections on the Prose of Dennis Lee." *Descant* 39 (1982): 103–17.

Bologh, Roslyn Wallach. *Dialectical Phenomenology: Marx's Method.* International Library of Phenomenology and Moral Sciences. London: Routledge, 1979.

Bowering, George. *A Way with Words.* Ottawa: Oberon, 1982.

Brown, Russell M. "Critic, Culture, Text: Beyond Thematics." *Essays on Canadian Writing* 11 (1978): 151–83.

Cameron, Barry. "Theory and Criticism: Trends in Canadian Literature." *Literary History of Canada.* 4 vols. Ed. W. H. New. Toronto: U of Toronto P, 1989. 4.

Cameron, Barry, and Michael Dixon. "Mandatory Subversive Manifesto: Canadian Criticism vs. Literary Criticism." *Minus Canadian: Penultimate Essays on Literature.* Ed. Cameron and Dixon. Spec. issue of *Studies in Canadian Literature* 2 (1977): 137–45.

Cappon, Paul, ed. *In Our Own House: Social Perspectives on Canadian Literature.* Toronto: McClelland, 1978.

Cohen, Leonard. *Beautiful Losers.* New York: Viking, 1966.

Crean, Susan, and Marcel Rioux. *Two Nations: An Essay on the Culture and Politics of Canada and Quebec in a World of American Pre-eminence.* Toronto: Lorimer, 1983.

Culler, Jonathan. *On Deconstruction: Theory and Criticism after Structuralism.* Ithaca: Cornell UP, 1982.

———. *Structuralist Poetics: Structuralism, Linguistics and the Study of Literature.* London: Routledge, 1975.

Davey, Frank. *From There to Here: A Guide to English-Canadian Literature since 1960.* Vol. 2 of *Our Nature—Our Voices.* Erin, ON: Porcépic, 1974.

———. *Surviving the Paraphrase: Eleven Essays on Canadian Literature.* Winnipeg: Turnstone, 1983.

Ducrot, Oswald, and Tzvetan Todorov. "Poetics." *Encyclopedic Dictionary of the Sciences of Language.* 1979. Trans. Catherine Porter. Oxford: Blackwell, 1981. 78–84.

Dybikowski, Ann, et al., eds. *In the Feminine: Women and Words/Les femmes et les mots.* Conference Proceedings 1983. Edmonton: Longspoon, 1985.

Eagleton, Terry. *Criticism and Ideology: A Study in Marxist Literary Theory.* London: Verso, 1978.

Frye, Northrop. *The Bush Garden: Essays on Canadian Imagination.* Toronto: Anansi, 1971.

———. "Conclusion." *Literary History of Canada: Canadian Literature in English.* Ed. Carl F. Klinck. Toronto: U of Toronto P, 1965. 821–49.

——. *Divisions on a Ground: Essays on Canadian Culture.* Ed. James Polk. Toronto: Anansi, 1982.

Godard, Barbara, ed. *Gynocritics/Gynocritiques: Feminist Approaches to Canadian and Quebec Women Writers.* Toronto: ECW, 1987.

——. "Other Fictions: Robert Kroetsch's Criticism." *Reflections: Essays on Robert Kroetsch.* Spec. issue of *Open Letter* 5.8–9 (1984): 5–21.

——. "Structuralism/Post-Structuralism: Language, Reality and Canadian Literature." Moss, *Future Indicative.* 25–51.

Grace, Sherrill E., and Lorraine Weir, eds. *Margaret Atwood: Language, Text, and System.* Vancouver: U of British Columbia P, 1983.

Harrison, Dick. *Unnamed Country: The Struggle for a Canadian Prairie Fiction.* Edmonton: U of Alberta P, 1977.

Hirst, Paul. *On Law and Ideology.* London: Macmillan, 1979.

Hood, Hugh. *Selected Stories.* Ottawa: Oberon, 1978.

Howells, Coral Ann. *Private and Fictional Words: Canadian Women Novelists of the 1970s and 1980s.* London: Methuen, 1987.

Irvine, Lorna. *Sub/Version: Canadian Fictions by Women.* Toronto: ECW, 1986.

Jones, D. G. *Butterfly on Rock: A Study of Themes and Images in Canadian Literature.* Toronto: U of Toronto P, 1970.

Kreisel, Henry. "The Prairie: A State of Mind." *Contexts of Canadian Criticism: A Collection of Critical Essays.* Ed. Eli Mandel. Patterns of Literary Criticism. Chicago: U of Chicago P, 1971. 254–66.

Kroetsch, Robert. *Creation.* Toronto: New, 1970.

——. *Robert Kroetsch: Essays.* Ed. Frank Davey and bpNichol. Spec. issue of *Open Letter* 5.4 (1983).

Kroker, Marilouise, and Arthur Kroker, eds. *Feminism Now: Theory and Practice.* Spec. issue of *Canadian Journal of Political and Social Theory* 9.1–2 (1985).

Lecker, Robert. *On the Line: Readings in the Short Fiction of Clark Blaise, John Metcalf, and Hugh Hood.* Toronto: ECW, 1982.

Lee, Dennis. "Cadence, Country, Silence: Writing in a Colonial Space." *Open Letter* 2.6 (1973): 34–53.

——. "Polyphony, Enacting a Meditation." *Descant* 39 (1982): 82–99.

——. "Reading Savage Fields." *Canadian Journal of Political and Social Theory* 3.2 (1979): 161–82.

——. *Savage Fields: An Essay in Literature and Cosmology.* Toronto: Anansi, 1977.

Macherey, Pierre. *A Theory of Literary Production.* Trans. Geoffrey Wall. London: Routledge, 1978.

Mandel, Eli. *Another Time.* Erin, ON: Porcépic, 1977.

——. "The Border League: American 'West' and Canadian 'Region.'" *Crossing*

Frontiers: Papers in American and Canadian Western Literature. Ed. Dick Harrison. Edmonton: U of Alberta P, 1979. 105–21.

———. *Criticism: The Silent-Speaking Words.* Toronto: CBC, 1966.

———. "'Life Sentence': Contemporary Canadian Criticism." *Poetry since 1950. Laurentian University Review* 10.2 (1978): 7–19.

———. "Northrop Frye and the Canadian Literary Tradition." *Centre and Labyrinth: Essays in Honour of Northrop Frye.* Ed. Eleanor Cook et al. Toronto: U of Toronto P, 1983. 284–97.

———. "Strange Loops: Northrop Frye and Cultural Freudianism." *Canadian Journal of Political and Social Theory* 5.3 (1981): 33–43.

Marchak, Patricia. "Given a Certain Latitude: A (Hinterland) Sociologist's View of Anglo-Canadian Literature." *In Our Own House: Social Perspectives on Canadian Literature.* Ed. Paul Cappon. Toronto: McClelland, 1978. 178–205.

Mathews, Robin. *Canadian Literature: Surrender or Revolution.* Toronto: Steel Rail, 1978.

McCourt, Edward A. *The Canadian West in Fiction.* Rev. ed. Toronto: Ryerson, 1970.

Moisan, Clément. *A Poetry of Frontiers: Comparative Studies in Quebec/Canadian Literature.* Trans. Linda Webber. Victoria: Porcépic, 1983.

Moss, John, ed. *Future Indicative: Literary Theory and Canadian Literature.* Reappraisals: Canadian Writers 13. Ottawa: U of Ottawa P, 1987.

———. *Patterns of Isolation in English Canadian Fiction.* Toronto: McClelland, 1974.

———. *Sex and Violence in the Canadian Novel: The Ancestral Present.* Toronto: McClelland, 1977.

Neuman, Shirley, and Smaro Kamboureli, eds. *A Mazing Space: Writing Canadian Women Writing.* Edmonton: Longspoon-NeWest, 1986.

Neuman, Shirley, and Robert Wilson. *Labyrinths of Voice: Conversations with Robert Kroetsch.* Western Canadian Literary Documents 3. Edmonton: NeWest, 1982.

New, W. H. *Articulating West: Essays on Purpose and Form in Modern Canadian Literature.* Toronto: New, 1972.

———. "Canadian Home Ground, Foreign Territory." *Among Worlds: An Introduction to Modern Commonwealth and South African Fiction.* Erin, ON: Porcépic, 1975. 101–29.

Olson, Charles. "Projective Verse." *Twentieth-Century Poetry and Poetics.* Ed. Gary Geddes. 2nd ed. Toronto: Oxford UP, 1973. 526–41.

Ondaatje, Michael. *The Collected Works of Billy the Kid: The Left-handed Poems.* Toronto: Anansi, 1970.

Ricou, Laurence. *Vertical Man/Horizontal World: Man and Landscape in Canadian Prairie Fiction.* Vancouver: U of British Columbia P, 1973.

Said, Edward. *The World, the Text, and the Critic.* Cambridge: Harvard UP, 1983.

Stouck, David. *Major Canadian Authors: A Critical Introduction.* Lincoln: U of Nebraska P, 1984.

Sutherland, Ronald. *The New Hero: Essays in Comparative Quebec/Canadian Literature.* Toronto: Macmillan, 1977.

———. *Second Image: Comparative Studies in Quebec/Canadian Literature.* Toronto: New, 1971.

Tallman, Warren. *Godawful Streets of Man.* Spec. issue of *Open Letter* 3.6 (1976–77).

Wiebe, Rudy. "New Land, Ancient Land." *The New Land: Studies in a Literary Theme.* Calgary Institute for the Humanities. Waterloo: Wilfrid Laurier UP, 1978.

Williams, Raymond. "Literature in Society." *Contemporary Approaches to English Studies.* Ed. Hilda Schiff. New York: Barnes, 1977. 24–37.

———. *Marxism and Literature.* Oxford: Oxford UP, 1977.

Wilson, Milton. "Recent Canadian Verse." *Contexts of Canadian Criticism: A Collection of Critical Essays.* Ed. Eli Mandel. Patterns of Literary Criticism. Chicago: U of Chicago P, 1971. 198–205.

David M. Hayne

THE EVOLUTION OF FRENCH-CANADIAN LITERATURE TO 1960

MODERN QUÉBEC, THE largest of the ten Canadian provinces, occupies an area more than twice that of Texas, lying on both shores of the St. Lawrence River, Canada's principal commercial waterway. The valley of the St. Lawrence, first explored by Jacques Cartier during his second voyage in 1535, was colonized by France in the seventeenth century. When New France was ceded to Britain during the Seven Years' War, its immense territory included most of present-day Canada and the entire Mississippi Valley. Yet the inhabitants of this vast empire amounted to only 65,000 persons, a fraction of the population of the English colonies in America at that date.

French immigration to Canada virtually ceased after the British Conquest of 1760, but the French-Canadian population multiplied at a remarkable rate, increasing tenfold every century to become a uniquely homogeneous demographic unit of more than six million Francophones in Canada today. In addition to their common ancestry, the new British subjects were united by a shared language and a traditional religious faith. Their speech was a blend of several French dialects that was already fairly uniform throughout the colony by the mid-eighteenth century, before French had become standardized in France itself. Their religion was an uncompromising Roman Catholicism inherited from New France, which had been an exclusively Catholic foundation.

After the conquest and the consequent departure of French troops and administrators, the parish priests assumed, by virtue of their superior education, leadership among a largely agricultural francophone population living, until 1854, under a seigniorial land-tenure system. Gradually, English-speaking immigrants—United Empire Loyalists fleeing from the United

States, Scottish families dispersed in the "clearings" of the highlands, impoverished English gentry, or Irish farmers driven out by the potato famines—were converging on Canada and making of it an anglophone country, in which the descendants of the original French settlers would find themselves a minority, but a minority determined to survive.

The French Regime, 1535–1760

French colonization of the St. Lawrence Valley began with the founding of Québec in 1608; smaller posts were created at Three Rivers in 1634 and on Montréal Island in 1642. Settlement proceeded slowly at first under the commercial monopolies granted by the French kings, so that in 1663 direct royal government was instituted, turning the tiny colony into an overseas province of France with its own governor and intendant. Immigration, early marriage, and large families were encouraged, and as settlements developed along the river, a few local industries were established. By 1700 the threat posed by unfriendly Amerindian tribes had declined, and the population had passed the 10,000 mark. Intermittent wars with England continued, however, and by the Treaty of Utrecht (1713) France lost Nova Scotia and Newfoundland to her rival. In the half-century of peace that followed, New France enjoyed increasing prosperity, until the Seven Years' War and the Peace of Paris (1763) finally brought the end of the French regime in North America.

During the two-and-a-quarter centuries of French power, not a single page of French was printed in New France, as there was no printing press in the colony until after the British Conquest. There is nevertheless a considerable literature of New France written in and about the colony, although published in Europe for a European audience.

The earliest texts were tales of discovery and exploration, like the voyages of Jacques Cartier and Samuel de Champlain. Later, a Recollect brother, Gabriel Sagard, described his travels in the interior; the Jesuits published forty-two annual *Relations* reporting on their missionary labors, and a courageous nun, Marie de l'Incarnation, wrote hundreds of letters recounting her experiences at the Québec post from her arrival there in 1639 until her death in 1672. The state of New France in 1663 was minutely described for the French court in a book-length account by Pierre Boucher. Subsequently, explorers like Pierre-Esprit Radisson, Louis Hennepin, and the La Vérendryes pushed southward and westward, recording their travels in their journals. Writers such as Joseph-François Lafitau; Chrestien Le Clercq; Claude-Charles Le Roy, *dit* Bacqueville de La Potherie; and Sister Marie Morin composed histories of the colony and of its religious institutions, while Louis-Armand de Lom d'Arce, baron de Lahontan, used his observation of Indian customs to criticize European practices and beliefs. The culminating point of French historiography during the old regime was the publication in 1744 of Pierre-François-Xavier de Charlevoix's monumental *Histoire et description générale de la Nouvelle-France.*

The printed literature of New France was supplemented by a substantial oral literature composed of folksongs in ancient musical modes, folk tales, and historical legends passed from generation to generation by parish folk-singers and storytellers. A huge collection of such material has been accumulated in the Archives de folklore created at Laval University by the internationally renowned folklorist Luc Lacourcière and his staff, who have produced numerous studies of their holdings.

The rich heritage of literary works and oral traditions preserved from the French regime has until recently been of interest chiefly to historians and folklorists. Only now is it being examined by students of literature in search of the origins of Québec thought and writing.

After the Conquest, 1760–1830

When no further reinforcements or supplies arrived from France in the summer of 1760, New France passed into British hands. The town of Québec had been bombarded for weeks, farms on the south shore of the St. Lawrence had been burned, French currency was hopelessly devalued, and the French military and administrative classes were obliged to return to France. For the three-quarters of the French population living in their rural parishes, however, the change of government had little significance. For practical purposes the British military (1760–64) and civil governments allowed them use of the French language, the practice of their religion, and the continuation of the seigniorial system. To ensure the loyalty of the French-speaking population as the American Revolution threatened, the civil status of French Canadians was clarified by the Québec Act of 1774, which allowed them access to public office, the protection of French civil law, tithing for support of the church, and guarantees of seigniorial rights. These privileges did not, however, sit well with the thousands of United Empire Loyalists who began arriving in 1783 from the new republic of the United States. In 1784 the province of New Brunswick was formed to accommodate the immigrants, and a few years later the whole country was reorganized under the Constitutional Act of 1791, which divided Québec into two provinces, Upper and Lower Canada, the former English-speaking; the latter, French. Each province was to have a two-chamber legislature, but the governor and his appointed executive council would control expenditures.

Now having their own provincial government, a few French Canadians began to take an active part in public life. Their numbers increased with the founding, in the early nineteenth century, of several new classical colleges providing education for the learned professions. Yet four-fifths of the French population, still largely illiterate, remained on the land, working hard, obeying their parish priests, and preserving their folkloric culture.

In such conditions of political and economic struggle, a disinterested literature was inconceivable. The first publications after the introduction of a printing press, in 1764, were utilitarian: newspapers, government documents, pamphlets, and sermons, all minutely described in Marie Tremaine's *Bibliography of Canadian Imprints, 1751–1800*. The first newspaper, the *Quebec Gazette* (1764), was a bilingual government periodical that appeared for more than a century, giving valuable weekly or triweekly information on the sociopolitical life of the time. The second newspaper was *La Gazette de Montréal* (1778), published by a French printer, Fleury Mesplet, with the collaboration of a second Frenchman who shared his republican sympathies. Both ended up in prison for their subversive views. The first journal of French-Canadian political opinion, *Le Canadien*, began to appear in 1806, but it was closed down several times by the British authorities. Both it and its more discreet rival, *La Minerve* (1826), lived on throughout the whole of the nineteenth century, whereas dozens of other French-language newspapers had shorter existences.

Simultaneously with the increase in numbers of newspapers, the first monthly review, the *Quebec Magazine* (1792), offered its readers a wide selection of articles on all imaginable subjects, reprinted from European books and periodicals. A generation later, the journalist and historian Michel Bibaud launched a series of four monthly magazines between 1825 and 1843, with the express purpose of raising the cultural level of the literate population. Much of the material in the magazines was written by Bibaud himself, including serialized chapters of his *Histoire du Canada*, the first to be written by a French Canadian.

The newspapers and magazines of the late eighteenth and early nineteenth centuries were also vehicles for the first literary efforts of their readers. Poems and songs, anecdotes, dialogues, legends, and even short stories were included in their pages, affording to aspiring writers an inexpensive opportunity of seeing their compositions in print. At first the most prolific contributors were visitors from France like Joseph Quesnel, whose numerous poems, although not his stage plays, appeared in the newspapers of the day, or Joseph Mermet, an officer sent to Canada during the War of 1812, who described Niagara Falls and recounted the battle of Chateauguay in long poems printed in the press. Canadians like Bibaud also published poems in the papers; much of the verse Bibaud was later to include in Québec's first published volume of poetry (1830) had previously been printed in his own newspapers and magazines.

Although the first years of British domination were hardly conducive to literary expression, journalistic activity was intense and extremely valuable for the French-speaking population. Before the invention of modern methods of communication, newspapers and magazines were the sole medium of mass communication and the only contact with Europe and the United States. In the struggle for political liberty and national rights, patriotic journals like *Le Canadien* and *La Minerve* were indispensable instruments of expression and channels for voicing demands. In addition, the press provided the earliest indications of a more developed national literature to come.

Beginnings of Literature, 1830–60

French-Canadian literature begins in the 1830s. Bibaud's *Epîtres, satires, chansons* appeared in 1830, the first French-Canadian novel is dated 1837, the first published stage comedy written by a French Canadian belongs to the same year, and the first published tragedy came a few years later, in 1844.

This apparently sudden appearance of a national literature had in reality been prepared by a number of developments. Efforts to organize both primary and secondary education in the first third of the century were producing a generation of young men with a good background in humane letters. Increasing, although indirect, contacts with France via London and New York made possible the occasional importation of French books and periodicals, and the works of French Romantic writers were on sale in the bookstores being opened in Québec City and Montréal about 1820. The first cultural societies were founded at about the same time: the venerable Québec Literary and Historical Society dates from 1824. The multiplication of newspapers attracted more printers, and several printing houses were soon available to publish new writings.

The 1830s were stirring times in Québec. The parliamentary conflicts of previous years, in which the new professional class led a campaign for responsible government against the British administration, were to culminate in ill-fated rebellions in both Upper and Lower Canada in 1837–38. After John Lambton, earl of Durham, had reported on the affairs of the colony, the Act of Union (1840) again united French Canadians in a single province with a growing anglophone population. Despite these setbacks, the political aspirations of younger French Canadians found support in the nationalism and individualism of European Romantic writings, and the link thus forged in Québec between literature and nationalism was to persist for generations. Its first important manifestation was the great *Histoire du Canada* published by François-Xavier Garneau in 1845–48, which painted a colorful fresco of the glories of the French regime in Canada and gave the lie to Durham's statement in his 1839 *Report* that French Canadians were "a people without a history." French-Canadian national pride reached unprecedented heights in the summer of 1855, when Napoleon III, taking advantage of his alliance with Britain in the Crimean War, sent a frigate, *La Capricieuse*, to Québec to restore commercial relations with Canada after an interruption of almost a century. The occasion was celebrated by the Québec bookseller and poet Octave Crémazie, in one of his most popular poems, "Chant du vieux soldat canadien." Years later, when he was living in financial exile in France, Crémazie made gentle fun of his earlier patriotic poems and of the Canadian public's naive taste for chauvinistic verse. Indeed, Crémazie's penetrating critical comments in his letters from France and his fascinating journal of the siege of Paris in 1870 suggest that he might in other circumstances have become an important prose writer. A short-lived contemporary of Crémazie's, Joseph Lenoir, was perhaps more gifted as a poet and less tempted by nationalistic subjects than Crémazie; Lenoir's tender lyricism and exotic themes allied him closely with the French Romantic poets writing a generation earlier.

In fiction this was the period of the first novels, nearly a dozen of which had been written by 1860. The earliest examples, like *L'influence d'un livre*, by Philippe-Ignace-François Aubert de Gaspé, Joseph Doutre's *Les fiancés de 1812*, or Eugène L'Ecuyer's *La fille du brigand* were, as their titles imply, melodramatic tales of adventure complete with stormy nights, buried treasures, disguises, abductions, melancholy heroes, and pale heroines. In 1845, however, the tone changed, perhaps in response to an appeal by the politician Louis-Auguste Olivier for less sensational and more typically Canadian writing. The next two novels by French Canadians, Patrice Lacombe's *La terre paternelle* and Pierre-Joseph-Olivier Chauveau's *Charles Guérin*, presented idealized portraits of rural life in Québec, in which the simple virtues and natural beauty of the countryside were opposed to the ugliness and materialism of the cities. This was the beginning of the subgenre known as the *roman du terroir*, which would serve for many years as a justification of the agricultural ideology being proposed for French Canadians. The transition in fiction is strikingly illustrated in George Boucher de Boucherville's *Une de perdue, deux de trouvées*: the first part of the novel, written in 1849, is an adventure tale of a Caribbean slave revolt; the second, published in 1864–65, is a more sober narrative of Lower Canada in the 1830s.

Novelists had no easy time in United Canada. They had to sell their books by advance subscription to cover printing costs, then compete with the more readable French fiction being imported, and, finally, defend themselves against the widespread notion that fiction was a frivolous, if not immoral, use of the reader's time. Only as the nineteenth century wore on did novels achieve even modest respectability.

The Québec Movement, 1860–90

Under the Act of Union of 1840, the single Parliament of the combined provinces of Upper and Lower Canada was an itinerant one, alternating between English-language and French-language centers. During the years 1859–65, it was located in Québec City, which was also the seat of the recently founded (1852) Laval University. The "old capital" thus became the home of a literary movement whose members were to produce a dozen noteworthy books in the next half-dozen years, until the Confederation of 1867 moved the national capital to Ottawa.

The Movement of 1860 was first and foremost an expression of French Canadian national sentiment. The adjective *canadien* (then reserved for French-speaking Canadians) appeared in almost every title published. It was also a retrospective movement, looking backward in time for its themes and giving preference to retrospective genres such as history, biography, memoirs, legends, and the historical novel. Lastly, the movement was a religious and didactic one. The ideology of the 1860s, influenced by the French historian Edmé Rameau de Saint-Père's theories, envisaged a providential mission for Roman Catholic French Canada in the midst of a Protestant and materialistic North American continent. The movement's writers therefore looked back to French Romanticism, espousing its national consciousness and historical perspectives, although rejecting its exaltation of individual passion and moral freedom.

The first joint project undertaken by the dozen members of the group was the founding of a monthly literary magazine, *Les soirées canadiennes* (1861–65). Two years later a splinter group founded its own review, *Le foyer canadien* (1863–66), which soon had more than two thousand subscribers. Shortly thereafter, a more substantial monthly, the *Revue canadienne*, was launched in Montreal. The publication of these three journals gave immediate circulation to the poetry and prose of local authors, and even some book-length bonus volumes were issued. These included a classic of the period, Philippe-Joseph Aubert de Gaspé's historical romance of the Seven Years' War, *Les anciens Canadiens*, later to be twice translated into English.

Within a few months of the publication of *Les anciens Canadiens*, two other important works of fiction were completed: Antoine Gérin-Lajoie's *Jean Rivard* and Joseph-Charles Taché's *Forestiers et voyageurs*. The former was a *roman à thèse* designed to encourage educated youths to undertake agricultural settlement in the Eastern Townships of Québec; the latter was a collection of lumberjack tales and reminiscences.

Two younger members of the group, Louis Fréchette and Pamphile Le

May, published their first volumes of lyric poetry in these years. A third poet of the group was the son of the national historian F.-X. Garneau, Alfred, who had the most delicate touch of the three, but was too modest ever to issue a collection of his verse.

Fiction and poetry were considered unworthy of priestly authors, who tended to specialize in history and biography. Abbé Charles-Honoré Laverdière produced scholarly editions of the *Jesuit Relations* in 1858 and of Champlain's *Voyages* in 1870. Abbé Jean-Baptiste-Antoine Ferland began issuing his *Cours d'histoire du Canada* in 1861 and 1865, and the animator of the 1860 movement, Abbé Henri-Raymond Casgrain, published in 1864 a life of Marie de l'Incarnation that circulated in Europe and was translated into German.

Although in the 1860s literary activity was centered in Québec City, the booming commercial city of Montréal was rapidly overtaking the capital. Terminus of a growing railway network, site of the first bridge over the St. Lawrence, and center for ocean and inland shipping, Montréal in 1861 already had ninety thousand inhabitants to Québec City's sixty thousand, and the Institut canadien de Montréal (1844) was the first "people's university" in the province. Some of the novels published in the previous decades had been printed in Montréal, and one of the most admired romances of the 1860s, Napoléon Bourassa's *Jacques et Marie*, was serialized in the *Revue canadienne*. Encouraged by the success of *Evangeline*, Bourassa constructed a simple but moving narrative around his Acadian heroine, her fiancé, and the latter's English officer rival. This triangular structure would recur in numerous other French-Canadian historical romances, particularly in those composed in the 1870s by the historian Joseph Marmette, whose most popular novel, *François de Bienville*, was based on Sir William Phips's attack on Québec in 1690. The best-selling historical romance of the 1880s came from the pen of an English-speaking Canadian, William Kirby, whose *Golden Dog* was read in French Canada in Pamphile Le May's French translation.

Historical romances fitted readily into the patriotic and retrospective ideology of the Movement of 1860. Other types of fiction were less successful, although Honoré Beaugrand's *Jeanne la fileuse* was an important document in the continuing controversy about the emigration of thousands of French Canadians each year to the textile mills of New England.

The most original novel of these years, *Angéline de Montbrun* by the pseudonymous Laure Conan, recounted the tribulations of an adolescent heroine, engaged to an exemplary young man, who breaks off the engagement after the death of her beloved father and her own disfigurement, and retires to a life of spiritual reflection. For readers of the time, Angéline was a model of Christian resignation. For today's biographical critics, however, the book is a disguised account of its author's only love affair; for Freudian readers, Angéline is the victim of an incestuous passion for her father. Thus a century after its publication, *Angéline de Montbrun* continues to intrigue its readers as no other Québec novel of its time has done.

Meantime, poetry was enjoying a second expansionary phase about 1875, as a generation of poets born in midcentury began to publish, complementing the continuing collections of the three older writers, Fréchette, Le May, and Alfred Garneau. Of these, Fréchette was the dominant figure, receiving an award from the French Academy in 1880 and completing, in 1887, his magnum opus, *La légende d'un peuple*, a series of forty-seven verse tableaux depicting Québec history from Cartier's explorations to the execution of Louis Riel, in 1885. Among the younger poets, William Chapman showed a predilection for two themes, the beauties of Canadian nature and the intellectual hegemony of France; his major collections appeared after the end of the century. Nérée Beauchemin, a country doctor practicing in Yamachiche, near Trois-Rivières, is chiefly remembered as the author of an anthology piece, "La cloche de Louisbourg" (1896). The most ironic poet of this generation, Eudore Evanturel, published only one slender volume, *Premières poésies* (1878), before leaving Canada to become secretary to the historian Francis Parkman.

Because it presupposes an urban society, a concentrated population, and a certain affluence, drama is normally the last literary genre to develop in a young country. In post-Confederation Québec these conditions were slowly being met, and one or two large theaters were built in both Québec City and Montréal. The Roman Catholic hierarchy viewed the theater with deep concern, both as a questionable institution and as the vehicle of French repertory tours, like that of Sarah Bernhardt in 1880, denounced by the bishop of Montréal. Plays written by French Canadians, on the other hand, were normally respectful of the church's teachings, and dramatizations of the historical romances of Aubert de Gaspé and Marmette were especially popular. The liberal-minded Fréchette found material in the 1837 rebellion for his plays *Félix Poutré* (1862) and *Papineau* (1880), but two later plays of his were discovered to be plagiarized from French writers. One of the more skillful comic dramatists of the time was a future prime minister of Québec, Félix-Gabriel Marchand, whose four lively social sketches were the Canadian equivalent of French boulevard comedy.

Two other kinds of writing emerged during this period: literary criticism and literary history. Criticism at first took the form of short passages in the prospectuses of literary magazines, in the prefaces of novels or verse collections, or in correspondences like those of Crémazie and Casgrain. More formal studies began to appear in the 1870s: Edmond Lareau's *Histoire de la littérature canadienne* (1874) was a remarkably well-informed reference work, and early anthologies of Québec poetry were issued in 1869 and 1881. One of the first papers read before the newly founded Royal Society of Canada was Chauveau's "Etude sur les commencements de la poésie française au Canada" (1882), and at subsequent meetings the French-speaking members frequently treated literary subjects.

As the final decade of the nineteenth century began, it was evident that the long union of ultramontane Roman Catholic spiritual power and Conservative political supremacy in Québec was weakening. The clergy's "undue influence" in elections had been condemned by the Supreme Court of Canada, and the Conservative hold on the provincial government had twice been threatened. On the intellectual front, too, cracks were showing by 1890. Little magazines were appearing that praised contemporary French writers like the *poète maudit* Paul Verlaine; one of them, *Canada-Revue*, openly defied the ecclesiastical authorities for a brief period. The long reign of French Romanticism in Québec was ending, but there was now no doubt that a French-Canadian literature existed and would continue to flourish.

Ecole littéraire de Montréal, 1890–1935

By the end of the nineteenth century, technological progress was changing the face of eastern Canada. Electric street lighting, electric streetcars, and the first automobiles appeared in the cities before the turn of the century, and the first cinema opened in Montréal in 1906. Long-standing Conservative governments in both Ottawa and Québec City were replaced by Liberal ones, and a French Canadian, Wilfrid Laurier, became prime minister of Canada. French Canadians were now alert to their important political role, particularly when Canada was drawn into Britain's wars against the Boers in 1899 and against Germany in 1914. French-language orators like Henri Bourassa attracted large audiences, and nationalistic associations were founded. Bourassa's own newspaper, *Le devoir*, launched in 1910, is still an influential journal of opinion today.

The confidence and bustle of this *belle époque* was reflected in its literature. After half a century of Romanticism, the younger writers—those born in the 1870s—were eager to try more modern forms of literature. The Movement of 1860 had been centered in Québec City; the new school would take its name from Montréal, already a metropolis of a quarter of a million inhabitants. The 1860 movement had been a handful of acquaintances meeting casually; the School of Montréal had more than sixty members, each nominated and elected. It held regular weekly sessions, kept detailed minutes, and organized four large public meetings that were widely publicized and fully reported in the press. The school continued to meet, intermittently in later years, for more than a quarter of a century, and its members published far more than their predecessors, albeit almost exclusively in verse. They read their compositions at the weekly meetings, criticized one another's work, and strove to improve their general culture and their knowledge of the French language. On three occasions, in 1900, 1910, and 1925, the Ecole published collective volumes of the writings of its members.

By the first decade of the twentieth century, it was apparent that the Ecole littéraire de Montréal harbored two contradictory tendencies. Its members were fascinated by contemporary French poetry and wanted to identify with the French tradition, yet many of them felt a patriotic urge to develop a Canadian poetry and to use Québec material. By 1910 the Ecole had split into two groups. A small minority of its members opted for the aesthetic tradition, some of them (Paul Morin, René Chopin, Guy Delahaye) going to Paris, where they frequented the salon of Countess Anna de Noailles. With the declaration of war in 1914, these expatriates returned to Québec, where they founded an ephemeral artistic magazine, *Le nigog* (1918). Their appeal was limited, however, and the majority of members of the Ecole remained faithful to their Canadian heritage and tried to write in Canadian terms.

Ironically, the "exotics" and the "regionalists," as the two factions came to be called, shared the principal concerns of the School of Montréal, but with differing emphases. Both, for example, were intensely interested in the French language. For the regionalists, the concern was a local one, stressing the peculiar dialectal, archaic, and popular characteristics of Canadian French. For the exotics, the French language was the vehicle of a centuries-long tradition of Latin culture, universal and indivisible.

Similarly, both groups took literature seriously, but with different convictions about its nature and purpose. The regionalists saw in it a form of social action, part of the struggle for national survival. Content was thus of fundamental importance. The exotics, for their part, considered literature an artistic activity like music or painting; their primary concern was with beauty of form and elegance of expression, and they were contemptuous of local references and quaint national subject matter.

The gulf between the two factions could not be bridged. But the battle was uneven: the regionalists greatly outnumbered the exotics, and their case was much more palatable in the anti-imperialist and nationalistic climate of Québec before and after the First World War. Yet, paradoxically, regionalist writing was almost exclusively rural and agricultural in its themes at the very time, from 1921 on, that Québec was becoming largely urbanized and industrialized.

Some twenty of the poets associated with the Ecole littéraire de Montréal

published collections of their verses, but their most outstanding representative did not. Unquestionably a genius, Emile Nelligan was the first Québec
poet able to bear comparison with his contemporaries in France. He wrote
all his poetry between the ages of sixteen and nineteen (1896–99) before
lapsing into madness. His poems "Le vaisseau d'or" and "La romance du
vin" are to be found in every anthology of Québec verse (see, for example,
Mailhot and Nepveu 161, 170). Nelligan's intricate and polished sonnets
and rondels, collected after his hospitalization by his friend Louis Dantin,
mark a sudden and surprising high point in the history of French-Canadian
poetry. There was to be no poet of comparable gifts and technical skill
until the 1940s.

Other leading figures among the poets of the Ecole littéraire were its
cofounder and historian Jean Charbonneau; Nelligan's bohemian friend
Arthur de Bussières; the painter-poet Charles Gill; a bed-ridden author,
Albert Lozeau; and the solitary poet of Canadian nature, Albert Ferland.
During the 1920s three other writers moved away from the concerns of the
Ecole littéraire and experimented in new directions. As early as 1920, Jean
Aubert Loranger composed prose poems that anticipated the coming of
modernism to Québec a generation later. Alfred DesRochers, a self-educated
jack-of-all-trades, combined regional observation and universal sentiment
in his depictions of the lives of lumberjacks and farmers. He was the
acknowledged leader of a literary movement centered in Sherbrooke in
the 1930s. Robert Choquette, both cosmopolitan poet and regional novelist,
was one of the first successful radio dramatists writing in French.

In fiction this was a period of cautious, and sometimes courageous,
experimentation. A prolific ultramontane apologist, Judge Adolphe-Basile
Routhier published the historical novel Le centurion; based on biblical
themes, the work had remarkable success and was translated into several
languages. Most historical novelists continued, however, to exploit the
French regime (Laure Conan, L'oublié) and the rebellion of 1837 (Ernest
Choquette, Claude Paysan), although with increasing objectivity (Robert
de Roquebrune, Les habits rouges). Two Montréal journalists, Rodolphe
Girard and Albert Laberge, defied convention by writing naturalistic tales
exposing rural life. Their books (Marie Calumet, La Scouine) were immediately denounced by the bishop of Montréal and disappeared from sight
for half a century. The unequaled best-seller of the period was Maria
Chapdelaine (Paris, 1914, published in Montréal in 1916), a stark and static
account of settlers' lives in the Lac Saint-Jean region, written by a French
visitor to Québec, Louis Hémon. Accepted hesitantly in Québec as a portrait
of rural life, Maria Chapdelaine was extensively promoted in France by the
publisher Bernard Grasset; it passed through hundreds of editions and was
translated worldwide. Inevitably, it influenced subsequent French-Canadian

fiction and prolonged the reign of the regional idyll in Québec. The most sympathetic treatment of the *terroir* theme was provided by Adjutor Rivard in *Chez nous* and *Chez nos gens*; the most durable, extended by long-running radio and television serials, was that of Claude-Henri Grignon in his novel *Un homme et son péché*.

The theater continued to be dominated by French touring companies until the outbreak of war in 1914, despite the fact that a relatively successful attempt had been made, with ecclesiastical approval, to encourage amateur theater performances in the series called "Les soirées de famille" (1898). During the 1920s, in the face of growing competition from the cinema and from radio drama, several French-Canadian plays had remarkably long runs (Louvigny de Montigny, *Le bouquet de Mélusine*, 1928; Léopold Houlé, *Le presbytère en fleurs*, 1929). The all-time favorite in parish hall performances was Petitjean and Rollin's heartrending melodrama of child persecution, *Aurore, l'enfant martyre* (1921). Also popular were the vaudeville turns, revues, and sketches performed on the stage of theaters like Montréal's Le Stella (1930–35).

Historiography was dominated in the 1920s and 1930s by the impassioned eloquence of Abbé Lionel Groulx, theorist of the right-wing nationalism of the time. Similarly, literary criticism was the province of Abbé Camille Roy, whose manuals of French-Canadian literature and volumes of essays communicated an enlightened but moralizing view of literature to generations of Québec college students.

The provincial Liberal governments in power from 1897 to 1936 encouraged cultural activities, subsidizing libraries and archives and establishing the first official literary prizes in the province. In the private sector, the Québec publishing industry was expanding to serve a better-educated population; newspapers put out Saturday literary pages, and magazines reviewed new books. Some of these innovations suffered a setback during the economic crisis of the 1930s, but a climate favorable to Québec writing had been created.

The Second World War and Postwar Period, 1935–60

The last quarter-century of our survey is characterized by two events: locally, by the long mandate (1936–60) of the Union nationale provincial government of Maurice Duplessis, and internationally, by World War II and its aftermath. In the 1930s Québec was already substantially industrialized and urbanized; nearly three-quarters of its people lived in cities and towns, a million of them in the Montréal area. The traditional rural and folkloric society of Québec was disappearing, and literary regionalism no longer corresponded to socioeconomic reality.

The signs of change in literature were apparent in all the major genres. In fiction the preponderance of rural novels was challenged by the publication in 1934 of Jean-Charles Harvey's anticlerical novel in an urban setting, *Les demi-civilisés*, promptly condemned by the archbishop of Montréal. In 1937 a young Montréal intellectual, Hector de Saint-Denys Garneau, assembled a collection of verse that had no discernible Canadian content, no punctuation, and no rhymes. In the same year the theater was reborn with the founding of Les Compagnons de Saint-Laurent, which presented stylized performances influenced by the French director Jacques Copeau. The change of climate was confirmed by the personalist articles published in *La relève* (1934–48); by an antiestablishment manifesto, *Refus global*, circulated in 1948 by the painter Paul-Emile Borduas and his circle; and by *Cité libre* (1950–66), an anti-Duplessis journal of political and economic comment. European ideas crossed the Atlantic more rapidly in the 1930s and 1940s, partly because of improved communications (television would come to Canada in 1952) but especially because the wartime occupation of France thrust Montréal into the role of a major French publishing center. The traditional time lag of a generation between intellectual fashions in France and in Québec was now greatly reduced.

Fiction evolved rapidly during these years. The rural novel reached its artistic peak in *Trente arpents (Thirty Acres)*, by Philippe Panneton (who used the pseudonym Ringuet), published in France. It traced the rise and decline of a farming family, offering a perceptive criticism of the agricultural ideology so uncritically accepted in French Canada. Rural novels continued to be written, those of Germaine Guèvremont (*Le survenant*) being particularly effective, but the days of this subgenre were numbered. The historical novel, too, had apparently had its day, despite the success of Léo-Paul Desrosier's epic of the fur trade, *Les engagés du Grand Portage*. Overt nationalist sentiment gave rise to a remarkable poetic narrative, Félix-Antoine Savard's *Menaud, maître-draveur*, but the achievement would not be repeated.

As the Second World War ended, it was evident that French-Canadian fiction was taking new directions in both its representation of reality and its psychological analysis. Roger Lemelin's *Au pied de la pente douce* and *Les Plouffe* did for the proletariat in Québec City what Gabrielle Roy's *Bonheur d'occasion* and Roger Viau's *Au milieu la montagne* would do for Montréal's working class: document in detail the daily struggle for existence of the impoverished urban masses. As the Québec novel began to address universal concerns, it became readable elsewhere. Translations and Parisian editions of Québec authors became more frequent, and in 1947 Roy was awarded the Prix Femina in France for *Bonheur d'occasion*.

Not all novelists were attracted to social realism, however, and the 1950s saw several writers producing introspective novels in which middle-class young men searched their souls in quest of purity and spiritual peace. Yet the outcome was, more often—as in André Giroux, *Au delà des visages*; Robert Elie, *La fin des songes*; and André Langevin, *Poussière sur la ville*, respectively—murder, suicide, or solitude. These interior novels displayed an awareness of the socioeconomic realities of the postwar years but were more experimental in their narrative techniques than the rather conventional novels of social observation. In short, the French-Canadian novel was profiting from the examples of Duhamel and Mauriac.

Finally, five novelists who would become major figures during the 1960s began writing and publishing at the end of this period. They are Gérard Bessette (*La bagarre*), Marie-Claire Blais (*La belle bête*), Anne Hébert (*Les chambres de bois*), Antonine Maillet (*Pointe-aux-Coques*), and Québec's most prolific writer of fiction, Yves Thériault (*La fille laide, Aaron, Agaguk*).

This was the first generation of modern poets, if by "modern" one means poets for whom poetry is a spiritual adventure and a quest for the absolute. The period was characterized first by four poets of stature and then by a wave of younger writers who undertook a collective poetry-publishing project.

The four influential poets, who were to become models for those coming after them—and for the first time it is Québec poets and not French ones who have this role—are Hector de Saint-Denys Garneau, Anne Hébert, Alain Grandbois, and Rina Lasnier. Each has a distinctive vocabulary and imagery, but all share certain themes: an anguished sense of solitude in an indifferent or hostile world, a haunting awareness of the ebbing away of life in the face of death or destruction, and a hopeless longing for an unattainable joy.

The first collective publishing movement in the history of Québec poetry was launched in 1953 when six poets formed a literary association called L'Hexagone. Over the next twenty years L'Hexagone, directed always by the energetic Gaston Miron, became the most influential force in Québec poetry, publishing by subscription dozens of collections of verse. Its members were active in founding literary magazines like *Liberté* (1959–) and in organizing poetry nights and annual gatherings of Québec poets. The Hexagone poets, Gaston Miron, Jean-Guy Pilon, Gilles Hénault, Roland Giguère, Paul-Marie Lapointe, Michel Van Schendel, Fernand Ouellette, Yves Préfontaine, and others, shared no common doctrine of poetry, but all were convinced of the centrality of poetry in a developing society, and they all would play their part in the literary renascence of the 1960s. French-Canadian poetry had until then been the work of isolated poets; henceforth Québécois poetry would be a collective national endeavor.

It is customary also to date the beginnings of modern Québec theater from this same decade of the 1950s, specifically from the performance of Gratien Gélinas's *Tit-Coq* in May 1948. Gélinas and Marcel Dubé were the most productive playwrights in Québec in the 1950s; their plays presented, in colloquial language, the problems of working-class and lower-middle-class characters imprisoned in a traditional Québec society. Other dramatists revived classical themes (Paul Toupin), introduced a new nationalism into their work (Jacques Ferron), or experimented with the theater of the absurd (Jacques Languirand). Permanent theaters (La Comédie-Canadienne, 1958) and companies (Théâtre du Rideau Vert, 1949; Théâtre du Nouveau Monde, 1952) were established in Montréal during this decade. Much indirect support for theatrical activities and personnel was provided by the French-language radio and television networks of the government-sponsored Canadian Broadcasting Corporation (Radio Canada) and by the French section of the National Film Board of Canada.

By the late 1950s conditions already existed that would result in a vast expansion and enrichment of Québec's cultural life during the following decade. With a population of more than five million Francophones, a highly industrialized economy, and a strong provincial government, Québec was preparing to play a major role in the Canada of the future. Fifteen years after the end of the Second World War, a generation of adolescents was growing up in Québec aware of their place in the global village, of the interests they had in common with former European colonies in the Third World then seeking independence, and of the dominant role of science and technology in the electronic and space age. In such a context the agricultural and clerical patterns of traditional Québec society required massive revision. This transformation of Québec life in the 1960s, arguably the greatest upheaval in the province's history, would constitute the so-called Quiet Revolution.

WORKS CITED

Aubert de Gaspé, Philippe-Ignace-François. *L'influence d'un livre.* 1837. Montréal: HMH-Hurtubise, 1984.

Aubert de Gaspé, Philippe-Joseph. *Les anciens Canadiens.* 1863. Montréal: Fides, 1967. *The Canadians of Old.* Trans. Georgiana M. Pennée. 1864. Trans. Charles G. D. Roberts. 1890. Toronto: McClelland, 1974.

Beauchemin, Nérée. *Son oeuvre.* Ed. Armand Guilmette. Montréal: PU du Québec, 1973–74.

Beaugrand, Honoré. *Jeanne la fileuse.* 1878. Montréal: Fides, 1980.

Bessette, Gérard. *La bagarre.* 1958. Montréal: Cercle du Livre de France, 1969. *The Brawl.* Trans. Marc Lebel and Ronald Sutherland. Montréal: Harvest, 1976.

Bibaud, Michel. *Epîtres, satires, chansons, épigrammes et autres pièces de vers.* 1830. Montréal: Réédition-Québec, 1969.

———. *Histoire du Canada sous la domination française.* 1837. *Histoire du Canada et des Canadiens sous la domination anglaise.* 1844. New York: Johnson, 1968.

Blais, Marie-Claire. *La belle bête.* 1959. Montréal: Cercle du Livre de France, 1968. *Mad Shadows.* Trans. Merloyd Lawrence. Toronto: McClelland, 1971.

Boucher de Boucherville, George. *Une de perdue, deux de trouvées.* 1849–65. Montréal: HMH-Hurtubise, 1973.

Bourassa, Napoléon. *Jacques et Marie.* 1865–66. Montréal: Fides, 1976.

Charlevoix, Pierre-François-Xavier de. *Histoire et description générale de la Nouvelle-France.* . . . 1744. Montréal: Elysée, 1976. *History and General Description of New France.* Trans. John Gilmary Shea. Chicago: Loyola UP, 1962.

Chauveau, Pierre-Joseph-Olivier. *Charles Guérin.* 1846–53. Montréal: Fides, 1978.

Choquette, Ernest. *Claude Paysan.* Montréal: Bishop, 1899.

Conan, Laure [Félicité Angers]. *Angéline de Montbrun.* 1881–82. Montréal: Fides, 1980. *Angéline de Montbrun.* Trans. Yves Brunelle. Toronto: U of Toronto P, 1974.

———. *L'oublié.* 1900. Montréal: Beauchemin, 1958.

Crémazie, Octave. *Oeuvres.* Ed. Odette Condemine. Ottawa: Editions de l'Université d'Ottawa, 1972–76.

Desrosiers, Léo-Paul. *Les engagés du Grand Portage.* 1938. Montréal: Fides, 1980. *The Making of Nicolas Montour.* Trans. Christina van Oordt. Montréal: Harvest, 1978.

Doutre, Joseph. *Les fiancés de 1812.* 1844. Montréal: Réédition-Québec, 1969.

Elie, Robert. *La fin des songes.* 1950. Montréal: Fides, 1968. *Farewell My Dreams.* Trans. Irene Coffin. Toronto: Ryerson, 1954.

Evanturel, Eudore. *Premières poésies.* 1878. Rpt. in *L'oeuvre poétique.* Ed. Guy Champagne. Québec: PU Laval, 1988.

Ferland, Jean-Baptiste-Antoine. *Cours d'histoire du Canada.* 1861–65. New York: Johnson, 1969.

Fréchette, Louis. *Félix Poutré and* Papineau. 1862, 1880. Montréal: Leméac, 1974. *Papineau.* Trans. Eugene Benson and Renate Benson. *Canadian Drama* 7.1 (1981): 51–110.

———. *La légende d'un peuple.* 1887. Montréal: Beauchemin, 1941.

Garneau, François-Xavier. *Histoire du Canada.* . . . 1845–48. Montréal: Amis de l'Histoire, 1969. *History of Canada.* Trans. Andrew Bell. Montréal: Lovell, 1860.

Garneau, Hector de Saint-Denys. *Regards et jeux dans l'espace.* 1937. Montréal: Fides, 1972. *Complete Poems of Saint-Denys Garneau.* Trans. John Glassco. Ottawa: Oberon, 1975.

Gélinas, Gratien. *Tit-Coq.* 1948. Montréal: Quinze, 1981. *Tit-Coq.* Trans. Kenneth Johnstone and Gratien Gélinas. 1950. Toronto: Irwin, 1967.

Gérin-Lajoie, Antoine. *Jean Rivard.* 1862–64. Montréal: HMH-Hurtubise, 1977. *Jean Rivard.* Trans. Vida Bruce. Toronto: McClelland, 1977.

Girard, Rodolphe. *Marie Calumet.* 1904. Montréal: Fides, 1979. *Marie Calumet.* Trans. Irene Currie. Montréal: Harvest, 1976.

Giroux, André. *Au delà des visages.* 1948. Montréal: Fides, 1979.

Grignon, Claude-Henri. *Un homme et son péché.* 1933. Ed. Antoine Sirois and Yvette Francoli. Montréal: PU de Montréal, 1986. *The Woman and the Miser.* Trans. Yves Brunelle. Montréal: Harvest, 1978.

Guèvremont, Germaine. *Le survenant.* 1945. Ed. Yvan Lepage. Montréal: PU de Montréal, 1989. *The Outlander.* 1950. Trans. Eric Sutton. Toronto: McClelland, 1978.

Harvey, Jean-Charles. *Les demi-civilisés.* 1934. Ed. Guildo Rousseau. Montréal: PU de Montréal, 1988. *Sackcloth for Banner.* Trans. Lukin Barette. Toronto: Macmillan, 1938. *Fear's Folly.* Trans. John Glassco. Ottawa: Carleton UP, 1982.

Hébert, Anne. *Les chambres de bois.* 1958. Paris: Seuil, 1985. *The Silent Rooms.* Trans. Kathy Mezei. Don Mills, ON: Musson, 1974.

Hémon, Louis. *Maria Chapdelaine.* 1914. Montréal: Fides, 1980. *Maria Chapdelaine.* Trans. W. H. Blake. Toronto: Macmillan, 1986.

Houlé, Léopold. *Le presbytère en fleurs.* 1929. Montréal: Lévesque, 1933.

Kirby, William. *The Golden Dog.* 1877. Toronto: McClelland, 1969. *Le chien d'or.* Trans. Pamphile Le May. 1884. Québec: Garneau, 1971.

Laberge, Albert. *La Scouine.* 1918. Ed. Paul Wyczynski. Montréal: PU de Montréal, 1986. *Bitter Bread.* Trans. Conrad Dion. Montréal: Harvest, 1977.

Lacombe, Patrice. *La terre paternelle.* 1846. Montréal: Fides, 1981. "The Ancestral Farm." Trans. Yves Brunelle. *French-Canadian Prose Masters: The Nineteenth Century.* Montréal: Harvest, 1978. 139–70.

Lafitau, Joseph-François. *Mœurs des sauvages amériquains comparées aux mœurs des premiers temps. . . .* 1724. Paris: Maspéro, 1983. *The Customs of the American Indians Compared with the Customs of Primitive Times.* Trans. William N. Fenton and Elizabeth L. Moore. Toronto: Champlain Soc., 1974.

Lahontan, Louis-Armand de Lom d'Arce, baron de. *Nouveaux voyages . . . dans l'Amérique septentrionale.* 1703. Montréal: L'Hexagone-Minerve, 1983. *New Voyages to North America.* Trans. unknown. 1703. Facs. ed. New York: Franklin, 1970.

Lambton, John George, earl of Durham. *Report on the Affairs of British North America.* 1839. Toronto: McClelland, 1963.

Langevin, André. *Poussière sur la ville.* 1953. Montréal: Tisseyre, 1975. *Dust over the City.* Trans. John Latrobe and Robert Gottlieb. Toronto: McClelland, 1974.

Lareau, Edmond. *Histoire de la littérature canadienne.* Montréal: John Lovell, 1874.

Le Clercq, Chrestien. *Premier établissement de la foi dans la Nouvelle-France. . . .* 1691. *First Establishment of the Faith in New France.* Trans. John Gilmary Shea. New York: Shea, 1881. AMS facs. ed., 1973.

L'Ecuyer, Eugène. *La fille du brigand.* 1844. Montréal: Bilaudeau, 1914.

Le May, Pamphile. *Essais poétiques.* Québec: Desbarats, 1865.

Lemelin, Roger. *Au pied de la pente douce.* 1944. Montréal: La Presse, 1975. *The Town Below.* Trans. Samuel Putnam. Toronto: McClelland, 1961.

———. *Les Plouffe.* 1948. Montréal: La Presse, 1973. *The Plouffe Family.* Trans. Mary Finch. Toronto: McClelland, 1975.

Lenoir, Joseph. *Oeuvres.* Ed. John Hare and Jeanne d'Arc Lortie. Montréal: PU de Montréal, 1988.

Mailhot, Laurent, and Pierre Nepveu. *La poésie québécoise des origines à nos jours: Anthologie.* Montréal: L'Hexagone, 1980.

Maillet, Antonine. *Pointe-aux-Coques.* 1958. Montréal: Leméac, 1977.

Marie de l'Incarnation. *Word from New France: The Selected Letters of Marie de l'Incarnation.* Trans. Joyce Marshall. Toronto: Oxford UP, 1967.

Marmette, Joseph. *François de Bienville.* 1870. Montréal: Beauchemin, 1924.

Montigny, Louvigny de. *Le bouquet de Mélusine.* Montréal: Carrier, 1928.

Morin, Marie. *Les annales de l'Hôtel-Dieu de Montréal, 1659–1729. . . .* Ed. Ghislaine Legendre. Montréal: PU de Montréal, 1979.

Nelligan, Emile. *Poésies complètes, 1896–1899.* Ed. Luc Lacourcière. Montréal: Fides, 1966. *The Complete Poems of Emile Nelligan.* Trans. Fred Cogswell. Montréal: Harvest, 1983.

Petitjean, Léon, and Henri Rollin. *Aurore, l'enfant martyre.* 1921. *Aurore the Child Martyr.* Trans. M. M. McManus. *Canadian Drama* 14.1 (1988): 83–125.

Rameau de Saint-Père, Edmé. *La France aux colonies. . . .* Paris: Jouby, 1859.

Ringuet [Philippe Panneton]. *Trente arpents.* 1938. Montréal: Fides, 1971. *Thirty Acres.* Trans. Felix Walter and Dorothea Walter. Toronto: McClelland, 1960.

Rivard, Adjutor. *Chez nos gens.* Québec: L'Action Sociale Catholique, 1918.

———. *Chez nous.* 1914. Québec: Garneau, 1976. *Chez nous (Our Old Quebec Home).* Trans. W. H. Blake. Toronto: McClelland, 1924.

Roquebrune, Robert de. *Les habits rouges.* 1923. Montréal: Fides, 1948.

Routhier, Adolphe-Basile. *Le centurion.* Québec: L'Action Sociale, 1909. *The Centurion.* Trans. Lucille P. Borden. St. Louis: Herder, 1910.

Roy, Gabrielle. *Bonheur d'occasion.* 1945. Montréal: Stanké, 1978. *The Tin Flute.* Trans. Alan Brown. Toronto: McClelland, 1980.

Sagard, Gabriel. *Le grand voyage du pays des Hurons. . . .* 1632. Montréal: HMH-Hurtubise, 1976. *The Long Journey to the Country of the Hurons.* Trans. H. H. Langton. 1939. New York: Greenwood, 1968.

Savard, Félix-Antoine. *Menaud, maître-draveur.* 1937. Montréal: Fides, 1982. *Boss of the River.* Trans. Alan Sullivan. Toronto: Ryerson, 1947. *Master of the River.* Trans. Richard Howard. Montréal: Harvest, 1976.

Taché, Joseph-Charles. *Forestiers et voyageurs.* 1863. Montréal: Fides, 1946.

Thériault, Yves. *Aaron.* 1954. Montréal: Quinze, 1981.

———. *Agaguk.* 1958. Montréal: Quinze, 1981. *Agaguk.* Trans. Miriam Chapin. Toronto: Ryerson, 1963.

———. *La fille laide.* 1950. Montréal: Quinze, 1981.

Tremaine, Marie. *A Bibliography of Canadian Imprints, 1751–1800.* Toronto: U of Toronto P, 1952.

Viau, Roger. *Au milieu la montagne.* Montréal: Beauchemin, 1951.

Patrick Imbert

FASCISM, MARXISM, LIBERAL DEMOCRACY: FIFTY YEARS OF QUÉBEC LITERATURE

> Just as Kundera characterizes the novel in communist
> countries as serving the ideological needs of the
> ruling elite, literature in capitalist countries often
> serves to reinforce the values of a dominant
> economic establishment.
>> D. C. Davies, *Literary Theory and the Novel*

"THE PROBLEMS TO be resolved here are much less complicated than in Europe. The social question does not exist in Canada and cannot exist in the present condition of our economic life," said Edmond de Nevers in 1896 (246).[1] Unlike European society, Québec was presented as a kind of unanimous conglomerate. Literature, in this context, has often been used as a tool for publicizing common goals or for making explicit a common ideal; it has frequently been a privileged agent of nationalism that allows a group to avoid any reference to class stratifications. It thus became possible to deny the fact that, if there were few powerful French-Canadian industrialists, there was a French-Canadian middle class that was disseminating, with or without the help of the Catholic church, an ideology designed to perpetuate the status quo:

> Capital is inextricably mixed with talents, those to which the Bible refers to as others do and also to hereditary and personal resources which are at the root of every civilization. (Pelletier 67)

Sylvie Bernier has observed that almost all the writers who were members of the Montréal literary movements La Relève (a group founded in 1934 that was trying to renew Catholicism) or L'Hexagone (a small publishing house active in the 1960s and still in existence that put out mostly modern poetry) were of middle-class origin. If not, they soon reached a middle-class status, thanks to the accumulation of cultural information and rewards that opened doors to the liberal professions. French-Canadian literature is linked to two complementary processes: involvement in nationalism and avoidance of the issue of class struggle. One of the characters in Pierre de Grandpré's novel *La patience des justes* is symptomatic of this situation when he asserts, seventy years after Edmond de Nevers, that "in this country the social question is the national question, there is no other one" (42). Such an aphorism is, in fact, reinterpreted in the same year (1966) by the influential cultural journal *Parti pris*. For this group, too—in keeping with a socialist approach to Québec society—the national question is the social question.

Fascism versus Class Struggle

Fascism

Two years after the beginning of the Depression, Jean Bruchési showed a strong sympathy to "necessary dictatorships." From Belgrade to Warsaw, from Budapest to Rome, the proclamation of nationalist principles produced a kind of consensus or united front against Communists, five million of whom would be sent to concentration camps along with Gypsies, intellectuals, Jews, and other opponents to these regimes. Bruchési opposed proletarianism and internationalism, both advocated by Moscow after the quasi-elimination of the Anarchists (except in Spain, a situation analyzed by Angelica Balabanoff in *My Life as a Rebel*). Bruchési goes as far as to say that internationalism is sometimes fostered "by American Jews with Bolshevists' faces" (45). This racist expression, which alludes to a broader context in which trade unions were said to be (and sometimes were) infiltrated by Bolshevists—specifically, fascination in North America with the Soviet Union (see Reed) and a certain economic cooperation between banks and industries in the United States and the Soviet Union—was ridiculed by Louis Dantin in *Gloses critiques* and "Complainte d'un chômeur," a violent text for its time. However, Dantin was largely ignored by critics. The only nationalism Bruchési rejected was Russian nationalism, because it was linked to world revolution and to the triumph of the people's interests. He never expressed concern about the economic crisis devastating

Europe and Canada; he only exalted the status quo and submission to hierarchy as incarnated by the ideology of the mother country and the mother church.

Bruchési's attitude had much in common with the political movement called L'Ecole Nationale Populaire, which published, among other works, the *Antibolchevic Manual* (March 1931). The group was concerned about the economic situation, however, and published a journal, also called *L'école nationale populaire*, until August 1936. Its writers regularly asserted, for instance, that Sunday labor would lead workers to communism. Such a concern is still alive, although the political coloration has changed. In 1986, big businesses wanted stores to be open on Sundays. However, the majority of the population, the church, and many small retailers were against this change in the municipal bylaws. Stores are still closed on Sunday.

In 1942 Rex Desmarchais published a novel, *La Chesnaie*, inspired by Salazar, dictator of Portugal, in which he violently criticized democracy:

> La démocratie parlementaire telle que pratiquée au Québec décomposait les forces de la nation, les pourissait toutes du haut en bas de l'échelle sociale. (200)

> Parliamentary democracy as practiced in Québec was decomposing the strength of the nation, which became rotten from the top to the bottom of the social ladder.

Fascism as a political movement was represented in Québec by Adrien Arcand, a nationalist who took his inspiration from Mussolini as well as from Salazar. Although its popular support was relatively small, Desmarchais's book was ideologically important in Québec. Its appeal derived from its portrayal of the disillusionment of a people who saw no alternative to the economic evil from which they were suffering.

Literature and the Social Question

During the "dirty thirties," the economic crisis had a devastating impact on Canada, but few French-Canadian literary works expressed any deep concern. (As Irene Baird, for instance, has shown, the situation was somewhat different in English Canada.) Censorship, fear, and ideology went hand in hand in fostering agriculturism, in exalting nationalistic roots, or in promoting a superficial exoticism related to art for art's sake.

One exception has to be noted: the publication of *Quand j'parle tout seul*, by Jean Narrache (under the name Emile Coderre), which sold six thousand copies in 1933. Although Coderre was sympathetic to the dreadful plight of those without jobs, he did not go so far as to criticize the economic system. Indeed, Coderre rejected trade unions and strikes and saw the real solution to the problems of the poor in the exaltation of eternal life. Populism never established any link whatsoever between theory and practice. Coderre published a second book in 1961, *J'parle tout seul quand Jean Narrache*, with a foreword reminding the readers of the Depression and of the conditions people then endured. But a back-cover comment by Rita Simard, geared toward nationalism and humanity in general, again obscures the possibility of seeing a social reality correctable by social laws:

> Jean Narrache is the Canadian poet who sang like Jehan Rictus of our customs, our defects, even our vices, but always in a subtle and good style.

One wonders if being poor and jobless is "a vice," as is often asserted by the cliché emphasizing that the unemployed do not want to work.

During the 1930s the Depression was not an important theme. Later, when it was no longer dangerous to propagate radical ideas and the Second World War had essentially solved the unemployment problem, the thematic of the economic crisis reappeared. Just after the war, however, it was still linked to a populist way of treating social problems, as is shown by *Le cathéchisme des électeurs* (published by Union Nationale sympathizers) and *Zirska immigránte inconnue*, by J.-M. Carette. Published in 1947 but set between 1929 and 1939, *Zirska* castigates immigrants for importing Bolshevist ideas. In so doing, Carette uses ideas that had already been applied in 1917, when immigrants from Austria and Hungary had been interned in camps, or in 1941, when the Japanese in Canada suffered the same fate. Similarly, Henri Degluyn, in his political novel *Les amours d'un communiste*, dedicates a chapter to the communists, who should be put into concentration camps in Québec. This is a solution for which Carette provides the problem:

> Par milliers les mineurs d'Outre-mer, qu'une progagande infâme avait arrachés à leur foyer, venaient chercher dans l'Ouest, l'or qu'on leur avait fait miroiter là-bas. Les compagnies de transport tâchaient d'éblouir la population des vieux pays par des mensonges effrontés. Pendant que l'immigrant se voyait porter par les faveurs du Gouvernement fédéral, les Nôtres se disputaient la vie avec peine et misère. C'est ainsi qu'un grand nombre de bolchévistes s'infiltrèrent chez nous, semant la révolte et l'incendie dans toutes les classes du corps social. (*Zirska* xii)

By the thousands, miners from overseas that an infamous propaganda pulled out of their homes came to the West to get the gold that was promised to them. Transport companies were trying to draw the populations from the old countries by outright lies. While immigrants were favored by the federal government, our people were struggling hard. This is why so many Bolshevists were infiltrating our homeland, sowing revolt and wreaking havoc among all the classes of society.

It is interesting to note a few contradictions in Carette's book. On the one hand, transport companies are resented for exploiting people with the encouragement of the federal government. On the other hand, Bolshevist immigrants are condemned for destroying the social peace. A racist and reactionary ideology is thereby crudely exposed. French Canada is presented as menaced by a double conspiracy of, first, the federal government and the big companies and, second, of agents of Moscow, including, indiscriminately, trade union organizers, intellectuals, and anyone criticizing the Québec government. This paranoia about the threat of communism was in keeping with legislation to repress most dissidents, enacted by the Québec government. The Loi du Cadenas, or Law of the Locker (1948), which was suppressed by the federal government in 1957, allowed the police to search and close down any store, apartment, or other place in which "seditious" literature was found.

But soon after the Second World War, other social theories started to gain credence. Many avant-garde intellectuals linked nationalism to the social question and argued the necessity of a movement of national liberation. A new generation was attaining prominence, including the painter Borduas—who, along with intellectuals and writers belonging to the automatist group (inspired by French surrealism), signed the manifesto entitled *Refus global*—and those publishing in journals like *Place publique, La nouvelle relève*, and particularly *Parti pris*. A new problematic, which would eventually give rise to the Quiet Revolution and to the overcoming of its shortcomings, was taking shape. (The Quiet Revolution—which started when Duplessis, head of the Union Nationale political party, died, in 1959—led peacefully to a redefinition of the values of Québec society as a whole, to the creation of modern institutions, and to the implementation of social programs.) Some advocates pointed out that the economic crisis was permanent because the economically weak lived in an environment in which deprivation was everywhere. Such views are clearly shown by Roger Viau in the novel entitled *Au milieu la montagne*. Thus, at the beginning of the 1950s, two main currents emerged: socialism and social democracy.

Social Question = National Question = Revolution

The Theoretical Texts

> Le chainon le plus faible qui fait sauter la chaîne, comme enseigne le
> camarade Staline, sûrement ce n'est pas cette histoire de traduction.
> Et puis se méfier du nationalisme. Mais utiliser chaque fois qu'on le
> peut les aspirations nationales. (Gélinas 197)

> The weakest link that causes the chain to break, as is taught by comrade
> Stalin, is certainly not this question of translation. Moreover, one has
> to be careful about nationalism. But one has to use national aspirations
> each time it is possible to do so.

As Pierre Gélinas emphasizes, Marxists are aware of the need to play on
both proletarian internationalism and the defense of local interests in order
to counter the internationalism of trusts, multinationals, and banks. This
problematic became acute after the Second World War, when a consumer
economy following the United States model was put into place in Québec.

At that time, there were violent quarrels over the means to be used to
reform or to revolutionize society. As liberal democracy emerged, replacing
the old Duplessist regime with thinkers like Gérard Pelletier and Pierre
Elliot Trudeau and literary and cultural journals like *La nouvelle relève*
and *Liberté*, a polemic raged between two radical groups, the Automatists,
represented by Paul-Emile Borduas and Claude Gauvreau, and those, like
Gélinas, who adhered to a more orthodox Marxism. Gauvreau criticizes
Zhdanovism, the official Soviet aesthetic doctrine linked to social realism:

> Zhdanovism was and still is an official aesthetic doctrine in the Soviet Union.
> Why is it so? It is so because the Soviet Union—for thirty-five years—has
> been a state capitalist society built by mediocre thinkers (among them the
> seminarist Djougachvili), established and maintained for the benefit of a new
> privileged class, a class of bureaucrats educated like petit bourgeois and
> whose conceptions and aspirations are those of a pre-Soviet society. (67)

This direct attack on the state, which in Québec was in the hands of the
private sector, caused some concern. As many saw, freedom could be
enjoyed only by well-off individuals who manipulated governments. Maurice Robillard pointed out that economic and cultural deprivations are
twins. *Place publique*, the journal in which his article appeared, was one
of the forerunners of *Parti pris*, with its clear-cut positions associating class
struggle, nationalism, and Marxism.

In the context of the cold war, the nationalist movements and the rise of national liberation fronts were a strategic weapon against free enterprise and liberal internationalism, the cultural framework of which can be linked to a definition of postmodernism (see, for instance, Scarpetta). Nobody, however, seemed to remember that Polish, Lithuanian, or Finnish nationalisms were efficiently used, during the Bolshevist revolution, against the class struggle and the Soviet Union. But at the time of the Referendum, in Québec, in 1976, a new conception of nationalism was surfacing. People were asked if they would agree to give the Parti Québécois a mandate to negotiate with the federal government an "entente" that could have led to a parting from the Confederation. The "no" side (Liberal Party) and the "yes" side (Parti Québécois, made up, from the start, of groups from the left, center-left, and right, like the Conservative and the Social Credit parties) were seen by the "truly" left wing and Marxist orthodoxy as two aspects of a fundamentally identical political and economical system. This view gains strength when one notes that the Parti Québécois succeeded in eliminating René Lévesque and most other left-leaning members of the party. For many, the consequence was that the political formation lost its social democratic appeal. Therefore, in 1976, Marxists advised voters to go to the polls but to write *J'annule* (I cancel). This gesture represented the only means to show, in this heated political context, the presence of the Nationalist class struggle, resting as much on provincial problems as on international ones.

The rejection of a simple duality ("yes" or "no" votes) is apparent in many articles published by *Parti pris*. Similarly, the model of the industrial and information society that creates wealth but also economic and cultural deprivation is almost as much criticized in its Soviet imperialist dimension as in its American one:

> [I]nterplanetary travels of Russians and Americans are causing starvation in India, as the Vietnam War is perpetuating black ghettos in Chicago, Los Angeles, and New York. (Gagnon 30)

The point of reference is displaced toward a Third World trying to reorganize. One rejects Goliath in order to save the nationalist and revolutionary David and to foster a national identity, synonymous, for a decade, with world revolution. The dualism between nationalism and internationalism is overcome by the use of dialectics, allowing a new synthesis even if Charles Gagnon is obliged to recognize that the majority of militants and workers are still far behind.

Literature and Revolution: Dissidence

Parti pris and *Place publique* are dedicated to publishing articles of sociopolitical importance as well as some literary texts. In the field of literature,

however—except for some poems and a few novels like *Ville rouge*, by
Jean Jules Richard; *Au milieu la montagne*, by Viau; or *Les vivants, les
morts et les autres*, by Gélinas—nothing of real social significance appeared
before the beginning of the 1960s. Then, throughout the sixties and seventies, *Parti pris* drew well-known writers like Jacques Ferron, whose left-
leaning social and political positions are reflected in his plays, novels, and
short stories. Thus the Quiet Revolution, fostered by the election of the
liberal government of Jean Lesage in 1960, led, after the strike at the
newspaper *La presse* in 1964, to a more radical conception of society, at
least among trade unionists, students, artists, and many intellectuals. Ferron (*La nuit*), Marie-France Dubois (*Le passage secret*), Pierre Gravel (*A
perte de temps*), Rémi Jodoin (*En d'ssour*), Francine Marcel (*Quarante-deux
ans de service*), and publishing houses such as Parti Pris, Editions Québécoises, and Editions de l'Aurore all demanded major social changes and
linked independence with both the class struggle and a renewal of literary
form and style.

But literature, in one way or another, still kept its distance from orthodox
lines and from bureaucratic policies. First, almost everything (novels, poems)
published by Editions Québécoises was considered by the critics as non-
literary, and books like those by Marcel (a worker who wrote militant
poetry) or Jodoin (a worker who told his life story) suffered the same fate.
Second, many writers and artists, like Gauvreau, contested or simply parodied any party line or group strategies, which they saw as static reflections
asserting, without subtlety, a crude truth. Most of the artists and writers
at this time worked for the Parti Québécois and its separatist program;
many of them were also deeply involved in the struggle to permeate the
new party with Marxist or Socialist ideas. However, they did not always
react positively to the sometimes bureaucratic minds of organizers, intellectuals, or syndicalists, who referred to a stricter orthodoxy or to precise
guidelines and tactics. In this situation, many writers employed irony to
assert freedom of expression as a basic right that had nothing to do with
orders:

Ses manuels révolutionnaires avaient été relégués dans une petite pièce du
sous-sol: 'ma bibliothèque' disait-il fièrement. Un peu avant la guerre, sé-
minariste, il s'était converti à Marx et à Lénine. Il vint à Montréal et fut reçu
comme l'envoyé de Dieu. Sans être prolétaire dans toute la force du mot, il
était à tout le moins un authentique indigène. Les camarades illico de le
promouvoir secrétaire du Parti. (Ferron, *La Charette* 27)

His revolutionary manuals had been relegated to a small basement room.
"My library," he said proudly. Before the war he was a seminarist and con-
· verted to Marx and Lenin. He came to Montréal and was acclaimed as an
envoy of God. Not being a proletarian in the full sense of the term, he was,

at least, an authentic indigenous. Comrades immediately promoted him party secretary.

In the novels, the discourse of the party was mocked, was seen as analogous to the religious ideology that had prevailed in Québec for a century. This attitude can be found, for instance, in such writers as André Major (*La chair de poule* 7), Serge Losique (*De Z à A* 37), and Réjean Ducharme (*L'hiver de force* 203). The analogy even allowed some writers to reject proletarian internationalism and class struggle in the name of a new unanimism. At a certain point, however, a scission appeared that opened the way to nationalism moving away from Third World and radical political positions.

Dissidence and Style

At the end of the 1960s, many writers followed a path explored by Gauvreau in what he called his "explorean" language. They decided to work on language itself, as a material base, a kind of material unconscious that, theoretically, receives its determination from production forces. This was a goal similar to what Wilhelm Reich had attempted to achieve forty years before:

> The way in which a social system reproduces itself structurally in human beings can only be grasped concretely, whether in theory or in practice, if we understand the way in which social institutions, ideologies, life-forms, etc., mold the instinctual apparatus. (20)

Exploring language was therefore seen as an important aspect of the revolutionary process, most notably in its popular and working-class dimension. The exploration, however, often led to a more literary deconstruction and to a split between intellectuals, artists, and workers. Thus language exploration, which gradually rejected the working-class sociolect and also a lower-middle-class or middle-class mimetic discourse, was more and more intertextualized, more and more turned inward to a tautological code. It became a fashionable way of writing that was theorized, for instance, by Jacques Derrida. The change was in keeping with a society that rests on a generalized exchange and has lost sight of the referent while stopping short of proposing any legitimate goal. The code validates itself through decontextualized intertextuality and language games, in a process analogous to the way the media do not really inform the public (see, for example, *Mass Media, Ideologies and the Revolutionary Movement*, by Armand Mattelart).

The absence of historical consciousness, as Orwell showed in *Nineteen Eighty-Four*, ineluctably shifts the problematic from the subject and his or her hopes to the overwhelming power of the system. The shift is illustrated by one of the preoccupations of the Trilateral Commission, a group of journalists, politicians, business executives, and professors who analyzed the state of democracies according to the philosophy of the Rockefeller family:

> What is in short supply in democratic societies today is thus not consensus on the rules of the game but a sense of purpose as to what one should achieve by playing the game. In the past, people have found their purposes in religion, in nationalism, and in ideology. But neither church, nor state, nor class now commands people's loyalties. (*Report* 159)

In this context, the aim of economists and politicians is to stress a democratic consensus that can be activated only by the realization of a common goal. Difficult times can provide this goal. Therefore, but without any mention of social classes, the theme of the new economic crisis shifted from social liberalism to a more conservative approach toward problems.

Dissidence and the Acceleration of the System

In the 1970s and 1980s many literary texts play the code for the code, exchange for exchange. Consider, for example, novels by Jean-Marie Poupart, Louis Gauthier, or Ducharme, which play on a kind of intertextuality often closely related to parody (Imbert). In this case, two possibilities are left open. Among those favoring Marxism and those inclined to liberalism, reactions are often analogous. When there is no belief in a referent anymore, when every text, moreover, is a lie, as Solzhenitsyn states, and this lie is covered up by the doctrine of socialist realism or by an emphasis on a discourse's claims to reality, the revelation of historical truths is seen as an absolute necessity. *August 1914* and *The Gulag Archipelago* are examples of this reaction because, as demonstrated by René Girard, a semantic and logical coherence is reinstated by the very possibility of exposing lie as lie through the revelation of genocide. In this regard, groups like Amnesty International can be seen as an important semantic enterprise showing that if it is impossible to discover the truth (an impossibility any dictatorship or any messianic ideology is prone to deny), it is still possible to point out a lie.

In the West those in favor of literary tradition and of bourgeois realism also reject the new literature that is seen as mere language games. For other reasons, too, those who, in the West, espouse Marxism or socialist realism reject this literary endeavor, which they see as bourgeois or as being easily recuperated by an imperialist internationalism, allowing it to evade the charge of social exploitation. These positions, which have been touched on by Roland Barthes in *Le degré zéro de l'écriture*, reject artistic and literary postmodernity.

Marxist countries understood earlier than democratic countries that artists, writers, social researchers, and intellectuals, all working in the so-called liberal art domains, were an important part of what was at stake in society. Such an understanding was one reason why writers like Aragon and Gide were invited to congresses in the Soviet Union. If liberal countries, and particularly the United States, invested money and energy in the sciences, administration, and the media in Europe after the Second World War, they tended to neglect the liberal arts. After students, intellectuals, and artists during the 1960s challenged the social order in Québec, in Europe (May 1968), and in the United States itself (against the Vietnam War), efforts were made, by the Trilateral Commission and other establishment groups, to win over the protestors or, at least, to contextualize their artistic or intellectual output. Their works could be interpreted through paradigms, through a set of meaningful readings by critics sympathetic to the dominant ideology. Interpretation is naturally redefined, from time to time, through the shifts in international relations from cold war, to peace, to Star Wars. This play on a context in evolution—which rests, at a deeper level, on an immutable semantic grid—represents a certain danger (as was well understood by the members of the Trilateral Commission) for society and for the intellectuals as well, who have no real control of the context.

The postmodern literature produced in Québec by Hubert Aquin (*Prochain épisode*), Jacques Brossard, and others accelerates the system of exchange of commodities or of exchange of significations and tries to escape from a fixed discourse tending to reduce that system to a meaning that, from the point of view of writers, is lost or, maybe, never was. In these texts the delegitimization of the narrative, of the rationalization processes, of the beliefs and of the theme of the economic crisis, takes place. Therefore they have to be *commented* on in order to fit once more into such and such an ideology. The constant interpretation and production of discourse is obviously more efficient, ideologically speaking, than the pure rejection of problematic texts through silence or censorship. Saturation is more powerful than elimination.

The year 1930 is said to have been linked to overproduction of goods. The seventies, as Jean Baudrillard notes, were linked to reproduction of the same patterns—economic patterns, signification patterns, and so on —and were at the origin of an economic and ideological crisis simulacrum serving the status quo. In a situation of production without any end in sight, thus without any meaning, a situation that contributed to the social criticism of the 1960s, "one had" to reinvent fear of deprivation by reviving Malthus—but Malthus transformed into an ecologist—and by spreading, with the help of an occidentalized orientalism, the successful doctrine of E. F. Schuhmacher and his followers.

However, lack and excess are two aspects of the same economic process, activating the power of production and the desire of consumption among the masses. This successful "show," produced twenty-four hours a day by the media, fuels *economism* and presents it as a universal. Thus the economic code explains everything, even itself, and gives a new meaning to production and to the stimulation (through advertising and marketing) of consumption. Reactivating values and slowing down the acceleration of the system hides the tautology inherent in this system, of which criticism and most literary productions are an integral part.

NOTE

[1] Unless otherwise indicated, all translations are my own.

WORKS CITED

Aquin, Hubert. *Point de fuite.* Montréal: Cercle du Livre de France, 1971.

———. *Prochain épisode.* Montréal: Cercle du Livre de France, 1965. *Prochain épisode.* Trans. Penny Williams. Toronto: McClelland, 1967.

Baird, Irene. *Waste Heritage.* Toronto: Macmillan, 1939.

Balabanoff, Angelica. *My Life as a Rebel.* New York: Greenwood, 1968.

Barthes, Roland. *Le degré zéro de l'écriture.* Paris: Seuil, 1953.

Baudrillard, Jean. *Pour une critique de l'économie politique du signe.* Paris: Gallimard, 1972.

Bernier, Sylvie. "Caractéristiques socio-économiques des mouvements littéraires québécois." *Réception critique des textes littéraires québécois.* Sherbrooke, PQ: Université de Sherbrooke, 1982. 7–41.

Brossard, Jacques. *Le sang du souvenir.* Montréal: La Presse, 1976.

Bruchési, Jean. *Aux marches de l'Europe.* Montréal: Lévesque, 1932.

Carette, J.-M. *Zirska immigrante inconnue.* Ste-Marie de Beauce, PQ: Brousseau, 1947.

Le catéchisme des électeurs. 2nd ed. Montréal: Saint-Martin, 1974.

Coderre, Emile. *J'parle tout seul quand Jean Narrache.* Montréal: L'Homme, 1961.

———. *Quand j'parle tout seul.* Montréal: Lévesque, 1933.

Dantin, Louis. "Complainte d'un chômeur." *Le jour* 1 July 1939: 4.

————. *Gloses critiques.* Montréal: Lévesque, 1935.

Davies, D. C. "Literary Theory and the Novel: Literature in a Political Context." *Atkinson Review of Canadian Studies* 2.1 (1984): 10–17.

Degluyn, Henri. *Les amours d'un communiste.* Montréal: 1965.

Derrida, Jacques. *De la grammatologie.* Paris: Minuit, 1967. *Of Grammatology.* Trans. G. C. Spivak. Baltimore: Johns Hopkins UP, 1976.

Desmarchais, Rex. *La Chesnaie.* Montréal: L'Arbre, 1942.

Dubois, Marie-France. *Le passage secret.* Montréal: Parti Pris, 1975.

Ducharme, Réjean. *L'hiver de force.* Paris: Gallimard, 1973. *Wild to Mild.* Trans. Robert Guy-Scully. Montréal: Heritage-Amerique, 1980.

Ferron, Jacques. *La nuit.* Montréal: Parti Pris, 1965.

————. *La Charette.* Montréal: Parti Pris, 1968.

Gagnon, Charles. "Pourquoi la révolution?" *Parti pris* 5.5 (1968): 18–30.

Gauthier, Louis. *Anna.* Montréal: Cercle du Livre de France, 1967.

Gauvreau, Claude. "Aragonie et surrationnel." *La Revue socialiste* 5 (1961): 67–68.

Gélinas, Pierre. *Les vivants, les morts et les autres.* Montréal: Cercle du Livre de France, 1959.

Girard, René. *Des choses cachées depuis la fondation du monde.* Paris: Livre de Poche, 1978. *Things Hidden since the Foundation of the World.* Trans. J. Messer. London: Athlone, 1987.

Grandpré, Pierre de. *La patience des justes.* Montréal: Cercle du Livre de France, 1966.

Gravel, Pierre. *A perte de temps.* Montréal: Parti Pris, 1969.

Imbert, Patrick. *Roman québécois contemporain et clichés.* Ottawa: Editions de l'Université d'Ottawa, 1983.

Jodoin, Rémi. *En d'ssour.* Montréal: Québécoises, 1973.

Lévesque, Andrée. *Virage à gauche interdit.* Montréal: Boréal, 1985.

Losique, Serge. *De Z à A.* Montréal: Jour, 1969.

Major, André. *La chair de poule.* Montréal: Parti Pris, 1965.

Major, Robert. *Parti-pris: Idéologies et littérature.* Montréal: HMH-Hurtubise, 1979.

Marcel, Francine. *Quarante-deux ans de service.* Montréal: Québécoises, 1973.

Mattelart, Armand. *Mass Media, Ideologies and the Revolutionary Movement.* Sussex: Harvester, 1980.

Nevers, Edmond de. *L'avenir du peuple canadien-français.* 1896. Montréal: Fides, 1964.

Orwell, George. *Nineteen Eighty-Four.* Harmondsworth: Penguin, 1954.

Pelletier, Albert. "Nos catholiques à la remorque de Moscou." *Les idées* 5.2 (1937): 65–73.

Poupart, Jean-Marie. *Que le diable emporte le titre.* Montréal: Jour, 1969.

Reed, John. *Ten Days That Shook the World.* New York: Modern Library, 1935.

Reich, Wilhelm. *Sex-Pol.* New York: Vintage, 1966.

Report on the Governability of Democracy to the Trilateral Commission. Ed. M. Crozier, S. P. Huntington, J. Watanaki. New York: New York UP, 1975.

Richard, Jean Jules. *Ville rouge.* Montréal: Tranquille, 1949.

Robillard, Maurice. "Le règne des castes." *Place publique* 3 (1952): 14–20.

Scarpetta, Guy. *Eloge du cosmopolitisme.* Paris: Grasset, 1979.

Schuhmacher, E. F. *Small Is Beautiful.* New York: Harper, 1973.

Solzhenitsyn, Aleksandr. *August 1914.* London: Bodley Head, 1972.

———. *The Gulag Archipelago.* New York: Harper, 1973.

Viau, Roger. *Au milieu la montagne.* Montréal: Beauchemin, 1951.

Mary Jean Green

THE NOVEL IN QUÉBEC: THE FAMILY PLOT AND THE PERSONAL VOICE

THE SUBJECTIVE VISION and personal voice that have become commonplaces of modern fiction were relatively slow to assume primacy in Québec. Almost until the 1960s, the era of modernization and secularization known as the Quiet Revolution, the focus of the Québec novel was not the isolated individual but the family group. The history of Québec fiction is thus very much the story of the evolution of what I will call the "family plot" and the way in which it has influenced developments in novelistic form.

Just as the large Québec family was closely linked to the agricultural economy that gave it sustenance, the family plot was originally associated with a literary form, unique to Québec, known as the *roman de la terre* (literally, the novel of the land). The first example of the *roman de la terre*, written by Patrice Lacombe and published in 1846, also provides the first articulation of the family plot, and its title clearly indicates the association of the land with the patriarchal family: *La terre paternelle*. A family, rather than an individual, is the novel's protagonist, and the central drama—as in so many *romans de la terre*—is the transmission of the heritage, the land, from father to son, an end that is finally attained after many obstacles have been overcome (Boynard-Frot 59). Like many nineteenth-century Québec writers, Lacombe seems more concerned with communicating his moral vision than the physical or psychological reality of life in rural Québec. But he provides a clear statement of a theme that would come to dominate the *roman de la terre*, as it was a central tenet of the dominant ideology: prosperity (or, in ideological terms, francophone cultural survival) is to be found only in close contact with the land and not in the corrupt and wretched cities. Equally in tune with the ideological discourse of his time is Lacombe's vision of the family, with authority vested in the father, as the basic unit of a hierarchical society (Laflèche 84–104).

The family plot set forth in almost schematic form by Lacombe persists through the nineteenth century and stands in the background of Louis Hémon's *Maria Chapdelaine*. Although written by a Frenchman who spent less than two years in Canada, *Maria Chapdelaine* must be considered in any discussion of the evolution of Québec novelistic form: it was proposed as a "model of Canadian literature" in the preface to its first Montréal edition, and critics did, in fact, use it as a standard of comparison for decades (Deschamps et al. 45, 210). Hémon's perspective as an outsider —a very sympathetic one—may account for the attention he gave to describing the details of daily life that had been overlooked by earlier writers. But, of course, this emphasis may also be attributed to the influence of the nineteenth-century French realist and naturalist traditions, from which writers in Québec had been cut off for political and ideological reasons. Hémon's attentiveness to reality also led him, for the first time in Québec literature, to portray the hardships, as well as the natural beauty, of life in a northern climate. The changing seasons, which provide the structure of the novel, are not all mystic moments of green fields and sparkling snow: Hémon describes swarms of summer mosquitoes, September drought, the barrenness and overt hostility of the winter landscape. It is this nuanced portrait of rural life that provides the conflicting forces in Maria's drama, when, after the death of her beloved François Paradis, she must decide between two suitors who represent the alternatives of remaining on the land or leaving for an easier life in the mill towns of the United States. In Maria's dilemma Hémon provides an allegorical representation of a problem facing the Québec people at the time—and, indeed, through the last half of the nineteenth century. And, surely not coincidentally, the mysterious "voices" that determine her decision repeat the arguments of generations of Québec clerics in favor of life on the land.

Despite his rather surprising sensitivity to contemporary Québec ideological discourse, Hémon effects several major displacements in the traditional family plot. Although he creates a strong and active father in Samuel Chapdelaine, the heritage is transmitted not from father to son but, really, from mother to daughter: the event that precipitates Maria's decision is the death of her mother, and the real basis of her choice is her determination to repeat her mother's life. Another significant change is Hémon's choice of protagonist: not the family as a whole, as in *La terre paternelle*, nor a strong male figure, as in Pierre-Joseph-Olivier Chauveau's *Charles Guérin* or Antoine Gérin-Lajoie's *Jean Rivard*, but a woman. And Hémon's heroine participates in the feminine virtues of the women of her time, as well as their limited sphere of action. These limitations are accurately portrayed in the novel itself, to the point where they serve as a characterization of Maria. When we contrast her activity with that of a male protagonist like Jean Rivard, who founds an entire community, or even that of her father, who is continually opening up new land, it becomes clear that Maria does not actually do much. Although Hémon devotes long, lyrical passages to the work of the fields and, particularly, the clearing of land, he does not linger on descriptions of women's housework. Maria's most frequent activity in the novel is that of waiting—waiting for the bread to bake, waiting for François Paradis to come back, waiting for the winter to end. Like her mother, Maria almost always remains shut up in the house (except for a few visits to the equally enclosed space of the church), and she is repeatedly shown looking at the outside world through a window that, most often, is rendered opaque by frost or the blackness of night. François offers her the sole avenue of escape from her enclosed world, as he accompanies her on the blueberry-picking expedition. But this possibility is shut off when François dies precisely because of his venturing off into the winter landscape. Maria chooses, in the end, to remain enclosed in space and also in time, whose repetitive nature is represented by the cycle of the seasons and the message of the "voices": "Au pays de Québec, rien ne doit mourir et rien ne doit changer" 'In Québec nothing must die and nothing must change' (213).

Maria's virtues are similarly unlike those exhibited by previous Québec male protagonists, or even by her adventurous father and fiancé. Like them, she is courageous and faithful to tradition, but she also displays qualities generally more valued in women than in men: patience, submissiveness, and resignation. It is possible to ask why, when previous writers had seen the representative Québec figure as an active man, Hémon chose to make his central character a submissive woman.[1] It may well have been a recognition, perhaps unconscious, of what later intellectuals would see as the victimized condition of the Québec people, whose effort to survive as a culture took the form of self-enclosure in a rural existence and stress on the passive virtues of resignation and submission to authority. Certainly, Hémon may have been influenced by the important female figures who dominated the nineteenth-century French novel, but such characters as Balzac's Eugénie Grandet, Flaubert's Emma Bovary, and Zola's Gervaise Lantier are also presented primarily as victims of an oppressive milieu. In Hémon's representation of Maria Chapdelaine, we have not only the first hard look at the conditions of rural existence in the Québec novel but also, perhaps, as has been suggested by Deschamps et al., the first critical appraisal of the plight of the Québec people.

But a novel's meaning is always determined in part by its readers. Québec critics at the time responded immediately to the familiar ideological theses evoked by Maria's choice and, particularly, by the ideal of the *défricheur* (clearer of new land) so heroically embodied in Samuel Chapdelaine. Hémon's novel quickly became an active element in the campaign to encourage settlement of northern lands as an alternative to emigration; in fact, Québec's minister of colonization in 1927 described an award-winning woman settler as "Maria Chapdelaine, l'épouse et la mère" 'a Maria Chapdelaine become wife and mother' (Deschamps et al. 21–37). Accustomed to reading the family plot according to the patriarchal model, Québec readers had no difficulty in giving primacy to the role of Samuel Chapdelaine, and they managed to ignore the way in which Hémon had effected a displacement of the family's center.

If Hémon's subtle implications could be ignored, direct contestation was another matter. Two years after the first Canadian edition of *Maria Chapdelaine*, Albert Laberge's *La Scouine*, a series of short episodes held together by the structuring principle of the family plot, appeared. The title character here is also a woman, a youngest daughter who never marries —a choice that points up Laberge's subversion of the proper family hierarchy. Physically and morally repulsive, Paulima has received the nickname *la Scouine* because she habitually smells of urine, as a result of her bed-wetting. Although she does not play as central a role as Maria Chapdelaine, her ugly and destructive spirit dominates the world of the characters.

Laberge ostensibly follows the normal development of the family plot, in that one of the sons inherits the family farm and runs it prosperously, although he never succeeds in founding a family. Each of the characters and episodes in the novel, however, becomes an inversion of its ideal form. The family meal with which the book begins approaches a parody of the happy family scenes described in *Maria Chapdelaine*. The mother, disfigured by a huge goiter and about to give birth to twins, drags herself around the kitchen. There is no water, and the children are immediately disgusted by the food, summed up in the image of the unappetizing bread that becomes a leitmotiv in the novel: "pain sur et amer marqué d'une croix" 'sour, bitter bread marked with a cross' (12, 142).

Episode after episode contradicts the ideal family hierarchy: the sons destroy the parents' orchard and strike their mother as she attempts to protect their helpless father. Even the beauty and prosperity of the rural landscape is disparaged by Laberge's dark vision. While the characteristic plot of earlier novels moves through hardship to a new equilibrium, the movement of *La Scouine* is essentially downward. In fact, each of the short chapters ends with an abrupt downward movement—even those that describe what promises to be a happy event. As Charles finishes building his new house, for example, he falls from the roof and is crippled for life. *La Scouine* approaches satire in the way in which it consistently turns the ideal vision on its head, but there is no room for humor in Laberge's dark vision.

Apart from a glimpse of the happy, loving family that appears to taunt his characters at the end, Laberge's picture of rural life is so negative that Québec critics found it totally unacceptable, even pornographic (Servais-Maquoi 100). As a result, Laberge published nothing further for many years. The family plot would not receive such an open challenge until the 1960s, when Marie-Claire Blais wrote her cruelly satirical *Une saison dans la vie d'Emmanuel*. But by then Blais could approach her subject with some humor, because it was no longer an object of belief.

Despite Laberge's alternative vision, the model of an even more idealized *Maria Chapdelaine* continued to haunt the Québec novel. Hémon's best-seller is specifically and repeatedly evoked by Félix-Antoine Savard in *Menaud, maître-draveur*. In the first scene Menaud is shown listening to his daughter as she reads the words of Maria's "voices," especially the message of unchanging fidelity to the past. Savard's plot follows the broad lines of Hémon's, as Menaud's daughter, not surprisingly named Marie, must choose between her suitors, le Délié, who has become an accomplice of foreign domination, and le Lucon, who has committed himself to carrying on Menaud's life and work after the death of the latter's son. Although Marie makes the correct choice, the end of Savard's novel is even less optimistic than *Maria Chapdelaine*, because the focus never really leaves the father. The last pages center on Menaud as he himself suffers the fate of Hémon's François Paradis by walking off to near-death and madness in the hostile winter landscape in an effort to assert his possession of the land. In the end, Menaud's values are transmitted (if only through his daughter and son-in-law), but the heritage—that is, the land—is no longer his to pass on. While earlier novels had seen inheritance in terms of the family farm, Menaud claims as his birthright the entire territory of Québec, which in the 1930s was being taken over by foreign interests (Monière 228). While he preserves the centrality of the patriarchal father, Savard shows the breakdown of the process of inheritance. In 1914 *Maria Chapdelaine* was an analysis of a contemporary situation; by 1937 *Menaud, maître-draveur* was already a lyrical lament for the lost past.

In a less polemical work than Savard's, Ringuet (the pseudonym of Philippe Panneton) structures his epic *Trente arpents* around the rise and fall of a patriarch, which he compares to the natural rotation of the seasons. Euchariste Moisan inherits his land, fathers a large family, and finally succumbs to reversals of fortune, old age, and dispossession by his son, ending his life in lonely exile in the United States. With his clear-seeing doctor's eye, Ringuet observes both the beauty and the hardship of agricultural life. His characters are not idealized, as were Hémon's, nor are they seen as inherently limited or depraved, as were those of *La Scouine*. Euchariste's bad fortune—his betrayal by the notary, his loss of the court case, the barn fire, the death of his oldest son—is not the result of his own deficiencies, although it does serve to point up the precarious bases of the whole ideal of rural prosperity. The real tragedy of Euchariste Moisan is the result of Ringuet's rewriting of the family plot. In *La terre paternelle* the eldest son inherits the land during his father's lifetime and goes on to mismanage and ultimately lose it. But the younger son, who has previously left home, returns to repossess the land and reunite the family in renewed prosperity. Similarly, in *Trente arpents* Euchariste cedes the land to his remaining son, who proceeds to care for it well—but to abandon the father. In a strange twist on the original plot, it is the old man himself who must go off to join the younger son in exile in the States. Like *Menaud, maître-draveur, Trente arpents* centers the family drama on the patriarchal figure and records his downfall. At a time when Québec's resources were being acquired by foreign capital, when the impoverished countryside was clearly no longer able to support growing rural families (if, indeed, it ever had been), and when the population center had irrevocably shifted to the cities, these writers were telling the story of the failure of inheritance, the end of a family line. Yet, as they do not alter the assumption that authority resides in the father, they do not question the cultural values that underlay the family plot.

Several major works of the postwar era began to call these values into question and, in so doing, made visible changes to the traditional plot. Germaine Guèvremont's two novels, *Le survenant* and *Marie-Didace*, are most appropriately considered as two parts of a single family cycle, as indicated by their publication in English as a single work, *The Outlander*. Although it is generally considered the last of the *romans de la terre*, Guèvremont's reinterpretation of the family plot is intimately related to that effected by Gabrielle Roy in *Bonheur d'occasion* and considered (along with Roger Lemelin's *Au pied de la pente douce*) as the first of Québec's urban novels.

Guèvremont preserves from the *Maria Chapdelaine* plot the figures of the strong patriarchal father (the robust Didace Beauchemin) and the radiant daughter (Marie-Amanda), who repeats her mother's life. As appealing as the traditional figures prove to be, they are progressively marginalized by the narrative and displaced by several additions to the family. The title character of the first novel, the Outlander, at first seems to be a modern avatar of François Paradis, claiming the hearts of the women and going off to die in the war. In Guèvremont's world, however, he is a profoundly disturbing force, primarily because he disappoints the expectations of the family plot. He replaces the weak son Amable in his father's affection but is unwilling to claim the heritage, just as he takes the heart of Angélina while refusing to marry and found a family. Connected with the Outlander is his friend, Blanche Varieur, whom Didace marries in the hope of producing a new heir. But her maternal bosom belies her real sterility, and she effectively displaces the one person who actually is able to carry on the Beauchemin line, Amable's frail and awkward wife, Alphonsine.

Phonsine clearly lacks the dynamic appeal of Didace and the Outlander, the characters most favored by readers and critics. Nevertheless, she is arguably the central character in the family drama, which ends when she succumbs to madness, leaving her little daughter, Marie-Didace, as the sole surviving Beauchemin. Phonsine is an orphan, a rarity in the Québec family novel before this time. Abandoned by her alcoholic father after the death of her mother, she has been deprived of parental guidance. She thus finds herself unable to cope with the demands of the womanly role so well fulfilled by her sister-in-law Marie-Amanda, who has received this legacy from her own mother, the much-lamented Mathilde Beauchemin. Phonsine, on the other hand, is profoundly alienated from her physical environment, to the point where she is unable to tolerate the very food she is condemned to serve. Even when pregnant she is unattractively thin, when the ideal of the Québec woman is, in the tradition of Maria Chapdelaine, appealingly plump. In her thinness, Phonsine is related to Roy's equally slender Florentine Lacasse, as both act out their rejection of the generously proportioned maternal figure; in her alienation, Phonsine suggests the even more alienated orphans who appear in the novels of Robert Charbonneau and André Langevin in the 1940s and 1950s. Guèvremont stresses the admirable qualities of traditional Québec ideals through her sympathetic portraits of Didace and Marie-Amanda. But through the increasingly dominant perspective of Phonsine, she shows the drudgery and boredom of farm existence, its overwhelming physical demands, and the way in which it suppresses individual aspirations to beauty and personal happiness.

At the end of the novelistic cycle, Didace is dead and has no living male heir, Phonsine has gone mad, and Marie-Amanda is left isolated on her island, worn down, like her mother, by the burden of her family. Clearly, the cycle of the rural family is drawing to a close. But there are a few survivors, and their choice is significant. The inheritor of the Beauchemin land is Didace's granddaughter and namesake, the little Marie-Didace. Her young age and her generational distance from the family patriarch reveal a momentary failure in the process of inheritance; her gender signals a change in the transmission of patriarchal authority. She stands, however, as an indication of hope in an ill-defined future. The guardian Guèvremont appoints for her is equally unexpected—not her capable aunt Marie-Amanda, but her old-maid neighbor, Angélina Desmarais. Loved and abandoned by the Outlander, Angélina has chosen not to follow the route of Maria Chapdelaine in accepting one of her local suitors; in her assertion of emotional autonomy, Angélina can trace her literary ancestry not to Hémon but to Laure Conan's nineteenth-century heroine, Angéline de Montbrun. It is thus a strong, independent woman who assumes the direction of the Beauchemin fortunes.

In Roy's *Bonheur d'occasion* the family plot is even more extensively rewritten. The family retains the same elements, but it has been removed to an urban environment in which the sense of incompetence and alienation so profoundly felt by Guèvremont's Phonsine is shared by all its members. In addition, the roles have been redistributed. The competent patriarchal figure, who has been a constant of these novels, has now been replaced by the well-intentioned but hopelessly weak Azarius Lacasse, and the burden of maintaining the family rests on the mother, the admirable Rose-Anna, and on the income of her oldest daughter, Florentine. The drama of inheritance is now, clearly, to be played out between mother and daughter rather than father and son.

The foregrounding of female figures that occurs in the postwar novel has profound implications for the representation of Québec society. It signals a breakdown in the traditional hierarchical structure, a breakdown that was already beginning to take place in the society itself, despite the persistence in power of the near-dictatorial Québec premier Maurice Duplessis (1936–39, 1944–59). In the difficulties experienced by the women characters as they assume unaccustomed roles as breadwinner and head of household can be seen the situation of an entire people, ill-equipped by their traditional upbringing to meet the demands of life in a modern urban economy.[2] The helplessness and marginality of the female protagonists created by Roy and Guèvremont undoubtedly corresponded to a feeling of alienation experienced by much of French-Canadian society.

Yet in Roy's novel a persistent bond between mother and daughter provides the continuity threatened by the failure of the male line. The relationship between Rose-Anna and Florentine Lacasse gives Roy an opportunity to reexamine not only the process of inheritance but the legacy itself. Here the daughter reenacts the role formerly given to the son(s), that of rejecting the heritage and subsequently returning home to enter into its possession. And, for the first time, the heritage is not the land but the family itself, which, Roy argues, is now jeopardized by the very ideological structures once developed to sustain it.

An ethic of love and care for the family is embodied in Rose-Anna, who is an admirable incarnation of the traditional maternal ideal—in fact, its most positive representation in all of Québec literature. Strangely enough, the prewar *romans de la terre*—with the single exception of *Maria Chapdelaine*—did not give an important place to the maternal figure, although she was in reality the source and center of the large rural family (Boynard-Frot 99). Ringuet's treatment of Alphonsine Moisan in *Trente arpents* is typical: she dies while producing the last of a long line of children, and her absence has little effect on either the family or the novel. It is only in the postwar period that strong mother figures begin to dominate Québec literature—at a time when the values with which they are associated have become problematic.

Despite Rose-Anna's ideal qualities (and it has not escaped notice that the book is dedicated to Roy's own beloved mother), she is incapable of providing for her numerous children, or even of satisfying their need for love and personal attention. Rose-Anna is portrayed as a martyred figure, and her most tragic failures as a mother are brought about by contradictions inherent in the large-family ethic itself. It is because she is in the final stages of yet another pregnancy that Rose-Anna is unable to be with her dying son Daniel in his last days, and it is her announcement of this pregnancy that calls forth the first overt statement of revolt from Florentine. Communication between mother and daughter is blocked not only by the overcrowded household but, more fundamentally, by shared vulnerability to a feminine condition they both recognize as oppressive.

Establishing her opposition to the ideal of Maria Chapdelaine, Florentine determines not to repeat her mother's life. But like Maria and almost all female figures in the Québec novel, her options for action reduce themselves to the choice of a husband. The role of François Paradis falls to the ambitious Jean Lévesque, who is carried off by a materialistic environment as hostile as the northern wilderness. Florentine's subsequent seduction of the compliant Emmanuel is hypocritical and manipulative, but, in a sense, her decision to provide for her unborn child by marrying a local boy is not very different from Maria Chapdelaine's. In the end, Florentine reaffirms her mother's values even as she succeeds in escaping the oppressive poverty of Saint-Henri. Finding a home for herself and her baby, she invites Rose-Anna and the younger children to join them, thus recognizing the shared condition of mother and daughter and providing a final image of family continuity.

Québec readers had been oblivious to the implications of Hémon's choice of an entrapped and submissive woman as his protagonist. Readers of *Bonheur d'occasion* were equally unwilling to see themselves in Florentine, and critics preferred to analyze male characters like Azarius Lacasse or Jean Lévesque, or the sympathetic and traditional Rose-Anna. Gabrielle

Roy was acclaimed for finally putting the Québec novel in touch with what had long been the essentially urban nature of Québec society. Less apparent, but even more radical an updating was the way in which she had rewritten the family plot.

Such rewriting could no longer be ignored when Anne Hébert published *Le torrent* in 1947. Although it is not quite long enough to be a novel, *Le torrent* occupies a crucial place in the evolution of Québec fiction: it has been termed by one critic "the first great classic of contemporary French Canadian literature" (Pagé 30). Writing in 1945, the year in which both Roy and Guèvremont published their first novels, Hébert directly attacks the oppressiveness of the traditional Québec value structure through her recognizably allegorical figures, as her protagonist openly revolts against his mother. Somewhat ironically, from the moment when the fictional mother had begun to assert her presence in the Québec novel, she quickly assumed an overbearing role in the family hierarchy (Paradis 65). This is true in Roger Lemelin's more realistic family portraits, particularly in *Les Plouffe*, but it is even more evident in *Le torrent*, in which the father has been totally effaced and the mother is left to stand for the whole traditional ideology. The process of inheritance that had been the moving force of the old family plot has been completely disrupted. Claudine Perrault has tried to make her son into an extension of her own life and values, a process evident in her gesture of passing on her old schoolbooks. But Hébert makes clear the destructive nature of such Maria Chapdelaine-like repetition. As is slowly revealed by the son's confused monologue, the mother's legacy has functioned to isolate him from the world, limit his vision, and finally beat him into deafness. Previous fictional protagonists had been dispossessed of their land or their country, but François Perrault claims himself "dispossessed of the world," as he states in the first words of the text. Rejecting the oppressive inheritance, the son also rejects the mother, finally acting out his desire to kill her. His violence not only prefigures the dramatic social and political changes of the 1960s but also inaugurates a new literary model of the family plot: Hébert's scenario would be echoed in such later works as Marie-Claire Blais's first novel, *La belle bête*.

Almost as if in response to the disintegration of the family, the protagonist of *Le torrent* speaks in his own voice. First-person narration had been rare in Québec fiction before the 1940s, and Hébert's confused, almost Faulknerian narrative voice sounds a distinctly new note. Although the subjective vision is a basic element of modern fiction, personal narratives had long received a cool reception in Québec. Interestingly enough, in the few instances in which the personal voice had tried to assert itself, it had been associated with a breakdown in the family plot.

Laure Conan's *Angéline de Montbrun*, one of the most important works in the nineteenth-century Québec canon, provides a striking and isolated example of the intrusion of a personal voice into a fictional text. Conan's novel initially gives the impression of subscribing to the family plot. In its first section, a series of letters reports the engagement of Angéline, only and adored child of Charles de Montbrun, to her best friend's brother, Maurice Darville. Despite the absence of the much-lamented mother, the family drama seems to be moving smoothly forward when an omniscient narrator abruptly intervenes to recount the death of Angéline's father, her own accident and resulting facial disfigurement, and her decision to end her engagement to Maurice. After this sudden disintegration of the family, Angéline is left alone, and she suddenly begins to speak in the first person about her own emotional reality. Reading Conan's novel against the political background of nineteenth-century Québec, Madeleine Gagnon has seen Angéline's enigmatic decision to break her engagement as an assertion of autonomy, which ends her status as a dominated object of patriarchal power (66). Angéline's withdrawal from the family plot would thus, clearly, be related to her newfound ability to speak in her own voice.

The voice of Angéline de Montbrun would have few echoes in Québec fiction, even in Laure Conan's own subsequent novels: her clerical mentors, apparently troubled by the personal note in her first novel, advised her to try her hand at historical fiction, which she did with great success. For years, the many Québec novels dominated by the family plot seemed almost universally to exclude first-person narration, or even the expression of an individual perspective. Like the oppressively silent Maria Chapdelaine, many characters in the traditional *roman de la terre* had to rely on other voices—generally that of the omniscient author, however it might be disguised—to give expression to their inner reality. This problem of self-expression seems to plague Québec fictional protagonists right up through *Bonheur d'occasion*. Even more successfully than Hémon, Roy attempted to incorporate local speech into her dialogues, but the characters seem incapable of expressing themselves to the reader or even to each other: one of the central problems in the world of *Bonheur d'occasion* is precisely this lack of communication. Through her effective use of point of view, Roy gives the reader direct access to her characters' minds, but they lack the ability to speak for themselves in their own familiar language.

Several writers had attempted to reintroduce the personal voice into Québec fiction in the period before 1940. If their efforts inspired little emulation, it was perhaps because first-person narration was often associated with a disruption of the family plot and contestation of its governing values. Two young women writers of the early 1930s, Jovette Bernier and Eva Senécal, made personal emotion the focus of their novels and, quite logically, wrote first-person narratives. Largely because their depiction of such subjects as unwed motherhood and extramarital passion did not correspond to traditional versions of the family plot, both women fell afoul of the critics, and they soon ceased writing altogether. An even more egregious case of ideological censure concerned the controversial novel of Jean-Charles Harvey, *Les demi-civilisés*. Harvey's contestatory protagonist is an orphan, and, perhaps not unexpectedly, he speaks in his own voice.

Orphans become more and more prevalent in Québec fiction of the 1940s and 1950s, and these new, alienated protagonists, cut off from their roots and traditional models (Falardeau 38–42), show a marked preference for the first-person pronoun. Robert Charbonneau's *Ils posséderont la terre* is ironically entitled, since the novel represents a complete rupture of the process of inheritance in the *roman de la terre*: the protagonist's first words express his desire to avoid resemblance to his dead father. In André Langevin's novels of the 1950s, the protagonists are similarly isolated—and their narratives are similarly subjective. In *Poussière sur la ville* the protagonist Alain Dubois analyzes his alienating experience in a voice reminiscent of the journal style of Jean-Paul Sartre's *La nausée*. Dubois and his wife have both lost their fathers, and their mothers fail to assert their presence. Cut off from their accustomed milieu in a barren mining town and isolated even from each other in a childless marriage, Langevin's characters provide an image of the fate of the family plot in this era. In 1960 the protagonist of Gérard Bessette's *Le libraire*, who is also writing a journal, does not even attempt to take a wife and seems at ease with his rootless state.

The way in which the family plot has functioned to suppress the individual voice becomes the explicit subject of Blais's *Une saison dans la vie d'Emmanuel*. The poet-son, Jean Le Maigre, is slowly suffocated by his oppressive milieu just as his first-person autobiography is engulfed by a third-person narrative that is clearly a parody of the traditional *roman de la terre*. By the 1960s the family plot has become an object of satire. The novel is set in the country, in a family of children so numerous they are assigned numbers and letters in lieu of names. Blais's depiction of the parents as anonymous figures mirrors the general effacement of the mother in the *roman de la terre* and the more recent disappearance of the father. On the other hand, the powerful and ambiguous Grand-Mère Antoinette is a reworking of the monstrous mother-figures who represent the traditional ideology in later fiction of protest and revolt, like *Le torrent* and Blais's own, very similar, *La belle bête*. Blais's confrontation with the family plot is more than a gratuitous exercise in satire. Rather, it seems to have been a necessary step in her own expression of a personal vision: *Une saison dans la vie d'Emmanuel* is almost immediately followed by the three volumes of *Manuscrits de Pauline Archange*, Blais's quasi-autobiographical first-person portrait of the development of a woman writer.

The more humorous dismissal of the traditional family structure that appears in Jacques Godbout's *Salut Galarneau!* also seems a necessary prelude to the protagonist's self-expression. The Galarneau family is no longer oppressive to its offspring, primarily because it has no inheritance to pass on. The father has responded to his loss of religious faith by retiring to drink beer on his boat: he finally goes down with the ship. The mother, who does little but eat chocolates and read pulp novels, finally leaves for the States. Even the protective grandfather can offer his grandson only an initiatory experience taken from the *Reader's Digest*. In Galarneau's world, the family plot and its ideological baggage have no more reality than does the baby dreamed up by his Québec City girlfriend in order to coerce him into a short-lived marriage. Almost effortlessly liberated from the old family ties, Godbout's hero is free to speak in his own voice, and one that is distinctly Québécois. His problem is no longer one of suppression by his milieu but, rather, of isolation: at the end of his story he has realized the importance of integrating art with life (a conclusion summed up in the composite verb *vécrire*) and of bringing his work back to the people who have formed his life.

The dominance of the family plot in Québec fiction well into the twentieth century testifies to the relationship of cultural ideology and literary form. As noted, the voice of the isolated individual so characteristic of other modern literatures did not make itself heard in the Québec novel until the 1940s and 1950s, the era in which a monolithic traditional ideology was beginning to lose its hold, and the rewriting and ultimate rejection of the family plot in the postwar period was the sign of a contestation of traditional values that extended to all areas of the society. The Québec novel has thus proven itself to be an important arena for the articulation and examination of cultural values.

The displacement of the family plot has not reduced Québec fiction to the solipsistic discourse of alienated individuals. After her bitter attack on the traditional family in *Une saison dans la vie d'Emmanuel*, Marie-Claire Blais's novels of the 1970s and 1980s—especially *Le sourd dans la ville* and *Visions d'Anna*—create networks of human relationships, even discovering new meaning in the much-maligned maternal role. The playwright Michel Tremblay, who dramatized the breakdown of family relationships in works like *Les belles-soeurs*, has shown them in a different context in his novels. Feminist writers like Louky Bersianik and Nicole Brossard have explored new modes of human interaction, within and outside the structure of the family. The dream of reconciliation with which Godbout leaves his François Galarneau suggests the direction of more recent novelistic developments: a new generation of Québec writers has begun to work out forms of fictional relationships capable of integrating rather than suppressing the individual voice.

NOTES

[1] Janine Boynard-Frot points out the many ways in which this novel, written by a Frenchman, constitutes an exception to the ideological assumptions of the *roman de la terre.*

[2] The situation of Roy's female characters corresponds to that of the Québec male worker in that era, as it has been described by Ben-Zion Shek: "The ex-farmer was faced with the highly competitive struggle in a new, impersonal work world for which his traditional education had not prepared him. He was placed in a subordinate position to an employer of another culture and language. This led to a loss of self-confidence and feelings of alienation" (19).

WORKS CITED

Bessette, Gérard. *Le libraire.* 1960. Montréal: Cercle du Livre de France, 1968. *Not for Every Eye.* Trans. Glen Shortliffe. Toronto: Macmillan, 1962.

Blais, Marie-Claire. *La belle bête.* 1959. Ottawa: Cercle du Livre de France, 1968. *Mad Shadows.* Trans. Merloyd Lawrence. Toronto: McClelland, 1971.

———. *Manuscrits de Pauline Archange.* Ottawa: Jour, 1968, 1969, 1970. *The Manuscripts of Pauline Archange.* Trans. Derek Coltman. Toronto: McClelland, 1980.

———. *Une saison dans la vie d'Emmanuel.* 1965. Montréal: Stanké, 1980. *A Season in the Life of Emmanuel.* Trans. Derek Coltman. New York: Farrar, 1966.

———. *Le sourd dans la ville.* Montréal: Stanké, 1979. *Deaf to the City.* Trans. Carol Dunlop. Toronto: Lester and Orpen Dennys, 1981.

———. *Visions d'Anna.* Montréal: Stanké, 1982. *Anna's World.* Trans. Sheila Fischman. Toronto: Lester and Orpen Dennys, 1984.

Boynard-Frot, Janine. *Un matriarcat en procès.* Montréal: PU de Montréal, 1982.

Charbonneau, Robert. *Ils posséderont la terre.* Montréal: L'Arbre, 1941.

Chauveau, Pierre-Joseph-Oliver. *Charles Guérin.* 1852–53. Montréal: Fides, 1978.

Conan, Laure [Félicité Angers]. *Angéline de Montbrun.* 1884. Montréal: Fides, 1974. *Angéline de Montbrun.* Trans. Yves Brunelle. Toronto: U of Toronto P, 1974.

Deschamps, Nicole, Raymonde Héroux, and Normand Villeneuve. *Le mythe de Maria Chapdelaine.* Montréal: PU de Montréal, 1980.

Falardeau, Jean-Charles. *Imaginaire social et littéraire.* Montréal: HMH-Hurtubise, 1974.

Gagnon (-Mahony), Madeleine. "*Angéline de Montbrun*: Le mensonge historique et la subversion de la métaphore blanche." *Voix et images du pays* 5 (1972): 57–68.

Gérin-Lajoie, Antoine. Jean Rivard, le défricheur, *suivi* de Jean Rivard, économiste. 1874, 1876. Montréal: HMH-Hurtubise, 1977. *Jean Rivard.* Trans. Vida Bruce. New Canadian Library. Toronto: McClelland, 1977.

Godbout, Jacques. *Salut Galarneau!* 1968. Paris: Seuil, 1979. *Hail Galarneau!* Trans. Alan Brown. Toronto: Longmans, 1970.

Guèvremont, Germaine. *Marie-Didace.* 1947. Montréal: Fides, 1980.

———. *The Outlander.* Trans. of *Le survenant* and *Marie-Didace.* Trans. Eric Sutton. New Canadian Library. Toronto: McClelland, 1978.

———. *Le survenant.* 1945. Montréal: Fides, 1974.

Harvey, Jean-Charles. *Les demi-civilisés.* 1934. Ottawa: L'Actuelle, 1970. *Fear's Folly.* Trans. John Glassco. Ed. John O'Connor. Ottawa: Carleton UP, 1982.

Hébert, Anne. *Le torrent.* 1950. Montréal: HMH-Hurtubise, 1974. *The Torrent.* Trans. Gwendolyn Moore. Montréal: Harvest, 1973.

Hémon, Louis. *Marie Chapdelaine.* 1914, 1916. Montréal: Fides, 1975. *Maria Chapdelaine.* Trans. W. H. Blake. Toronto: Macmillan, 1965.

Laberge, Albert. *La Scouine.* 1918. Montréal: Quinze, 1981.

Lacombe, Patrice. *La terre paternelle.* 1848. Montréal: Fides, 1981.

Laflèche, François-Louis. *Quelques considérations sur les rapports de la société civile avec la religion et la famille.* Montréal: Senécal, 1866.

Langevin, André. *Poussière sur la ville.* 1953. Montréal: Tisseyre, 1975. *Dust over the City.* Trans. John Latrobe and Robert Gottlieb. New Canadian Library. Toronto: McClelland, 1974.

Lemelin, Roger. *Au pied de la pente douce.* 1944. Montréal: La Presse, 1975. *The Town Below.* Trans. Samuel Putnam. New Canadian Library. Toronto: McClelland, 1961.

———. *Les Plouffe.* 1948. Montréal: La Presse, 1980. *The Plouffe Family.* Trans. Mary Finch. New Canadian Library. Toronto: McClelland, 1975.

Monière, Denis. *Le développement des idéologies au Québec.* Montréal: Québec/Amérique, 1977.

Pagé, Pierre. *Anne Hébert.* Ottawa: Fides, 1965.

Paradis, Suzanne. *Femme fictive, femme réelle.* Québec: Garneau, 1966.

Ringuet [Philippe Panneton]. *Trente arpents.* 1938. Montréal: Fides, 1976. *Thirty Acres.* Trans. Dorothea Walter and Felix Walter. New Canadian Library. Toronto: McClelland, 1960.

Roy, Gabrielle. *Bonheur d'occasion.* 1945. Montréal: Stanké, 1978. *The Tin Flute.* Trans. Alan Brown. Toronto: McClelland, 1981.

Savard, Félix-Antoine. *Menaud, maître-draveur.* 1937. Montréal: Fides, 1982. *Master of the River.* Trans. Richard Howard. Montréal: Harvest, 1976.

Servais-Maquoi, Mireille. *Le roman de la terre au Québec.* Québec: PU Laval, 1974.

Shek, Ben-Zion. *Social Realism in the French-Canadian Novel.* Montréal: Harvest, 1977.

Tremblay, Michel. *Les belles-soeurs.* 1968. Montréal: Leméac, 1972. *Les Belles-Soeurs.* Trans. Bill Glassco and John Van Burek. Vancouver: Talonbooks, 1974.

Camille La Bossière

PAST AND PRESENT:
THE NEOBAROQUE NOVEL
IN FRENCH CANADA

Infinis esprits se treuvent ruinez par leur propre force
et soupplesse.

Montaigne, *Apologie de Raimond Sebond*

... une encyclopédie qui viserait d'abord à
l'autodétermination et à l'autosuffisance de
chacun de ses lecteurs.

Michel Bélair, *Franchir les miroirs*

THE TITLE OF Gérard Tougas's *Destin littéraire du Québec*, a follow-up to his *Puissance littéraire des Etats-Unis*, is certainly weighty. It seems ironic as well. *Le destin*, in the sense of the necessary succession of events that are independent of the human will, is far from apposite to the future Tougas's history envisions and embraces. In fact, *Destin littéraire* is anything but a call for humility or resignation before the edicts of history and fate, exhorting as it does Québec's *littérateurs* to follow in the American way of cultural self-reliance and independence from imitation. With such critics as Henry S. Canby and F. O. Matthiessen for exemplars, they are retrospectively to invent their great writers by remaking them in their own image (177). The future makes the past, and Québec's history is ripe for creation according to the wills of its writers, pronounces Tougas: "Ce n'est pas le passé qui nous instruit sur le passé, mais le futur" (147). In this respect, Tougas's *destin* is a principle no less active than the predestination fundamental to the Manifest Destiny informing Whitman's 1856 "Letter to

Ralph Waldo Emerson": the poet's reaching out to take Montréal and Havana into his and America's embrace is prologue here to a proximate future history of "A Hundred States" (1: 2038). And the acted-upon responds to, as it records, the presence and activity of the will to inventiveness. Delivered in a place made pliant to Whitman's visionary imagination, Thomas D'Arcy McGee's exhortation to the members of the Montréal Literary Club (November 1867)—that they and the new Dominion resist imitation of a Bostonian literary culture assuming "the American democratic system to be the manifestly destined form of government for all the civilized world, new as well as old" (66)—reaffirms the concept that destiny American-style, like Tougas's *destin*, is a principle for action, of mind over matter and history, and not, ironically, a counsel to resignation before the limitations of time and place.

Understandably, then, *Destin littéraire* tends to privilege the critic as artist in the process of making particular works and national literatures—so much so, that the disjunction Tougas outlines between American literature in the nineteenth century and the American Renaissance conceived in the twentieth appears strong. For example, Emerson's *American Scholar* (1837), a declaration of the need for his country's authors and students to break free of imported books and ideas, fell largely on deaf ears, according to *Destin littéraire* (16). The sovereignty precious to Emerson was to be achieved only in the next century. Similarly, Melville's struggle to give life to "le nouvel homme" proved abortive, since contemporaries greeted his works after *Omoo* (1847) for the most part with rejection, a prelude to neglect. The status of *Moby-Dick* as representative American book and universal work of genius is "une invention de la critique américaine contemporaine" (137). The point is well taken and instructive in what it makes explicit. Tacitly conveyed is a related history no less instructive, serving to remind one that American criticism in the autogeneal-autotelic mode has taken important lessons from Emerson and Melville or their likes. For example, *"Moby-Dick" as Doubloon*, edited by Hershel Parker and Harrison Hayford, whose introduction concludes with a celebration of the inviolable privacy of Melville's enterprise and that of his readers—the fiction, like its Spanish coin, is a mirror for self-reflection—testifies as much. Autonomy calls unto autonomy, invention unto invention.

American criticism as creative art has a history of formation, is shaped by a tradition of considerable age. For all the topsy-turvydom, all the twists and turns in Emerson's whimsical reflections, their emphasis on the mind's imperial power is constant enough to be clear: "Perception makes" (*Journals* 13: 51). "What's a book?" Emerson asks himself and gives the answer—by now a cliché—to students of self-consuming artifacts: it is "everything or nothing. The eye that sees it is all" (*Journals* 5: 93). In the words of his 1830 sermon "Self-Culture," "The world is but a mirror in which every mind sees its own image reflected" (*Young Emerson Speaks* 101). On that score at least, Melville is of a mind with Emerson. If we see as in a glass darkly, as he relentlessly speculates, what we read there is of our own making. "The world revolves upon an I," according to *Mardi* (2: 279), Melville's eclectic, genuine romance picturing a pursuer pursued over an endless sea; and *Moby-Dick*, his epic invention that should not be taken for veritable gospel cetology or history, logically follows. When set within the context of the literature it reads, then, the inventiveness of twentieth-century criticism in the United States seems old hat, as J. C. Rowe's *Through the Custom-House* confirms: contemporary critics follow in the steps of the authors they make, of the autodeconstructed writings they dismantle to reinvent. "Nous nous promenons sur nos pas" 'We walk in our own footsteps,' from Montaigne's *Essais* (13: 122), would make a good epigraph for Rowe's charting of the modern critic's progress.[1] If the future writes the past, the past writes the future. If the critic or reader is artist, the artist is critic or reader, too.

Emerson and Melville as readers are in a position not substantially at variance with that of the twentieth-century American criticism invoked by Tougas. They too have their antecedents and mentors, their time and place and tradition. Both variously respond to and register the transatlantic fluxions of that post-Kantian idealism founded on doubt that feeds on as it stimulates the nineteenth-century's appetite for reviving Renaissance and baroque texts. Among those texts most privileged, as Schopenhauer's *World as Will and Idea* serves to remind, are Montaigne's *Essais*, Shakespeare's *Tempest*, and Calderón's *La vida es sueño* (*Life Is a Dream*): each proclaims the imagination's power of metamorphosis, affirming that "life and dreams are leaves from the same book," a truth inscrutable to the Aristotelian realism and linear logic of "the dreary Middle Ages" (1: 22, 62, 463–65). In the readerly world of dreams, relativity, improvisation, and uncertainty, where distinctions between illusion and reality, self and other fade in ambiguity, the somnambulist travels not in a straight line but in a circle, the cardinal figure for the baroque logic of unreason that rules life's book. "Les contraires se rejoignent" recapitulates the endlessly reflexive grammar of contradiction governing Montaigne's *Essais* and the literature of "l'âge baroque" that follows in Europe (Rousset 27). The example of the dreamy Renaissance skeptic's private and therefore circular enterprise is efficacious in the United States as well. "Saint Michel de Montaigne"—so "this prince of egotists" is canonized in 1850 by Emerson's *Representative Men*—announces the Sage of Concord's perennial wisdom (*Complete Works* 4: 162, 173). "Extremes meet: there is no straight line," Emerson repeats time and again (see, for instance, *Journals* 8: 397) and figures that logic in "cold fire" (*Complete Works* 3: 171). Their presence detected in Shake-speare's "Montaignism" (Leyda 1: 291), the *Essais* enact a coincidence of opposites consonant with the syntax described in Melville's retrospective "Art," a poem privately printed a few months after his reading of *The World as Will and Idea*: "What unlike things must meet and mate: / A flame to melt—a wind to freeze" (*Poems* 270). The student of baroque literature is on familiar, if shifting, ground here, in the dizzying roundabout dreamworld of contradiction appropriated by nineteenth-century idealism on both sides of the Atlantic.

Nor does the student of baroque literature—any more than Emerson and Melville before the mirror of Montaigne's oneiric autobiography, or contemporary autoscopic critics before the writings of Emerson and Melville—have reason to feel *dépaysé*, lost in terra incognita, in the pres-ence of the mental infinity-box (de)constructions of the postmodern novel. The inventiveness that contemporary fiction or criticism in the newest manner generates, within itself and in its sympathetic reader, has a history that goes back more than four centuries. In terms of its salient speculative underpinnings and artistic practices, writing in the postmodern manner is no less antique than the history of the neobaroque novel in French Canada, which shares in that mode's literary-philosophical ancestral provenance. Intellectual genealogy suggests that the rapprochement of contemporary French-Canadian and United States literature is a matter less of future than of past development. If Québec's critics still have some way to go in the American way of autonomic creation, a number of Québec's contemporary novelists have already made the round trip, albeit indirectly at times and at great expense. Like Emerson and Melville, these writers of fiction precede the van of readerly criticism that takes up their lead. Accordingly, the following commentary on a few of the many contemporary novels from French Canada will suggest their role as critical *éclaireurs*. The selected fictions represent major contributions to the French-Canadian Renaissance and to the instauration of the baroque literature of subjectivity and circular unreason that gives that cultural rebirth its proper expression. With the publication of Gérard Bessette's fourth novel, *L'incubation*, and Hubert Aquin's first, *Prochain épisode*, both in 1965, the age of invention comes to Québec fiction with force. *L'incubation*, a recent literary dictionary rec-ords, marks a clean break with the traditional realism Bessette himself had practiced in his earlier novels (Dorion 428).

Life is "*a tale told by an idiot*," Herr Professor Wilhelm Ricard Bar-tolomeus Weingerter avers to Lagarde, the narrator of *L'incubation* (64). Lagarde's rumination of his own life, in which are entangled the dimly recollected tales of Weingerter and others similarly encoiled in the "problematic" of remembering their past coherently and giving it finite expression, does not belie the professor's self-confirmed wisdom. No less than theirs, the text of Lagarde's experiences during World War II and the present, in London (England), Montréal, Toronto, and a place named Narcotown, is rife with indeterminacy. *L'incubation*, like its narrator's life, haltingly dramatizes the unknowing that full privacy makes invincible: "la vida es sueño" (Tougas 42) and its semantic performance a delirious dreaming. The toils of Bessette's noctambulists to allay the torment of their suffocation and to have done with interminable soliloquizing are necessarily vain, trapped as the characters are in a mind-cage without exit, "cette ovoïde boîte crânienne sans issue" (150). Merely one among other visually impaired subterranean wanderers and alone in a world conceived as a dark labyrinth of mirrors, Lagarde is kin to "the blind moles" babbling their lives in the Melvillean universe (*Pierre* 246) and to the mental prisoner sketched in the grim tribute paid to Montaigne and Hume by the 1868 "Conclusion" of Pater's *Renaissance*: "Experience ... is ringed round for each one of us by that thick wall of personality through which no real voice has ever pierced on its way to us.... Every one of those impressions is the impression of the individual in his isolation, each mind keeping as a solitary prisoner its own dream of the world" (196). Neither reason nor the language of sense can penetrate the shell of Lagarde's solitude. "Le monde est ma représentation" (162). What his endlessly sounding tale may *express* is hard to know or tell with any certainty, for Lagarde is snared in the web of words spun out of his own bowels (15, 35), as Bessette repeats Montaigne's figuration of the solipsized interpreter (*Essais* 3: 278). Bessette's narrator must consequently rely on obliquity, more on the resonance than the sense of words, to relate what he can of his vague impressions. Written in the manner of a surrealist poem (Lauzière and Bessette 20), *L'incubation* has the eloquence as well of the symbolist's *poème-silence*. Significance is unspeakable in a fiction of invincible ignorance and solitude.

   Inherent in the inquisition of the self by the self about the self in *L'incubation* is a logic of the kind remarked in the "Late-Baroque" chapter of Wylie Sypher's *Four Stages of Renaissance Style*: "Every proposition *implies* the existence of its opposite; consequently every affirmation involves a contradiction" (294). It is the logic of the Ouroboros. Always vexing to Melville (see *Mardi* 1: 295) and to Emerson sometimes so (see *Journals* 8: 246), that Renaissance emblem of the snake with its tail in its mouth graphs the self-contradiction that impels Montaigne's writing (Glauser 152) and aptly gives Louis Lasnier's article on Bessette its title, "L'Ourobouros est un serpent qui se mord la queue." *L'incubation* answers closely to the double sense built into the snaky circle. If the action of paradox is infinitely reflexive, as Rosalie L. Colie's *Paradoxia Epidemica* parses the syntax of the Ouroboros, it is also "self-canceling" (40). The snake with its tail in its mouth figures at once a never-ending revolution of opposites and their mutual cancellation: infinity and zero. In *L'incubation* the wheels of the closed railway car taking Lagarde nowhere inscribe the pattern of his mental traveling, "un cercle une spirale sans fin" (72). Necessarily endless, the circular logic of *L'incubation* is self-annihilating as well. An anaconda "wound round and round its own neck" images the God of Suicides in Melville's *Mardi* (2: 26–27), and Lagarde's narration analogically pays homage to that deity. One reflection nullifies its opposite, and paralysis follows: "veux pas veux veux pas" 'want not want want not' (103). The only way out of paradoxy's interminable discoursing, Lagarde ponders to himself in the last pages of *L'incubation*, is suicide. The death of the Englishwoman Néa-Antinéa, by a self-administered overdose of sleeping pills unwittingly provided by Weingerter, enacts the one kind of concluding possible in the world of Bessette's novel. In a fiction begun by a narrator gazing into the stagnant pools of another dizzy narrator's eyes, these reflecting a bar ceiling ornate with tangled vines, Néa-Antinéa's suicide frees her of entanglement in paradox, brings her interior circling to term, and stops the decay that the paralysis of contradiction visits on its prey. Her final act concludes the decomposition that the quick must continue to endure in their suffocating self-enclosure.

As in *L'incubation*, the opening page of Aquin's *Prochain épisode* pictures a narrator picturing himself in a watery mirror, sinking in the envelope of his words. From this, his first novel, to *Neige noire* (English title: *Hamlet's Twin*), his last, Aquin does not leave that mirror. It is the instrumental cause of his fictive enterprise and a device the multiple uses of which continuously engage his inventiveness. "His books," a commentator summarizes, "are ironic melodramas couched in the self-reflexive forms of the nouveau roman, complicated in the telling by every baroque device of allusion and illusion, every inner duplication, or outer artifice, every shift from one identity to another, or even from 'character' to 'text,' that Aquin's fertile imagination could devise" (Merivale 11). Implicit in the eloquent summary is the subtext of Aquin's work as a whole: the grammar of the Narcissus mirror. A review of his ingenious, perhaps even thorough, exploitation of the thematic-structural possibilities built into the device provides a way of sketching the major lines of neomodern and baroque speculation that his fiction traces and retraces and to which his thought constantly returns.

Ideologically contextualized by past and present civil wars in Greece, Latin America, Africa, and Québec, Aquin's first novel is indeed "revolutionary." All things work in circles of self-reflexiveness, of creation and destruction proceeding together in "un cercle prédit" (*Prochain épisode*

59). Actually written in the summer of 1964, when its author was a prisoner of the Royal Canadian Mounted Police, *Prochain épisode* is the composition of a narrator sitting in a prison dreaming the circumstances leading to his incarceration. "My book writes me," as a critic cites from Penny Williams's translation of *Prochain épisode* (Merivale 11), which itself translates from Montaigne's "Du dementir": "mon livre m'a faict" (*Essais* 2: 326). Writing the writer is dizzying business, as Borges, Barth, Nabokov, and Barthes more recently confirm. Revolution, as Aquin's narrator reflects on his own vertiginous creation, is neither rational nor sober: its dialectical proceeding cannot be explained "comme un syllogisme" (125). The spiraling descent into the mirror of the self that *Prochain épisode* narrates, an activity perilously like "une noyade écrite" 'a written drowning' (27), duplicates the endless self-pursuit of Narcissus. Fortunately for the narrator, a Separatist agent assigned to track down and erase a counteragent in Switzerland, he is unsuccessful in his task, for the would-be assassin and his target bear an uncanny resemblance. The suicidal mission remains happily unaccomplished, and *Prochain épisode* ends inconclusively. Revolutionary pursuit and invention can go on indefinitely, in countless episodes.

Aquin's mirror play continues in *Trou de mémoire* (English title: *Blackout*), a tale of textual obsession written "dans le style 'pur baroque' " (25). Diaries and diarists, editors and manuscripts, actors and spectators, persons and characters embrace as they read and write each other in a "révolution permanente ... qui peut se comparer à la rotation terrestre" (58). Paradox abounds and there are high jinks galore in *Trou de mémoire*, to the astonishment, dismay, and delight of the fiction's participants. The editor RR, for example, is made pregnant by the narrator in the text she is putting together. But *Trou de mémoire*, for all its high-spirited theatrics, marks an increase in darkness from *Prochain épisode*. Each text inscribed in the novel is a "miroir noir" (82), a mirror for somber self-reflection and in which, Narcissus-like, one can drown. At the end of *Trou de mémoire*'s story, both the narrator Magnan and his mysterious double, an inverted mirror image of himself, commit suicide. Like the uppers and downers that govern the teller's interior life, he and his opposite cancel each other out: taken together, their effect is reduced "à zéro" (32). Similarly fatal is the identification of reader and read in Aquin's third novel, *L'antiphonaire*, in which the violence in (and of) a Renaissance text destroys a historian whose life in modern Québec becomes inseparable from the sixteenth-century Italian text she is reconstructing. Her fate signals the peril of being at once the pursuer and the pursued—the condition of Aquin himself as the prisoner of contradiction who writes the literary-philosophical speculations gathered together in his *Point de fuite*.

Neige noire is the story of a director's remaking of *Hamlet* and his own life. "Le monde est un rêve et le rêve est un monde" 'the world is a dream and the dream is a world' (184), speaks the new Hamlet; the text sums up the substance of Aquin's novel, rendered more epigrammatically still in the oxymoron of its title. Recalling Anaxagoras's "black snow" and Montaigne's use of the figure in an extended jeu d'esprit on the paradoxes generated by epistemological perspectivism (*Essais* 2: 169), *Neige noire* embodies the dreamer's logic, the *coincidentia oppositorum* also dramatized in Shakespeare and Calderón (Cope 126; Smart). In the dreamworld of Aquin's novel, everything is inseparable from its inverted or reversed image. Life and death, love and hate, pleasure and pain, darkness and light, illusion and reality, freezing and burning—each is united with its opposite by the mirror's synthetic logic, "cette circularité" that makes up the fiction's underlying grammar and "la structure voilée" of the film giving Hamlet yet another life (138). "At his most blackly romantic" here (Merivale 16), Aquin advances his claim for the universality of that logic. If "une parabole dans laquelle toutes les oeuvres humaines sont enchâssées" 'a parable-parabola in which all human enterprises are inscribed' (264), Aquin's last novel writes a lesson as dark as its topsy-turvy mirrorings. What surcease or concluding there can be to exhausting and interminable circling in paradox can come but one way. As Aquin himself observes in a lucid essay written in 1962, double agents embroiled in the "civil war" of endless self-contradiction, a "deadly" struggle, are steadily drawn to seek the peace of "nirvana through self-dissolution" ("Cultural Fatigue" 75). In the light of Aquin's neobaroque inventions, his suicide in March 1977 seems tragically logical.

Labyrinthine as Aquin's neobaroque fictions are, they seem almost straightforward next to the virtuoso performance of radical subjectivity that is Réjean Ducharme's first novel, *L'avalée des avalés* (*The Swallower Swallowed*). Like a hermetic poem in its gorgeous semantic playing, recondite allusiveness, and conscious cultivation of enigma, the book resists anything approaching satisfactory translation. That resistance, in a sense, is what *L'avalée des avalés* is about. "Je suis seule" 'I am alone' is the constant avowal and plaint of the novel's narrator and protagonist, the young Bérénice. Hers is a readerly philosophy *à outrance*, denying the text of "the other" any existence other than the one she gives it. Perception makes, there is no life outside the mind, the world is a Narcissus mirror. The militant idealist's self-reflexiveness ensures her solitude and that full independence that absolute self-reliance confers. Her will bent on (de)construction, Bérénice grants herself the power to ra(i)se buildings in the twinkling of an eye. The swallower swallowed, she is like a statue sculpting itself; and like the maker of self-consuming artifacts, she is ever at war with herself. The complexly mannered efforts of Ducharme's text to ensure a privacy cognate with Bérénice's make the translator's lot an unenviable one. Traducing increases as solitude deepens.

Bérénice's philosophy accords well with an aesthetic of limitless invention. In the absence of external reference or knowledge, anything goes. Kant's dubitative, anticipated by Montaigne's Socrates and followed by Emerson's Montaigne, that perhaps we cannot even know that we know that we know nothing, abridges the conundrum bedeviling Ducharme's characters (Imbert 233). "Qu'est-ce que je sais?" Ducharme repeats the ancient question (*Le nez qui voque* 182)—and "un ludisme constant" gives the artist's response (Imbert 235). Bérénice plays with the universe as with a bauble, while her author subverts received semantic structures and the conventions of linear history to make a language and a narrative that are *sui generis*. *L'avalée des avalés*, like its heroine, is Promethean in its ambitions. Exulting in her self-conferred liberty, Bérénice imagines herself a new Icarus, free as an eagle flying into the sun at will. Daedalus Ducharme implicitly claims a prerogative no less categorical.

But the liberty conferred by Promethean self-reliance comes at a cost, for creature and artist alike. Bérénice is free to do as she pleases, but at the price, ironically, of self-entrapment. A penned wolf, a trapped rat, sardines in a can, and a caged squirrel, for example, figure the lot of Bérénice in "le cul-de-sac" of her mind (230). And with solitude comes inanition. Left with only herself to feed on, she starves for want of outside nourishment. Bérénice knows from experience the truth of the couplet heading Emerson's essay "Heroism":

> The hero is not fed on sweets,
> Daily his own heart he eats.   (*Complete Works* 2: 249)

The inhabitant of a world in which linear logic and realism have no place is bound to endless self-consumption and self-contradiction, forever to travel in circles, "à tourner en rond" (165) in a hell of fire and ice. Suicide would bring the infernal whirligig to a stop and give her (and Ducharme's) narration a concluding, as Bérénice entertains. But she wills to soldier on, knowing full well the consequences of pronouncing the mind its own place. Unlike Marlowe's Faustus, the extravagantly learned Bérénice—Renaissance travel books are all her delight—squarely faces the torment that boundless audacity exacts.

Ducharme goes on as well, with *Le nez qui voque*, *L'océantume*, *La fille de Christophe Colomb*, and *Les enfantômes*. The diary of egocentricity's travails begun with *L'avalée des avalés* continues through these novels, the principal characters of which unite in themselves the lover and the beloved, "l'amoureux et l'amoureuse," in the words of the masturbating teenager Mille Milles (*Le nez qui voque* 261). But the luxuriant mannerism seems pro forma after *L'avalée des avalés*. Ducharme repeats and caricatures himself, returning always to the "literary recipes" that produced his initial work, as Tougas observes (*Destin littéraire* 31). Why so? Robbe-Grillet, Ducharme's familiar and an éminence grise for Bessette and Aquin as well, suggests an answer: if the world is a labyrinth of mirrors, duplication and reduplication are unavoidable. And repetition induces ennui, which itself can become a subject for neobaroque jesting. "Etc..., etc..., etc...," Robbe-Grillet responds to his own killing reduplication in *Maison de rendez-vous* and so spares himself the task of rewriting and his public of rereading once again the novel's repeated single episode (La Bossière 30). The life of Iode Ssouvie, the youthful heroine trotting the globe of her mind in Ducharme's *L'océantume*, writes in small the larger cultural history of which Robbe-Grillet's joking is a part: hers, she reckons, is an age of ennui and vanity, "des voyageurs immobiles" (96). Iode has cause to agree with the prescient Emerson too, when, glossing Montaigne's "Des coches"—we travel round and round, in our own footsteps (*Essais* 3: 122)—he avers that the quest of the "new Narcissus" leads nowhere: "the world is a treadmill" (*Journals* 7: 22). Infinite as it is, then, and as Ducharme concurs, the inventiveness that unremitting reflexiveness permits also consigns the self-reliant to poverty of invention. Self-repetition, like running on (the spot) without end, must prove exhausting and cramping. Melville confirms the diagnosis. The plaint of his Ishmael—"Such is the endlessness, yea, the intolerableness of all earthly effort" (*Moby-Dick* 1: 73)—issues from a condition familiar to the self-styled drunken sailor spinning the universe and his life out of his own mind in Ducharme's *Les enfantômes*. Alone in an attic room lit by a single candle, Vincent Falardeau finds himself lost in the words of his diary and log, going round and round "au fond de mon trou ... de l'enfer" 'at the bottom of my hole ... of hell' (280). Ducharme's solitary peripatetic sees that he is effectively "immobile" (189): advance as he will, Vincent always arrives "à la même place" (232). Like creature, like author. Narrated by dreamers immobile in their abyss of unrest, Ducharme's fictions are hermetic diaries composed with magic monotony.

    The rapprochement of the French-Canadian and United States Renaissance explicitly informs the novels of Victor-Lévy Beaulieu, the author of book-length treatments of Kerouac (1972) and Melville (1978). And in no Québec novel are the problems attendant on *la renaissance* more prominently and poignantly put on display than in Beaulieu's 1974 metafiction, *Don Quichotte de la Démanche (Don Quixote in Nighttown)*. Abel Beauchemin, its author-narrator, owns dozens of copies of *Moby-Dick*, in a variety of languages, none of which he can translate. The inscrutability of Melville's book is confirmed by Abel's inarticulate response: he babbles his way through it, sometimes from end to beginning. So cognate are the two solitudes, of reader and text, that Abel can claim he knows *Moby-Dick* by heart. The joke is in deadly earnest, for Abel's "reading" of Melville's epic of communal narcissism exemplifies the paradox that always vexes Beaulieu and drives the writing of *Don Quichotte*. Beaulieu and his novel about writing that novel aim to create new life, but the work itself is a solitary's production: the inventiveness generated by the identification of reader and text, conceiver and conceived, comes at the price of infecundity. So snared in a contradiction of end and means, the artist is bound ever to work at cross-purposes. The wrenchings undergone by Beaulieu as an autogeneal-autotelic artist who would make something other than himself correspond to "the difficult and painful birth-pangs of a nation on the verge of creating and inventing itself" (Mezei 44). Like Beaulieu's many other novels—no French-Canadian author has added more to neobaroque fiction's population of uneasy spectral dreamers—*Don Quichotte* enacts an artist's toiling to cut himself free of the trammels of self-enclosure and to express what his inviolable privacy makes inexpressible.

Don Quichotte narrates the story of its own gestation by an author who sees himself as a prey "au monde baroque de ses images" (25). Set to paper by a somnambulist lost in a subterranean world ruled by "l'impérieux pouvoir de l'imagination" (157), the novel reads like an encyclopedia of neobaroque perplexities: Abel's writing is "un acte créateur abolissant toute réalité" (157). Like masturbating before a mirror (128), it is an act performed in perfect self-enclosure. His words he likens to black snakes on a field of white, their configuration the perfectly circular field of his anguish, "un champ d'angoisse parfaitement circulaire" (13), and his sentences remind him of hundreds of boot laces each knotted end to end. Kin to Ducharme's Bérénice, Abel is a swallower swallowed, and his self-consuming act of self-creation finds its logical term in death. The author-narrator of *Don Quichotte* sees himself spiraling down to hell with the *Pequod*, an effect of Promethean narcissism; and the book-child of his invention is stillborn, the product of a solitary's self-conception. As his narration ends, the feverish Abel imagines himself freezing, stock-still as he spirals in the innermost circle of his mind, trapped in his solitude. Like Melville's Ishmael, Beaulieu's Abel effectively finishes his tale a solitary "orphan," in the last word of *Moby-Dick*, himself his own mother and father.

If the work is a veritable exemplum of self-creation postmodern-style, its disposing causes and their effects, *Don Quichotte* does not augur well for the rebirth by self-invention awaited by *Destin littéraire du Québec*. The novelist lights the way for the critic, and the future looms dark. Bessette, Aquin, and Ducharme likewise serve as *éclaireurs*, providing obscure yet revealing illumination to those who would follow in the way of boundless autonomy. The solipsistic entrapment, sterility, inanition, ennui, and suicide variously featured in their neobaroque novels sign French Canada's belated entry into the age of rebirth and invention. Such gloom is not as

inevitable as destiny, however, at least for those who find themselves closer
to home in a literary culture prizing liberty of a less cramping kind. It is
worth remembering that inventiveness in the contemporary French-Canadian novel is not limited to its neobaroque practitioners. There is another
tradition, popular, older, and less somber, of a narrative literature made
for reading in community. It continues, for example, in Antonine Maillet's
Crache à Pic (English title: *The Devil Is Loose!*). This imaginary chronicle
of Acadian bootlegging during Prohibition, of seafaring thaumaturges practicing their dizzying improvisations, sets out to rebuild the world in a
carousal of fabulation. But the inventiveness that *Crache à Pic* celebrates
is held in community, and the skills of improvisation that Maillet puts to
use, like the stories she imagines, are ancestral. Working in the spirit of
Albert the Great's *Liber de alchima*, she shares in the power to transform
passed on from narrator to narrator in *Crache à Pic*, from generation to
generation. The spirit blows where it will, and Maillet follows its life-giving
inspiration, an eau-de-vie, wherever it takes her, just as she sees her people
to have done from their very beginning. Sociability and inventiveness go
hand in hand in *Crache à Pic*, which near its end narrates the witnessing
of an Acadian community before a judge who cannot understand their
language nor follow their sprightly logic. Blessed with the vigor of the
medieval homo ludens, each witness performs ably, to the delight and
profit of the collectivity. Each teller is part of a whole, *Crache à Pic* emphasizes: "Chacun se sentait bien dans la peau de l'autre, et n'aspirait pas
à l'autonomie" 'Each felt at home in the other, and did not aspire to autonomy' (333)—a condition alien to the restless solitaries at sea in the
neobaroque novel of French Canada. Maillet, according to Tougas in 1982,
can but repeat herself ("ne peut rigoureusement que se répéter"), tied as
she is "à la langue folklorisante des Acadiens" (*Destin littéraire* 32). *Crache
à Pic*, published two years later, argues otherwise. The past has gifts for
the future and, in this case, it will be a lively one made possible by the
renewal of an ancient and unifying faith.

NOTE

[1] All translations in this essay are mine.

WORKS CITED

Aquin, Hubert. *L'antiphonaire*. Montréal: Cercle du Livre de France, 1969. *The An-
tiphonary*. Trans. Alan Brown. Toronto: Anansi, 1974.

———. "The Cultural Fatigue of French Canada." *Contemporary Quebec Criticism.* Ed. and trans. Larry Shouldice. Toronto: U of Toronto P, 1979. 55–82.

———. *Neige noire.* Montréal: Cercle du Livre de France, 1974. *Hamlet's Twin.* Trans. Sheila Fischman. Toronto: McClelland, 1979.

———. *Point de fuite.* Montréal: Cercle du Livre de France, 1971.

———. *Prochain épisode.* Montréal: Cercle du Livre de France, 1965. *Prochain Episode.* Trans. Penny Williams. Toronto: McClelland, 1967.

———. *Trou de mémoire.* Montréal: Cercle du Livre de France, 1968. *Blackout.* Trans. Alan Brown. Toronto: Anansi, 1974.

Beaulieu, Victor-Lévy. *Don Quichotte de la Démanche.* Montréal: L'Aurore, 1974. *Don Quixote in Nighttown.* Trans. Sheila Fischman. Toronto: Porcépic, 1978.

———. *Jack Kérouac [sic].* Montréal: Jour, 1972.

———. *Monsieur Melville.* 3 vols. Montréal: VLB, 1978.

Bélair, Michel. *Franchir les miroirs.* Montréal: Parti Pris, 1977.

Bessette, Gérard. *L'incubation.* Montréal: Déom, 1965. *Incubation.* Trans. Glen Short-liffe. Toronto: Macmillan, 1967.

Colie, Rosalie L. *Paradoxia Epidemica: The Renaissance Tradition of Paradox.* Princeton: Princeton UP, 1966.

Cope, Jackson I. *The Theater and the Dream.* Baltimore: Johns Hopkins UP, 1973.

Dorion, Gilles. "*L'incubation.*" *Dictionnaire des oeuvres littéraires du Québec.* Ed. Maurice Lemire et al. Montréal: Fides, 1984. 4: 428–30.

Ducharme, Réjean. *L'avalée des avalés.* Paris: Gallimard, 1966. *The Swallower Swallowed.* Trans. Barbara Bray. London: Hamilton, 1968.

———. *Les enfantômes.* Paris: Gallimard, 1976.

———. *La fille de Christophe Colomb.* Paris: Gallimard, 1969.

———. *Le nez qui voque.* Paris: Gallimard, 1967.

———. *L'océantume.* Paris: Gallimard, 1968.

Emerson, Ralph Waldo. *Complete Works.* Ed. Edward Waldo Emerson. 12 vols. Boston: Houghton, 1903–04.

———. *Journals and Miscellaneous Notebooks.* Ed. W. H. Gilman et al. 16 vols. Cambridge: Belknap–Harvard UP, 1960–82.

———. *Young Emerson Speaks.* Ed. A. C. McGiffert, Jr. Port Washington: Kennikat, 1968.

Glauser, Alfred. *Montaigne paradoxal.* Paris: Nizet, 1972.

Imbert, Patrick. "Révolution culturelle et clichés chez Réjean Ducharme." *Journal of Canadian Fiction* 25–26 (1979): 227–36.

La Bossière, Camille R. " 'En sens inverse': The Traditional Imagery of Alain Robbe-Grillet's New Art." *Selecta (PNCFL)* 1 (1980): 29–31.

Lasnier, Louis. "L'Ourobouros est un serpent qui se mord la queue." *Le Québec littéraire* 1 (1974): 92–116.

Lauzière, Arsène, and Gérard Bessette. "Gérard Bessette: L'art de préciser pour (s') (m') (l') expliquer." *Journal of Canadian Fiction* 25–26 (1979): 11–25.

Leyda, Jay. *The Melville Log: A Documentary Life of Herman Melville (1819–1891)*. 2 vols. New York: Harcourt, 1951.

Maillet, Antonine. *Crache à Pic.* Montréal: Leméac, 1984. *The Devil Is Loose!* Trans. Philip Stratford. Toronto: Lester and Orpen Dennys, 1986.

McGee, Thomas D'Arcy. "The Mental Outfit of the New Dominion." *Canadian Anthology.* Ed. Carl F. Klinck and Reginald E. Watters. 3rd ed., rev. and enl. Toronto: Gage, 1974. 63–66.

Melville, Herman. *Mardi.* 1849. 2 vols. New York: Russell, 1963.

———. *Moby-Dick.* 2 vols. New York: Russell, 1963.

———. *Pierre.* New York: Russell, 1963.

———. *Poems.* New York: Russell, 1963.

Merivale, Patricia. "Hubert Aquin." *Dictionary of Literary Biography: Volume 53. Canadian Writers since 1960: First Series.* Ed. W. H. New. Detroit: Gale, 1986. 8–17.

Mezei, Kathy. "The Literature of Quebec in Revolution." *The Human Elements.* Ed. David Helwig. Ottawa: Oberon, 1978. 31–51.

Montaigne, Michel de. *Essais.* Ed. Alexandre Micha. 3 vols. Paris: Garnier-Flammarion, 1969.

Parker, Hershel, and Harrison Hayford, eds. *"Moby-Dick" as Doubloon: Essays and Extracts, 1851–1970.* New York: Norton, 1970.

Pater, Walter. *The Renaissance.* New York: Modern Library, 1899.

Rousset, Jean. *Circé et le paon: La littérature de l'âge baroque en France.* Paris: Corti, 1954.

Rowe, J. C. *Through the Custom-House: Nineteenth-Century American Fiction and Modern Theory.* Baltimore: Johns Hopkins UP, 1982.

Schopenhauer, Arthur. *The World as Will and Idea.* Trans. R. B. Haldane. 3 vols. London: Routledge, 1883–86.

Smart, Patricia. *"Neige noire:* Hamlet and Coinciding Opposites." *Essays on Canadian Writing* 11 (1978): 97–103.

Sypher, Wylie. *Four Stages of Renaissance Style.* New York: Doubleday, 1955.

Tougas, Gérard. *Destin littéraire du Québec.* Montréal: Québec/Amérique, 1982.

———. *Puissance littéraire des Etats-Unis.* Lausanne: L'Age d'Homme, 1979.

Whitman, Walt. "Letter to Ralph Waldo Emerson." *Norton Anthology of American Literature.* 2nd ed. New York: Norton, 1979. 1: 2032–41.

Karen Gould

WRITING AND READING "OTHERWISE": QUÉBEC WOMEN WRITERS AND THE EXPLORATION OF DIFFERENCE

A SIGNIFICANT DEVELOPMENT in Québec literature since the early 1970s has been the emergence of a group of women writers whose experimental efforts to reshape language and textual production in the feminine have turned conventional writing practice upside down. Writers such as Nicole Brossard, Louky Bersianik, Madeleine Gagnon, and France Théoret have ushered in a new era of textual experimentation and feminist theorizing on women's writing and the difference(s) that women's experiences and perspectives make in the language of the text. Although remarkably diverse in tone, style, themes, and structure, their works exemplify the efforts of a growing number of Québec women writers for whom the political concerns of contemporary feminism, the experimental forms of literary modernity, the particular position(s) women occupy in language, and the question of the specificity or difference of women's writing today appear to be inextricably bound.

Women writers in Québec who have engaged in various forms of self-consciously gender-marked writing since the 1970s have sought to undermine the presumed universality of literature written through male eyes and to shatter patriarchy's sphere of influence over language and thought. Many of their "newly born" (Cixous, *La jeune née*), women-centered texts stand in bold contrast to traditional literary forms and conventional literary objectives that, in the minds of many Québec feminists, have served to censor women's words, to devalorize "feminine" forms of inscription, and, in general, to hinder critical appreciation of the significant otherness of women's writing. In a vigorously modern way, Brossard, Bersianik, Gagnon, Théoret, and others have celebrated women's "new" entry into language by exposing the traps and conventions of phallocentric discourse, and by asserting the centrality of female experience in writing. Inspired by feminist thought in Québec, France, and the United States, the voices encountered in these texts analyze the nature of women's oppression and alienation in patriarchal society, endeavor to delegitimize patriarchal authority by undermining its discourse, explore the multiple sources of female pleasure, and locate the most fertile sites of their own feminine creativity through language.

Recognizing the collective nature of their creative efforts and acknowledging their historic ties to other women writers, Brossard, Bersianik, Théoret, and Gagnon have used a variety of literary techniques to underscore the plurality of women's voices that traverse their own literary explorations. While Bersianik and Brossard have cited Mary Daly, Adrienne Rich, Monique Wittig, and Gertrude Stein in their work, and Théoret has conjured up the presence of Marie-Claire Blais, Virginia Woolf, Colette, and the silent aunt whose words were kept under wraps, Gagnon has looked to Annie Leclerc, Eva Forest, Marguerite Duras, her own grandmother, and to women collectively for inspiration, literary companionship, and solidarity:

> We're going to tell them what resemblances we share. How we repeat ourselves, plagiarize one another; how our writings become collective.... We all speak your words: me too, me too; I could have written it; I'll write it for you; you'll write it for me. Others and others still.[1]   (Gagnon, preface 9–10)

Strictly speaking, attempts by Québec women writers to inscribe the feminine do not constitute a literary movement per se, particularly since individual political perspectives, narrative strategies, poetic design, linguistic forms, rhythm, and thematic lines of development differ so widely from one writer to the next. Moreover, some writers, such as Gagnon, are understandably wary of labels and resist characterizing the experimental texts of Québec feminists as anything resembling a literary school or distinctly classifiable avant-garde (Gould, "Ecrire" 137). Yet few in Québec would dispute the fact that since the mid-1970s, the efforts of a growing number of Québec women writers to approach writing in a different voice have signaled a major shift in focus in women's literary production and an increased interest on the part of Québec feminists in radical textual experimentation.

During the 1970s, the project of "writing like a woman" (Ostriker)—that is to say, from a woman's vantage point, from a woman's body, and in a language that could be regarded as primarily woman-made—emerged as a new and transgressive mode of political intervention. For feminists sensitive to the inherent complicity under patriarchy between discourse and power, between the father's word and institutional authority, the project of writing "otherwise"—against and possibly even outside paternal reason, truth, and phallic desire—can be viewed as a radical attempt to destablize and ultimately dislocate the phallocentric hierarchy, both real and symbolic. It also constitutes an attempt to "derange" patriarchal discourse by overthrowing its syntax, "by suspending its eternally teleological order, by snipping the wires, cutting the current, breaking the circuits, switching the connections, by modifying continuity, alternation, frequency, intensity" (Irigaray, *Speculum* 142).

To date, the regions of the new territory of feminine inscription appear to be boundless, the terrain constantly fluctuating. Experimental efforts to write in the feminine have unveiled an ever-shifting linguistic field of female discovery not unlike what French theorist Luce Irigaray has referred to as the "flowing," "fluctuating," "excess" of women's discourse (Irigaray, *Ce sexe* 76) or the haunting depths of Hélène Cixous's oceanic expanses and the liberating "flight" (*vol*) she attributes to women who dare to "steal" (*vole*) the words of men and make them their own (Cixous, "Le rire" 49). In the face of a hostile and oftentimes intolerable patriarchal environment, the poet and theorist Brossard considers the notion of a gender-marked *écriture au féminin* as both an imaginative site on which to construct a new female identity and an indication of the desire of contemporary women to transform themselves, both individually and collectively. For Brossard, writing in the feminine entails the inventive mapping of women's expansiveness and *ouverture* through the act of writing. The process of writing also provides a radical opening in the world, where the woman writer's personal and political aspirations may finally conjoin in the creative expression of an "unutterable will to change life, to change her life" (*La lettre aérienne* 44).

The political urgency of writing through a feminist consciousness as a way of exploring and ultimately heightening women's consciousness is, of course, a progressive stance for our time—whether in Québec or elsewhere. Beyond the political necessity of conveying the realities of women's lives and the range of their creative abilities, however, the notion of writing in the feminine as a writing of difference is clearly a complex and potentially problematic one, even for the most sympathetic feminist readers. Well aware of the thorny issues associated with the question of difference in women's experimental writing in Québec, I should, nevertheless, like to address the subject in this essay. More specifically, this discussion will focus on the theoretical underpinnings of *l'écriture au féminin* and on how the notion of difference has circulated in particular texts.

Both contemporary Québec feminism and the ensuing literary experiment of writing in the feminine have developed from the convergence of social, literary, and intellectual currents in Québec during the late 1960s and early 1970s. The efforts of women writers to voice the *différence* of women's experience are firmly grounded in feminist analyses of gender politics in patriarchal culture, in the related political debates of the left on racism, imperialism, and nationalism, and in important political and philosophical discourses of our time—Marxism, psychoanalysis, and deconstruction in particular. Québec feminists were also influenced by increasing political attention to the analysis and cultural affirmation of the francophone experience in North America, and by the appeal to the "modern" (both modernization and, subsequently, *modernité*) ushered in during Québec's cultural revolution and its aftermath in the late 1960s. Women activists in the 1970s were inspired, as well, by the political currents within the feminist movement itself, including socialist feminist perspectives. The early writings of Gagnon (*Pour les femmes* and *Poélitique*), for instance, reflect the significant impact of Marxist thought and labor solidarity on a number of Québec feminist writers of the period.

Québec nationalism, for which a number of Québec writers became "the privileged articulators" (Schwartzwald 46), would offer feminists a political and theoretical language in which to investigate their particular sense of oppression and alienation as women. Both the political nature of the discourse of decolonization in Québec and the seriousness of the language question associated with that discourse underscored the crucial ties linking language, oppression, and cultural hegemony. The writings of Gaston Miron, Paul Chamberland, Jacques Godbout, Michèle Lalonde, and others provided a social as well as a literary forum for the expression of political and cultural discontent. Moreover, the desire for radical change explicit in much of this literature was an expressed desire for change in the relations of power outside as well as within Québec society itself.

In terms of Québec feminism, the decolonization paradigm created an international frame of reference for women's political analyses through its identification with Third World liberation movements—Algeria, Chile, Vietnam, Argentina were frequently cited in the socialist feminist journalism of the time. Both Gagnon and Théoret have linked women's oppression under patriarchy with the struggles of developing countries subjected to the dominance of foreign capital. Thus, even at the height of her experimentation with the female "body text" and alongside her critique of Lacanian psychoanalysis, Gagnon continued to make the connection between feminism and Third World resistance to Western imperialism. In her important theoretical text "Mon corps dans l'écriture," the female body is the site of an erupting force of resistance to political oppression as well as sexual repression. Her weapon of revolt is a form of writing that moves from the personal (the female writer) to the political (the exploited body politic):

> Mon corps est maux. Mais du fond de ma nuit, il est volcan qui commence à gronder, il est lumières qui commencent à luir: de partout, de tous les pays, je viens raconter cette nuit. Je me lis d'une contrée à l'autre, j'assiste à mes mouvements de libération—d'Amérique, de Chine, du Portugal, de France ou d'Espagne, du Cambodge, du Viêt-nam et de plus loin encore—je me mets à bouger et l'on me voit du dedans. (64)

> My body is pain. But from my nocturnal depths, it is a volcano beginning to rumble, it is lights beginning to glimmer: from everywhere, from every country, I come to describe this night. I read myself from one country to the next, I witness my movements of liberation—from America, from China, from Portugal, from France or from Spain, from Cambodia, from Vietnam and from farther away still—I begin to move and people see me from the inside.

By the late 1960s, while many Québec writers and critics focused on the national question and the related thematics of country and collective identity, Brossard, Marcel Saint-Pierre, Jan Stafford, and Roger Soublière had formed what was to become the most important review devoted to literary modernity in Québec for over a decade.[2] Theoretically transgressive in its modern posture of experimentation over tradition, *La barre du jour* (1965–77) exemplified the keen interest of a small but increasingly visible portion of Québec's literary avant-garde in the materiality of language and in the possibilities of subversion and play that writing provides. Nurturing the intense self-consciousness of more formalist writers, *La barre du jour* became an oasis for some of the more subversive and theoretically oriented explorations of *modernité*, a place where the popular political themes of the time lay relatively dormant, where the hierarchical and arbitrary divisions of conventional literary genres and the literary canon itself were openly contested, and where the practice and pleasure of writing would be continually reinvestigated. (While the notion of *modernité* in French is usually translated in the United States as *postmodernism*, the particular emphasis in Québec on the radically new—hence positively modern—is not sufficiently rendered by the term *postmodern* [Gould, *Writing* 17–24].)

For Brossard, the posture of literary modernity at *La barre du jour* was, in fact, "resolutely modern." Echoing an increasing weariness on the part of a number of Québec intellectuals with the nationalist themes and overtly political forms of writing that had dominated the literary scene during the early 1960s, Brossard articulated a set of theoretical positions for the review that would challenge the conventional semantic system as a whole and would resist the internal consumer logic of bourgeois literary production:

> Something in the thematics of the country irritated us. Politically speaking, we supported by and large the texts of *Parti pris*. But from a literary point of view, we had the "impression" of a void ... we wanted to approach and question literature differently. We had a lot of pretension to subversion. We wanted the spirit of protest to enter literature as well. We wanted to approach literature from a formal point of view, from the point of view of writing.[3]
>
> ("Ce que pouvait être" 71)

For Brossard and later for Théoret, who also worked for a time at *La barre du jour*, the emphasis on the materiality of language brought with it an awareness of language as social construction and, in turn, fueled the exploration of writing as an ongoing process of imaginative and unconventional discovery. This modern sensibility encouraged an indulging self-reflexivity on the part of the writer; it also heightened awareness of how words, linguistic structures, and literary forms emit prescriptive cultural codes for organizing reality and fiction. Literature was thus found to be subject to the same ideological pressures toward conformity as other forms of cultural production.

In Québec, and at *La barre du jour* in particular, the loss of confidence in traditional bourgeois values and the general doubt of modernity led to a radical *mise en question* of representational art and of the mimetic abilities of language itself. Many of the experimental writers publishing in *La barre du jour* during its early years worked to deprive words of their presumed essence, since words themselves could no longer be revered as objects of predetermined meaning or *signification*. As a palpable object, Brossard wanted the word to become familiar "in the bursting, in the rupture. It's a question of constructing the passkey word that no longer refers merely to emotional and intellectual notions, but that mainly creates its own variants: the word-consciousness in opposition to the word-convention" (editorials 45). By exploding conventional meanings, stripping language bare, hollowing it out, and leaving openings where meanings are as yet undetermined, Brossard hoped to dismantle the old logic of writing and of conceptualizing and, at the same time, to expand the semantic system dramatically.

In texts published by Brossard and others in the early issues of *La barre du jour*, the notion of distinct genres gradually withered away, while *textualité* and later *écriture* became the theoretical passwords. At the same time, the general orientation of the review was increasingly marked by the influence of new theoretical discourses in France, by Barthes's semiological practice and Blanchot's discussions of literary modernity, by the disruptive force of Derridian deconstruction, and later by Cixous's modernist sensibility and radical philosophy of feminine desire. Yet despite the general suspicion and distancing between reader, writer, and the written word in Brossard's early texts, and despite a kind of experimental neutrality (anonymity?) that she initially assigned herself as a writer—consequences that would later pose serious problems for Brossard, Théoret, and other feminists disturbed by the apparent erasure of gender identity in the texts associated with Québec's literary modernity—Brossard's notion of "the pleasure of the text" spilled out beyond the boundaries of the page, creating an intimate complicity between an as-yet-fractured, gender-neutral speaker and a reader whom she continually invited to participate in the seduction of reading ungrammatically and in new ways, of reading differently.

With the publication in 1970 of two volumes of poetry, *Suite logique* and *Le centre blanc*, Brossard's exploration of a language of neutrality and excess was at its apex. Conveying an ever-increasing bareness of vision, she stripped away the last traces of realistic description and emptied her poems of conventional punctuation and syntax. The key verb in both texts is, in fact, *dénuder*, with its sense of stripping, laying bare, and of uncovering as well: "dénuder le sens sa non-évidence" 'strip/uncover meaning its non-evidence/unclearness' (*Le centre blanc* 194). Ellipses, holes, "deferred" meanings are abundant in Brossard's poetry at this point. Surface, fragment, void, fiction, text, become her primary exploratory themes. This ultramodern poetry is both deconstructive and forward-looking; it is also a highly intellectual poetry in which anticipated meanings are neutralized, formal structures are fractured, and the first-person pronoun is eclipsed through what Normand de Bellefeuille refers to as "the negation of the grammatical subject" (94).

In place of continuity, solidity, hierarchy, and certainty, Brossard constructs a discourse of instability and doubt in which

> l'exil s'impose radical
> la certitude n'est que vérifiable
> en ce moment la démesure renverse   (*Le centre blanc* 155)
>
> exile is radically imposed
> certainty is only verifiable
> at this time excess overthrows

In short, Brossard's resolutely modern writing in 1970 projects a certain Derridian indeterminacy and unreadability, characteristics that many critics now consider the hallmarks of postmodern writing. Yet both the temporal break with the past and the textual indeterminacy Brossard sought to explore failed to produce the kind of experimental neutrality she had initially envisioned, for the very notion of "neutrality" in the acts of reading and writing denies the overriding force of determinants that both writer and reader bring to any text. This troublesome ruse of neutrality is one that Brossard has since acknowledged as problematic in her early works. As Mary Jacobus notes, "Privileging indeterminacy ... risks ignoring powerful determinants on the readings which a text may generate, one of these determinants being the question of sexual difference (whether signaled by its presence or its absence)" (290).

Suite logique and *Le centre blanc* announced the beginning of the end for the lengthy courtship of the real and the representational in modern Québec literature. For Brossard and others writing in *La barre du jour*, the entire mimetic enterprise of conventional art was, in effect, being called into question, while their new focus became the process and pleasure of writing itself. In the early to mid-1970s, however, a number of Québec feminists, including Théoret, challenged modernity's refusal to distinguish between fiction and reality together with its need to "bracket off the referent or real historical world" (Eagleton 140) and thereby bracket off the political forces that could conceivably promote social change.

From a woman's point of view, the evacuation of the real and of the real speaking subject from many experimental texts could only encourage self-denial, a dilemma that ultimately led a number of feminist writers to rethink the cultural bases and social implications of *modernité* for women in general. Théoret has candidly acknowledged her feelings of failure as a writer during her association with *La barre du jour*: "One wasn't permitted to be a woman. If one was a woman, one introduced something about the order of existence into writing and that was 'semanticizing' writing, returning to representation. It was necessary, in fact, to flee representation. That was not allowed to take place in any fashion" ("Le fantasme" 89). By the mid-1970s, Brossard herself readily admitted the serious risks for women in a writing of modernity that effaced the historical and the female speaking subject, while blurring the distinctions between fiction and the reality of women's daily lives.

The impact, however, of Brossard's initial concerns with textual production and with language as a forever new space of ecstatic, if solitary, invention can still be traced in her most radically woman-centered writing. Even in a text as recent as *Picture Theory*, we find repeated evidence of her earlier efforts to undermine anticipated meanings, to confront the void or dense "whiteness," as she initially termed it, of unnarratability, and to demonstrate how the text "works"—how it proceeds, falters, is condensed, and overflows the recognizable semantic field. In fact, Brossard's extreme literary self-consciousness and fundamental questioning of virtually every aspect of the writing process have never ceased, even though the act of writing itself has also become a way of exploring female sexuality and feminist consciousness and of articulating women's desire for one another and for other ways of organizing reality:

> Quelle forme peut bien prendre une pensée contemporaine qui donnerait aux mots une autre tournure d'esprit, car le corps a ses raisons. Comment garder ses distances avec les mots sans pour autant donner sa place, sans en arriver à se neutraliser dans son texte, sans perdre de vue une image de soi enfin libérée de sa négativité, sans négliger ce qui la reflète (les femmes et le sens de l'honneur, comme le dirait Adrienne Rich) et qui toujours aussi la transforme et en déploie le sens. (*Le lettre aérienne* 51)

> What form can a contemporary thought best take that would give words another cast of mind, for the body has its reasons. How to keep one's distance with words without for all that relinquishing one's place, without reaching the point of neutralizing oneself in the text, without losing sight of an image of self liberated at last from negativity, without neglecting what reflects it (women and the sense of honor, as Adrienne Rich would say) and also what always transforms it and reveals its meaning.

While replete with contradictions for the project of writing in the feminine, the move to inscribe *la modernité* in Québec, as Brossard herself had promoted it, thus brought language to the foreground, not as an item primarily attached to a specific political agenda (the way some nationalist writers had characterized it), but rather as a site of rupture and continual beginnings and as a source of abstract pleasure in the infinite possibilities of creativity itself—even if the traces of gender were to a large extent obfuscated and even if the text did not appear to be historically grounded. The demanding ethic to "inaugurate" rather than to "repeat," which the critic Suzanne Lamy associated with the most innovative examples of *l'écriture au féminin*, certainly has its roots in the conscious position of transgression and invention that modernity assumed (56). Likewise, the combined emphasis of Québec's literary modernity on theory and writing practice prepared the way for the textual integration of various theoretical positions within feminism into women's writing. With the languages of poetry, prose, and theory no longer distinct, no longer assigned different value in many experimental texts, the door was opened for feminists to challenge the traditional marginalization of "other" forms of *écriture* as well, such as diaries, journals, letters, and autobiographical writing in general.

Various strands of the sensibility we most associate with literary modernity in Québec greatly influenced the theoretical orientations of Brossard, Théoret, and Bersianik, as well as others. By the mid-1970s, however, women writers already interested in *modernité* were increasingly inspired by the political concerns of the feminist movement in Québec, as well as in France and in the United States. A number of them began to experiment with approaches to writing that could address—both theoretically and poetically—the problematic position and historic absence of the female subject in language and in writing. Concerned with linking modernity with the political agendas of various feminist groups, they began to consider the relationships between political theory (traditionally male) and cultural production (also predominately male), between language and gender (historically male constructions), between the realm of the symbolic (inaccessible to women, says Lacan) and the concrete realm of women's daily lives, between a long-repressed sexuality and the authorative power of the male word. Cixous's much-discussed invitation to women to "write themselves" in an-other language captures the point of departure for women's writing in Québec after 1975: "Woman must write her self: must write about women and bring women to writing, from which they have been driven away as violently as from their bodies—for the same reasons, by the same law, with the same fatal goal. Woman must put herself into the text—as into the world and into history—by her own movement" ("Le rire" 875).

Marcelle Brisson has defined the advent of experimental feminist writing in Québec as a writing of the body (*écriture du corps*), in which the writer inscribes her body in order to discover and recover herself, hence a politically motivated affirmation of women's physical difference:

> Woman's writing says to us: This is my body. It starts from there and returns there. It is a constant in this writing, regardless of whether or not we situate it before or after the avant-garde philosophical movements of its time. Woman writes from her own hills and from her caverns and from her mountains.... If there is no reference to the body, there is no feminist writing. (27)

Although extreme in its emphasis on the corporeal in feminist writing in Québec, Brisson's description underscores the crucial and highly visible centering of the female body in numerous women's texts since 1975. Moreover, despite the wide range of structures, thematics, and generating symbols Québec women writers have employed to inscribe their sexual difference, it is from, to, and through women's bodies that some of the most radical forms of feminine inscription have taken place.

In 1977, three texts appeared that exemplified the corporeal grounding of experimental attempts at feminine inscription. While dissimilar in many ways, Gagnon's poetic essay "Mon corps dans l'écriture," Brossard's radical theoretical fiction in *L'amèr* (*These Our Mothers*), and Théoret's first important text, *Bloody Mary*, marked a turning point in feminist literary experimentation. By strategically linking the exploration and celebration of women's bodies—previously repressed in writing as in life—with a theoretical discourse on language and difference, they combined modernity's move toward transgression and rupture with overtly political issues such as abortion, rape, violence toward women, cultural and institutional sexism, sexuality and motherhood, and lesbian rights.

Released from centuries of statuesque silence—like the Carayatids of the Acropolis whom Louky Bersianik would delightfully bring to life and to language two years later—the female bodies in *L'amèr, Bloody Mary*, and "Mon corps dans l'écriture" yearn, cry out, even 'bleed' for a language of their own, a language capable of subverting and breaking up both the fictional (discursive) and the real (institutional) order of things. All three texts develop the compelling analogy between women's historical absence from the political and cultural spheres and the silenced female body. And in each case, writing the female body brings forth new forms of corporeal imagery, distinctly female thematics centering on the vitality, insurgent libidinal desires, and creative power of women's bodies, new and more "fluid" structures suggestive of women's physical fluids, and a ruptured syntax that signals a radical break with logocentric discourse and the unifying authority of phallocentrism. Yet while the specificity of *écriture féminine* in these texts appears to be located increasingly in biological difference, a closer look suggests that the theoretical considerations underlying these inscriptions of the female body are as firmly rooted in political analyses of the various forms of women's oppression as they are in the more essentialist paradigms of biological difference, inspired by Cixous and Irigaray in particular.[4]

In "Mon corps dans l'écriture," Gagnon argues for an approach to women's writing that would displace patriarchy's phallic "conceit" by putting female sexuality and feminine desire back at the center of women's discourse. For Gagnon, the historic repression of women's sexuality and desire in male-centered discourse has resulted in the continual repression of the female form and of feminine creativity itself. In this pivotal essay, Gagnon calls for the birth of a "body writing" that is gender-marked, intimately personal, and politically astute.

Echoing feminist Adrienne Rich, who has also urged women to "touch the unity and resonance of our physicality, our bond with the natural order, the corporeal ground of our intelligence" (21), Gagnon considers the link between textuality and corporeality an essential one in the struggle to revolutionize women's consciousness. As women write the female body, so will they write the female form, and thereby reconceptualize her infinite possibilities. By writing with and through the desiring female body—a body in search of the multiplicity and fullness of life in all its forms—Gagnon hopes to destroy the false binary opposition of reason (intellect) and sexuality (body) that has long dominated phallocentric discourse in the West. From her vantage point, the knowledge that has (mis)guided Western thinking for centuries is "structured by a discourse without sexuality: without drives or fantasies. It's a knowledge without desire" ("Mon corps dans l'écriture" 83).

Gagnon's commitment to write the female body and establish a direct relationship between her body and the unfolding text rests with the belief that the scriptorial, the corporeal, and the political are essentially one. The socialist revolution she espoused in earlier works has thus taken a back seat to a revolution of women struggling to reach beyond their social isolation, class differences, and physical distance in patriarchal-heterosexual society and to reach toward a political union with other women. Since no viable models for such a revolution exist, Gagnon urges women to recapture the power and inherent multiplicity of lost female forms through an exploratory language that traces the inscriptions of an infinite number of differences on women's flesh, in their varied fantasies, in their groping words, and in the farthest recesses of what might be termed a collective feminine unconscious:

> Nos révolutions vont sourdre de toutes parts. Visqueuses, défilées, emmêlées, nouées ou tendues. Mon cerveau n'est pas linéaire; mon sexe est circulaire, il se plie, se délie et décrit des circonvolutions; mes yeux sont ronds, mes oreilles compliquées à déjouer toute description; ma langue tordue, mes langues d'écritures étranges et semblables.... (115–16)

> Our revolutions are going to gush from all sides. Viscous, filing past, entangled, tied together or strained. My brain is not linear; my sex is circular, it bends, unties itself and depicts circumvolutions; my eyes are round, my ears intricate enough to elude all description; my tongue twisted, my languages of writing strange and similar....

In "Mon corps dans l'écriture," the vision of an approach to writing grounded in the uniqueness of women's physical being thus becomes not only an individual act of self-possession but of collective reappropriation as well. What keeps Gagnon's emphasis on the physicality of women's writing from returning too easily to the old reductive masculinist categories of woman = body + Nature (vs. man = mind + Culture) is the extent to which the female body in Gagnon's writing relates to various aspects of human experience, including the most intellectual and abstract of human activities. Gagnon's efforts both in this essay and in subsequent texts to weld together intellectual theory, remarkably intimate narrative descriptions, and poetic reflections on her own life are an indication of her ability to resist categorizing and limiting women's experience in writing and in the world.

Nowhere in contemporary Québec writing, it seems, is the pain resulting from women's alienation in language more acute than in Théoret's *Bloody Mary*. The focus here is on an urgent search for words that might give the female speaker a physical presence (a face and a body in the mirror) and might somehow express the censored realities of women's lives. For Théoret, any successful move to articulate a woman's life involves penetrating the masks of social convention and thereby hastens the transgression of all social codes. In Théoret's early writing, this need to write translates as a crying out for recognition of women born in poverty, raised in self-depreciation, and harshly conditioned in self-denial. The female voice in *Bloody Mary* imagines her pencil in the form of a knife or stake as she sharpens her tongue and dreams of tearing through traditional phallocentric discourse with the force of an angry slash. The extreme physicality of this gesture is a prime example of the convulsive manner in which the female body struggles to write itself in Théoret's text by "slicing" through the smooth surfaces of the master's discourse.

For French-speaking readers, the title of *Bloody Mary* is itself a form of linguistic and cultural assault, evoking both the rude English words and the unpopularity of an English queen (Mary I, 1553–58) whose troubled reign and strong ties to Catholicism resulted in religious persecution and civil unrest. Théoret's title can also be read as a vulgarized evocation of the Virgin Mary, whom the Catholic church has traditionally associated with purity and with the absolute absence of blood, of the physical, of the sexual, of the real. The polysemic richness of the English word *bloody* gives Théoret room to explore the variable and contradictory meanings the term evokes in her text. While the Mary of Catholic dogma has been purified to the point of transparency and muzzled into perennial silence, Théoret's female writer emerges as a new Mary whose words are "bloody" in every conceivable sense of the term: cruel, murderous, stained with blood, cursed, damned.

Women's blood circulates on a variety of levels in this text, but always in connection with women's awkward, untenable position in language. Indeed, for Théoret, the words women might speak were they free to do so would be marked in blood, the blood of their menses (which must not be mentioned), the blood of secret abortions, of rape, all of which produce 'stains' that society prefers to ignore. Unlike the numerous deconstructive attempts to "cut up" the language of the father in this text—causing paternal blood to flow—these bloody references to the female body are less abstract and much closer to the everyday reality of women's bodies and women's lives. They also point to the various ways in which women's language is, of necessity, concealed, "cleaned up," and yet remains stubbornly stained in red. The material appearance of *Bloody Mary* is also visibly "bloodied," since each of the three fragments included in the text is introduced by blank pages stained with a bloodlike ink, as is the text's cover.

Women's words and the blood from women's bodies leave subversive traces that Théoret wants to expose rather than mop up. To speak as a woman—both in and from a female body—means to let the blood flow, to resist the censorship of a language that is deemed unfit, unclean by the dominant culture. Most shocking of all, Théoret suggests that the language women have been schooled in, harnessed in, and have then unwittingly used at their own expense is itself a form of rape:

> L'engorgée la possédée l'enfirouapée la plâtrée la trou d'cul l'odalisque la livrée la vierge succube fend la verge fend la langue serre les dents. Des passes je me fais la passe, je suis ma propre maison de passe. (11)

> The choked the possessed the bound in fur the painted up the ass hole the concubine the servant the virgin demon the penis penetrates the tongue penetrates grit your teeth. Passes I make a pass at myself, I am my own brothel.

The syntax and rhythm in the passage are chopped up like the inherited masculine language Théoret wants to axe and be done with. Moreover, the vulgarity inherent in the sexual stereotypes attributed to women is so insistent that, ultimately, we are left numb. Her violation is our violation, the ravishing pace and intent of these mocking patriarchal words are both alien and uncomfortably familiar. In the end, the female speaker admits to her own complicity. The whole textual event leaves her (and the female reader) limp and speechless. The remainder of the page is blank. Théoret's female voice has silenced herself.

For the female voice struggling to speak in *Bloody Mary*, both body and language, outside and inside, have come to resemble alien ground. Thus, in Théoret's text, writing in the feminine requires coming to terms with the real as well as with the symbolic violation of women in patriarchal culture, for it is only then that women can begin to "unspeak," to wear down little by little the structures of a "forced" discourse that, as Patricia Smart has also suggested, sequesters women and divides them from one another (Smart 153).

The physical and linguistic alienation Théoret explores in *Bloody Mary* is further developed in Brossard's powerful dramatizing of a woman writer's resistance to the language of the father in *L'amèr*. And like Théoret's insistence on "un-speaking" and Irigaray's "disconcerting of language," Brossard's call for women's "de-conditioning" with regard to language involves a radical process of linguistic and social unlearning, a setting fire to all previous discursive constraints. *L'amèr* provides an entry into a world of proliferating maternal words and discursive spaces in which the lost warmth, regenerative power, and repressed desire of the mother are uncovered and linguistically reconstituted. Brossard searches for the buried "maternal tongue" through the female child who, in a bid for subjectivity, has chosen to align herself with the father's language and authority at the expense of maternal ties.

Brossard's writing in *L'amèr* is first and foremost an act of reparation that invests the mother figure with a physical freedom and discursive force previously denied her in fiction and in reality. Situating herself between two generations of women—a mother and daughter—Brossard undertakes an imaginative rewriting of the mother figure by reappropriating both the physically productive attributes of the mother's body and the symbolic domain of the maternal archetype: "J'ai tué le ventre et fait éclater la mer" (12) 'I have killed the womb and exploded the sea/our sour mother' (14). Brossard's urgent need to liberate the female body from the traditional burden of sexual reproduction forms the textual imperative of *L'amèr*, which is, in essence, the construction of a discourse capable of transmitting the maternal body and the maternal voice to a new generation of daughters who will resist any impregnation—physical, intellectual, artistic—that might enslave them. For woman's submission to the father, husband, lover, brother, argues Brossard, has invariably led to her own painful illegitimacy.

The deconstructive strategies Brossard employs to rethink women's identity outside the traditional biological sphere have been both courageous and influential. Brossard's poetic success at stripping the mother figure of her "domesticated" breasts and womb, and thereby transforming her into a powerful and effective symbol of resistance to male domination and man-made language, is yet another example of the defiant character of her writing: "On ne tue pas la mère biologique sans que n'éclatent tout à la fois la fiction, l'idéologie, le propos" (21) 'The biological mother isn't killed without a simultaneous explosion of fiction, ideology, utterance' (23).

In her desire for the mother who has been idealized and silenced, Brossard finds her own form and discovers the mouths and bodies of other women as well. The mother thus becomes a beacon for a female-centered vision of language, textual production, and social organization. Ultimately, *L'amèr* reads as a positive lesbian utterance as well as an invitation to reflection, an intellectual yet poetic attempt to engage the reader in a series of contemporary reflections on women as mothers, daughters, and lovers of other women. Above all, *L'amèr* offers both a deconstructive and an affirmatively lesbian approach to writing in the feminine that has paved the way for Brossard's later theoretical fiction. Here and in the works that follow, Brossard's writing risks all in its efforts to inscribe feminine differ-ence intensely and to trace the contours of women's desires in the political, emotional, and physical realms of fiction and daily life:

> Prendre des risques en dedans, avec le doigt dans la gorge pour faire vomir la muse endormie. De voir surgir. En même temps, les mythes foisonnants, la faune oscillante. Le creux des poitrines. La fille les regarde au loin les femmes: mirage. Pour en arriver là en personne, contemporaine. (82)

> Take risks inside, with the finger in the throat to make the sleeping muse vomit. To see it come up. At the same time, myths abounding, fauna swaying. The hollow of the breasts. The girl looks at the women far away: mirage. To reach that point in person, contemporary. (84)

Although unquestionably diverse in style, tone, and political perspective, the three works—"Mon corps dans l'écriture," *Bloody Mary*, and *L'amèr* —exemplify the affirming movements from women's bodies to writing and from theorizing to being-in-the-world that have characterized attempts to write in the feminine in Québec since the mid 1970s. And despite significant changes in narrative development, in their poetic symbolisms, and even in the political orientations of these writers, subsequent texts by Brossard (*Amantes, Le sens apparent, Picture Theory, Domain d'écriture, La lettre aérienne, Le désert mauve*), Théoret (*Une voix pour Odile, Nécessairement putain, Nous parlerons comme on écrit, Entre raison et déraison, L'homme qui peignait Staline*), and Gagnon (*Antre, Lueur, Pensées du poème, La lettre infinie, Les fleurs du catalpa*) underscore the specificity of women's relationships to language and to the process of writing. Most important, the strength of their respective poetic visions as well as their efforts to undo and remake the text suggest that women's writing today—and in Québec in particular—may provide a provocative social forum for exploring dif-ferences and for imagining another kind of future.[5]

NOTES

[1]All translations are my own unless otherwise indicated.

[2]During its twelve years in print, *La barre du jour* published fifty-seven issues. For an informative discussion of the history and evolution of *La barre du jour* and its sequel, *La nouvelle barre du jour* (1977–90), see the special issue devoted to it in *Voix et images* 10.2 (1985).

[3]*Parti pris* was an influential literary and cultural review, published from 1963 to 1968, that brought together the writings of left-wing intellectuals (poets, novelists, political theorists) around the themes of nationalism, socialism, and revolution. As Louise Forsyth has noted, "Brossard shared the immediate socio-political goals of the *Parti pris* generation and was also in agreement with many of its views and priorities: nationalism must confront the problems of the present and make an absolute break with past traditions; analysis is essential to any effective form of political action; a people alienated from its language is without the means to envisage and affirm its freedom and autonomy; the real problem is interiorized fear and defeat" (159).

[4]The move to recognize the biological as one of the creative sources of *écriture féminine* (particularly the centrality of the maternal body in Cixous's early work) has been hotly debated by a number of critics in the United States, including Ann Rosalind Jones and Domna Stanton, who have pointed out some of the philosophical and political pitfalls of privileging difference by means of what appears to be an essentialist argument.

[5]This essay is drawn from my study *Writing in the Feminine: Feminism and Experimental Writing in Quebec*, which examines the literary projects of Nicole Brossard, Madeleine Gagnon, Louky Bersianik, and France Théoret.

WORKS CITED

Bellefeuille, Normand de. "Suite logique." *La nouvelle barre du jour* 118–19 (1982): 91–98.

Bersianik, Louky. *Le pique-nique sur l'Acropole*. Montréal: VLB, 1979.

Brisson, Marcelle. "Femme et écriture." *Arcade* 11 (1986): 26–32.

Brossard, Nicole. *Amantes*. Montréal: Quinze, 1980. *Lovers*. Trans. Barbara Godard. Montréal: Guernica, 1986.

———. *L'amèr: Ou, le chapitre effrité*. Montréal: Quinze, 1977. *These Our Mothers: Or, The Disintegrating Chapter*. Trans. Barbara Godard. Toronto: Coach House, 1983.

———. *Le centre blanc*. Montréal: L'Hexagone, 1978.

———. "Ce que pouvait être, ici, une avant-garde." *Voix et images* 10.2 (1985): 68–85.

———. *Le désert mauve*. Montréal: L'Hexagone, 1987.

———. *Domaine d'écriture*. Montréal: NBJ, 1985.

———. Excerpts from political editorials published outside *La barre du jour*. *Voix et images* 10.2 (1985): 41–46.

———. *La lettre aérienne*. Montréal: Rémue-Ménage, 1985. *The Aerial Letter*. Trans. Marlene Wildeman. Toronto: Women's, 1988.

———. *Picture Theory*. Montréal: Nouvelle Optique, 1982.

———. *Le sens apparent*. Paris: Flammarion, 1980.

Cixous, Hélène. *La jeune née.* Paris: Union Générale, 1976. *The Newly Born Woman.* Trans. Betsy Wing. Minneapolis: U of Minnesota P, 1986.

———. "Le rire de la Méduse." *L'arc* 61 (1975). "The Laugh of the Medusa." Trans. Keith Cohen and Paula Cohen. *Signs* 1.4 (1975): 875–99.

Eagleton, Terry. *Against the Grain.* London: Verso, 1986.

Forsyth, Louise. "Beyond the Myths and Fictions of Traditionalism and Nationalism: The Political in the Work of Nicole Brossard." *Traditionalism, Nationalism, and Feminism: Women Writers of Quebec.* Ed. Paula Gilbert Lewis. Westport: Greenwood, 1985. 157–72.

Gagnon, Madeleine. *Antre.* Montréal: Herbes Rouges, 1978. *Lair.* Trans. Howard Scott. Toronto: Coach House, 1989.

———. *Les fleurs du catalpa.* Montréal: VLB, 1986.

———. *La lettre infinie.* Montréal: VLB, 1984.

———. *Lueur: Roman archéologique.* Montréal: VLB, 1979.

———. "Mon corps dans l'écriture." *La venue à l'écriture.* Paris: Union Générale, 1977.

———. *Pensées du poème.* Montréal: VLB, 1983.

———. *Poélitique.* Montréal: Herbes Rouges, 1975.

———. *Pour les femmes et tous les autres.* Montréal: L'Aurore, 1974.

———. Preface. *Cyprine.* By Denise Boucher. Montréal: L'Aurore, 1978.

Gould, Karen. "Ecrire au féminin: Interview avec Denise Boucher, Madeleine Gagnon et Louky Bersianik." *Québec Studies* 2 (1984): 125–42.

———. *Writing in the Feminine: Feminism and Experimental Writing in Quebec.* Carbondale: Southern Illinois UP, 1990.

Irigaray, Luce. *Ce sexe qui n'en est pas un.* Paris: Minuit, 1977.

———. *Speculum of the Other Woman.* Trans. Gillian C. Gill. Ithaca: Cornell UP, 1985.

Jacobus, Mary. *Reading Woman.* New York: Columbia UP, 1986.

Jardine, Alice. "Opaque Texts and Transparent Contexts: The Political Difference of Julia Kristeva." Miller 96–116.

Jones, Ann Rosalind. "Writing the Body: Toward an Understanding of *l'écriture féminine.*" *Feminist Criticism and Social Change.* Ed. Judith Newton and Deborah Rosenfelt. New York: Methuen, 1985. 86–101.

Lamy, Suzanne. *d'elles.* Montréal: L'Hexagone, 1979.

Miller, Nancy K., ed. *The Poetics of Gender.* New York: Columbia UP, 1986.

Ostriker, Alicia. *Writing like a Woman.* Ann Arbor: U of Michigan P, 1983.

Rich, Adrienne. *Of Woman Born: Motherhood as Experience and Institution.* New York: Norton, 1976.

Schwartzwald, Robert. "Literature and Intellectual Realignments in Quebec." *Québec Studies* 3 (1985): 32–56.

Smart, Patricia. "Quand la fille du bar se met à parler: La poésie de France Théoret."

Dalhousie French Studies: La poésie québécoise depuis 1975. Ed. Eva Kushner and Michael Bishop. 1986. 153–62.

Stanton, Domna C. "Difference on Trial: A Critique of the Maternal Metaphor in Cixous, Irigaray, and Kristeva." Miller 157–82.

———. "Language and Revolution: The Franco-American Dis-Connection." *The Future of Difference.* Ed. Hester Eisenstein and Alice Jardine. Boston: Hall, 1980. 73–87.

Théoret, France. *Bloody Mary.* Montréal: Herbes Rouges, 1977.

———. *Entre raison et déraison.* Montréal: Herbes Rouges, 1987.

———. "Le fantasme de la BJ, c'est la théorie." *Voix et images* 10.2 (1985): 87–92.

———. *L'homme qui peignait Staline.* Montréal: Herbes Rouges, 1989.

———. *Nécessairement putain.* Montréal: Herbes Rouges, 1980.

———. *Nous parlerons comme on écrit.* Montréal: Herbes Rouges, 1982.

———. *Une voix pour Odile.* Montréal: Herbes Rouges, 1978.

D. G. Jones

THE HEXAGON POETS AND THE CONTINUING REVOLUTION IN QUÉBEC POETRY

> Toute écriture de fiction est une stratégie pour affronter le réel, pour transformer la réalité, pour en inventer une autre.
>
> All fictional writing is a strategy for confronting reality, transforming reality, inventing another reality.
>
> Nicole Brossard, La lettre aérienne

QUÉBEC POETRY IN the second half of the twentieth century can be divided into two successive movements: the first associated with Gaston Miron, the poets publishing in *Liberté* (1959–) and *Parti pris* (1963–68); the second with Nicole Brossard and the poets publishing in *La barre du jour* (1965; after 1977, *La nouvelle barre du jour*) and *Les herbes rouges* (1968–).

The first movement appears to be dominated by men, to draw on socialism, surrealism, and existentialism to revolutionize traditional French-Canadian poetry and culture—to liberate a "nation," or *l'homme québécois*. The second, essentially the work of women, draws on the new formalism and feminism to revolutionize the patriarchal discourse of the Western world, to liberate not only *la femme québécoise* but all women.

The first group speaks of poetry, and the work tends to be *lisible*, or readable. The second group is as likely to speak of *l'écriture* and to be deliberately *illisible*, or unreadable. One might simply say that the first is modern, the second postmodern.

Such magisterial simplification is, as usual, misleading, as several observations will demonstrate.

One may note that the earlier movement, insofar as it is represented by the painter Paul-Emile Borduas and the manifesto *Refus global* (1948), participates in an international surrealist revolution. Its rejection of an inherited culture, whether theocratic or technocratic, ruled by *l'intention*, or the will to rational design, linear, causal, and presumably objective, and its promotion of a new culture that would favor the aleatory and the synchronic, the poetic and the erotic, corresponds in a number of points to the program of Brossard and her generation.

Moreover, prominent among the poets published by *Les herbes rouges* are Claude Beausoleil, Normand de Bellefeuille, François Charron—all men.

One may also point out that a principal poet of the 1940s and 1950s is Anne Hébert, that in the title poem of *Le tombeau des rois*, in which her protagonist is drawn into the tomb to be raped by the ancestral dead, Hébert in effect exposes and rejects a patriarchy that would make her merely a vessel to perpetuate its own life or "reality." And in the later poem "Eve," Hébert revises the Edenic myth, to justify woman, nature, the incarnate world of sex and death—and of love, birth, and sensuous delight as well.

Hébert seeks to rework her inherited "reality" by revising biblical myth, by emphasizing the Incarnation and the myth of the creative word. The duty of human kind, like the duty of the French Canadian, is to repeat or perpetuate the word not as scripture or commandment engraved in stone but as act. This version of the "Mystère de la parole" (*Poèmes*) revolutionizes traditional French-Canadian culture with its official motto, "Je me souviens" or "I remember"—and the implication that in Québec nothing ever changes. In the terms of Brossard's generation, Hébert insists on speaking and not merely being spoken.

Thus in the prose statement that prefaces her new poems, Hébert can write:

> Notre pays est à l'âge des premiers jours du monde. La vie ici est à découvrir et à nommer; ce visage obscur que nous avons, ce coeur silencieux qui est le nôtre, tous ces paysages d'avant l'homme, qui attendent d'être habités et possédés par nous, et cette parole confuse qui s'ébauche dans la nuit, tout cela appelle le jour et la lumière. (*Poèmes* 71)

> Our country has arrived at the first days of creation. Life here is a matter of discovering and naming; our shadowy features, our mute hearts, the whole landscape that lies before us to be inhabited and possessed, and these confused utterances that erupt in the night, all cry out for definition in the light of day.[1]

Hébert is not alone in the emphasis on the myth of the word. Witness a few titles. Besides "Mystère de la parole" we have Roland Giguère's *Age*

de la parole, Yves Préfontaine's *Pays sans parole,* and Gatien Lapointe's
Le premier mot.

Indeed, Paul Chamberland's ambitious article "Founding the Territory"
argues that the whole body of poetry between Hébert and himself tends
to be structurally organized in terms of a myth of origins, of the founding
of a land or nation. Increasingly alienated—economically, socially,
culturally—French Canadians, he suggests, reject their old identity and
begin to imagine a new one. Poetry becomes exorcism and incantation. It
announces a new beginning, a return to the elemental, the primitive, to
the *illo tempore,* the central place and the first morning of the world. One
dies into winter, earth, ocean—one passes through the ordeal of baptism
and initiation—emerging reborn with a new identity and community, that
of the Québécois.

If one emphasizes the parallel between Hébert's statement and the epigraph by Brossard, one can see the whole period as a continuing project,
informed by the conviction that in revising the text one is revising the
world.

It is also worth noting that, as the poets were joined in the 1960s by
singers, actors, students, politicians, and voters, reality changed. A token
of that change is the fact that the literature took a new name. For example,
in 1942 Guy Sylvestre published an anthology with the title *Anthologie de
la poésie canadienne d'expression française;* after five more editions, in
1974 it became *Anthologie de la poésie québécoise.* In a real sense, the
French Canadian has ceased to exist.

Such a change has its consequences for the poets who began writing in
the later 1960s and 1970s. A transformation of the traditional French-Canadian
culture has in many respects been realized. The celebration of the land
and a new collective identity has itself become a convention. And further
changes have also taken place. Structural linguistics and Jacques Derrida's
poststructuralist critique of Western discourse have ostensibly expelled
substance from language and exposed all myths of origin as illusory. Jacques
Lacan, following Derrida, has revised Freud, defined desire as impossible,
and declared all language an Oedipal formation embodying the power of
the phallus—in effect, the patriarchy.

Thus, if Hébert's use of the myth of the word links her with Brossard, it
also divides. For many of the younger writers, any collective myth, all
canonized literature, loses its mystique, becomes suspect as ideology. For
some, poetry itself may become problematical. There are only forms of
writing, those that confirm and those that subvert the reigning discourse.

That said, I would like to concentrate the discussion on certain poets
of the older generation, the so-called Hexagon poets.

One may argue that it was not until the 1960s, even the 1970s, that the achievement of these writers became fully manifest. Though Paul-Marie Lapointe, for example, published his first book in 1948, he did not publish his second until 1960. Gilles Hénault, one of the oldest of the group, began publishing in the mid-1940s, but he was out of the province, working as a labor organizer in northern Ontario, during the late 1940s and early 1950s. Roland Giguère put out a number of small volumes on his own press during the 1950s, but these were not widely circulated, and he too was absent for seven years between 1954 and 1964, working in France. It was not until Hexagon published his first major selection, *L'âge de la parole*, that many readers had a clear sense of his work. Gaston Miron refused to publish his major poems in book form—until the editors of the review *Etudes fran-çaises* and the University of Montréal Press did it for him, bringing out *L'homme rapaillé* in 1970. And Fernand Ouellette has been publishing steadily, from *Ces anges de sang* to *Eveils*. The work of these poets remains, I think, central to the period, and a more detailed look at certain aspects of the poetry in relation to the larger context of French-Canadian poetry may be helpful.

As a poetry of revolt and re-creation, their work is fueled by frustrated desire and dreaming desire, by rage and aspiration. Thus in the 1940s, Paul-Marie Lapointe writes:

> Je suis un homme qui dévorait un mur jaune. Panneaux, barricades, armoires de débauches, cadavres érigés, puanteurs de fer. Je suis un homme. Un mur ne garde plus mes portes. (*Le réel absolu* 79)

> I am a man chews up a yellow wall. Partitions, barricades, cupboards of corruption, upright corpses, cast iron stinks. I'm a man. A wall no longer guards my door. (*Fifth Season* 17)

He also writes: "I am a hand dreaming of a wall of flowers / of wallflowers / of tall flowers" (9). And in the early 1950s, Giguère writes in "La vie dé-visagée":

> la vie face aux murs prend figure de défaite
> s'il n'y a dans quelque fissure l'apparence d'un espoir
> l'espoir de l'amour l'espoir de la liberté
> l'espoir qu'un jour nous vivrons tous pour aimer.
>   (*L'âge de la parole* 21)

> life lived between walls takes on the mask of defeat
> if in some crack there isn't a gleam of hope
> the hope for love the hope for freedom
> the hope that in time we will live all of us live to
> love.

If one's cultural house is a prison, one may respond with a destructive rage. Gilles Hénault begins his poem "Bestiaire" with a series of animal cries, "grogner, chuinter, miauler, bêler, aboyer, hennir" 'grunting, hooting, meowing, bellowing, barking, neighing.' He calls for a poetry of such visceral cries, rather than one that would "bercer l'âme" 'cradle the soul.'

He exclaims, "Je veux rogner tous les dieux, demi-dieux et quarts-de-dieux ... Je veux que ma colère se transforme en pierres sous mes paumes" 'I would tear apart all gods, half-gods and quarter-gods ... I would have my anger transformed into stones beneath my palms.'

The immediate target of this anger is the ideology of conservation that became central to French-Canadian culture and to a line of poets going back to Octave Crémazie and his narrative poem "Le drapeau de Carillon."

Written in the 1850s, the poem became famous. For nearly three generations it was taught in the schools. It tells the story of an old soldier of New France who guards his regimental battle flag after the British Conquest. He takes it to France, hoping to persuade the king to restore Canada to his empire. Failing, he returns, climbs the snow-covered hillside at Fort Carillon (now Fort Ticonderoga in New York State) and dies, wrapped in the flag. He thus rejoins his fallen comrades and recovers all that makes life worth living—in the grave. For the living, for Crémazie's readers, there remains the flag, a kind of holy text that reveals the glorious past. Here is an assured identity, since it has been removed from historical time and become part of the eternal, which the narrator enjoins readers to remember and to preserve without adulteration of any kind.

For Crémazie, it is an identity defined by the collective childhood of New France, by the mother culture, the mother tongue, and the mother church. For Emile Nelligan in the next generation, it is defined by his childhood, by the virtues of his actual mother or, more poignantly, his mother as she was in her youth, as a maiden. This is to identify with the dead, a beloved or a "reality" that is always absent, elsewhere, purely and strictly ideal. From Nelligan to Alain Grandbois to Hector de Saint-Denys Garneau, French-Canadian poetry, one may suggest, plays variations on Gérard de Nerval's "El desdichado" 'The disinherited.' In the words of the critic Gilles Marcotte (Shouldice 117–21), it becomes a poetry of exile.

And a poetry of romance. Nelligan's "Clair de lune intellectuel" invokes a "pays angélique" 'an angelic country' (41). Elsewhere he asks his soul mate to fly with him to the castle of their white or pure ideals (191). Grandbois declares himself a widower of an invisible land, and in "Fermons l'armoire" he confesses that his miraculous gardens and aureoled women have left him bewitched, only to turn around and invoke just such a feminine figure walking across the waves, diademed with the stars, and leading him to a rendezvous with the archangel. Saint-Denys Garneau (*Poésies complètes*) keeps watch for a problematical star ("Faction"). He professes a love so pure it cannot be communicated without fear of disturbing the pure being of the beloved ("Accueil"). And although the beloved walks through a valley, she remains as unapproachable as if she inhabited the celestial Athens in Nelligan's "Clair de lune intellectuel" or the impregnable city of virgins in his "Châteaux en Espagne."

This is the mode of romance, but by the time we reach Hébert, if not before, it is clearly gothic romance. Look, says Hébert, the castle is empty: no carpets, no table, no fire, only mirrors reflecting a ghostly double (*Poèmes* 54). Drawn into closed rooms, half bridal suite and half torture chamber —drawn finally into the burial crypt, she says, I'm being raped by the dead (42–43, 59–61).

Giguère, poet, painter, and typographer, recognizes the mode. "La main du bourreau finit toujours par pourrir" invokes the world of the three-headed ogre, the wicked giant who turns his castle into a prison and lays waste the surrounding countryside. The ogre is made more vivid by metonymy and the use of anaphora:

> Grande main qui pèse sur nous
> grande main qui nous aplatit contre terre
> grande main qui nous brise les ailes
> > (*L'âge de la parole* 17)

> Heavy hand that weighs upon us
> heavy hand that flattens us against the earth
> heavy hand that breaks our wings

And as the focus narrows, the violence increases:

> grands ongles qui nous scient les os
> grands ongles qui nous ouvrent les yeux
> > commes des huîtres
> grands ongles qui nous cousent les lèvres
> > grands ongles d'étain rouillé
> > grands ongles d'émail brûlé   (17)

> great nails that rip through our bones
> great nails that pry open our eyes
> > like oysters
> great nails that would rivet the tongue in our mouths
> > great nails of rusty tin
> > great nails of baked enamel

Only slightly surreal, it is the fairytale or nightmare image of the hand of power, whether one relates it to Maurice Duplessis's Québec, Stalin's Soviet Union, Pétain's France, or any number of current regimes.

But, the poem prophesies, the hand of power contains the seeds of its own destruction—here an aptly chosen disease, *panaris*, the whitlow. The *panaris* will be our panacea. The whitlow will come, the joints will shatter like glass, the nails will fall off:

> la grande main pourrira
> et nous pourrons nous lever pour aller ailleurs. (17)

> the heavy hand will rot
> and we will be able to get up and go on our way.

Of course, as other texts suggest, we may help things along by active subversion or demolition. Giguère's "Nos châteaux livrés au feu" appears to respond directly to Hébert's "Vie de château":

> Les temps est venu de passer par le feu
> doubler la flamme à l'instant fatal
> pour n'avoir des châteaux que l'essentiel
>
> des châteaux de cartes la cendre
> d'une main les lignes
> d'un doigt l'anneau
> de la vie le souffle
>
> et un peu de chaleur au front
> une fièvre pour tout ranimer. (*L'âge de la parole* 24)

> The time has come to go through the fire
> to double the flame at the fatal instant
> to retain of these houses the essential alone
>
> of the houses of cards the ash
> of a hand the lines
> of a finger the ring
> of life the breath
>
> and a little warmth in the brow
> a fever rekindling all (*Ellipse* 2 [1970]: 28–29)

Giguère's "Roses et ronces" is a tour de force that resists translation because of its insistent play on sounds. Here even the fire under the ashes appears to go out, the last spark flaring at the foot of the bed. The twentieth century is presented as a period of violent and inevitable change, a time not of roses but of thorns. Towers collapse amid the cries of the victims; the wind rips up trees, the waves erode cliffs; civilized forms, our very features, disintegrate, resemble a storm-wrecked beach, the twisted roots, the bare shingle, pounded by breakers. Everything is confounded, levelled, roses, rushes, and thorns, sedges and sledges, spring water and slough water, in a series of pounding internal rhymes. The world is reduced to its mineral base, bits of copper and tin, iron filings, needles of asbestos, flakes of mica, which mix with the salt waves to become a universal sludge.

This is winter. The end of castles in Spain and intellectual moonlight. The bird sits in a crown of thorns with only the memory of a nest. The West is in ruins, and the problem with ruins is that they are inhabited. For those who survive the breaking of mirrors, the burning of houses, the plunge into the volcano, the general reduction, there can only be a primitive dawn, a possible spring—a return to essentials, perhaps to their senses. The hand begins dreaming of walls of flowers.

Hénault's "Temps des aurores du temps," having evoked a landscape of caves and fossils, flints and tom-toms, having left behind a bewildering "forêt de miroirs" 'forest of mirrors,' concludes abruptly:

> La petite fille était pieds nus dans la glace fondante
> Son coeur comme une lanterne. (*Signaux* 105)

> The young girl barefoot in the melting ice
> Her heart a lantern. ("Time")

Similarly, Giguère's "Adorable femme des neiges" (*L'âge de la parole*), a sequence of twelve poems, has the lady turning up on the speaker's doorstep, in section 6, like a spring maiden—the last remnants of winter are consumed by the hem of her flame. She bears traces of earlier feminine figures, is a guide, polestar, cosmic and haloed. But if she draws the speaker to his destiny, it is not a meeting with the archangel; he is drawn by his loins, not his soul. The figure is being deliberately revised. There is an allusion in section 7 to Nelligan's "Le vaisseau d'or" (*Poésie*; Glassco), which tells of a spiritual shipwreck, apparently precipitated by sirens, by the Venus figure carved on the bowsprit. Giguère sees the lady on the bowsprit, after the wreck, become a local or familiar goddess, and the reef becomes decked with tributary flowers.

We return to the figure of desire, perhaps divine, but also carnal and incarnate in local space. Giguère's speaker roots himself in that feminine abyss. So, too, the speaker in Hénault's "Le jeu de l'amour" would bathe in the universal lymph, lie with his love in the great maternal night, his desire making a nest in the tree of her veins.

The poetry of Hénault and Giguère speaks to the Western reader generally, but it also speaks specifically to a French-Canadian tradition, which it rewrites and transforms.

Gaston Miron, the principal founder of Hexagon Press, presents us with a slightly more realistic muse in his "Ma désolée sereine":

> Ma désolée sereine
> ma barricadée lointaine
> ma poésie les yeux brûlés
> tous les matins tu te lèves à cinq heures et demie
> dans ma ville et les autres
> avec nous par la main d'exister   (*L'homme rapaillé* 23)

> My sad one and serene
> my distantly withdrawn stream
> my poetry with the snow blind eyes
> every morning you get up at five
> in my city and others with you
> drawn by the hand to survive   (*March to Love* 25)

Nature's wild energies are exhausted in a working-class fate. She is his "ma poésie le coeur heurté" 'poetry of the battered heart' and "ma poésie de cailloux chahutés" 'of the rattling stones,' an image that is ambiguous and harsh yet suggestive of a sudden release of mountain springs.

Voltaire dismissed New France as a few acres of snow, a phrase Crémazie echoes sardonically. Yet the final irony of "Le drapeau de Carillon" is that it confirms Voltaire's view. The snow-covered waste is meaningless, except for the flag the dead soldier bequeaths.

Miron ignores the flag and confronts the waste. In "Les siècles de l'hiver" he addresses his ancestral land:

> Le gris, l'agacé, le brun, le farouche
> tu craques dans la beauté fantôme du froid
> dans les marées de bouleaux, les confréries
> d'épinettes, de sapins et autres compères
> parmi les rocs occultes et parmi l'hostilité   (*L'homme rapaillé* 51)

> Grey land and furious, brown and savage
> split in the ghostly beauty of the cold
> in tides of birch, in brotherhoods
> of spruce and pine, and in your similars
> of hidden rocks, of enmities   (*March to Love* 17)

The land may be rude, its "des milles de patience à bout" 'infinite patient miles' may flow into poverty-stricken towns, "nos amours vidées de leurs meubles" 'our empty and unfurnished loves'; the people may be sustained only by the slow fire burning in their backs. Yet it is real, elemental, a base on which to build.

The first lines of the original may echo Mallarmé, but generally Miron opens the poem to the referential and discursive, the political and the personal. And rather than working forward through surrealism, Miron tends to work backward through the whole of French poetry to François Villon, to Rutebeuf, toward a rooted speech.

His strategy is to begin by confessing his poverty. One of the principal, if alien, mirrors of a French-Canadian identity in Miron's Montréal is English. What he sees there is not a glorious inheritance. What he hears there is "Pea Soup" "Pepsi" "Frog" "dishwasher" "floorsweeper" "bastard" (*L'homme rapaillé* 127).

Positively, he claims only the basic vitality of the land, the people, and the language of his mother and father, a language of threads and stitching, of tools and of work. His image of the collective identity is not Mother France, not the mother church; it is, borrowing from Bertholt Brecht, Mother Courage (*March to Love* 79). And the figure of a man that emerges from his work is consonant: he is harassed by society and exposed to the elements. Soaked by the rain, cuffed by the wind, whipped by the snow, he staggers, rests, goes on, the promise of love like wildfire round his knees.

As the critic G.-André Vachon indicates, the presumably empty space begins to fill up with living particulars. It becomes articulate in metonym and metaphor. The speaker is born in the old grated mountains of the north; he draws his strength from mountain springs. As a lover he is a buffalo, a moose, belling in the night; he is backboned like the rock bass; his courage is a spruce; he unfolds in his love's warmth to the long cries of the cicada; he begets in his love the frenzies of the spawning grounds of the Ottawa; the cry of the nighthawk comes to beat in her throat. Nearly all these images are found in "La marche à l'amour" (*L'homme rapaillé* 36–41; *The March to Love* 55–73). In Miron's poetry, Aphrodite's bird is neither sparrow nor dove; it is *la corneille*, the raven or crow. "La corneille" concludes:

> Tu me fais prendre la femme que j'aime
> du même trébuchement et même
> tragique croassement rauque et souverain
> dans l'immémoriale et la réciproque
> secousse des corps
> Corneille, ma noire   (*L'homme rapaillé* 78)

> You make me take the woman I love
> with the same quavering and with the same
> tragic, raucous and sovereign cawing
> in the jolt of bodies
> in that immemorial and mutual tremor
> Raven, my black beauty   (*March to Love* 75)

Saint-Denys Garneau had set out to celebrate the play of the eye in space, a world illumined by a spiritual light, where one could look but not touch. Miron's world is aural, tactile, haptic, a world of bodily energies. He celebrates their collisions, their intercourse. It is a world of things made, shaped. His world is rasped and planed; his life becomes timber and heaped brush; he shivers in his whole frame; he becomes the gravel crusher of despair or he finds a thousand horsepower beating in his heart. And the syntax becomes equally dynamic; sentences sweep from line to line, pile image on image, strain to become encyclopedic, making it difficult at times to quote less than a poem.

Like the parables of Giguère, Miron's poems speak with a collective voice. However important the "I" and the "you," especially in the love poems, they cannot be separated from the "we" or "us," from the more political themes of the land and the people. The private world is a function of the public world; love's fulfillment depends on the collective fulfillment, though it is the former that motivates and guides the latter.

Miron is a Québec nationalist; he has worked not only as a poet but as a facilitator, organizer, lobbyist to revitalize and expand the French-speaking culture and life of Québec. But as Pierre Nepveu insists in *Les mots à l'écoute*, in Miron's work *le pays*, the land, the nation, is ultimately a form of the future tense, a symbol of desire, or a potential human order, and not of a fixed or exclusive national identity. Miron has invented a rhetoric whose largeness and largesse can speak to all people. In "Compagnon des Amériques" Miron concludes:

> mais donne la main à toutes les rencontres, pays
> ô toi qui apparais
>   par tous les chemins défoncés de ton histoire
> aux hommes debout dans l'horizon de la justice
> qui te saluent
> salut à toi territoire de ma poésie
> salut les hommes des pères de l'aventure   (*L'homme rapaillé* 57)

> give a hand to all encounters, country
> land, O you who have emerged
>   from all the pot-holed roads of your history

to all upright men on the horizon of justice
who salute you
hail to you *territoire de ma poésie*
hail, men born of the fathers of adventure   (*March to Love* 83)

Paul-Marie Lapointe, whose career in journalism led to his becoming
director of the news service of Radio Canada, is explicitly international in
a number of his poems of the 1960s: "Le temps tombe," "ICBM," "Mission
accomplie." The surrealistic exuberance of *Le vierge incendié* is muted,
the tone darker. "ICBM," for example, begins plainly:

> chaque jour étonné tu reprends terre
> cette nuit n'était pas la dernière   (*Le réel absolu* 259)

> each day astonished you land up on earth
> this night was not your last   (*Fifth Season* 59)

Here, the atomic cloud is a toad that "agrippe sa terre / et l'embrasse à
petits coups répétés" 'squats on its earth / squeezes it with small repeated
hugs.' The text ends with sardonic echoes of bedtime prayers:

> un bombardier repose à tes côtes
> tes nuits sont assurées!
>
> ô président ô pasteur
> général des îles et des lunes
>
> les enfants se recroquevillent comme des feuilles brûlées   (259)

> a bombardier stretches out at your side
> your nights are secure
>
> O President O Good Shepherd
> General of the Islands and of the Moons
>
> the children curl up like burnt leaves   (59)

Lapointe moves freely between irony and lyricism, between myth and
realism. Certain of his poems from the 1970s return to the Egyptian world
of the dead—touched on in Hébert's "Le tombeau des rois"—and use two
different modes. One group from 1974 are almost documentary descriptions
of mummies in a museum. The text called "Groupe anonyme (IVe Dy-
nastie)" describes a couple who have been fused in an embrace; it concludes:

```
        seul
        de ce bois désemparé
        de cette épave
        n'est point rongé le geste d'aimer   (Tableaux 58)

        alone
        of all this dismantled wood
        this wréckage
        undevoured is the gesture of love   (Fifth Season 73)
```

The slightly later series of thirteen poems in *Bouche rouge* (trans. in *Fifth Season*) moves into the mythical mode, playing variations on the night journey of death and rebirth. Highly erotic, it celebrates the goddess, the "mouths" of the goddess, who swallows the sun, cradles the sun in her womb, gives birth to the sun, again and again.

A unifying feature of Lapointe's work, from the earliest surrealist poems to the latest experimental of formalist *Ecritures*, is its improvisational and paratactic character. Thus, while his major poem, "Arbres," serves as do many of Miron's poems to articulate a previously inarticulate space, it does so in a different manner. Further, it rewrites or transforms a traditional motif in French-Canadian poetry.

Where English-Canadian and United States culture has tended to emphasize continuity in space, French-Canadian culture has stressed continuity in time. Since the 1830s and François-Xavier Garneau's poem "Le vieux chêne," the tree, especially with a bird in its branches, has been a symbol of the continuity—or break in continuity—between past and present, between the temporal and the eternal. Lapointe's "Arbres" both continues and revises this motif.

The initial intertext for this poem is a government publication on the trees of Canada, and in its basic structure the poem remains faithful to the structure of the catalog, running through the list from evergreens to deciduous trees, from nut trees to fruit trees to ornamental shrubs. But on this metonymical base Lapointe weaves a host of free associations, an increasingly metaphorical structure that links nature and culture, time and space:

```
        j'écris arbre
        arbre d'orbe en cône et de sève en lumière
        racines de la pluie et du beau temps      terre animée

        pins blancs      pins argentés      pins rouges et gris
        pins durs à bois lourd      pins à feuilles tordues
        potirons et baliveaux
        pins résineux      chétifs et des rochers      pins du lord
```

pins aux tendres pores   pins roulés dans leur neige
traversent les années   mâts fiers voiles tendues
sans remords et sans larmes   équipages armés
pins des calmes armoires et des maisons pauvres
bois de table et de lit
bois d'avirons de dormants et de poutres   portant le
    pain des hommes dans tes paumes carrées
                              (*Le réel absolu* 171)

I write tree
tree spinning rings into cones   sap into light
roots of the rain and of fair weather   animate earth

pine   the white and the red   Norway and Jack pine
tough heavy-wooded pine   pine with long twisting needles
winter squash and saplings
pitch pine   dwarf and rock   lordly pine
    pine with tender pores   pines traversing time
    wrapped in their snows   proud masts stretched sails
    dry-eyed and remorseless   armed companies
pines of quiet cupboards   of simple houses
wood for tables and for beds
wood for paddles frames and beams   men's bread
    rising from your squared palms   (*Terror* 29)

The writer's pencil links the tree and the text: "génévrier qui tient le plomb des alphabets" 'juniper keeping the plumb of alphabets.' Substance, form, or function link "croix de construction   d'épée   de fusil   croix de bombardier   téléphone   haut fourneau" 'crossbar   swordhilt   gunstock/bombsight   telephone   blast furnace'—the skyscraper and the doghouse. Here "cerisier" 'cherry' leads naturally to jam, and also to "mamelons des amantes" 'nipples of amorous women.' The world of the text comprehends the cross and the hope chest, the housebreaker and the gendarmes, Hurons with hatchets and Franciscans with tonsured heads—the fox, the bear, the albatross, the lark.

In the last five lines the poem moves finally from its solid realistic base into myth, the world as forest, its branches full of nests full of children—a kind of Yggdrasil, nourishing the whole creation:

les arbres sont couronnés d'enfants
tiennent chauds leurs nids
sont chargés de farine

dans leur ombre la faim sommeille
et le sourire multiple ses feuilles

the trees are crowned with children
keep warm their nests
are loaded with fine flour

hunger sleeps in their shade
and smiles multiply their leaves

The lark, or *alouette*, figures in one of the best-known French-Canadian folksongs, where the singers pluck the songbird, verse by verse, from head to tail. Fernand Ouellette writes a poem "L'alouette" (Mailhot and Nepveu), in which the bird's role lies somewhere between that in the song and that in Shelley's "To a Skylark." The speaker recalls standing with friends amid a chaos of rock overlooking the sea, when suddenly, high above, the lark unlooses the cadences of the sun, opening space like a flower of time. Then the bird falls, as if dead, yet burying the listeners in the brilliant shards of its song. Just so, we read in parentheses, eternity may blitz us and untune itself. *La fulguration*, an essentially divine breaking and spending of energy, radiance, is central to this poetry.

Ouellette, a producer at Radio Canada and one of the founders of *Liberté*, helped to transform the Québec writers conferences into an international affair; he has been called the most European of the modern Québec poets. And of all the Hexagon poets he continues most directly the tradition of French-Canadian poetry that would evoke, in a basically symbolist manner, an absolute reality. Early poems reflect an interest in surrealism, in the music of Edgard Varèse, even in Henry Miller—note the titles "Oxygène" and "Quatuor climatisé." But his essentially religious concern is exemplified by his longstanding interest in the French poet Pierre-Jean Jouve and the German poet Novalis. Ouellette also touches on the theme of a "national" renaissance or resurrection, but the issue broadens into a larger spiritual concern, whether in an earlier volume like *Le soleil sous la mort* or a later one like *Ici, ailleurs, la lumière* which includes "L'alouette" and which, more successfully than Saint-Denys Garneau, speaks of a world irradiated by divine energy.

If Ouellette is more successful than Saint-Denys Garneau, it is because he, like Hébert, insists on an incarnate divinity and on creation as process. He has spent his life, he says, resisting the tendency of his inherited culture toward a Manichean division of spirit and flesh. If he pursues angels, they are, as in the title of his earliest book, angels of blood. He sees the divine, no doubt with encouragement from Teilhard de Chardin, as an evolutionary unfolding. Thus we read in "Le fleuve vertical":

Longtemps
la verticale a germé dans l'argile

Puis le fleuve se tint debout
    comme un long mâle se refuse
    au silence des gisants.

Le fleuve devint l'arbre,
    le verger qui monte
    allégé
    par la liesse des fleurs (*Poésie* 90)

A long time
    the vertical lay spawning in the ooze.

The river rose
    erect, as the long male flame
    leaps from the trunk of the fallen wood.

The river was tree
    was orchard rising
    lightened
    by the gaiety of flowers

Animated by the vertical, space becomes the womb of an emergent spiritual life—though it entails the fact that "viendra, la mort sous la morsure du soleil" 'death comes with the bite of the sun.'

For Ouellette, such an evolution appears to involve not only an increasing individuation but an increasingly severe rupture as individual forms are forced to break or abandon themselves to enter into even larger and more complex wholes. This, for Ouellette, is the experience of the obscene, of those extremes of abandon, in death or in love. And it is this amorous "obscenity" that he explores again and again in the volume *Dans le sombre*, its deliberate eroticism clearly intended to confront and to revise the tradition of French-Canadian poetry.

"Naufrage," in Mailhot and Nepveu, echoes and rewrites various earlier texts, notably Saint-Denys Garneau's "Après les plus vieux vertiges" (*Poésies*) and, again, Nelligan's "Le vaisseau d'or." Once more, a Venus figure, stretched out on the cool sheet, seemingly amorphous as a river among reeds, uses her silence and passivity to seduce the male—angel, crow, fiery aggressor—who ravishes her with the cries of his hands and polishes her with his tongue and yet ends by disappearing as effectively as some Icarus. Indeed, there is a shipwreck, with the female apparently plundering the male's spiritual treasure. The figure who rights herself in the conclusion is no longer inert and formless. She has become an amphora of flame, her translucent skin mottled like mother-of-pearl with the flotsam of the shipwrecked mind. The Garneau poem ends with the lady "Portant ma coeur sur sa tête / Comme une urne restée claire" 'Bearing my heart upon her

head / Like an urn that kept its radiance.' But Ouellette's poem, especially
in the context of his work as a whole, demands a shift in point of view,
one that identifies with neither the defeated male nor the triumphant female, but with a third figure, the hermaphrodite who rises from the shipwreck.

Were there space, I would conclude this discussion of the earlier generation with a close look at the work of Jacques Brault and Paul Chamberland. Suffice it to say that after the richly elegiac as well as ironic
Mémoire, Suite fraternelle, and *La poésie ce matin,* Brault moves away
from the collective theme via a new (for Québec) interest in translation,
the discovery of self through the other—which may bear analogy to Ouellette's rupture and reintegration, and which is, at any rate, a form of decentering. Most immediately, Chamberland's "editorial poems," *L'afficheur
hurle* and *L'inavouable,* mark an extreme of violence, in theme and form,
coming close to Hénault's animal cry.

Chamberland leads into the explosion of poetry into concrete, mixed
media, the happening or "show"—the work of Raoul Duguay and the band
l'Infonie, and "La nuit de la poésie," an all-night performance with readings,
songs, and music that involved hundreds of people, the whole affair documented by the National Film Board of Canada.

The Quiet Revolution in Québec was reinforced by that of the 1960s
generation in the United States and Europe: the Beatles, pot, flower power,
and protest marches. Michèle Lalonde's "Speak White" uses English with
irony, identifies with the blacks of Birmingham and Watts and with the
Third World, and ends by incorporating, this time without irony, the familiar
refrain, "We shall overcome."

It is in this climate that Chamberland revolts against himself. He drops
the revolutionary Marxism central to many contributors to *Parti pris,* and
advocates peaceful protest, the power of Eros, the need for a new spiritual
vision. He continues, in his fashion, the program of *Refus global,* by de-
nouncing a culture that he sees as everywhere breeding aggression and
violence and by announcing the new apocalypse, a cosmic ecology, both
natural and divine. He creates a collage of citations, photos, drawings—
from children, journalists, poets, songwriters, philosophers, and, of course,
his own hand. He speaks partly in the language of the electronic age, calling
for a horizontal, computerized information grid that will subvert the hierarchical structures of power, and partly in the language of the
alchemists—he too celebrates the new hermaphrodite.

But other writers entering the 1980s hardly shared Chamberland's sense
of the great work. Michel Beaulieu or Pierre Nepveu, writing out of their
immediate experience of the urban world, find little evidence of a communal
purpose or of a divine ground. Their world appears hardly more substantial

and probably more incoherent than the one that flashes across the television screen. Beaulieu's titles themselves suggest a fragmented, certainly a decentered, world: *Erosions, Variables, Desseins,* and *Kaléidoscope.* The collective "we" is displaced by "you" and "I," and the "I" itself becomes divided in Beaulieu, who frequently addresses himself as "you" or even "he." Nepveu begins a poem:

> Je ne fais plus ce que je sais faire, je n'ai plus d'objets sûrs, ils me ressemblent trop, ont souffert ce que j'ai souffert, épaves de la catastrophe, déchets touchés. ("Je ne fais plus")

> I no longer do what I know how to do, I no longer possess reliable objects, they bear too much resemblance to me, have suffered what I have suffered, wreckage from the catastrophe, useless remnants. ("I no longer do")

In "L'oeuvre démantelée" he speaks of the words he uses, the things they refer to, himself finally, as becoming insubstantial. Though he begins with the phrase "Au plus profond des mots" 'At the deepest level of words,' the depth is silent, void.

Gilles Marcotte notes that in Jacques Brault's *Moments fragiles* the metaphor of depth disappears ("Poésies" 243). This may partly reflect Brault's interest in Japanese poetry, but it probably indicates a more general change. Eli Mandel argues that in English-Canadian poetry over the last decade there has been "a change in the psychology of depths or surfaces to a field of linguistic texture" (47). Poetry enters a Derridean world where there is no hidden meaning—no mysterious substance, source, or author above or beneath or behind the text.

Normand de Bellefeuille asks the question:

> faut-il désormais que la mère, sans figure pourtant au bord de ma pensée, tienne lieu, au tout dernier moment, de mystère étoilé? ... ni mère ni fille à jupe ni char imaginaire, ni mère ni plomberie douce de l'inconscient ... faut-il vraiment que la mère, sans figure toujours au bord de ma pensée, tienne lieu au tout dernier moment, de mystère étoilé? (Mailhot and Nepveu 520)

> must the mother, faceless however at the edge of my mind, henceforth take the place, at the very last moment, of the starry mystery? ... neither mother nor girl in skirts, neither mother nor a naively embroidered metaphysics, neither a girl in skirts nor a fantasized chariot, neither mother nor the sweet plumbing of the unconscious ... must the mother, still faceless at the edge of my mind, take the place, at the very last moment, of the starry mystery?

Must all those "deep images," Giguère's lovely lady of the snows, Grandbois's woman walking on the waves, crowned with stars, Nelligan's mother, maiden, sister, or saint be reduced to nothing but a paradigm of human desire, clichés to be shuffled and reshuffled by the jaded poet?

Perhaps, says Ouellette in "Janvier" (Mailhot and Nepveu), in an age of warring ideologies and global violence, the time has come to pull up the whole tree, To let the earth grow white with the discourse of winter—to let it breathe and find new voices.

A revolution is defined, in part, by what it revolts against. There is continuity in negation. Québec poetry has been rewritten to comprehend space and process, and that rewriting continues, especially as women grope to articulate a feminine body of discourse—which is no doubt one of the reasons de Bellefeuille feels compelled to question "mother," "girl," "sweet plumbing of the unconscious." But there persists a concern, even in the depthless world of semiotic systems, to go beyond the social and secular, to identify with and to participate in, even if by negation, a starry mystery.

Some of the new writing may appear to be a rather prosaic metalanguage, a kind of eroticized grammar. Yet metaphor and even myth appear inescapable. What is France Théoret's walking woman but a further revision of the essentially mythical figure who walks through the pages of Nelligan, Grandbois, Giguère, Hénault? A revision that makes her less like an angel or biblical Eve and more like a Homeric Helen of Troy:

> elle a la délicatesse d'un jardin japonais cependant elle ne rend aucun service. Sauf d'exister d'agir sans le savoir comme un révélateur de la violence humaine. (Mailhot and Nepveu 457)

> She has the delicacy of a Japanese garden yet renders no service. Except by existing and acting and without even knowing it she serves to reveal human violence.

Even in her prose Brossard speaks of the new feminine reality as emerging from an airmail letter, as generating a spiral that will lead out of the circle of purely patriarchal discourse, as a new hologram (emerging from the interference pattern of different discourses?). Speaking of the role of the reader, of what the reader wants to find, wants to become, by virtue of the words or the structures that the words reveal, Brossard concludes:

> Vraiement, l'effet sensationnel de la lecture est une sensation que nous ne pouvons pas exprimer, sinon qu'en soulignant. *L'intime de l'éternité est une intrigue que nous inventons á chaque lecture.* Toute lecture est une intention de spectacle qui nous donne espoir.

> Truly, the extraordinary effect of reading is a sensation that we cannot express, except in italics. *Intimacy with the eternal is a plot we invent with each reading.* We read, each time, to discover images, to discover a drama that gives us hope. (154)

Let us hope that there is a relation between producing text and producing world.

NOTE

[1]Quotations in French are followed by page numbers in the French texts; where published translations exist, page references are given. When no page number is given for the English, the translation is mine.

WORKS CITED

Beaulieu, Michel. *Desseins: Poèmes 1961–1966.* Montréal: L'Hexagone, 1980.

———. *Erosions.* Montréal: Esterel, 1967.

———. *Kaleidoscope.* Saint Lambert, PQ: Noroît, 1983. *Kaleidoscope.* Trans. Arlette Francière. Toronto: Exile, 1988.

———. *Spells of Fury / Charmes de la fureur.* Trans. Arlette Francière. Toronto: Exile, 1984.

———. *Variables.* Montréal: PU de Montréal, 1973.

Brault, Jacques. *Mémoire.* Paris: Grasset, 1968.

———. *Moments fragiles.* Saint Lambert, PQ: Noroît, 1984. *Fragile Moments.* Trans. Barry Callaghan. Toronto: Exile, 1985.

———. *La poésie ce matin.* Paris: Grasset, 1971.

———. *Suite fraternelle.* Ottawa: Université d'Ottawa, 1969.

Brossard, Nicole. *La lettre aérienne.* Montréal: Rémue-Ménage, 1985.

Chamberland, Paul. "Founding the Territory." Shouldice 122–60.

———. Terre Quebec *suivi de* L'afficheur hurle *et de* L'inavouable. Montréal: L'Hexagone, 1985.

Crémazie, Octave. "Le drapeau de Carillon." *Poésies.* Vol. 1 of *Oeuvres complètes.* Ed. Odette Condemine. Ottawa: L'Université d'Ottawa, 1972–76.

Ellipse: Oeuvres en traduction/Writers in Translation. Box 10, Faculty of Letters, University of Sherbrooke, PQ J1K 2R1, Canada.

Garneau, Francois-Xavier. "Le vieux chêne." *Le répértoire national 2.* Ed. J. Huston. Montréal: Valois, 1893. 206–09.

Garneau, Hector de Saint-Denys. *Poésies complètes.* Ed. Robert Elie. Montréal: Fides, 1949. *Complete Poems of Saint-Denys Garneau.* Trans. John Glassco. Ottawa: Oberon, 1975.

———. *St.-Denys Garneau and Anne Hébert: Translations/Traductions.* Trans. F. R. Scott. Vancouver: Klanak, 1962.

Giguère, Roland. *L'âge de la parole: Poèmes 1949–1960.* Montréal: L'Hexagone, 1965.

———. "The Age of the Word." Trans. D. G. Jones. *Ellipse* 2 (1970): 28–29.

———. *Rose and Thorn: Selected Poems of Roland Giguère*. Trans. Donald Winkler. Toronto: Exile, 1988.

Glassco, John. *The Poetry of French Canada in Translation*. Toronto: Oxford UP, 1970.

Grandbois, Alain. *Poèmes*. Montréal: L'Hexagone, 1963.

———. *Selected Poems*. Trans. Peter Miller. Toronto: Contact, 1964.

Hébert, Anne. *Anne Hébert: Selected Poems*. Trans. Al Poulin, Jr. Toronto: Stoddart, 1988.

———. *Poèmes*. Paris: Seuil, 1960. *Poems by Anne Hébert*. Trans. Alan Brown. Don Mills, ON: Musson, 1975.

———. *St.-Denys Garneau and Anne Hébert: Translations/Traductions*. Trans. F. R. Scott. Vancouver: Klanak, 1962.

———. *Le tombeau des rois*. Québec: Institut littéraire du Québec, 1953.

———. "Vie de chateau" 'Manor Life.' Trans. F. R. Scott. *Poems of French Canada* 25.

Hénault, Gilles. "Bestiaire" 'Bestiary.' Trans. D. G. Jones. *Ellipse* 18 (1976): 37–39.

———. "Le jeu de l'amour" 'Love Game.' Trans. Barbara Belyea. *Ellipse* 18 (1976): 41–43.

———. *Signaux pour les voyants: Poèmes 1941–1962*. Montréal: L'Hexagone, 1972.

———. "Temps des aurores du temps" 'Time of the Dawn of Time.' Trans. G. M. Lang. *Ellipse* 18 (1976): 25.

Lalonde, Michèle. *Défense et illustration de la langue québécoise suivi de Prose et poèmes*. Paris: Seghers, 1979.

———. "Speak White." *Ellipse* 3 (1970): 24–31.

Lapointe, Gatien. *Le premier mot*. Montréal: Jour, 1967.

Lapointe, Paul-Marie. *Bouche rouge*. Montréal: L'Obsidienne, 1976.

———. *Ecritures*. 2 vols. Montréal: L'Obsidienne, 1980.

———. *The Fifth Season*. Trans. D. G. Jones. Toronto: Exile, 1985.

———. *Le réel absolu: Poèmes 1948–1965*. Montréal: L'Hexagone, 1971.

———. *Tableaux de l'amoureuse suivi de Une, unique; Art égyptien; Voyage et autres poèmes*. Montréal: L'Hexagone, 1974.

———. *The Terror of the Snows: Selected Poems*. Trans. D. G. Jones. Pittsburgh: International Poetry Forum, 1976.

Mailhot, Laurent, and Pierre Nepveu, eds. *La poésie québécoise*. Montréal: L'Hexagone, 1986.

Mandel, Eli. "Contemporary Canadian Writing." *Arrivals: Canadian Poetry in the Eighties*. Spec. issue of *Greenfield Review* 13.3–4 (1986): 46–59.

Marcotte, Gilles. Introduction. Brault, *Fragile Moments*.

———. "Poésies de novembre." *Voix et images* 35 (1987): 239–49.

———. "The Poetry of Exile." Shouldice 117–21.

Miron, Gaston. *L'homme rapaillé*. Montréal: PU de Montréal, 1970; Paris: Maspero, 1981.

——. *The March to Love.* Ed. D. G. Jones. Byblos Editions 10. Pittsburgh: International Poetry Forum, 1986.

Nelligan, Emile. *Poésies complètes (1896–1899).* Ed. Luc Lacourcière. Montréal: Fides, 1952.

——. "Vaisseau d'or" 'Ship of Gold.' Trans. A. J. M. Smith. Glassco 42.

Nepveu, Pierre. "Je ne fais plus." 'I no longer do.' Trans. Kathy Mezei. *Ellipse* 32 (1984): 36, 37.

——. *Les mots à l'écoute: Poésie et silence chez Fernand Ouellette, Gaston Miron et Paul-Marie Lapointe.* Québec: PU Laval, 1979.

——. "L'oeuvre démantelée" 'The Work Dismantled.' Mailhot and Nepveu 496–97.

Ouellette, Fernand. *Ces anges du sang.* Montréal: L'Hexagone, 1955.

——. *Dans le sombre.* Montréal: L'Hexagone, 1967.

——. *Eveils.* Montréal: L'Obsidienne, 1982.

——. "Le fleuve vertical." *Poésie* 90. "The Vertical Stream." Trans. Kathy Mezei. *Ellipse* 10 (1972): 37.

——. *Ici, ailleurs, la lumière.* Montréal: L'Hexagone, 1977.

——. "Naufrage." *Poésie* 174; Mailhot and Nepveu 348–49.

——. *Poésie: Poèmes 1953–1971.* Montréal: L'Hexagone, 1972.

——. *Le soleil sous la mort.* Montréal: L'Hexagone, 1965.

Préfontaine, Yves. *Pays sans parole.* Montréal: L'Hexagone, 1967.

Scott, F. R. *Poems of French Canada.* Burnaby, BC: Blackfish, 1977.

Shouldice, Larry, ed. and trans. *Contemporary Quebec Criticism.* Toronto: U of Toronto P, 1979.

Sylvestre, Guy. *Anthologie de la poésie canadienne d'expression française.* Montréal: Valiquette, 1942. *Anthologie de la poésie québécoise.* 1974.

Théoret, France. "La marche." Mailhot and Nepveu 455–58.

Vachon, G.-André. "Gaston Miron: Or, The Invention of Substance." *Ellipse* 5 (1970): 38–54.

Jane Moss

DRAMA IN QUÉBEC

THE HISTORY OF Québec theater is inextricably entwined with the history of French Canada. The evolution of drama reflects changes in the social institutions and the political status of Canada's Francophones, from French colonists to English subjects to French Canadians to Québécois. While it is true that there has been theatrical activity since the early days of Nouvelle France, the conditions conducive to the development of a distinctive national dramaturgy have existed only since the 1940s. A brief survey of theater in French Canada will serve as a preface to a fuller analysis of Québec drama as it has emerged since the early 1970s.

As Jean Béraud, Baudouin Burger, Jacques Cotnam, John Hare, and other theater historians have pointed out, most theatrical activity during the seventeenth and eighteenth centuries took place in salons or military barracks, where amateur thespians performed French classical plays, or in the *collèges classiques*, where students staged religious, didactic, or allegorical works. The first theatrical production in French Canada was *Le théâtre de Neptune* by Marc Lescarbot, an allegorical spectacle on land and water produced at Port Royal d'Acadie in 1606. In 1640, French colonists in Québec City staged a tragicomedy to celebrate the birth of the dauphin, the future Louis XIV. The role played by the Catholic church in controlling theater cannot be overemphasized. Wary of what it considered profane drama and of the immoral behavior often associated with actors, the church kept a close watch over dramatic activity, insisting that boys play female roles to discourage potentially sinful contact between the sexes, regularly issuing official condemnations of theater, and occasionally banning plays. The most famous incident of church censorship, the *Tartuffe* Affair, took place in 1694, when Monseigneur de Saint-Vallier, the bishop of Québec City, forced Governor Frontenac to cancel a production of Molière's play.

The threat of excommunication that was used to ban *Le Tartuffe* effectively prevented further public performances until after the Conquest of New France by the British in 1760, limiting dramatic activity to church-controlled seminaries or schools. After the Conquest, amateur productions of French classical plays resumed, often performed by English officers in Montréal. In 1789, the Théâtre de Société was set up in that city as a playhouse for French-language plays. Among the works presented at this informal theater were those of Joseph Quesnel, a naturalized Canadian born in France, whose operettas and social comedies were written in the tradition of eighteenth-century French salon comedy or vaudeville.

During the early nineteenth century, anglophone theater in Montréal began to flourish, but francophone theater was still limited by a number of social, economic, and political factors such as the lack of an educated public, the absence of cultural contact with France, the opposition of the clergy, and insufficient capital (Burger 7–25). Lord Durham's *Report on the Affairs of British North America* (1839) mentioned the fact that the French population of Lower Canada could not support a national stage. In response to the stinging criticisms of the report, a number of native-born French Canadians took it on themselves to celebrate the heroes of the province in patriotic historical dramas. Antoine Gérin-Lajoie's *Le jeune Latour*, performed in 1844 by students of the Collège de Nicolet, was a three-act tragedy in verse glorifying the struggle against the English enemy and fidelity to Québec's French heritage. The nationalist spirit sparking the Patriots' Rebellion also inspired *Félix Poutré* (1862), *Papineau* (1880), and *Le retour de l'exilé* (1880), three historical dramas by Louis-Honoré Fréchette based on the heroes and events of 1837–38. It is interesting to note that nationalistic historical plays, so important in the rise of a distinctive French-Canadian theater in the nineteenth century, would also play a key role in the renewal of Québec dramaturgy during the Quiet Revolution of the 1960s. But whereas the early French-Canadian theater presented an idealized image of Québec and preached patriotism, nationalism, and cultural survival, the truly national drama that emerged in the twentieth century does not worship the past; rather, it reexamines the past as part of the quest for a more authentic expression of Québec's collective identity.

Not all theatrical activity in nineteenth-century Québec had a political message. Québec's first native-born playwright, Pierre Petitclair, made a career of writing light comedies in the tradition of Molière's farces and comedies of character. Other dramatists catered to the public's taste for vaudeville, melodramas, and folklore sketches, thereby avoiding conflict with ecclesiastical authorities. Visiting troupes of United States, English, and French actors attracted appreciative audiences in Montréal and Québec City throughout the century. The success of touring foreign artists such as the great French tragediennes Rachel in 1855 and Sarah Bernhardt in 1880, 1891, and 1917 seemed only to underscore the need for professional theater in Québec—that is, for permanent playhouses and professional actors. Despite continued opposition from the Catholic clergy to anything other than didactic, moralizing dramatic exercises, the years 1894–1914 saw a flowering of French-Canadian theater including the establishment of a number of permanent playhouses. Unfortunately, the plays produced during this period were mostly French works and mediocre French-Canadian imitations. Only the patriotic historical dramas displayed any distinctive national qualities.

After World War I, theater had to compete with the growing popularity of three new forms of entertainment: the cinema, burlesque, and radio. A number of theater historians (Germain; Godin, "Les gaietés"; Hébert; Usmiani) have argued convincingly that the "new" Québec theater that emerged in the 1960s had its roots in the burlesque shows so popular in growing urban areas between the two world wars. Touring United States vaudevillians and the great comic actors of the Hollywood cinema introduced burlesque and slapstick to Québec, but soon French-Canadian troupes were performing their own variety shows, using the language of working-class Montréal. Starting from simple plot outlines, the burlesque actors improvised comedies incorporating songs, dances, and humorous sketches filled with bawdy jokes. Despite the scorn of highbrow critics, burlesque remained enormously popular until television replaced it in the 1950s. Radio also played an important role in preparing the way for native Québec dramaturgy. During the economic crisis of the 1930s and 1940s, many French-Canadian actors and writers earned their living and perfected their craft working for CBC and Radio Canada. In the meantime, serious drama was struggling, its survival made all the more difficult by continued church censorship and the dearth of good French-Canadian plays.

The year 1937 marks a turning point that at first glance appears to be a fork in the road toward creating a national dramaturgy. In this year, Gratien Gélinas created Fridolin, the street-smart, witty kid who poked fun at contemporary Québec society in annual satiric revues called *Fridolinades*. Also in 1937, Father Emile Legault founded the Compagnons de Saint-Laurent, a group dedicated to improving the professional quality of theatrical production and to bringing classical and avant-garde French plays to Québec. The enormous popularity of Gélinas's revues made it clear that to be a viable art form, Québec theater had to reflect its own context, had to speak to the audience about their shared experience and in their language. At the same time that Fridolin was bringing French-Canadian life to the stage, the Compagnons de Saint-Laurent were producing continental plays with the aim of giving the audience an aesthetic and spiritual experience.

In the long run, Gélinas's cultural specificity, his realistic portrayal of Québec society, was more important to the creation of a national repertory,
but Legault's influence was decisive in determining the technical aspects
of Québec theater. During and after World War II, a number of professional
companies were formed (many by former disciples of Legault) based on
the amateur model of the Compagnons de Saint-Laurent. Among these
groups were the Théâtre de l'Equipe (Pierre Dagenais, 1943), Théâtre du
Rideau Vert (Yvette Brind'Amour and Mercédes Palomino, 1949), Théâtre
du Nouveau Monde (Jean Gascon and Jean-Louis Roux, 1952), and Théâtre
Club (Monique Lepage, 1954). Although these troupes presented mostly
foreign plays, they laid the groundwork for native dramatists by improving
the quality of productions and by attracting large audiences to serious
theater. The success of these groups encouraged others, such as the Ap-
prentis-Sorciers (Jean-Guy Sabourin, 1955) and the Egrégore (Françoise
Berd, 1959), both devoted to avant-garde theater.

In their enthusiasm for innovation, the avant-garde groups were soon
joined by a number of French-Canadian writers whose experimental plays
were influenced by surrealism, *automatisme*, and the French theater of the
absurd. The works of Claude Gauvreau (*La charge de l'orignal épormyable*,
1956; *Les oranges sont vertes*, 1968) and of Jacques Languirand (*Les insolites*,
1956; *Les grands départs*, 1958) are important in the development of drama
not so much for their quality as for their rejection of the conventions of
bourgeois realism and of rationalism, and their experimentation with language. Other forms of experimentation followed the Brechtian model. Gilles
Derome (*Qui est Dupressin?*, 1961) and Jacques Duchesne (*Le quadrillé*,
1964) used songs, placards, choruses, masks, and other distancing techniques. Perhaps the key event in the renewal of drama was the founding
of the Centre d'Essai des Auteurs Dramatiques in 1965 by Duchesne and
Robert Gurik. Since its inception, the Centre d'Essai has been dedicated to
the promotion of Québec dramaturgy; it has organized public readings and
workshops, published texts and a newsletter, and lobbied for vital government subsidies.

Paradoxically, it was the fusion of avant-garde dramaturgy with popular
language and Québécois subject matter that gave rise to the new theater
of the 1970s. But before that could happen, French-Canadian drama had
to go through a period of apprenticeship, a phase of social realism that
prepared the way for the antinaturalistic reaction. Transforming a 1946
Fridolin sketch into a full-length drama, Gélinas inaugurated the era of
dramatic realism in 1949 with *Tit-Coq*, the sad story of a soldier whose
romantic dreams are destroyed by his illegitimate birth. Having been brought
up in an orphanage, Tit-Coq yearns to become part of a family; when he
meets Marie-Ange, an army buddy's sister, he falls in love not only with

her but with an idealized vision of family life. Marie-Ange breaks her promise to wait for Tit-Coq while he is overseas fighting the war; she gives in
to family pressure and marries someone else. When he returns, Tit-Coq
asks her to run away with him, but the two unhappy lovers are persuaded
by a priest that this act of passion would lead to further unhappiness. In
addition to being alienated from her family, they would be cut off from a
society that would condemn them as adulterers and their children as bas-
tards. *Tit-Coq* presents many of the themes that were to dominate French-
Canadian theater for the next twenty-five years: the alienation of the average
French Canadian, the repressive nature of Québec's conservative social
institutions, the poverty of language that frustrates the expression of passion and ideas. Like Gabrielle Roy's novel *Bonheur d'occasion, Tit-Coq*
poignantly expresses French Canada's growing awareness of the gap between its folklore and its reality, between the traditional self-image projected by the *romans du terroir* and the daily poverty and humiliation of
its urban and rural inhabitants.

Several years after *Tit-Coq*, another playwright captured the attention
of Canadian theatergoers by dramatizing the pathetic plight of young French
Canadians who had little hope of escaping from poverty, ignorance, and
repressive social conditions. Marcel Dubé's successful career as a writer
of stage and television plays was launched by his hit *Zone*, which won first
prize at the 1953 Dominion Drama Festival. *Zone* is the story of a gang of
Montréal East End teenagers trying to make better lives for themselves.
Unfortunately, they delude themselves into thinking that cigarette smug-
gling is a way out of poverty. After the gang leader accidentally kills a
customs officer, he is denounced by a fellow gang member, imprisoned,
and killed in an escape attempt. While Gélinas's theater maintained elements of social satire from his Fridolin days, Dubé's brand of social realism
is distinguished by its penchant for poetic symbolism. To emphasize the
themes of imprisonment and aborted escape, he sets his plays in closed
spaces: behind walls, in prisons, back alleys, walled gardens, and living
rooms. It should be said, however, that neither Gélinas nor Dubé was
particularly daring in terms of dramatic technique. Both use sentimental,
somewhat melodramatic plots to examine idealistic characters whose dreams
and rebellions are crushed by a repressive and hypocritical society.

The movement of Dubé's plays from back alleys to bourgeois living rooms
(*Les beaux dimanches*, 1965) reflects the changing climate of the province
during the period known as the Quiet Revolution, when the growing frustrations of a long-suffering people made revolt against economic exploitation, repressive social institutions, and a reactionary political system
inevitable. Dramatists often translate the rejection of the recent past into
generational conflict—that is, a son's revolt against a despotic father. When

the son is illegitimate (as in the case of Tit-Coq) or ashamed of a weak father (as is the protagonist of Dubé's *Simple soldat*, 1958), the sense of alienation reveals Québec's growing awareness of its oppressed colonial status. The social realist drama of this period mixes comic and tragic elements in its portrayal of the failed attempt at liberation from a pathetic quotidian existence. Leaving behind the youthful characters and vernacular of Montréal's slums, Dubé and Gélinas, like other Quebecers, turned from questions of social and economic survival to the political question of separatism and the existential question of *le mal d'être*. The drama of the 1960s often takes the form of a search for personal identity, freedom, and happiness conducted within the family home. The middle-class characters of Dubé's *Bilan* (1960) and *Les beaux dimanches* (1965) and those of Françoise Loranger (*Une maison . . . un jour*, 1965; *Encore cinq minutes*, 1967) are forced into self-awareness, into recognizing the anguish and malaise of their boring lives in a hypocritical, superficial, materialistic society. These bourgeois psychological dramas suggest that the root of the problem, at once a difficulty of being and an incapacity for love, is the moral vacuum of a Québec society that has lost its sense of collective destiny. The political implication of this existential malady seemed obvious to many Quebecers: personal freedom depended on Québec's independence.

The nationalist sentiments impelling the growth of the independence or separatist movement found expression in the political and historical dramas of the 1960s. As early as 1958 in *Les grands soleils*, Jacques Ferron had used the 1837 Patriots' Rebellion to provoke a reexamination of the past and a discussion of Québec's status as an oppressed country. Ferron's next political play, *La tête du roi* (1963), uses Louis Riel's ill-fated insurrection as a reminder of the historical emnity between Canada's two founding nations. The main character is the prosecutor, who has tried to balance his loyalty to his French heritage with his career as a servant of the crown. Now his career is threatened by his son's involvement in an act of anti-British vandalism, the decapitation of the statue of King Edward VII. In Dubé's *Les beaux dimanches*, Olivier, the pro-separatist character, traces Québec's social and psychological ills back to the Conquest of 1760. He blames the Catholic church, the English, and capitalists for the deprivation and humiliation of French Canadians. Personal freedom, says Dubé's separatist, must be preceded by political freedom. Like Dubé, Gélinas also moved from social to political themes during the 1960s. In *Hier, les enfants dansaient* (1966), the federalist-separatist debate dividing the province takes place between two generations of the Gravel family. Pierre Gravel's ambition to become part of Lester Pearson's Liberal government is ruined by his two sons' participation in acts of separatist terrorism. As the play ends, the older Gravel beings to understand the need to throw off the colonial mentality. In Robert Gurik's political parody, *Hamlet, prince du Québec* (1968), the Shakespearean characters are replaced by contemporary politicians who play out the betrayal of the province. Gurik's dying Hamlet (symbol of Québec) predicts the birth of a new Québec, freed from the weight of the past. Françoise Loranger entered the political arena with two polemical plays: *Le chemin du roy* (1968) and *Médium saignant* (1970). *Le chemin du roy*, written in the wake of de Gaulle's 1967 visit to Québec, pits English and French Canadians against each other in a theatrical hockey game. René Lévesque leads the Québec team toward the goal of independence, making fools of the Ottawa team's efforts to unite the opponents. *Médium saignant* also elicits an emotional response from spectators who are asked to exorcise their collective fears and hatred. The play's subject, the use of French versus the use of English, reflects Québec's bitter public debate over language legislation and the tensions between the francophone majority, the anglophone minority, and immigrants forced to choose sides.

At the same time that these political plays were advocating collective exorcism and independence, the avant-garde theater was urging total liberation—political, psychological, cultural, and sexual. By the end of the 1960s, the popular and the avant-garde currents were moving toward the fusion that would create a dynamic national dramaturgy. The spark that united the two movements was Michel Tremblay's *Les belles-soeurs*, first produced by the Théâtre du Rideau Vert in Montréal in 1968. The play provoked a loud public debate on the issue of Québécois French because it was the first drama written in *joual*, the popular language of Montréal's East End. Twenty years later, when the stage use of *joual* was commonplace, *Les belles-soeurs* had become a repertory classic because of its grimly humorous insights into the social, emotional, and sexual problems of the average Quebecer and because of the innovative blending of lyricism and stark realism. The action takes place in Germaine Lauzon's kitchen, where fourteen neighbors and relatives—all women—have been invited to help paste a million trading stamps into booklets. Germaine, who has just won the stamps in a contest, plans to refurnish her apartment with luxury items from the premium catalog. As they paste stamps and gossip, the women become increasingly jealous of Germaine's good fortune. In monologues, dialogues, and choruses, they complain about the drabness of their household drudgery, too many unwanted pregnancies, coarse husbands, senile mothers-in-law, and restrictive moral codes. Although the women are angry and resentful, their only outlet is prayer or gossip, and their only diversion is bingo. They vent their frustrations by quarreling, exchanging insults, and stealing Germaine's stamp books. The play ends with a battle royal over the stolen stamps, which rain down on the stage as the women sing a derisive chorus of the national anthem, "O Canada." For all its verbal comedy and farcical touches, *Les belles-soeurs* is a tragedy about the alienation of the average Quebecer. The characters, pathetic and grotesque, express their sense of powerlessness, loneliness, and despair, yet they never hear each other.

Elitist critics were shocked by Tremblay's sordid dramatic vision of Québec society and by his use of vulgar slang. For the author, it was a matter of authenticity; he was presenting the people of his old neighborhood expressing themselves in their own language. But Tremblay was not striving for simple realism; he is an artist who transforms the stage into metaphors for social and psychological realities and who creates strangely affecting poetry through the use of *joual*. His innovative dramatic technique combines elements of classical tragedy, Brechtian dramaturgy, musical composition, burlesque, and avant-garde antirealism. In *Les belles-soeurs*, for example, normal conversation is frequently interrupted by monologues highlighted by spotlights and by choral recitations composed like musical comedy numbers. Tremblay occasionally demonstrates his virtuosity by constructing two or more dialogues in counterpoint. In his masterful work *A toi, pour toujours, ta Marie-Lou* (1971), the contrapuntal conversations span a ten-year period. Space rather than time is transcended by the solos, duets, trios, quartets, sextets, and octets that make up the operatic structure of *Bonjour, là, bonjour* (1974). Moreover, Tremblay rarely falls back on conventional plot structures or realistic techniques: *La duchesse de Langeais* (1970) is a monologue; *Demain matin, Montréal m'attend* (1970) is a musical comedy; *Damnée Manon, sacrée Sandra* (1976) is composed of parallel monologues. In his continuing experimentation with dramatic forms, Tremblay has five actresses simultaneously portray one character at five stages of her life in *Albertine, en cinq temps* (1984).

One of the unique aspects of Tremblay's work is his creation of a distinctive cast of recurring characters who appear in his novels and in the early plays that comprise the cycle of *Les belles-soeurs*. These are the people of the plateau Mont-Royal: unhappy housewives, pious spinsters, foul-mouthed waitresses, cheap nightclub performers, prostitutes, pimps, madmen, and transvestites. Just as *joual* symbolizes the breakdown of language and communication, so the paucity of strong male characters and the lack of "normal" sexual behavior symbolize the breakdown of social institutions in an emasculated society. Tremblay has always been frank in his treatment of sex. The sexuality of his women characters has been repressed by the puritanical morality of the Catholic church: wives complain bitterly about having to submit to the clumsy and aggressive lovemaking of their husbands, while spinsters sublimate their desires through quasi-erotic religiosity. The outrageous behavior of his transvestites seems to imply that in Québec it is difficult to be a man. The marginality of the transvestite symbolizes the marginality of all Quebecers; his sexual confusion becomes a metaphor for the uncertainty of Québec's collective identity. Alcoholism, insanity, perverted piety, crass materialism, and delusions of show-business stardom seem the only ways out of this sordid environment, the only possible avenues of escape from the stifling influences of the family and the church.

The oppressive and repressive influences of the church, the family, and poverty in Québec are also the major subjects of another playwright, Jean Barbeau. Born near Québec City and educated at Laval University, Barbeau followed Tremblay's lead in using popular speech, elements of popular culture, and antirealistic techniques to dramatize the reality of life for the average Quebecer. In his early plays, Barbeau frequently explored the political and cultural implications of the language question. *Le chemin de Lacroix* (1970) was written in response to police repression of protests against Bill 63, which gave Québec Anglophones the right to send their children to English schools. In the work, a latter-day Passion play, Rodolphe Lacroix is arrested, interrogated, and beaten by the police without cause. But Québec's power elite is not the only source of Lacroix's humiliation; the cultural elite reminds him constantly of his inferiority and his ignorance. Having been told so often that he speaks French badly, he has enlisted the aid of a Frenchman to correct his grammar, vocabulary, and pronunciation. The grammar coach, Thierry, makes fun of Lacroix's *joual* and reduces him to silence by playing the police officer's role. Just as oppressive as social and economic injustice, cultural elitism deprives the Quebecer of dignity and a sense of identity. Barbeau uses humor to examine the psychosexual implications of *joual* in two one-act plays, *Manon Lastcall* (1970) and *Joualez-moi d'amour* (1970). Both plays suggest that *joual* is a sign of the vitality and virility of the Québec people and that it can be a language of love. The playwright satirizes those who imitate Parisian accents and worship French culture, portraying them as pompous, pretentious, impotent, and effeminate.

The adverse effect of elite and foreign cultural influences is also demonstrated by Barbeau's *Ben-Ur* (1971), a comic allegory about a young Québécois man whose psychological development is stunted by overexposure to the heroic myths of American comic books. When real life fails to satisfy him, he retreats to the attic, where he can act out the adventures of the Lone Ranger, Tarzan, and Zorro. Although he regrets the fact that his heroes are Americans rather than Québécois, he does not reject foreign role models until he recognizes the violence that underlies American heroic myths. Still, finding no native heroes to replace those of American popular culture, he sees no escape from his banal existence. In *Le chant du sink* (1973), Barbeau dramatizes the Québec writers' need to assert their linguistic and cultural identity by rejecting French and American influences. The protagonist is Pierre, a would-be playwright suffering from writer's block and driven to a mental breakdown by the presence of four personal muses. The "anti-muses" who stifle his creativity represent the influence of the Catholic church, French classical culture, revolutionary politics, and United States consumerism. Not only do they haunt his imagination; they have materialized to haunt his apartment. Before Barbeau's alter ego can find his own voice, he must find his identity and overcome his sense of cultural inferiority. The antirealistic techniques of *Ben-Ur* and *Le chant du sink* mitigate the depressing social realities portrayed in the two works. Some of the techniques seem inspired by Brecht, others by Ionesco. In *Ben-Ur*, for example, Barbeau uses songs and choruses to comment on the action of the play, divides the stage into areas representing different aspects of Ben-Ur's life, satirizes his characters by labeling them with placards and symbolic objects, and makes fantasies come to life in comic-book adventure scenes. In *Le chant du sink*, Pierre's muses materialize on stage in the form of four women: a saintly representative of the church, Esther Larousse (of dictionary fame), a leftist guerrilla, and a Barbie doll complete with inflatable breasts and bouffant wig. The antirealistic techniques create a distance between the spectator and the stage, a distance that calls theatrical illusion and social reality into question and forces the spectator to adopt a critical attitude.

The mixture of avant-garde dramaturgy and Québécois subject matter in Barbeau and Tremblay is the distinctive feature of the nationalistic theater of the 1970s. Renate Usmiani describes the *nouveau théâtre québécois* as a literary *théâtre d'auteurs*, primarily concerned with demythification of Québec's past and the creation of a national identity (108). The alternative theater movement (*jeune théâtre*) that flourished during the same period shared many of the same dramatic techniques and sociopolitical issues. The difference as Usmiani sees it is that *jeune théâtre* was committed to Marxist philosophy and based on improvisation and collective creation (109–17). It was popular theater that gave the people a political message and involved them in an aesthetic experience. *Jeune théâtre* saw itself as part of the counterculture, militant in its rejection of authority and hierarchy and dedicated to experimentation and research. The organization of alternative theater companies founded in 1972, the Association Québécoise du Jeune Théâtre (AQJT), was an outgrowth of the Association Canadienne du Théâtre d'Amateurs (ACTA), founded in 1958. The new organization included various radical groups influenced by different political and artistic ideas. The Grand Cirque Ordinaire (founded in 1969, disbanded in 1978), the Eskabel (founded in 1971), the Pichous, the Enfants du Paradis (1975), and the Grande Réplique (1976) experimented with methods of creation, often based on the theories of Artaud, Brecht, and Piscator. Groups such as the Théâtre . . . Euh! (1970), the Théâtre de Carton (1972), the Groupe de la Veillée (1973), the Théâtre de Quartier (1974), and the Théâtre Parminou (1973) produced plays influenced by Marx and Brecht, with emphasis on political and social issues. The Théâtre des Cuisines (1974), feminist cells of the Eskabel and the Organisation ô, the Commune à Marie (1978, organized as the Centre d'Essai des Femmes in 1977), and the Théâtre Expérimental des Femmes (1979) dramatized feminist concerns using the *jeune théâtre* techniques of improvisation and collective creation.

Jean-Claude Germain and his Théâtre d'Aujourd'hui seem to bridge the gap between *nouveau théâtre québécois* and *jeune théâtre*. After founding the troupe in 1969 as the Théâtre du Même Nom, Germain became its artistic director, resident playwright, and lead actor. The company's first production, *Les enfants de Chénier dans un autre grand spectacle d'adieu* (1969), was a collective creation that proclaimed the anticolonial historical consciousness and the anticlassical cultural nationalism that are the chief characteristics of Germain's aesthetic. In essays and interviews, Germain has expressed his determination to demolish the classical French repertoire and conventional realistic performance styles. He wants to create accessible theater that speaks the language of the people and shares their social, historical, and cultural traditions ("Entretien[s]" 58–62). His main objective is to replace the folkloric, precultural forms of self-expression typical of a colony with the authentic culture and history characteristic of a nation (15). Such an aesthetic does not have to result in mass culture, nor does it imply a Marxian political stance. Germain insists that the tradition of Québec drama begins not with the elitist, continental influence of Père Legault but rather with the music hall reviews of Gélinas (13–14, 21–22). In his persistent efforts to democratize, demythify, and desanctify theater, Germain has used the weapons of burlesque: satire, parody, and farce. His Brechtian distancing techniques create spectacles that are series of tableaux; the characters are actors who constantly are changing roles. What makes Germain's theater distinctive is his playful use of language, his ear for the accent and rhythms of popular speech, his parodic imitiation of classical French, his penchant for word plays. Above all, Germain's spectacles make audiences laugh.

Since the late 1960s, Germain has been Québec's most prolific playwright, often producing two or more new spectacles in a single theater season. The early plays, centered on the family, use grotesque farce à la Ionesco to denounce the social institutions and the cultural heritage of traditional Québec. The caricatural portrayal of the archetypal family in *Diguidi, diguidi, ha! ha! ha!* (1969) and *Si les Sansoucis s'en soucient, ces Sansoucis-*

ci s'en soucieront-ils? Bien parler, c'est se respecter! (1971) points to the gap between the idealized self-image and the reality of society. The satirical denunciation leads to a call for liberation from the repressive mentality of the past and to a call for Québec independence. In his next works, Germain reminded Quebecers that, Lord Durham's report notwithstanding, they do have a history, a tradition of independence, and a collective identity. In *Un pays dont la devise est je m'oublie* (1976), two itinerant actors portray various episodes of Québec history, reserving the best roles not for Frenchmen like Jacques Cartier or General Montcalm but for native-born folk and popular heroes such as the *Canadien errant*, the *coureur des bois*, the *habitant*, strongman Louis Cyr, and hockey star Maurice Richard. The optimistic conclusion predicts that one day Québec will remember that it is already a country with heroes (*Un pays* 138). *Mamours et conjugat* (1978), subtitled "scènes de la vie amoureuse québécoise," is a series of farcical vignettes tracing the sexual history of Québec. As in *Un pays dont la devise est je m'oublie*, the episodic structure of the tableaux telescopes time, reinterpreting the past in light of the present. But here there is less optimism; *Mamours et conjugat* suggests that the political and religious history of the province, the legacy of colonialism and Jansenism, is responsible for the frustration and personal unhappiness of contemporary Quebecers. Germain calls his third historical work, *A Canadian Play/une plaie canadienne* (1979), "un exorcisme collectif" (26), an attempt to correct the negative image of Québec presented by Lord Durham's report.

Just as Germain uses the theater to demythify social institutions and history to reconstruct Québec's self-image, so he uses it to demythify the elitist concept of "culture" to effect the transition from folklore to national culture. In *Les hauts et les bas dla vie d'une diva: Sarah Ménard par eux-mêmes* (1974), Germain takes aim at opera and classical tragedy, the ultimate symbols of highbrow European culture. Sarah Ménard, modeled on Sarah Bernhardt and the Québec opera singer Emma Albani, performs a series of monologues and songs as she reviews her long career as an international star. The price she has paid for celebrity is the loss of her Québec language and identity. Lamenting her sense of alienation, Germain's diva rejects foreign culture and seeks her roots in the traditional fiddle music and jigs of her village. In the sequel, *Les nuits de l'indiva* (1980), Sarah has found freedom and happiness as a cabaret singer. *L'école des rêves* (1977), sequel to *Un pays dont la devise est je m'oublie*, reexamines the role of theater in building a national identity.

At the same time playwrights like Germain, Barbeau, and Tremblay were creating a distinctive Québécois dramaturgy that expressed the aspirations of Quebecers in language they could understand, another oppressed group was making itself heard: women. During the 1970s, feminist theater groups, actresses, and others began writing plays that dramatized the concerns of the women's liberation movement: economic and sexual exploitation, the repressive stereotypes (virgin-mother-whore) imprinted on girls, the fears that reduce women to silence or madness, the need for self-expression and communication with others. An outgrowth of the alternative theater movement, women's theater initially depended on improvisation techniques and collective creation. The work of the Théâtre des Cuisines, an amateur Montréal group with a Marxist orientation, illustrates the process. The group chose a topic that was then discussed and researched before improvisational sessions begin. The final production was a series of tableaux loosely connected by the main theme. The Théâtre des Cuisine's first play, *Nous aurons les enfants que nous voulons* (1974), takes on the issue of abortion on demand; the second, *Môman travaille pas, a trop d'ouvrage* (1975) deals with payment for housework; the third, *As-tu vu? Les maisons s'emportent!* (1980), depicts the double burden of home and job.

The first major event for Québec women's theater took place in 1976, when *La nef des sorcières* reached a popular audience during its successful run at the Théâtre du Nouveau Monde. *La nef* is composed of eight monologues by seven well-known actresses and writers: Marthe Blackburn, Luce Guilbert, France Théoret, Odette Gagnon, Marie-Claire Blais, Pol Pelletier, and Nicole Brossard. The monologues express the women's sense of alienation in a male-dominated society, the desire for self-possession, independence, and sexual liberation. The message of the play, set out in the preface to the published edition (7–13), is that women must appropriate a language of their own that allows them to speak about themselves and their bodies. Feminist dramatic discourse bears witness to a *prise de conscience* and a *prise de parole* that liberates women from their fear, silence, and solitude. Brossard's monologue of the Writer makes it clear that writing is a sexual act, by which she takes possession of her body, and a political act, by which she proclaims her solidarity with other women in an effort to claim their rightful place in history (74–75, 78).

Rejection of traditional female roles was seen as the first step toward liberation; this is the subject of Denise Boucher's *Les fées ont soif* (1978), and of *A ma mère, à ma mère, à ma mère, à ma voisine* (1978) by the Théâtre Expérimental des Femmes (Gagnon et al.). Boucher wrote her play to exorcize the Catholic church's repressive female archetype, the Virgin Mary. The play's three characters—the statue of the Virgin, Marie the Mother, and Madeleine the Prostitute—represent three faces of the archetype, the woman who cannot enjoy sex. *Les fées* became a succès de scandale when conservative members of the Greater Montreal Arts Council tried but failed to block its performance by withdrawing a $15,000 subsidy to the Théâtre du Nouveau Monde. In alternating monologues, the three women lament their status as silenced, beaten, alienated, violated, demented, lost. Coming together to share their feelings and anger in dialogues and songs, they finally decide to refuse to be victims. This movement from denunciation of sexual repression to triumphant liberation structures many plays by women, including *A ma mère*, which begins with a physical and verbal assault on the patriarchal woman (a mummified mother figure) and ends with a demonstration of unity and force by a chorus of Amazon warriors. Through words and gestures, these plays focus attention on the female body, the matrix of sexuality and sexual difference, the primary generator of the dramatic text. Placed at center stage, the female body is exposed, demystified, reclaimed, rehabilitated, and reintegrated.

Writing the body, creating a female dramatic discourse, is the key to Québec women's theater. Just as male dramatists adopt *joual* as the medium for a decolonized national theater, so women subvert polite, "ladylike" speech to find their own voices. They violate taboos to speak about their fears, their fantasies, and their sexuality. Often, madness accepted as a form of liberation from rational male order (what Derrida calls *phallogocentrisme*) allows women to decondition themselves, to speak more freely about their sexuality. The madwoman has appeared in different guises in many Québec feminist plays; she becomes the neurotic Marquise of Marie Savard's *Bien à moi* (1969), the witches of *La nef des sorcières*, the fairies of *Les fées ont soif*, and the writers of Jovette Marchessault's dramas. In her plays on writers of Québec (*La saga des poules mouillées*, 1981), France (*La terre est trop courte, Violette Leduc*, 1982), and the United States (*Alice & Gertrude, Natalie & Renée et ce cher Ernest*, 1984; *Anaïs, dans la queue de la comète*, 1985), Marchessault suggests that madness can be a poetic experience that calls forth the mythic visions trapped within, releases creative energy, and leads to communion with other women artists. These plays reenact the trauma of artistic creation, which is akin to self-creation, and depict the pain inflicted by male critics. By her choice of lesbian writers such as Violette Leduc, Gertrude Stein, and Renée Vivien —who dared to write about homosexual eroticism—Marchessault deliberately violates acceptable female expression in the search for a uniquely female discourse.

Other women playwrights used more conventional dramatic forms to explore the reality of women's lives in Québec. Historical plays such as *Dernier recours de Baptiste à Catherine* (1977) by Michèle Lalonde, *Ils étaient venus pour* ... (1981) and *C'était avant la guerre à l'Anse à Gilles* (1981) by Marie Laberge, and *En ville* (1984) by Elizabeth Bourget dispel the myth of *Maria Chapdelaine* and portray the women of Québec's past as strong, patriotic characters who struggled against oppression. A number of dramas by Laberge, Bourget, Maryse Pelletier, Jeanne-Mance Delisle,

Jocelyne Beaulieu, and others examine the personal lives of contemporary women in sympathetic depictions of the difficulty of being daughters, lovers, wives, and mothers. These plays have contributed to the rejection of female stereotypes and the creation of more authentic female characters.

It may be said that women's theater led to the decline of the nationalist obsession of Québec theater in the 1970s. As the decade drew to a close, political events, educational reforms, and economic improvements ameliorated the conditions that had been targets of the *nouveau théâtre québécois* and the *jeune théâtre*. The Catholic church lost much of its influence, the Parti Québécois government made French the primary language of the province and was asserting its rights in the Federal Government at Ottawa, the standard of living of the average Quebecer rose markedly, and the condition of women improved. Much of what the counterculture theater had called for had been achieved, including a consensus that Québec had a national history and culture and a collective sense of identity. Counterculture had become established culture. The defeat of the referendum on sovereignty association in 1980 seemed to mark the end of politicized, nationalist drama in Québec, as Bernard Andrès, Gilbert David, Adrien Gruslin, and others have remarked. Quebec theater in the 1980s was increasingly universal, fragmented, modernist, and theatrical.

The couple (married, unmarried, or homosexual) has become a favorite dramatic subject in the light of the changes wrought by the feminist and sexual liberation movements. Starting in the late 1970s, women playwrights turned from the monologue of alienation of early feminist theater to the couple's dialogue, in works such as Bourget's *Bernadette et Juliette ou la vie, c'est comme la vaisselle, c'est toujours à recommencer* (1978) and its sequel, *Bernadette et Juliette (suite)* (1986); Janette Bertrand's *Moi Tarzan, toi Jane* . . . (1981); Laberge's *Deux tangos pour toute une vie* (1984); Maryse Pelletier's *Duo pour voix obstinées* (1985). Men have also dramatized the changes in gender relations. In two comedies, *Faut divorcer!* (1981) and *Faut se marier pour* . . . (1985), Bertrand B. Leblanc depicts traditional males adapting to sexual equality and liberating themselves emotionally; Jean Barbeau has written several light comedies dealing with couples and family relations, including *La Vénus d'Emilio* (1980), *Coeur de papa* (1981), and *Les gars* (1983). Jean-Raymond Marcoux studies couples from the male point of view in *Bienvenue aux dames, ladies welcome* (1983) and *La grande opération* (1984). André Ricard's *Le tir à blanc* (1983) explores the tensions created by modern sexual mores. The problems of homosexual couples have been the focus of Michel Tremblay's *Les anciennes odeurs* (1981), Michel Marc Bouchard's *La contre-nature de Chrysippe Tanguay, écologiste* (1984) and *Les feluettes* (1987), and René-Daniel Dubois's *Being at Home with Claude.*

In an interview in the mid-1980s, Gilbert David bemoaned the depoliticization of experimental theater in the province and described the new preoccupation with theatricality and scenic language as modernist (17). Such experimental theater has been more concerned with exploring the possibilities of performance and the inner worlds of dreams and imagination than with representing quotidian reality. The communal improvisations of experimental theater groups—a process the Nouveau Théâtre Expérimental calls *autogestion*—make it clear that the physical aspects of performance (body movements, theatrical space) are more important than the author's text. This is theater as spectacle, theater as research laboratory, theater as ludic epic, theater as carnival. Refusing to allow the spatiotemporal limitations of conventional theater to restrain his epic imagination, Jean-Pierre Ronfard invited his audience to participate in an outdoor production of all six plays in the cycle *Vie et mort du Roi Boiteux* (1982), a festive spectacle that lasted all day. This kind of experimentation establishes new relationships between actors and audiences, stage and space (Lavoie 115–17); it also redefines the practice of theatrical writing. Ronfard defines theater, in opposition to film and television, as three-dimensional action in time and space that plays off the physical reality of actors on the stage against the false illusion of simulated events (Ronfard, "Qu'est-ce que le théâtre?" 227–28). Subordinating text to mise en scène, the Nouveau Théâtre Expérimental concentrates its creative energy on new ways of dramatizing classics such as *Lear* (1977), *Les mille et une nuits* (1984), and *Le Cyclope* (1985). Other groups participating in this modernist theater research—which is influenced by Brecht, Artaud, and Grotowski —include Carbone 14 (formerly, the Enfants du Paradis), Eskabel, the Groupe de la Veillée, Omnibus, and the Théâtre de la Manufacture. While critics may applaud their sophisticated productions as proof that Québec theater is no longer introverted and regional, it should also be noted that few of these stagings are of original plays. Many are adaptations of works by Euripides, Aeschylus, Machiavelli, Shakespeare, Cervantes, and Peter Weiss. The goal of creating a distinctively Québécois dramatic repertoire has been overshadowed by the preoccupation with performance.

Notwithstanding the trends toward universal subject matter, international repertory, and experimentation, there are still original dramatic authors in the province. Two Montrealers, Normand Chaurette and René-Daniel Dubois, stand out as the leaders of the generation of playwrights replacing those who created the notion of Québec theater in the 1970s. Although their styles and techniques differ, Chaurette and Dubois have much in common. They both subvert the conventions of realistic theater by presenting bizarre or mad characters in nightmarish hallucinations open to multiple interpretations. The mad characters of Dubois and Chaurette are not the oppressed or repressed victims of Québec society who people earlier plays analyzed by Pierre Gobin's *Le fou et ses doubles* (1978). Theirs is an existential madness brought on by the unbearable banality of the real world and a literary madness that deconstructs reality through the act of writing. The psychodramas of Chaurette and Dubois are mind games conducted by mad characters. Realistic decor, linear plot, unified personality, and simple meaning are discarded in favor of minimalist settings, dream logic, fragmented and multiple personalities, and multiple levels of meaning. Their drama exposes theatrical conventions, brings author and text onto the stage, and emphasizes its own intertextuality with ironic humor.

The fact that Chaurette's mad characters are often writers points to the danger of artistic dreams. *Rêve d'une nuit d'hôpital* (1980) takes place in a mental asylum where the fragmented memories, visions, and infernal nightmares of the poet Emile Nelligan are acted out. Time and space have no meaning in this unbalanced world of hallucinatory reality and poetic dream logic. Textuality and intertextuality are stressed by quotations from Nelligan's poems and by references to Baudelaire and Rimbaud. Chaurette's second play, *Provincetown Playhouse, juillet 1919, j'avais 19 ans* (1981), is a play within a play, the one-man show of a lunatic imprisoned for nineteen years in a hospital for the criminally insane. The mad playwright demystifies theatrical illusion in the opening scene by introducing himself as an actor-playwright and by showing the audience the text of his play. The performance is further disrupted by memory blanks, late-arriving spectators, references to other dramatists, and a defense of the play addressed to critics. The central character of *Fêtes d'automne* (1982) is also author, narrator, and actor in her own text. Joa narrates the text from the foreground of the bare stage, conjuring up players and props through the powers of writing and imagination. The play she creates is a mystical mélange—part adolescent diary, part erotic fantasy, part biblical vision, part sacred ceremony—that radically undermines the rationalism and sacred myths of Western culture.

While Chaurette's characters drift into madness when they realize that their dreams of pure artistic creation and their thirst for the ideal cannot be satisfied in the real world, Dubois's characters often seem caught in a cacophonous nightmare of doubt, solitude, and inanity. Their confusion is symptomatic of chaos; their disintegration of being reflects the disconnectedness of modern life; their verbal delirium echoes the dissonance of world politics. Given the absence of logic, purpose, and meaning, there can be no representation of unity; there can only be a collage of fragmented characters speaking in different voices, accents, and languages. Dubois's first published play, *Panique à Longueuil* (1980), is a bizarre modern version of Dante's descent into hell played out in a suburban apartment building. Having locked himself out on the balcony of his seventh-floor flat, Monsieur Arsenault descends to the basement where the elevator will bring him back up. On the way, he meets a strange collection of neighbors (representing the seven cardinal sins) who lead him to self-examination, self-doubt, and existential panic. In *Adieu, docteur Münch* (1981), the search for identity and meaning leads the solitary character to delirium. As the recently deceased Doctor Münch takes stock of his life, obsessions, fragmented memories, ideas, and artistic images besiege him in a deluge of words. As the monologue becomes a diatribe against modern life, Münch explodes and disintegrates into a hallucinated cast of others. His derangement deconstructs the text, undermining logic and reason, creating polyphonic dissonance. Dubois's third published play, *26 bis, impasse du Colonel Foisy* (1983), is a self-conscious text that ridicules its own theatricality, questions author-character-spectator relationships, and comments on other plays. The lone character is an aging Russian princess (to be played by a male actor in drag) who frequently interrupts her monologue to complain about the text, the author, the critics, the audience, and her memory lapses. The monologue is a collage of obsessive memories, flashbacks, a poem, literary commentaries, digressions, and intrusions leading to her preannounced, melodramatic murder by a desperate lover. Later, Dubois decided that since difficult and dense texts such as *Adieu, docteur Münch*; *26 bis*; and *Ne blâmez jamais les Bédouins* (1984) did not attract big audiences, he would write more conventional plays. *Being at Home with Claude* (1986), a murder mystery, and *Le printemps, Monsieur Deslauriers* (1987) were produced in large theaters, although the critics were not overly enthusiastic.

The works of Laberge, Tremblay, Chaurette, and Dubois bear witness to the fact that Québec theater has come of age. After two centuries of imported drama, one century of colonial drama, and fifty years of nationalist drama, Québec theater has matured to the point that its playwrights, directors, and actors can claim their places in the international theater community. As the political sentiments and collective sense of identity that helped it flourish in the 1960s and 1970s waned, Québec drama found new creative directions and talented playwrights to take it through the 1980s. Never completely ignoring its social, historical, and cultural context, and never repudiating its unique language, Québec drama has begun to explore universal questions that will enable it to transcend its specificity and to become world-class drama.

WORKS CITED

Andrès, Bernard. "Notes sur l'expérimentation théâtrale au Québec." *Etudes littéraires* 18.3 (1985): 15–51.

Barbeau, Jean. *Ben-Ur.* Montréal: Leméac, 1971.

——. *Le chant du sink.* Montréal: Leméac, 1973.

——. *Le chemin de lacroix.* Montréal: Leméac, 1971, 1977. *The Way of Lacrosse.* Trans. Laurence R. Berard and Philip W. London. Toronto: Playwrights Co-op, 1972.

——. *Coeur de papa.* Montréal: Leméac, 1986.

——. *Les gars.* Montréal: Leméac, 1984.

——. Manon Lastcall *et* Joualez-moi d'amour. Montréal: Leméac, 1972. *Manon Lastcall.* Trans. Philip W. London and Susan K. London. Montréal: Centre d'Essai des Auteurs Dramatiques, 1973.

——. *La Vénus d'Emilio.* Montréal: Leméac, 1984.

Béraud, Jean. *Trois cent cinquante ans de théâtre au Canada français.* Montréal: Cercle du Livre de France, 1958.

Bertrand, Janette. *Moi Tarzan, toi Jane. . . .* Montréal: Inédi, 1981.

Blackburn, Marthe, Marie-Claire Blais, Nicole Brossard, Odette Gagnon, Luce Guilbeault, Pol Pelletier, and France Théoret. *La nef des sorcières.* Montréal: Quinze, 1976. *The Clash of Symbols.* Trans. Linda Gaboriau. Toronto: Coach, 1979.

Bouchard, Michel Marc. *La contre-nature de Chrysippe Tanguay, écologiste.* Montréal: Leméac, 1984.

——. *Les feluettes, ou la répétition d'un drame romantique.* Montréal: Leméac, 1987.

Boucher, Denise. *Les fées ont soif.* Montréal: Intermède, 1978. *The Fairies Are Thirsty.* Trans. Alan Brown. Vancouver: Talonbooks, 1982.

Bourget, Elizabeth. *Bernadette et Juliette ou la vie, c'est comme la vaisselle, c'est toujours à recommencer.* Montréal: VLB, 1979.

——. *En ville.* Montréal: VLB, 1984.

Burger, Baudouin. *L'activité théâtrale au Québec (1765–1825).* Montréal: Parti Pris, 1974.

Chaurette, Normand. *Fêtes d'automne.* Montréal: Leméac, 1982.

——. *Provincetown Playhouse, juillet 1919, j'avais 19 ans.* Montréal: Leméac, 1981.

——. *Rêve d'une nuit d'hôpital.* Montréal: Leméac, 1980.

Cotnam, Jacques. *Le théâtre québécois, instrument de contestation sociale et politique.* Montréal: Fides, 1976.

David, Gilbert. "Un théâtre en pleine dérive: Entretien avec Gilbert David." With Lorraine Hébert. *Jeu* 36 (1985): 17–24.

Derome, Gilles. *Qui est Dupressin?* Montréal: Leméac, 1972.

Dubé, Marcel. *Les beaux dimanches.* Montréal: Leméac, 1968.

———. *Bilan.* 1968. Montréal: Leméac, 1978.

———. *Un simple soldat. Le temps des lilas.* Québec: Institut Littéraire, 1958. Rpt. Montréal: L'Homme, 1967.

———. *Zone.* Montréal: Cascade, 1956. Rpt. Montréal: Leméac, 1968.

Dubois, René-Daniel. *Adieu, docteur Münch.* Montréal: Leméac, 1982.

———. *Being at Home with Claude.* Montréal: Leméac, 1986.

———. *Ne blâmez jamais les Bédouins.* Montréal: Leméac, 1984.

———. *Panique à Longueuil.* Montréal: Leméac, 1980.

———. *Le printemps, monsieur Deslauriers.* Montréal: Guérin, 1987.

———. *26 bis, impasse du Colonel Foisy.* Montréal: Leméac, 1983.

Duchesne, Jacques. *Le quadrillé.* Montréal: Leméac, 1975.

Ferron, Jacques. *Les grands soleils. Théâtre I.* Montréal: Déom, 1969. 11–109.

———. *La tête du roi. Théâtre II.* Montréal: Déom, 1975. 63–152.

Fréchette, Louis-Honoré. *Félix Poutré.* Montréal: Leméac, 1974.

———. *Papineau.* Leméac, 1974. *Papineau.* Trans. Eugene Benson and Renate Benson. Wagner 141–202.

———. *Le retour de l'exilé.* Montréal: Leméac, 1974.

Gagnon, Dominique, Louise Laprade, Nicole Lecavalier, and Pol Pelletier. *A ma mère, à ma mère, à ma mère, à ma voisine.* Montréal: Remue-Ménage, 1979.

Gauvreau, Claude. *La charge de l'orignal épormyable. Oeuvres complètes.* Montréal: Parti Pris, 1971. 637–754.

———. *Les oranges sont vertes. Oeuvres complètes.* Montréal: Parti Pris, 1971. 1363–1488.

Gélinas, Gratien. *Les Fridolinades. 1945 et 1946.* Montréal: Quinze, 1980.

———. *Les Fridolinades 1941 et 1942.* Montréal: Quinze, 1983.

———. *Les Fridolinades 1943 et 1944.* Montréal: Quinze, 1981.

———. *Les Fridolinades 1938, 1939, 1940.* Montréal: Leméac, 1988.

———. *Hier, les enfants dansaient.* Montréal: Leméac, 1968.

———. *Tit-Coq.* Montréal: Beauchemin, 1950. Trans. Kenneth Johnstone and Gratien Gélinas. Toronto: Clarke, 1967.

Gérin-Lajoie, Antoine. *Le jeune Latour.* Montréal: Réédition-Québec, 1969. *The Young Latour.* 1844. Trans. Louise Forsyth. Wagner 111–40.

Germain, Jean-Claude. *A Canadian Play/une plaie canadienne.* Montréal: VLB, 1983.

———. *Diguidi, diguidi, ha! ha! ha! and Si les Sansoucis s'en soucient, ces Sansoucis-ci s'en soucieront-ils? Bien parler, c'est se respecter!* Montréal: Leméac, 1972.

———. *L'école des rêves.* Montréal: VLB, 1979.

———. "Entretien(s)." With Gilbert David and Francine Noël. *Jeu* 13 (1979): 9–81.

────. *Les hauts et les bas dla vie d'une diva: Sarah Ménard par eux-mêmes.* Montréal: VLB, 1976.

────. *Mamours et conjugat.* Montréal: VLB,

────. *Les nuits de l'Indiva: une mascapade.* Montréal: VLB, 1983.

────. *Un pays dont la devise est je m'oublie.* Montréal: VLB, 1976.

Gobin, Pierre. *Le fou et ses doubles: Figures de la dramaturgie québécoise.* Montréal: PU de Montréal, 1978.

Godin, Jean-Cléo. "Les gaietés montréalaises: Sketches, revues." *Etudes françaises* 15.1–2 (1979): 143–57.

Godin, Jean-Cléo, and Laurent Mailhot. *Le théâtre québécois: Introduction à dix dramaturges contemporains.* Montréal: HMH-Hurtubise, 1970.

Gruslin, Adrien. "Le théâtre politique au Québec: Une espèce en voie de disparition." *Jeu* 36 (1985): 32–39.

Gurik, Robert. *Hamlet, prince du Québec.* Montréal: Leméac, 1977. *Hamlet, Prince of Quebec.* Trans. Marc F. Gélinas. Toronto: Playwrights, 1981.

Hare, John. "Panorama des spectacles au Québec: De la Conquête au XX siècle." *Le théâtre canadien français.* Ed. Paul Wyczynski, Bernard Julien, and Hélène Beauchamp-Rank. Archives des lettres canadiennes 5. Montréal: Fides, 1976.

Hébert, Chantal. *Le burlesque au Québec: Un divertissement populaire.* Montréal: HMH-Hurtubise, 1981.

Laberge, Marie. *C'était avant la guerre à l'Anse à Gilles.* Montréal: VLB, 1981.

────. *Deux tangos pour toute une vie.* Montréal: VLB, 1984.

────. *Ils étaient venus pour. . . .* Montréal: VLB, 1981.

Lalonde, Michèle. *Dernier recours de Baptiste à Catherine.* Montréal: Leméac, 1977.

Languirand, Jacques. *Les grands départs.* Montréal: Cercle du Livre de France, 1958.

────. *Les insolites.* Montréal: Cercle du Livre de France, 1962.

Lavoie, Pierre. "Nouveau Théâtre Expérimental: Le 5-10-15 de l'expérimental." *Jeu* 36 (1985): 114–18.

Leblanc, Bertrand B. *Faut divorcer!* Montréal: Leméac, 1981.

────. *Faut se marier pour. . . .* Montréal: Leméac, 1985.

Lescarbot, Marc. *Le Théâtre de Neptune en la Nouvelle France. Histoire de la Nouvelle France.* Paris, 1609. *The Theatre of Neptune in New France.* Trans. Eugene Benson and Renate Benson. Wagner 35–44.

Loranger, Françoise. *Le chemin du roy.* With Claude Levac. Montréal: Leméac, 1969.

────. *Encore cinq minutes.* Montréal: Cercle du Livre de France, 1967.

────. *Une maison . . . un jour.* Montréal: Cercle du Livre de France, 1965.

────. *Médium saignant.* Montréal: Leméac, 1970.

Marchessault, Jovette. *Alice et Gertrude, Natalie et Renée et ce cher Ernest.* Montréal: Pleine Lune, 1984.

────. *Anaïs, dans la queue de la comète.* Montréal: Pleine Lune, 1985.

————. *La saga des poules mouillées.* Montréal: Pleine Lune, 1981. *The Saga of the Wet Hens.* Trans. Linda Gaboriau. Vancouver: Talonbooks, 1983.

————. *La terre est trop courte, Violette Leduc.* Montréal: Pleine Lune, 1982.

Marcoux, Jean-Raymond. *Bienvenue aux dames, ladies welcome.* Montréal: VLB, 1985.

————. *La grande opération.* Montréal: VLB, 1988.

Pelletier, Maryse. *Duo pour voix obstinées.* Montréal: VLB, 1985.

Petitclair, Pierre. *La Donation.* L'Artisan 1.20 (15 Dec. 1842); 21 (19 Dec. 1842); 22 (22 Dec. 1842); 23 (26 Dec. 1842); 24 (29 Dec. 1842).

————. *Une partie de campagne.* Québec: Joseph Savard, 1865.

Quesnel, Joseph. *Colas et Colinette ou le Bailli dupe: Comédie-vaudeville.* Québec: John Neilson, 1808. *Colas and Colinette: Or, The Bailiff Confounded.* 1790. Trans. Michael Lecavalier and Godfrey Ridout. Wagner 53–95.

————. *Les républicains français.* La barre du jour 25 (1970): 64–88. *The French Republicans: Or, An Evening in the Tavern.* 1800–01. Trans. Louise Forsyth. Wagner 96–110.

Ricard, André. *Le tir à blanc.* Montréal: Leméac, 1983.

Ronfard, Jean-Pierre. *Les mille et une nuits.* Montréal: Leméac, 1985.

————. "Qu'est-ce que le théâtre?" *Etudes littéraires* 18.3 (1985): 227–31.

————. *Vie et mort du Roi Boiteux.* Vols. 1 and 2. Montréal: Leméac, 1981.

Roy, Gabrielle. *Bonheur d'occasion.* Montréal: Stanké, 1978. *The Tin Flute.* Trans. Hannah Josephson. New Canadian Library. Toronto: McClelland, 1958.

Savard, Marie. *Bien à moi.* Montréal: Pleine Lune, 1979.

Le Théâtre des Cusines. *As-tu vu? Les maisons s'emportent!* Montréal: Remue-Ménage, 1981.

————. *Môman travaille pas, a trop d'ouvrage!* Montréal: Remue-Ménage, 1976.

Tremblay, Michel. *Albertine, en cinq temps.* Montréal: Leméac, 1984.

————. *Les anciennes odeurs.* Montréal: Leméac, 1981. *Remember Me.* Trans. John Stowe. Vancouver: Talonbooks, 1984.

————. *Les belles-soeurs.* Montréal: Théâtre Vivant 6 (1968). Montréal: Leméac, 1972. Trans. John Van Burek and Bill Glassco. Vancouver: Talonbooks, 1974.

————. *Bonjour, là, bonjour.* Montréal: Leméac, 1974. Trans. John Van Burek and Bill Glassco. Vancouver: Talonbooks, 1975.

————. *Damnée Manon, sacrée Sandra.* Montréal: Leméac, 1977. Trans. John Van Burek. Vancouver: Talonbooks, 1981.

————. *Demain matin, Montréal m'attend.* Montréal: Leméac, 1973.

————. *La Duchesse de Langeais. Hosanna.* Montréal: Leméac, 1973. Trans. John Van Burek. La Duchesse de Langeais *and Other Plays.* Vancouver: Talonbooks, 1976.

————. *A toi, pour toujours ta Marie-Lou.* Montréal: Leméac, 1971. *Forever Yours, Marie Lou.* Trans. John Van Burek and Bill Glassco. Vancouver: Talonbooks, 1974.

Usmiani, Renate. *Second Stage: The Alternative Theatre Movement in Canada.* Vancouver: U of British Columbia P, 1983.

Wagner, Anton, ed. *Colonial Quebec: French-Canadian Drama, 1606–1966.* Vol. 4 of *Canada's Lost Plays.* Toronto: York U, 1982.

Barbara Godard

CRITICAL DISCOURSE IN/ON QUÉBEC

WHAT NARRATIVE TO relate? This is a fundamental question to be addressed by the literary critic faced with a vast body of material, a pluralistic critical scene, a border/line position both inside and outside the critical institution in question, and the limitations of the form imposed by the present venue. Narrative will inevitably emerge, for, as Lyotard has suggested, narrative is the preeminent mode in the formulation of customary knowledge (19).[1] Although opposed to scientific knowledge in that it is not skeptical, its truths having no recourse to argumentation and proof, narrative knowledge is not separate from scientific knowledge. Indeed, the "return of the narrative in the non-narrative" (27) is a part of the language game of science. A scientist communicating a "discovery" relates a quest narrative or epic about the research. Narratives—of speculation or of emancipation—are modes of legitimation, statements of truth whose own legitimation is effected in the very act of transmission, through "performativity" (41).[2] With the upsurge in technologies and techniques, however, these "grand narratives" of unification have lost their credibility (37). Instead of the coherence of the historical discourse of modernism, described by Jean-Pierre Roux as "seek[ing] the intelligible in the play of temporalities and the flow of a narrative deliberately constructed, intrigue, sequence and progress, the three rules on which has flowered modernist dramaturgy" (qtd. in Perron 84), we are confronted with the contesting narrative of delegitimation, characterized by its ruptures and dis/placements, its interrogation of the narrating instance, in which the narrator is cut off from the narratee and the story being told—in short, "the investigative language game" of the "postmodern world" (Lyotard 41). The choice of narrative mode in which to frame this story of contemporary Québec critical discourse is of crucial importance, for narratives "formulate prescriptions that have the status of norms. They therefore exercise their competence not only with respect to denotative utterances concerning what is true, but also prescribe utterances with pretentions to justice" (31).

But in selecting a narrative to frame this discourse of scientific knowledge, a critical discourse on critical discourses, the freedom of the critic is already limited. As Lyotard points out, an institution imposes constraints that "function to filter discursive potentials, interrupting possible connections in the communication network: there are things that should not be said. They also privilege certain classes of statements (sometimes only one) whose predominance characterizes the discourse of the particular institution: there are things that should be said, and there are ways of saying them" (17). Jacques Dubois has defined literature as an institution on three levels, as "autonomous organization, as socializing system, and as ideological apparatus" (*Institution de la littérature* 34). A tendency of this institution, according to Bourdieu, is for criticism "to take as its task not the production of instruments of appropriation ever more imperative for the work in function as it is distanced from the public, but to supply a 'creative' interpretation for the use of its 'creators' " (56–57). The limits the institution imposes on potential language "moves" are never established once and for all, nor are they universal, but are themselves "the stakes and provisional results of language strategies, within the institution and without" (Lyotard 17). In the present discursive instance, in which the institutional boundaries are compounded by linguistic frontiers and national border/lines—English-Canadian–based narrator of Québec critical discourse to a United States narratee—the institutional limits are multiplied and fractured. Which narrative to choose? The narrative of intelligibility emanating from the Ecole des Hautes Etudes Pratiques in Paris, where, in developing a "structural anthropology" (Perron 83) for Québec literature, numerous Québec critics have located a discursive formation in the writing of Roland Barthes, Julia Kristeva, Gérard Genette, and other structuralists? Or should I choose the new discursive practice in the form of discontinuous, delegitimating narratives, which challenge the master narratives and legitimate poststructural knowledges along the model of English-Canadian critics who, like their peers in the United States, have made steps to the Ecole Normale Supérieure, where presides the archdeconstructionist Jacques Derrida (Godard, "Other Fictions," "Structuralism")?

Plus ça change, plus ça reste pareil. A glance at the trajectory of literary criticism in Québec since the 1950s would seem to bear out the truth of this venerable adage, forcefully reiterated in such classic Québec novels as Louis Hémon's *Maria Chapdelaine* and Felix-Antoine Savard's *Menaud,*

Maître-draveur, that nothing ever will or ever should change in the province of Québec. The notion is suggested also by Robert Giroux:

> To judge by recent theoretical discourses on Quebec poetry—think of the numerous articles signed P. Haeck, C. Beausoleil, F. Charron, N. Brossard, to name the best known from *La Barre du jour, Dérives, Hobo Québec, Les Herbes rouges*, etc.—it seems that the movement begun towards the end of the sixties to displace the question of literature from an ideological level to a level of so-called scientific knowledge, it seems this movement is in the process of being reversed. After the difficult and loaded descriptive techniques of those holders of a linguistic and logical perspective—"formalist" —on the subject of the analysis of poetic texts, we are witnessing a return to contemplation, to the real poetic text as an object for aesthetic consumption, to writing as the lived experience of gifted individuals, to reading as a ludic practice which is exclusive and incommunicable. (Giroux and Dame 29)

He points out that the structuralist enterprise, focusing on the function of codes in the production of meaning and on cultural conventions, has given way in the 1980s under discursive subversion and deconstructive virtuosity to a focus on subjectivity.

A rapid scan of the horizon would confirm this reversal. Jean Ethier-Blais is once more writing a literary chronicle for *Le devoir* after fostering academic criticism during his tenure at McGill University. Whether his current reviews will have the impact of his earlier work is a moot point. Published in the three-volume collection *Signets*, this criticism is typical of that practiced in Québec periodicals before the development of academic criticism. Aesthetic values are of secondary interest: literary criticism is above all a criticism of life, a search for humane and spiritual values (Marcotte 345). French-Canadian literature is an "important sociological phenomenon in our lives," because it leads us to recognition of ourselves. Writers "describe us as we are" and "without fear of losing ourselves, we can plunge into [their works'] mirror" (*Signets* 2: 20, 5). Another sign of a return is the flourishing interest in the sociology of literature and the literary institution, as exemplified in the special issues of *Etudes françaises* (1984) and *Sociologies et sociétés* (1985) that mapped the terrain of contemporary sociological theories of literature and culture (*Sociologies, Sociologie critique*). Other signals of change were the innumerable publications of the research groups at the University of Sherbrooke and University of Laval that studied the institutionalization of literature in Québec—for instance, *Structure, idéologie et reception du roman québécois de 1940 à 1960*, edited by Jacques Michon; Joseph Bonenfant's *A l'ombre de Desrochers*; and Maurice Lemire's *L'institution littéraire*. Exploring the teaching, publishing, and reception of

Québec literature, its relationship to government and the press, collective studies like Lise Gauvin and Jean-Marie Klinkenberg's *Trajectoires* testified to the vitality and range of interest in the literary fact. But sociology of literature was already the major critical narrative on Québec literature in the early 1960s, when the literature was first being institutionalized, as manifest in the collaborative venture *Littérature et société canadienne-française*, edited by Fernand Dumont and Jean-Charles Falardeau, and in the Marxist criticism of *Parti pris* (1963–68). While studies from the 1980s belong to what André Belleau has called " 'professional' sociocritique," this continuum suggests a "traditional 'sociocritique,' a sort of general sociologizing discourse practiced forever by journalists, writers, professors, who tend to consider each important work that appears as a moment, successful or not, in a literary evolution inseparable from national and political evolution," the two series, to use Russian formalist terms, considered to be in an isochronic relationship ("Le démarche" 302, 300). The nationalist issue has in fact remained the touchstone for literary evaluation since the nineteenth century.

Additional evidence of an eternal return is to be found in a 1987 review of critical studies of Québec literature, Agnes Whitfield's "La modernité." In answer to the question of how to link the seeming incongruities of Roger Chamberland's phenomenological study of the poetry of Claude Gauvreau, Marie-Andrée Beaudet's intertextual reading of Langevin, and *A double sens*, a dialogue between Hugues Corriveau and Normand de Bellefeuille on the current views on modernity, Whitfield picks up the thread of modernism.[3] Had she focused on the theories implicit in these studies rather than on their content as common denominator, she too might have heralded the return of the subject and a personal, though not impressionistic, criticism in the exchange between the two poet-critics, who question the limits of formalism with regard to what modernity has excluded—that is, with regard to the concepts of the author, style, and meaning. Corriveau and de Bellefeuille confront the impossibility of excluding writers' anthromorphologic relation to their own words. Corriveau especially argues for the rehabilitation of neglected concepts, notably *l'émotion* (158–59). Chamberland's study, too, is premised on the subjectivity of the author and the critic. Adopting the approach of the Geneva school, especially the criticism of Jean Starobinski, Chamberland's phenomenological reading of Gauvreau is grounded in a constant movement between the literary work and the consciousness of the reader, to outline the transformations that occur in the theme of the gaze. Drawing also on the work of Maurice Blanchot, he connects the gaze to the theme of eroticism and the metaphysical and aesthetic dimensions of the poet's "exploréen" language. Intended not as future-oriented critique of the positivism of formalism and structuralism,

Chamberland's focus on the subjectivity of writer and reader, like Corriveau and de Bellefeuille's text, hearkens back to the heyday of phenomenology in the 1960s, when thematic criticism of space and time dominated the literary scene. Along with criticism of the themes of Anne Hébert's world by Lucille Roy, and Maurice Edmond's explorations of the poet's symbolic universe, which listen attentively and trace the meanders of images and themes to uncover a vibrant, dynamic world of her imagination, Chamberland's study testifies to the continuing presence of phenomenology on the Québec scene.

The reader's subjectivity is also a concern in Beaudet's book on Langevin. For Beaudet, too, criticism is conceived as an encounter between "the sensibility and the experience of the reader" and the "trajectory of the creator" (6). But in answer to questions about transformations of style, Beaudet offers explanations grounded not in the authorial function but in the text understood in its global sense—in this case, in the intertextual relations with the *roman du terroir*. Drawing on the work of Russian formalists and French structuralists, Beaudet argues with Maurice Blanchot that the work develops in complicity with the "literary space" that contains it and is contained by it, and with Julia Kristeva that literature is born of literature, that every text is a "mosaic" of quotations, textuality being the absorption of texts by other texts, or intertextuality (16). Here is a clear enunciation of the preeminence of text over author or reader in the production of meaning. The battle of the subject has occurred in Québec, as elsewhere, between phenomenology and structuralism, as the focus of critical activity has shifted from author to text to reader as locus of meaning. Whatever reinscription of the subject may be taking place on the Québec critical scene, the text has not been entirely excluded from the discourse. Indeed, the lessons of structuralism have been well learned. To a much greater degree than in English Canada, Québec critics acknowledge the structuring force of language in the constitution of knowledge, a characteristic trait of post-Saussurean discourses. Contemporary Québec criticism is indeed poststructuralist. Subjectivity is not grounded in the humanist understanding of the subject as a free agent but as constructed and positioned within discourse(s) whose codes are legitimated by social institutions.

Rather than reading this article teleologically—as I have been in the footsteps of Giroux, looking for a narrative thread like that of the romance quest for becoming and being or of the epic of discovery, focusing on the moment of mythic return, to describe the development of contemporary Québec criticism—I could read it as a grid or field of lines and forces, metaphorically an emblem of the pluralistic nature of critical theory in Québec. For like Whitfield's, my reading of these three books together is happenstance. My narrative would no longer emphasize historical continuity and privilege these three texts as metonymies of successive phases of Québec criticism since 1960: thematic, structuralist, poststructuralist. Instead, it would read these texts as a play of competing discourses framed in a disjunctive narrative that would challenge the totalizing and homogenizing claims of all narratives. Instead of giving oneself up to the pleasure of reading (which implies a pleasure in discussing the text based on familiarity with the "message" of the text or the author), one becomes implicated in the negative operation of language, seeing irony in the ephemeral meanings crystallized in the face of the writer's death drive, as described by Kristeva. To follow Giroux: "It is no longer a question of recalling the structures of language or a group of theoretical concepts and textual manipulations: finished with preexistent models, codes, cultural conventions, the text as an object to construct as an object of knowledge; make way for the individuality, the originality of the text, for discursive subversion, for the virtuosity of deconstruction. Too bad for unreadability, theoretical contradictions, numbilical metadiscourse" (Giroux and Dame 29–30). A sarcastic dismissal of deconstruction's unfixing of the transcendental signifier and decentering of the subject in the free play of meaning, Giroux's statement is representative of a certain disjuncture between writing and criticism in Québec, the deconstructive moment in the former confronting the formalist-structuralist practices of the latter. But then, as the discourse analysis of Lyotard and Foucault has shown us, the free play of signifiers is an illusion. The institution—through the authorial function or the critical function, in the case of critical fictions—fixes and defines meaning. The prescribed narrative on the Québec critical scene probes the discourses authorized by the academy to expose their hidden assumptions and ideologies. While many critical discourses proliferate in books of criticism, not all are equally privileged by the literary institution itself, as evidenced in the reviewing patterns of *Lettres québécoises* and, more significant, of *Voix et images*, two periodicals devoted exclusively to Québec literature.

In isolating the hegemonic discourses in Québec criticism, I shall make use of Raymond Williams's concepts of dominant, residual, and emergent discourses (121–27). Inevitably, since the 1960s, the dominant discourse of one moment has become the residual of another in the dialectics of genre, antigenre, and renewal of genre. This model, in which residual may form the grounds for emergent discourse, avoids the teleology and singularity of the historical narrative and the currently unspeakable aleatory processes of the deconstructive challenge to narrative and representation. In this exploration, one must re/construct the critical dynamics of the early 1960s, to establish the residual humanist discourse against which the new academic institutional criticism of sociological and phenomenological persuasions emerged. The trajectory of one critic, André Brochu, whose career coincides with the development of the critical academy in Québec, is grounded in the Marxist sociocritique of *Parti pris*, later turning to the structuralist and semiotic approaches that came to dominate in the universities. Here, though, I shall explore only the emergent critical discourses, notably discourse analysis and feminism that draw on semiotics to analyze ideological signifying practices. To speak of these as emergent in the light of the recent deaths of the two most eminent practitioners, André Belleau and Suzanne Lamy, seems to be a logical contradiction worthy of the most assiduous deconstructivist critic. In this case, I write in the future perfect, in the promise of works in progress.

As in English Canada, the history of critical discourse in Québec is for the most part a history of literary criticism and not of poetics. No literary theorist of the stature of Northrop Frye has emerged in Québec. Québec critics have followed the theoretical modes of France with more or less precipitation, selectively, it should be noted. Critical fashions in the United States have gone unnoticed by Québec critics, especially the passage of New Criticism. Nor, despite translations of works by Northrop Frye and Marshall McLuhan, has Anglo-Canadian theory had a significant impact. Eclectic critics like Gilles Marcotte reveal a knowledge of their theory (Brochu and Marcotte) but do not apply it in their critical analyses of individual texts. Significantly, a body of literary theory has emerged in Québec, especially in the field of feminist theory, through the work of creative writers like Nicole Brossard and Madeleine Ouellette-Michalska, whose deconstructive dismantlings of the master discourses of Western society—Freudianism, Marxism, and structuralism—have provided a highly innovative theory combining the theoretical concerns of French and United States feminism. Brossard has coined the term *fiction/theory* for her work, breaking down the boundaries between these two discourses in her theorization of gender, which has served as a model for other Québec avantgarde writers associated with the periodical *La nouvelle barre du jour*. Their "exploréen" fictions have initiated poststructuralist theory, continuing a line of writing as rupture that began with the emergence of the *nouveau roman* in 1964, "a brusque mutation" that led Jean Marcel, summing up the critical production of the year, to deplore the absence of what was most exciting and original in France, "la nouvelle critique," despite the vitality and variety of the year's criticism (23).

While structuralism is positioned in this narrative as a moment of rupture and discontinuity in which a dominant humanist focus on the subject and meaning is challenged, another narrative, one of continuity, would emerge, if we paid strict attention to dates. Just when structuralist analyses of texts began appearing in the 1970s, a counterchallenge was launched. Earlier, in Europe, Bakhtin criticized the Saussurean model for its failure to deal with the speech act and diachronic analysis: in Québec, in the early 1970s, Belleau launched his critique of structuralism and positivism in the name of Bakhtin's theories of dialogism and the carnivalesque. Writing in the Marxist periodical *Stratégie* in 1974 on "littérature et politique," where he discusses the complex interrelationships of poetics and politics, Belleau acknowledges his debt to Marxist concepts of culture, especially those of "totality, multiplicity, becoming, etc."—"critical concepts, favoring the multivocal over the univocal and rejecting any fragmented, mutilated, or alienated vision of man" (*Surprendre* 75). Although Belleau foregrounds his adhesion to Theodor Adorno's view that literature is not "integrable," is not effective, and serves at most to prepare an intellectual and psychological terrain pertinent to the emergence of certain social changes, the reader recognizes in Belleau's language the concepts of Bakhtin—heteroglossia, polyphony, multivoiced discourse—that elsewhere Belleau sees as characteristics of Québec culture.

Criticism may now be perceived as a genre with its own dialectics peculiar to its established taxonomies: genre, antigenre, renewal of genre. Belleau's role in launching Québec criticism back into its perennial concern with the sociology of literature is primarily that of theoretician. As voice of an emergent critical discourse, Belleau holds a contradictory position. In that the majority of his critical production occurs in the form of brief, familiar essays that have appeared, for the most part, in nonacademic periodicals, Belleau is a direct inheritor of the impressionist criticism dominant in Québec until the 1960s. Indeed, Belleau began as a general cultural critic advocating the engagement of intellectuals in social change ("Action" 695), moving into academe in mid-career, when the academy became the central legitimating institution of that criticism. But *Le romancier fictif*, his study of the emergence of a genre of fiction, the novel about the novelist, as well as his discussion of the literary and social codes working in Québec literature ("La démarche") indicates that Belleau has thoroughly absorbed structuralist theory. He uses it as a *bricoleur*, however, as heuristic device, his final aim being not merely the description of the rules of the literary artifact but the elucidation of its social meaning. Plus, not minus, Québec.

Thoroughly dialectalized, Belleau's advocacy of the study of literature as a signifying practice, focusing on an exploration of the instance of enunciation with recognition of the heterogeneity of the discourses working the text and of the operation of the literary institution in shaping these discourses, accommodates the residual quest for the specificity of Québec literature and classification of the *homo quebecensis* to the dominant structuralist paradigm, metonymy of a new critical discourse. Following these currents, Québec critics such as Maroussia Hajdukowski-Ahmed and Joseph Bonenfant are turning their attention to the prevalence of the carnivalesque, to the exploration of dialogism and research in literary pragmatics, and to the study of the literary institution, the "code of codes," according to Belleau, which, presiding over the choice of codes as "obligatory mediation," intervenes between the mass of discourses composing the social discourse and the literary text, reorienting this heterogeneous linguistic material to the ends of the literary success of the text (*Surprendre* 188–89). Belleau recognizes the complexity of the mediation intervening in this intertextuality; his concept of the sociology of literature bears little resemblance to the sociology of the 1960s, which he has so vociferously attacked ("La démarche").

As godfather to the new ideological criticism, Belleau has waged war on the positivism of the Québec literary institution. "Literologist" is how he described himself in 1979 in an academic institution obsessively focused on result-oriented research (*Surprendre* 91). A change has taken place in the preceding decade so that the situation that existed when he began to teach at the university in 1970 (when the titles "Professor of literature, Journalist, Frenchman, Intellectual, Poet were interchangeable") has been transformed into one in which the professor is a "specialist in texts," engaged in a limited activity whose technicity is adapted from the social sciences (91). In this context, Belleau joins in the quarrel of *la nouvelle critique*, which opposes Barthes to Picard on the question of semiotics versus literary history. Railing against "an ingenuous semiotics which conceives literary works like musical cigarette boxes and believes in their [textual] closure," Belleau protests the irony that nobody in Québec was doing real literary history before the vogue for semiotics (93). Developing the polemic in a later essay, Belleau denounces the unwillingness of literary departments to examine their own epistemological presuppositions, which he categorizes as "naively positivist" (*Surprendre* 212). The objects of their research they take as natural, not as "constructed." The hidden presuppositions of the reigning positivist and scientistic ideology are camouflaged by a more immediate pressure, that of electronic communications. The arrival of the computer coincides with the discovery, by the Québec Ministry of Education, of Jakobson's linguistic theories with their model of the communicative act. The result, he fulminates, is the substitution of the word *emitter* for the word *writer* in the educational world (214). The death of the subject, the rise of the author function. Belleau concludes that theory is inevitably technicist and produces the same "anaesthetizing" effect as technology. The "logic of the informational machine" (215) is manifest in the proliferation of linguistic and semiotic theory in the educational institution. Elsewhere, exploring the ambiguous relations between mass culture and literary institution, he observes that confusion between mass culture and popular culture is knowingly fostered by a literary institution (publishers' catalogs and bookstores) that tends "increasingly to model itself on engineer-salesmen of standardized or prefabricated cultural products" (*Surprendre* 152).

Belleau's critique of the Québec literary institution is formulated in the terms of the Frankfurt school's advocacy of a critical culture that alone grounds an "authentic art." This stance is mediated by the work of Fredric Jameson, whose analysis of postmodernism as the proof of consumer culture, not its critical negation, Belleau adopts in attacking the mechanized mass culture of late-capitalist, postmodern Québec (*Surprendre* 200). In opposition to the positivist semiotics and narratology à la Gérard Genette, Mieke Bal, and Gerald Prince, practiced in Québec by critics like Jean Fisette, Pierre Hébert, Patrick Imbert, and Janet Paterson, Belleau advances the example of Bakhtin in *Esthétique et théorie du roman* as the basis for a new, critical narratology where the "grotesque body" would be everywhere (201). It is not the carnival as semantic content that is key to Bakhtin's theory, Belleau contends, but the carnivalesque or dialogic—that is, "what concerns the 'reproduction' and 'the aesthetic transfiguration' (in Bakhtin's words) of the heterogeneity of interacting discourses'" (*Surprendre* 94–95). In short, the type of artistic discourse called a novel, grounded in this concept of carnival, has as its concern not the life of society but the life of the enunciation (197). Carnivalization implies three registers of simultaneous oppositions: the binary oppositions (head-bottom, death-life, etc.) in popular culture; the double-voiced discourse of the popular carnivalesque culture in opposition to the singular discourse of the "official" culture; and the textual transposition of the first two carnival systems (196). The question of the carnivalesque cannot be separated from that of "poetics throughout history" (199). In this, in its efforts to describe the roles of the narrator as a function of the observation of properly discursive phenomena, narratology on the Bakhtinian model moves beyond the positivist illusion of current narratology, which limits its analysis of the signification of texts solely to linguistic characteristics: "time, mood, aspect and voice" (202). Belleau does not carry out this textual analysis, though he made a start on such a project—a critical description and reading of a transtextual phenomenon, an attempt at "sociotextual analysis"—in *Le romancier fictif*. His aim of linking the social meaning of the novels with their context involves a consideration of "society" not as an essence but as a "text" (*Romancier* 17). In this, he isolates the ideology *of* the text, the ideology in the aesthetic codes that mediate the relationship of the text to the social discourse. Belleau's discussion of the carnivalesque is paradoxically presented as theory—paradoxical because theory is offered as a textual strategy in opposition to theory denounced as "technicist"! One may read Belleau's critique as the traditional Marxist emphasis on the relationship between base and superstructures and the privileging of diachronic over synchronic analysis.

Although most critics engaged in the sociology of literature have chosen to focus on the literary institution, a study of the manifesto by Jeanne Demers and Line McMurray, *L'enjeu du manifeste/Le manifeste en jeu*, indicates that interest in the ideology of the text has not been eclipsed by attention to the legitimating instances of discourse. In fact, as the authors conclude, the manifesto is the ideology of the text carried to the ultimate: it is "the commentary of the institution," its way of speaking aloud about what happens silently within the institution (155). The manifesto makes precisely manifest the institutional character of literature—that is, its dimension as social practice, with its own sphere of activities as well as a number of codified relations to other aspects of social life. The literary manifesto may range along the scale between action and written text. The manifesto is a "bomb" strategically placed within the system of literary history, as Wlad Godzich describes it in his introduction to *L'enjeu* (7), underlining the role of the manifesto in the crisis and renewal of literary genres and movements.

This inseparability of text and discourse corresponds to the definition of the literary institution according to Giroux and Lemelin: "The institution is the inseparability of the body and the text, the undecidability of a boundary between the two and between the course of development and the discourse or between the story and the narration; [an] institution whose becoming-constitution is assured by the discipline" (8–9). In order to approach literature—"the process of reading, literature is nothing else but the spectacle of literature" (8)—it is not enough to add a sociology to an aesthetics, or a sociology to semiotics to come up with a sociosemiotics. For to do so would be to accept the closure of the text, to take the literary corpus as a given not to be questioned, to support a view that poetry has aesthetic or linguistic specificity when textual semiotics has shown that literature shares its special features with other systems, linguistic, symbolic, and social. What is needed to replace structuralist poetics with their focus on synchrony and the bounded text, Giroux and Lemelin suggest, is a "non-sociological theory of the social," "a generalized pragmatics" that will be a pragmatics of the perlocutory as well as of the illocutory and focus on the complete instance of enunciation, on the reception as well as the production of texts. The concept of the institution itself is the necessary sociohistoric theory that "breaks with the logic and dialectic of production as (re)creation or (re)solution of literature by writing" (8). It understands literature to be the process of reading and institutional mechanisms. Reading makes writers—not the inverse. The process of reading distinguishes writers who sometimes write very little from nonwriters who often write a great deal, literary writers from scribblers who are not literary (9). Consequently, in this collective study, the focus is on the institutional aspects of reading, on those facets of literary activity that link the institution and the discipline of literary studies—namely, publishing, promotion, teaching, research, labeling, and distribution. Jean-Marc Lemelin offers a number of narratives of pragmatics—on the text, on its publishing, its promotion, on teaching, and on distribution—and a history of the discipline of literary studies in Québec, focusing on the intellectual and scientific fields in relation to the literary, the relationship between the university and other agents of diffusion—periodicals, presses—areas of struggle for knowledge and power (Giroux and Lemelin). The collection opens with a study by Robert Giroux on the social and economic status of the writer— the ideological representation of the writer, the legal fiction of the writer, and the figure of the writer in the public imagination. There is clearly a difference in approach in these studies from that in studies by Belleau and by Demers and McMurray. Whereas Demers, McMurray, and Belleau are text-oriented, with "text" understood in its enlarged Derridean sense, in which there is no "hors-texte," no extratextual dimension, or in the Bakhtinian sense of the dialogic (where text and reception are dialectized), Giroux and Lemelin are exclusively focused on reception. Meaning is created by the receiver of the text as shaped by social codes.

This distinction is introduced by Jacques Michon in his contribution to the Québec-Belgium dialogue on the institution when he contrasts the outmoded "sociology of the work" with the new "sociology of literature." Whereas the former considered literature as an expression or reflection of the social conscience, the latter studies literary conventions and the way they function. Rejecting broad-ranging studies of society, class, and ideology, this new sociology focuses on the "mechanisms of mediation" through which the social constraints are translated into literary terms, mechanisms of production, and reception—namely, publishers, periodicals, criticism, prizes, all the apparatuses that keep the literary institution going and that "participate in reading, at least by strategies of orientation and recognition" (Michon 117). Quoting in these final words the sociologist Jacques Dubois, Michon acknowledges the éminence grise of this Montréal–Brussels encounter. Whereas the Québécois in the 1960s headed to Paris to do a doctorate in semiotics, aspiring critics in the 1980s rushed to Belgium to learn how to analyze the literary institution. Dubois is not the only influence on the new sociology of literature. In outlining his method for studying Québec avant-garde periodicals and the questions he planned to ask of them—questions regarding the relative numbers of university and religiously funded periodicals, the place they accorded Québec literature, the fraction of intellectuals they represented, the ideological positions implied by their aesthetics, and their interaction as the avant-garde—Michon accepts Dubois's distinction of the avant-garde as that group which introduces the idea of crisis into the literary institution. He also grounds his analysis in Pierre Bourdieu's definition of the avant-garde as a "production for producers elaborated in a restricted circle that contests the dominant cultural legitimacy by admitting new categories of aesthetic perception" (118). The combination of Dubois's institutional analysis and Bourdieu's theory of the market in symbolic goods has generated a number of Québec studies of literary production and reception.

Through a close analysis of the educational reforms of the 1960s—changes in exams, programs, essay themes—Joseph Melançon demonstrates the increasing role of the teaching of Québec literature in the production of the consumer goods that are literary texts, resulting in an increase from 233 in 1971 to 791 in 1981 with no change in the quality of texts or in financial support for their writing or publication (Gauvin and Klinkenberg 190). This flourishing situation coexists with the problematic identified by Lise Gauvin in her essay, in which Québec literature is threatened with appropriation and assimilation by the Canadian literary institution as exemplified in the Appelbaum-Hébert report, which fails to name Québec culture as a distinct entity and pairs its most famous authors with Anglo Canadians in a list of celebrated "Canadian" writers (Gauvin and Klinkenberg 30). Healthy or threatened with extinction? Facts in support of either conclusion are garnered in these studies of the institution from government documents, publishers' accounts—a series of texts not hitherto read intertextually with experimental fiction.

While there has been a proliferation of institutional analyses in the 1980s, they build on data accumulated over the years. Melançon's work on Québec pedagogy began in the late 1970s in collaboration with the Institut Supérieur des Sciences Humaines at the University of Laval in a research group on Québec literature coordinated by Fernand Dumont. This group cosponsored a conference on literature and ideologies in Québec in which the institution was first scrutinized. Many of the same participants returned to Laval for another conference on the institution in 1985. This conference covered the customary terrain of institutional analysis: the double allegiance of Québec literature, the infrastructure of publishing and prizes, the problem of the avant-garde, as well as the requisite reflections on the concept of the institution. New there, however, were explorations on the role of translation in Québec theater by Annie Brisset and a study of regionalism in Québec literature by Antoine Sirois outlining the objectives of the Association des Auteurs des Cantons de l'Est, organized in 1977 to defend the literary interests and make known the productions of writers of this region. What both these writers establish is the complexity and diversity of the literary institution in Québec—not monolithic in its French purity and Montréal aerie, as the earlier studies have suggested, but open to the competing pressures of several languages and urban centers, whether Sherbrooke, Hull, Moncton, or Winnipeg. Missing as yet from this opening to comparative studies of the "national" boundary is any understanding of the role of the literatures of linguistic and ethnic minorities in the Québec cultural institution.

That such explorations would prove fruitful in illuminating the ways in which the Québec institution establishes hegemony, makes its exclusions that determine who is and is not a writer, what is and is not literature, has been demonstrated by the emergence in Québec of feminist theory that has pointed out the patriarchal bias of these mechanisms and the marginal position of women writers and their literary productions. Closely connected to the social and institutional analysis, this other emergent discourse takes a new direction, foregrounding gender.

Feminist analysis is an instance of reading and construction of meaning in a troubling relationship with the literary institution. As Suzanne Lamy elaborates in "Les écritures au féminin," her contribution to the Brussels conference, the emergence of women's writing has accompanied the proliferation of alternative structures—in publishing, diffusing, and teaching this literature—that began in the mid-1970s with the founding of Les Têtes de Pioche by the poets Nicole Brossard, France Théoret, and others. The need for such alternatives was felt after the October crisis of 1970, when women became radicalized to the power that language wields and to the sexism of social institutions. While feminists aim to topple the dominant culture and replace it with a *culture au féminin*, a women's culture, according to Lamy, in the same collection Demers and McMurray identify the feminist manifesto as exhibiting an aim of perpetual marginality. Integration or separation? Develop a feminist critique of patriarchal institutions or create alternate structures for women?

This central/peripheral issue with respect to power and knowledge is at the heart of Québec feminist theory, whether of deconstructionist or of radical persuasion, these being the two dominant feminist discourses in Québec (Godard, "Flying," *Mapmaking*). Participating in the poststructuralist enterprise, with its focus on the logos, writing, discourse, and meaning, feminist theoreticians and critics struggle to decenter the dominant discourse in a perpetual movement of *différance* and, paradoxically, simultaneously attempt to inscribe the feminine subject in discourse, to name women's experiences in their own language. The emergence of a feminine subject raises questions for literary theory and for the theory of discourse in general regarding the articulation of the subject in language and the reintegration of the referent in textual theories. It also raises questions about power and authority in language and institutions. As for Foucault, the major point of departure for all feminist reading and criticism is: Who speaks? To whom? In what circumstances? In the subsequent denunciation of the narratives of mastery/the master narratives of our civilization (Freud, Marx, etc.), whose loss is a symptom of our postmodern condition, the feminist project has developed an extensive critique of the totalizing am- bitions of theoretical discourse that claims to account for all forms of social experience. Feminism has challenged theory over the distance it maintains between itself and its objects, a distance that objectifies and masters. It has especially challenged modernism's rigid opposition of ar- tistic practice and theory. The resulting *fiction/theory*, to use Brossard's term, is at the forefront of postmodernism.

The importance of the emergence of a feminist discourse on/in the Québec literary institution has been underlined by many observers. Jean Royer, among others summarizing the literary production of the 1970s, noted the innovative elements of feminist discourse as the most important in challenging and changing the course of literature in that decade: "wom- en's writing ... questions writing itself." From its first appearance, this writing was preeminently theoretical. In October 1975, *Liberté* organized an international meeting of women writers on the theme women and writ- ing. Nicole Brossard, as editor of *La barre du jour*, extended the debate in launching *Women and Language*, the first of many special issues on women, with a question: "How can the woman who uses words daily ... make use of a phallocratic language which from the beginning is against her" ("Pré- liminaires" 8–9). The texts submitted for that issue were rich and varied, ranging from poetry through prose and drama, but united in their radical opposition to dominant ideology and in their pursuit of formal experi- mentation. The search for her own forms and symbols led the woman writer to a rupture with the forms of language. As Brossard describes this in her preliminary remarks: "Tenter la femme à son propre jeu de *maux*" 'Try woman at her own game of ills/words' (9). In her other contribution to the issue, "E muet mutant" 'Silent *e* Mutating,' Brossard insists on the political importance of writing. In contrast to women's speech, which is inconsequential and evanescent, women's written words are public. "Writ- ing is making oneself visible. To show all sorts of forms and experiences. To impose upon the gaze of the other before he gets a chance to" (49). The gesture of writing is concrete and takes the form of a book. "It enters into history. It participates in the collective memory." The woman who writes "becomes a subject" and "imposes her subject," "transgressing masculine discourse" (13). Concisely framed here is the use by Québec feminist writers of negativity to interrupt the organic unity and cultural hegemony of dominant or "master" discourses. The negative impulse is a transformative strategy, as Brossard's text illustrates, for the results are productive and generative, resulting in a diversity of stylistic and genre "corruptions" especially with respect to the emergence of the feminine in language. The silent *e* protests against the dominance of the masculine in grammar, as Louky Bersianik has, and in the process renews the resources of language as Brossard has done with *amantes* and *l'amèr*. Concurring in the Saussurean paradigm of the primacy of language as a symbolic mode for human communication, these Québec feminists, with their French sisters Julia Kristeva, Monique Wittig, Hélène Cixous, and Luce Irigaray, with whom their theorizing is so closely connected, change language so as to transform relations of communicative and cultural exchange.

The emphasis on negativity evident in fiction/theories like Brossard's *L'amèr* (written both against and with the mother) and Bersianik's *L'euguélionne* (a utopian carnivalization of the Bible and Freud) reveals the deconstructionist bent of Québec feminist theory imprinted with the differential analysis and focus on the margin of Jacques Derrida, Gilles Deleuze, and Michel Foucault. Difference, deferral, discourse analysis—in Québec these terms were present from the first feminist theory in the 1970s, unlike in anglophone North America, where they have only recently come to challenge liberal feminist theory with its emphasis on images of women. Madeleine Gagnon raised the issue of women's *différence* in her speech at the 1975 International Writers' Conference. Residing in alterity and the unspoken in a state of lack of being to the self, a state of "oppression" under the "narcissistic representation of the same" of the "phallocentric" logos whose power is inscribed in her, she is "double" and her speech is "subversive" ("La femme et l'écriture" 251). Gagnon expands on this in her contribution to the first feminist issue of *La barre du jour*, in which she links structuralist, psychoanalytic, and Marxist discourses to analyze women's oppression in language. Language being a code, a social contract the dominant make for the dominated, it becomes yet another of the instruments of domination, another form of capitalist exploitation ("La femme et le langage" 46). Against the code, women inter-vene in anecdotes and pretexts, through ellipses, gaps, displacements, and metonymies that mark their attempt at subverting le "Nom du père" (the name, the no, the law of the father) through which the subject is positioned under patriarchal discourse (47–49). Biological difference is not the grounds for the oppression of women (51–52). The antagonism of men and women is constructed through the subject's interpellation by/in ideology, Gagnon contends, extending the analysis of Althusser to the question of sexual difference. Rather than seeking leadership positions in the social order by speaking out about their oppression, women should ally themselves with other oppressed elements in society to engage in a critique of institutions and the way they reproduce the relationships of domination. Gagnon briefly describes what such action of the "mistresses" against the "masters" would be like in the educational institution from which she speaks. Framed as norm and positive value, silence is not death but a temporary exile from which writing will begin again and re-create. In conclusion, Gagnon cautions that while it is important, in preparing a feminist revolution, to seize the opportunity to speak, to work upon language from her decentered position, the revolution must be carried out on the level of "real power, economic, political, ideological" (57).

Silence is at the heart of Nicole Brossard's concerns too, silence not on the near side of language in the unspoken but on the far side of language in the numinous. "Le centre blanc," the white center, is the nodal point of Brossard's writing, the place where language turns back on itself to allow space for the reader/hearer to become aware of herself in the act of enunciation and self-reflexively to subvert mimesis and the representation of the female body. Brossard's theory has its grounding in the work of Wittgenstein on language and his foregrounding of the spectacle of language, its materiality and its paradoxes, especially Godel's theorem regarding self-referentiality. Brossard sets out to deconstruct patriarchal language, by voicing the silent *e*, which, though changing pronunciation, had itself remained silent, and by subverting singular meanings through polysemous word play—paradoxes, puns, elisions—that frustrate attempts to arrive at binary oppositions. Brossard's work on paradox is nourished by the deconstructionism of Gilles Deleuze. For Brossard, too, repetition is always difference and deferral in a process that challenges the rule of noncontradiction at the basis of Western logic and metaphysics. In her critique of origins, she draws on the work of Derrida, especially on the concepts of undecidability and oscillation to develop a theory of feminist writing as mobility and the spiral. These cohere in her critique of representation, the fixed identifiable product of the book that represents an originary moment being displaced in a mimesis of process, of a work always in becoming, "in the trajectory of the species" (*Our Mothers* 101).

Here Brossard's project overlaps that of Irigaray and her theory of mimesis as an intentional miming of identity that overwhelms it. The feminine deploys the feminine self-reflexively, and in so doing reveals it to be a construct of patriarchal logic and explodes boundaries and categories in the refractory mirror of the speculum/simulacrum. Brossard's texts are characterized by boundary play that challenges the categories and classification, the rules of logic, on which the dominant Western—read patriarchal—discourses are founded. Like Gagnon, she plays with the paradoxical positioning of insider/outsider in undermining the fixed category of "woman" to allow for the emergence of women in all their plurality and diversity. Here, as in Gagnon, the female body is metonymy, not metaphor, in a text of contiguity or, as Cixous has framed it, an "endless" female text ("sans but ni bout") of the circulation of female desire (18). Brossard's theory has encouraged many feminist critics of Québec writers to explore the rhetorical strategies and linguistic patterns of women's writing to isolate an alternative lineage, a "fil/ial" lineage, of "casse-textes," 'puzzles' in a deconstructive practice of the play of the signifier.

Most wide-ranging in its laying bare of the aporias of the dominant discourse is *L'échappée des discours de l'oeil*, by Madeleine Ouellette-Michalska. Taking on each of the intellectual disciplines in turn—philosophy, anthropology, history, psychoanalysis, and literature—Ouellette-Michalska reveals how all fields of Western knowledge have been characterized by a narcissistic game of mirrors and surfaces whereby the masculine eye establishes the dominance of its gaze. Woman is "interpellated to constitute the negative term of a binary system." In this process of differentiation, she becomes "the silent sign of a masculine principle which is omnipresent and vocal. Immutable and static, she incarnates the fixed place of origins. Unspeakable, she is the blank in discourse where the ashes of the sign accumulate," the token in exchanges facilitating the transfer of goods or knowledges (73). Fixed at the origin, she expresses nonbeing and nonplace. Projected to mythic poles outside of time, she represents time. "To possess her, is to possess time. To close the Eye and take one's pleasure in the origin" (147). Between what was and what will be, between her virginity and her death, is interposed narrative, the sublimation of male sexual pleasure, symbolic capture able to transcend time. Woman is the mirror in which identity is reflected. In preventing the Eye from "stumbling on the scandal of the void and the gap," she upholds the Law of the Father, the omnipresence of the phallus, transcendental signifier. As token of exchange, she effects the grafting of the social body onto the biological body: "The text cements the relationship of nature/culture in the communication system" (152). The textual body is substituted for the visceral body and enters into a game of (dis)simulation. The signs are fixed in their linearity and re-create the world by a game of substitution. Writing fills gaps in the network of mediation. But the unnamable must be named. "The literary institution is born from this desire and from the impotence of citing the unnameable" (233). Throughout the history of literature, as Ouellette-Michalska shows, woman has held the function of conveyer of "mystery, ecstasy, and duration" (257). Object of exchange, and not subject, woman is fixed as mother or whore, witch and hysteric.

To explore these spaces, silence and hysteria, the excesses of the unnamable and absent feminine, is, Ouellette-Michalska demonstrates in her concluding chapters on the work of women writers, "to destroy the Eye forever," to shatter the effects of the mirror, the reflection of the same, through "fetal contamination" with the mother's voice and through symbolic inversion (295). Woman no longer serves as absent token of exchange in the transmission of patriarchal discourse. The absence of intellectual rigor, the impressionistic collage, the absence of a logical problem, these are some of the characteristics of women's cultural productions that expose "the weak points and make a blot on the Eye" (309). Illustrating the politics of inversion that she describes as a feature of writing in the feminine, Ouellette-Michalska concludes her study of patriarchal discourse with a prologue in which she prepares to write her first sentence. *L'échappée des discours de l'oeil* was awarded the Governor General's Award for prose, signaling the valorization of feminist theory in the literary institution in the 1980s.

The critic who most eloquently advocated a new mode of feminist criticism as *fiction/theory* was Suzanne Lamy, who, in *d'elles* and *Quand je lis, je m'invente*, evolved a new mode of writing that is a blend of critical analysis and creative writing, narrative, poetry, personal essay, diary. As in Brossard's work, these multiple texts are in/formed by the practice of Irigaray in *This Sex Which Is Not One* and by Roland Barthes's theory and practice in *The Pleasure of the Text*. For Lamy too, criticism is an intermediary between literary science and reading, a place of diverse encounters where desire circulates. A loving relationship or the search for pleasure is most frequently the initial impulse of her criticism. The texts in *d'elles* in which the affectionate bond is played out to its fullest irrupt in the Québec critical discourse with a new vitality.

Lamy's analytical approach identifies instances linking speech and writing, the social and the literary, and explores the multiple determinants and meanings of the instance of enunciation. In each text, the sociohistorical element is foregrounded. According to Lamy there is no essential woman ("De corps parlant, il n'y a pas" [*Quand je lis* 12]). Rather, the feminine is a social and linguistic conjunction, both the trace of a millennial culture and the effect of women's violent will to break with traditional forms, "whose adoption is never innocent" (32). Who is speaking? In whose interest? These are the questions that initiate Lamy's analysis. Since the desire to break with the dominant order is understood to be a collective venture of women within a certain historicopolitical configuration, Lamy focuses her analysis in each essay on a group of writers. Consequently, the key term among the critical concepts is complicity, like Brossard's synchronicity, a phrase to describe the position of the woman critic engaged in loving dialogue with the woman writer, producing a text both about and with the latter's text.

Lamy's analyses of women's literary productions focus on the specificity of their writing. She identifies a number of linguistic facts that are also social facts. Coming to writing has been difficult for women, but it is with the voice that all begins, Lamy agrees with Gagnon. Speech expresses the relationship to the real, to power, and outlines the social imbrication and immediacy of women's writing. Lamy identifies a number of oral modes specifically with women's speaking that account for its social origins in marginality and the forms their writing will take: gossip, dialogue, litany, polytonality, and intertextuality. Sub/version is how she describes the litany, an intermediate form, "ritualized, overexploited" (*d'elles* 99), which women are using intentionally in a parodic manner to rupture old forms. This polymorphic quality makes feminist discourse an *écriture à deux*, "a dialogue in the full sense of the word" (39, 45). Dialogic, the one-within-the-other in the Bakhtinian sense of the polyphonic text, feminist discourse works to subvert the monologism of the dominant discourse. Suzanne Lamy's criticism embraces the same dialogic forms as the texts she writes about, subverting critical discourse.

The twinning of critical and creative text is evident in another sphere. Lamy writes only about contemporary texts. She distinguishes between "feminist writings, feminine literature, texts by women where there is 'writing' " (*Quand je lis* 12). Lamy is interested only in the third category, though admitting that Christine de Pisan, Madame de Staël, and others were subversive in their time (*Quand je lis* 6). Writing is an evaluative concept that determines her corpus. Nowhere does she engage in the feminist critique of the canon and re-visionary reading of women's texts of the past that have become the staples of United States and, to a large extent, Canadian feminist criticism.[4]

Quoting Pierre Nepveu, Lamy relates women's search to rediscover the body, daily life, and minorities to a "dis/placement, an unforeseen development of the theories of modernity" (*Quand je lis* 32, 42). Belgian feminist Françoise Collin situates feminism more precisely in the "crisis of modernism," last avatar of the modernist world, symptom of a postmodernist one (qtd. in *Quand je lis* 26). In describing how she would read otherwise, approaching from the other slope of life, Lamy offers a critique of the limitations of the theories that have in/formed her work: sociological criticism, structuralism, Marxism, and psychoanalysis, none of which adequately addresses women's specificity. Moreover, her reintroduction of the referent, the subject, and the reading process opens breaches in these dominant critical paradigms. "Interrogations" of modernity is how Lamy categorizes feminist writing and re-writing (criticism). Against Lacan's view of the real as impossible, feminist reading strategies oppose "the weight of the real, the reality of texts, the reality of their texts" (84).

This coherent position adopted by Québec feminists has had an impact on anglo-Canadian feminist theory as evidenced in *In the Feminine: Women and Words/Les femmes et les mots* and *Tessera* number 3 on *fiction/theory* (Dybikowski; *Tessera*). Bilingual, like all Canadian feminist critical periodicals, these publications testify to the liveliness of the dialog between the two language groups. Indeed, the convergence of perspectives around postmodernist performance, deconstructive undoing, by feminist critics of both language groups is unique in the trajectory of critical discourses in Canada and Québec. While criticism has evolved independently in the two cultures, the reaching out exemplified by feminist theory is characteristic of a general opening of Québec criticism, an opening that is dis/placing the binary mode of framing difference long a feature of Québec discourse. No longer exclusively bound up in its *différend* with Paris, Québec literature and criticism is exploring its alterity in comparison with another minor francophone literature, that of Belgium, in *Trajectoires: Littérature et institutions au Québec et en Belgique francophone*. It is also exploring its Americanity. The process is dialectical: American interest in Québec is also increasing, as demonstrated in the issue of *Yale French Studies* entitled *The Language of Difference* (Godard, "Reading Difference"). In an international colloquium, Québec critics reclaimed a prodigal son, Jack Kerouac, whose fiction is being translated into the Québec urban dialect, *joual*.

But America does not stop at the United States: it extends south over an entire hemisphere. The new focus of Québec studies is revealed in *Voix et images*, with its list of foreign correspondents including representatives from Brazil and Mexico as well as the United States and various European countries. Moreover, the issue devoted to English-Canadian literature (Fall 1984) was followed by an issue two years later charting relations with Latin America. "La littérature québécoise, une littérature du tiers monde?" 'Québec literature, a Third World literature?' asks Gilles Thérien, exploring "the position of third," the "included third" of colonialism, the "excluded third" of revolutionaries, a situation of detachment, a theme of dispossession. This north–south comparison foregrounds the issue of comparative literature and the heterogeneous element in Québec literature(s): a similar voice, though different languages. In this confusion of languages, Québec criticism may explore not its social impotence but its cultural and social ubiquity. This is an option for a society whose cosmopolitan inhabitants have colonized large areas of the Florida winterscape and who are familiarly known in Mexico as "los tabarnacos" for the uniqueness of their swearing, a society, moreover, that has initiated a change in its institutions, voting no to separatism and to the Parti Québécois. With a realignment of institutions inexorably comes a shift in discursive practices and a change in the discourse of literary criticism. Or vice versa. Genre yields to antigenre in a process of renewal.

NOTES

[1] Lyotard's *La condition post-moderne* was written in Québec, commissioned by the Ministry of Education.

[2] All translations in this text are my own unless otherwise indicated in the list of works cited.

[3] I use the term *modernity* here as a literal translation of the French. As used in Québec, the word describes the period termed *postmodern* in English Canada, but it also refers to the preceding period of high modernism. The designation of periods in Québec corresponds to that in France, where dada and surrealism were a central part of modernism.

[4] Interestingly, most of the feminist criticism, the readings of texts by Québec women writers, has been the work of feminist scholars living in English Canada and the United States. Québec feminists have concentrated on fiction/theory.

WORKS CITED

Bakhtin, Mikhail. *Esthétique et théorie du roman.* Paris: Gallimard, 1978.

Barthes, Roland. *The Pleasure of the Text.* Trans. Richard Miller. New York: Hill, 1975.

Beaudet, Marie-Andrée. *L'ironie de la forme: Essai sur "L'élan d'Amérique" d'André Langevin.* Montréal: P Tisseyre, 1985.

Belleau, André. "Action et enracinement." *Liberté* 3 (Nov. 1961): 691–97.

———. "La démarche sociocritique au Québec." *Voix et images* 8.2 (1983): 299–309.

———. *Le romancier fictif.* Sillery: PU du Québec, 1980.

———. *Surprendre les voix.* Montréal: Boréal, 1986.

Belleau, André, Manon Brunet, and Greg M. Nielsen, eds. *Sociologies de la littérature.* Spec. issue of *Etudes françaises* 19.3 (1984): 3–4.

Bersianik, Louky. *L'euguélionne.* Montréal: La Presse, 1975. *The Euguélionne.* Trans. Gerry Denis, Alison Hewitt, Donna Murray, and Martha O'Brien. Victoria: Porcépic, 1981.

Bonenfant, Joseph, Janine Boynard-Frot, Richard Giguère, and Antoine Sirois. *A l'ombre de DesRochers: Le mouvement littéraire des cantons de l'est, 1925–1950.* Sherbrooke: La Tribune and PU de Sherbrooke, 1985.

Bourdieu, Pierre. "Le marché des biens symboliques." *L'année sociologique* 22 (1971): 49–126.

Brochu, André, and Gilles Marcotte. *La littérature et le reste.* Montréal: Quinze, 1980.

Brossard, Nicole. *L'amèr: Ou, le chapitre effrité.* Montréal: Quinze, 1975. *These Our Mothers: Or, The Disintegrating Chapter.* Trans. Barbara Godard. Toronto: Coach, 1983.

———. "E muet mutant." *La nouvelle barre du jour* 50 (1975): 10–27. Excerpts. Trans. M. L. Taylor. *Ellipse* 23–24 (1979): 45–63.

———. "Préliminaires." *La nouvelle barre du jour* 50 (1975): 6–9.

Chamberland, Roger. *Claude Gauvreau: La libération du regard.* Québec: CRELIQ, 1986.

Cixous, Hélène. "Textes de l'imprévisible: Grâce à." *Les nouvelles littéraires* 2534 (26 May 1976): 18.

Corriveau, Hugues, and Normand de Bellefeuille. *A double sens: Echanges sur quelques pratiques modernes.* Montréal: Herbes Rouges, 1986.

Demers, Jeanne, and Line McMurray. *L'enjeu du manifeste/Le manifeste en jeu.* Longueuil: Préambule, 1986.

Dossier comparatiste Québec-Amérique Latine. Spec. issue of *Voix et images* 12.1 (1986).

Dubois, Jacques. *Institution de la littérature.* Paris: Nathan-Labor, 1978.

———. Introduction. "L'institution littéraire II." *Littérature* 44 (1981): 3–7.

Dumont, Fernand, and Jean-Charles Falardeau, eds. *Littérature et société canadiennes-françaises.* Québec: PU Laval, 1985.

Dybikowski, Ann, et al. *In the Feminine: Women and Words/Les femmes et les mots.* Edmonton: Longspoon, 1985.

Ethier-Blais, Jean. *Signets.* 3 vols. Montréal: Cercle du Livre de France, 1965–73.

———. "Our Pioneers in Criticism." Trans. Larry Shouldice. *Contemporary Quebec Criticism.* Ed. and trans. Shouldice. Toronto: U of Toronto P, 1979. 21–36.

Gagnon, Madeleine. "La femme et l'écriture." Actes de la rencontre québécoise internationale des écrivains. *Liberté* 18.4–5 (1976): 249–54.

———. "La femme et le langage: Sa fonction comme parole en son manque." *La barre du jour* 50 (1975): 45–57.

Gauvin, Lise, and Jean-Marie Klinkenberg. *Trajectoires: Littérature et institutions au Québec et en Bélgique francophone.* Montréal: PU de Montréal, 1985.

Giroux, Robert, and Hélène Dame, eds. *Sémiotique de la poésie québécoise.* Cahiers d'études littéraires 5. Sherbrooke: Département de français, Université de Sherbrooke, 1981.

Giroux, Robert, and Jean-Marc Lemelin. *Le spectacle de la littérature.* Montréal: Triptyque, 1984.

Godard, Barbara. "Flying away with Language." *Lesbian Triptych.* By Jovette Marchessault. Toronto: Women's Press, 1985. 9–28.

———. Introduction and "Mapmaking: A Survey of Feminist Literary Criticism in Canada/Quebec." *Gynocritics/Gynocritiques: Feminist Approaches to Canadian and Quebec Women Writers.* Ed. Godard. Toronto: ECW, 1987.

———. "*La nouvelle barre du jour*: Vers une poétique féministe." *Fémininité, subversion, écriture.* Ed. Suzanne Lamy and Irène Pagès. Montréal: Remue-Ménage, 1983. 195–205.

———. "Other Fictions: Robert Kroetsch's Criticism." *Open Letter* 5th ser. 8–9 (1984): 5–21.

———. "Reading Difference: Views of/from Quebec." *Borderlines* 2 (1985): 38–41.

———. "Structuralism/Post-Structuralism: Language, Reality and Canadian Literature." *Future Indicative: Literary Theory and Canadian Literature.* Ed. John Moss. Reappraisals: Canadian Writers 13. Ottawa: U of Ottawa P, 1987. 25–51.

Godzich, Wlad. "Préface: La littérature manifeste." *L'enjeu du manifeste/Le manifeste en jeu.* By Jeanne Demers and Line McMurray. Longeuil: Préambule, 1986. 7–19.

Hémon, Louis. *Maria Chapdelaine.* 1914. Paris: Grasset, 1924. Trans. W. H. Blake. Toronto: Macmillan, 1921.

Irigaray, Luce. *This Sex Which Is Not One.* Trans. Catherine Porter. Ithaca: Cornell UP, 1985.

Lamy, Suzanne. *d'elles.* Montréal: L'Hexagone, 1979.

———. "Les écritures au feminin. Un désir de perversion." Gauvin and Klinkenberg 33–44.

———. *Quand je lis, je m'invente.* Montréal: L'Hexagone, 1984.

The Language of Difference: Writing in Quebec(ois). Spec. issue of *Yale French Studies* 65 (1983).

Lemire, Maurice, ed. *L'institution littéraire.* Québec: Institut Québécois de Recherche sur la Culture, 1986.

Littérature canadienne-anglaise. Spec. issue of *Voix et images* 10.1 (1984).

Lyotard, Jean-François. *The Post-Modern Condition: A Report on Knowledge.* Trans. Geoff Bennington and Brian Massumi. Theory and History of Literature 10. Minneapolis: U of Minnesota P, 1984.

Marcel, Jean. "Les forces provisoires de l'intelligence." *Livres et auteurs canadiens.* 1965. 23–32.

Marcotte, Gilles. *Le temps des poètes.* Montréal: HMH-Hurtubise, 1969.

Melançon, Joseph. "The Writing of Difference in Quebec." *Yale French Studies* 65 (1983): 21–29.

Michon, Jacques. "Les revues littéraires d'avant-garde au Québec de 1940 à 1979." Gauvin and Klinkenberg 117–28.

———, ed. *Structure, idéologie et reception du roman québécois de 1940 à 1960.* Sherbrooke: Département d'Etudes Françaises, Université de Sherbrooke, 1979.

Ouellette-Michalska, Madeleine. *L'échappée des discours de l'oeil.* Montreál: Nouvelle Optique, 1981.

Perron, Paul. "Structuralisme/Post-Structuralisme: Québec/Amérique." *Dalhousie French Studies* 10 (1986): 72–90.

Royer, Jean. "Regards sur la littérature québécoise des années 70." *Le devoir*, cahier 3 (21 Dec. 1981): 1.

Savard, Felix-Antoine. *Menaud, maître-draveur.* Montréal: Fides, 1937.

Sociologie critique et création artistique. Spec. issue of *Sociologie et sociétés* 17.2 (1985).

Sociologies de la littérature. Spec. issue of *Etudes françaises* 19.3 (1984).

Tessera 3: Feminist Fiction Theory. Spec. issue of *Canadian Fiction Magazine* 57 (1986).

Thérien, Gilles. "La littérature québécoise, une littérature du tiers-monde?" *Voix et images* 12.1 (1986): 12–20.

Whitfield, Agnes. "La modernité: Des formes qui (s')inquiètent." *Lettres québécoises* 46 (1987): 56–58.

Williams, Raymond. *Marxism and Literature.* Oxford: Oxford UP, 1977.

Philip Stratford

NO CLEAR STRAIT OF ANIAN: COMPARING JACQUES POULIN AND MATT COHEN

IN A BOOK called *All the Polarities* I tried to balance conflicting views about Canadian literature. The poles are represented by pioneer comparatist Ronald Sutherland, who subscribes to the mainstream theory, and sociologist Jean-Charles Falardeau, who proposes what one might call, still using geographical terms, the theory of the great divide. Sutherland contends that between Canadian literatures in French and English there exists a strong current of similarity. "French-Canadian and English-Canadian novels of the twentieth century," he writes in *Second Image*, "have traced a single basic line of ideological development, creating a whole spectrum of common images, attitudes and ideas" (23). In contrast, Falardeau, in *Notre société et son roman*, contends that the two literatures are diametrically opposed. "English-Canadian literature," he says, "finds its basic tensions along a horizontal axis, studying man and his milieu or man and society. French-Canadian, on the contrary, is situated along a vertical axis where relations between man and his destiny or man and the absolute predominate" (58). These antithetical views are not new; they are nearly as old as Canada itself. Just a few years after Confederation, Ontario novelist William Kirby wrote that he hoped the two literary traditions of France and England would be united "in one great floodstream of Canadian literature" (268), while at the same time Québec's first prime minister, man of letters Pierre-Joseph-Olivier Chauveau, opined that the literatures of the two groups were so estranged that they reminded him of the double-spiral staircase at the Château de Chambord, which two people can mount without ever meeting until they reach the top (335).

In my own study I tried to test these hypotheses by comparing a dozen well-known contemporary novels. I compared Hugh MacLennan's *Two Solitudes*, for example, with *Bonheur d'occasion*, by Gabrielle Roy; Sinclair Ross's *As for Me and My House* with André Langevin's *Poussière sur la ville*; Margaret Laurence's *Diviners* with Anne Hébert's *Kamouraska*; I also paired novels by Alice Munro, Robert Kroetsch, and Margaret Atwood with ones by Marie-Claire Blais, Roch Carrier, and Hubert Aquin. I found much evidence to support both Sutherland's and Falardeau's theories and came to the median conclusion (an island in mid-mainstream, straddling the divide) that in comparing novels in Canada's two official languages, one would have to respect poles of difference as well as the axis of similarity —hence my title.

Perhaps in the long run I found more differences than likenesses. After analyzing the six pairs of novels, I tried to codify my results into general definitions of what the typical English-Canadian novel and the typical *roman québécois* seemed to be. Here, in abbreviated form, are the main features of those definitions:

> The English-Canadian novel tends to be the story of something that happened to someone in a distinct time and place. Its sense of historical realism is heightened by the treatment of characters as individuals and by attention to detail. The reader is persuaded to identify with the hero by reference to the minutiae of that character's life. Symbolism is seldom explicit, rarely emerging more clearly than as the presence of a certain atmosphere. The upshot of the story is frequently moralistic, although its impact is usually diffuse. The role of the novelist is not to universalize but to particularize; that of the reader to learn to side with the eccentric hero.

And now a look at the other side:

> *Le roman québécois* is a tale not generally tied to a specific time or place. The sense of historical realism is replaced by an intensely personal and present apprehension of reality, heightened by a sparse and selective use of detail. Characters tend to be representative or symbolic. The reader is urged to enter intimately and uncritically into the hero's state of mind, sharing the character's daydreams and nightmares. Symbolism has free rein and replaces moral suasion. The role of the novelist is to convert the raw material into captivating patterns; the role of the reader is to submit.

The novels that provided me these deductions were mainly written in the 1960s or before, and their authors are well-established figures. What I would like to do in the present essay is to test the continuing validity of the definitions by pushing on to examine works by younger, less well known writers from the following generation, namely Matt Cohen and Jacques Poulin.

Cohen is an inventive, energetic writer who has published eight novels and four collections of short stories since 1969. While his style varies widely from short to long fiction, *Wooden Hunters*, his fifth novel, can be taken to represent a writer whom W. H. New calls "the most accomplished of the young experimental stylists" (262). Poulin is a little older, and although he began to write at about the same time, he has been less prolific (in the same period he has published six novels). He is considered, by Laurent Mailhot among others, to be "a very important, unjustly neglected young writer" (675). *Les grandes marées* is his fifth novel also and won the Governor General's Award for fiction in 1978.

My choice of these two novels is not fortuitous. For a comparison to have some chance of success, the two sides must initially share some common ground, and more than chalk and cheese. In this case the common ground is the setting of the novels, for in each work the author has chosen an island, a distinctive geographical space that strongly influences its inhabitants and thus the character of the fiction. So the first step in the comparison must be to reconnoiter these islands.

Apart from size they are quite similar, set along a north-south axis with habitations at either end, a road or path linking them across an interior wilderness. Cohen's island is much bigger; it is situated in the Queen Charlottes in the Pacific Ocean off the coast of British Columbia; it has a summer population of six hundred, which drops to half that in winter, a logging town at its north end joined by a rough road to an airstrip at the south, with some Indian villages midway on the east side. Poulin's island, Ile Madame, lies in the St. Lawrence River off the northeast shore of Ile d'Orléans; it is only two kilometers long and to begin with has a caretaker population of one; a large house at its north end is joined by a path to a cottage at the south, with a tennis court midway; a helicopter can land at either end, if the tides are favorable.

Already the intricate play of sameness and difference begins to draw us deeper, for these novels are not only on but about islands. The first sentence in *Les grandes marées*, "In the beginning he was alone on the island," sets the right Crusoe-like, Genesis context. In the end "he" is forced to leave the island, swimming off into the cold St. Lawrence, where he meets death. In between, the tale develops like *Ten Little Indians* in reverse. To start, there is only one, Teddy Bear, code name for *traducteur de bandes dessinées* (T. D. B., hence Teddy Bear), a translator of comic strips. He has been offered this island retreat by his employer, a vigorous entrepreneur who owns a chain of Québec newspapers. The "boss" is the deus ex machina of the novel; his machine is the private helicopter he pilots from Montréal every Saturday with provisions for Teddy and a fresh batch of comics to translate. His sole aim, he says, is to make people happy, and to this end he ferries in a series of companions for wistful Teddy until eventually the island paradise is overpopulated with ten people, a chihuahua, and five cats. The islanders (as they are now called) turn on Teddy and expel him.

The first companion the boss provides for his island Adam is a girl, Marie, who climbs down a ladder out of the air with a tabby for the translator's old tom. Next the boss introduces his wife, code named Featherhead, to play mother hen to the young couple. He then supplies intellectual companionship in the persons of the "Author," a surly Québec nationalist, and Professor Mocassin, a Sorbonne anthropologist who is an expert in the history and aesthetics of the comic strip. As an antidote, the next visitor is known simply as the "Ordinary Man." He is followed by the "Organizer," a specialist in group dynamics; by a visit from a doctor; and finally, since things are obviously not going well, by a thaumaturge, Old Gélisol, whose primitive therapy consists in holding a patient on his lap in a rocking chair and exuding heat.

From this brief description it is immediately apparent that we are not dealing directly with the ordinary world. The *Pushkin* goes by in the channel, the lights shine from the opposite shore, the boss flies off to board meetings in Québec City and inspection tours of plants at Rimouski and Sept-Iles, but life on the island goes on in its own fantastic way, hardly more real than life on the island of the Katzenjammer Kids. The style of the narrative is in fact closely related to the comics. With the possible exception of Teddy and Marie, all the characters have comic strip traits. Professor Mocassin, with his glasses on the end of his nose, his hearing problems, and his absent-mindedness, is explicitly modeled on Professor Tournesol in the well-known Belgian comic albums *Tintin*. The others, with their nicknames, their tics, and their caricatural features, also resemble the population of the funnies. They have allegorical status and represent various types and attitudes, all of them incapable of alleviating the translator's essential solitude. Their dialogue is succinct, its movement erratic; it bobs like comic strip balloons, and the novel progresses in forty-three brief chapters like weekly installments. A convention of unreality is clearly established, and the novelty of fantasy is its staple. At one point Teddy's actions follow the sequence of the narrative but it turns out that he has imperceptibly crossed a threshold and dreams the close of the episode. It is that kind of fiction.

In *All the Polarities* I discovered that the Québec novels examined made little attempt "to create a convincing external view of reality or to reflect the autonomous, believable world" (98). More recent works by the same authors—Aquin's *Neige noire*, Hébert's *Héloïse*, Carrier's *La dame qui avait des chaînes aux chevilles*, Blais's *Visions d'Anna*—still take us swiftly into the depths of the characters' psyches, without introduction or explication, present us with surreal images of their traumas, make us privileged observers of their most intimate dreams (or, for that generation, perhaps we should say nightmares). In the 1970s the delirium grew somewhat less intense. Although there has always been a manic gleam of black humor in Québec fiction, with Poulin some of the blackness dissolves, the humor becomes gentler, more pervasive, and relaxes into drollery and nonsense. One can observe the same phenomenon in works by some of Poulin's contemporaries, in Michel Tremblay's novels, in Yves Beauchemin's *Le matou*, in Jacques Godbout's later fictions, and in Louise Mauheux-Forcier's stories. But whether comedy or tragedy predominates, whether nightmare or fantasy, the premise and logic of this fiction seems to be that of dream.

Trying to differentiate more specifically between the two types of fiction written in Canada, I observed in the definitions that English-Canadian novels were basically wedded to realism and paid great attention to detail. Unlike some of his antecedents, Poulin writes abundantly detailed fiction. His characters' states of mind and heart are not delivered directly in the typically abstract vocabulary of Québec fiction but are displayed in conjunction with a set of facts and objects completely exterior to them. But how are these details presented? Often by lists: the contents of Marie's suitcase, for example; a list of what was carried on ten trips from the North House on the island to the South House; the reproduction, verbatim and typographically, of telescripter messages, of signs, of a recipe for graham cracker pie; one chapter is completely devoted, in instruction-manual prose, to advice on how to deliver the best forehand and backhand strokes in tennis. The world of objects coexists with the world of the characters but in dislocation. The objects are not natural projections of the human but have a strange, separate existence, like the contents of Winnie's handbag in Beckett's *Happy Days*, or the isolated units in Ionesco's stilted verbal universe.

Cohen's universe is detailed in a different way. Here is an example, chosen at random:

> He reached into his pocket, to find the candle he had taken from the kitchen. The jacket was new, or at least different, a blue-black serge jacket from Harry Jones's infinite supply to replace the one that had been torn in the explosion last night. This one had all its pockets still intact. In one of them he had found a yellowed ferry ticket, both departure and destination erased by age. He set the candle on the sill beside the bottle, and started searching around in the pockets again, this time for tobacco and papers.   (95)

Nothing special is happening here, yet unlike the eccentrically autonomous objects in Poulin's fiction, these commonplace items are related in time to character or plot. The new jacket harks back to the old one, reminding us of a central incident in the story, the blowing up of an old logging camp tractor; the mention of its previous owner recalls Johnny Tulip's family; the faded ticket emphasizes the remoteness of the island setting; even the insignificant candle stub appears half a dozen times in the next few pages as Johnny walks through the sleeping house holding it up to illumine now this room, now that, each one evoking a different set of memories. Cohen's use of detail is tendentious; Poulin's, discontinuous. Cohen's is continental, Poulin's, islanded. The details in Cohen's fiction relate to the past, are connected to memory, form part of a history. Poulin's, in contrast, are atemporal. Typically, Québec fiction tends to be first-person, present-tense narration; *Les grandes marées* is told in the third person and the past tense, but the presentation of detail produces the typical effect: details exist, odd and surprising, in a timeless present, like objects in a dream.

The same is true of character. Take the two enigmatic heroines, for example. Laurel Hobson of *Wooden Hunters* has more than a full name; she has a past. Part of it is obscured by drugs and alcohol, but she does relive memories of parents and childhood and of her life with her Indian lover, Johnny Tulip, and his family. In fact, a good half of what we know of her is provided by reminiscence, and her story makes up almost half the novel. But Marie, her equivalent in *Les grandes marées*, has no surname (none of the characters do) and no appreciable past either. All we know of her background is that her father liked hunting and her mother was a long-distance swimmer. No question is raised about her past; she exists self-substantial, her mystery intact, in and for the present, like the objects in Poulin's tale. She arrives, in fact, as an answer to Teddy's fantasizing:

> Teddy pensait à une autre personne: une fille; elle n'existait pas dans la réalité, mais ses traits et son allure commençaient à se fixer dans sa tête. (15)

> Teddy was thinking about someone else too: a girl. She didn't exist in reality, but her features and appearance were beginning to take shape in his mind. (13)

She arrives from the air and disappears into the sea.

In each novel one of the main interests is romantic. I have referred to Poulin's hero, Teddy the translator; now a few words about Calvin, Cohen's male protagonist. Like Teddy he is a newcomer to the island; we are initiated to it and to its inhabitants through his eyes. Perhaps because he fills the role of initiate and initiator, he is not a strong character, a witness rather than an actor, and more a foil to Laurel than an equal partner, although at the end of the novel he has a chance to prove himself, as does Teddy.

There are the same number of secondary characters in the two novels, but Cohen's are more fleshed out. Here, the role of deus ex machina is played by C. W. Smith, once a Montana grain merchant who now owns the hotel at the north end of the island, the setting for some monumental brawls and the shootout that closes the work. Like 'the boss' in *Les grandes marées*, he is the prime mover, although not from concern for others' happiness but from jealousy and, as ugly American, by greed. His collusion with government officials and the timber company to arrange the logging off of ancestral Indian burial grounds, and his brutal affair with the Indian waitress, Mary Gail, are the specific reasons for the growing emnity he inspires, but his malevolence, unlike the boss's benevolence, is not simply given: he is accorded two full chapters in which to explain himself. Johnny Tulip—Laurel's former lover, Mary Gail's brother, and a representative of Indian rights—is also given two chapters, and other less important characters are provided with proper names and particular histories, unlike the cleverly stylized characters of Poulin's fiction.

The convention behind Cohen's novel is obviously realism. But what kind? Interestingly enough, Cohen's variation displays some attributes of Québec fiction. Eschewing stock-in-trade realism, he does not simply depict characters from the outside or detail stream-of-consciousness responses but penetrates deeper, revealing half-states of thought, emotion, dream, sensual perception, physical sensation, and visceral reaction. Some of the phrases in my definition of the typical *roman québécois* referring to the re-creation of a state of mind, "an intensely personal and present apprehension of reality," could be applied accurately to Cohen's style. Since style dictates subject as much as the other way around, the novel contains many scenes of violence suited to display primitive reactions. In chapter 1, for instance, Calvin's first night on the island, the lovers shoot a deer by night, a flashlight strapped to the rifle barrel to blind the animal; they haul it back to the campsite, string it up, and butcher it in graphic detail. Later they wade through a rushing stream netting salmon, gut them, and make love on the bank, smeared with blood and eggs. Every chapter has its quota of drunkenness, fighting, or sex, giving the narration its headlong impetus.

But despite the physical violence, the narrative turbulence, the frequent use of dreams, and a nonrational bias that frequently presents the characters in a state of semistupor, the premise and progress remain realistic. The characters, even minor ones, are treated as individuals, not types. Their lives are inscribed in space and time and contribute to the general history of the island. However eccentric they are or however briefly they are evoked, they intermesh in a credible way; they belong, although perhaps reluctantly and marginally, to a recognizable society. They are thus situated in the central realistic tradition that nourishes nearly all English-Canadian novelists from Laurence, Robertson Davies, Munro, and Atwood to Rudy Wiebe, Jack Hodgins, W. P. Kinsella, and Kroetsch.

Were we to compare these major contemporary English-speaking novelists with one another, the variety of their styles and the novelty of their experimentation within the central tradition would invite examination. But when we compare them with Québec writers, no matter what characteristics they may at first seem to share with their francophone counterparts, in the long run it is their common traits that predominate and the essential difference between the two groups that demands commentary. The difference in the case at hand is as great as that between the two islands, the crude, untamed West Coast island I have just described and that other island in the St. Lawrence, where characters are ciphers, where domestic objects have a life of their own, where events follow a dreamlike development, where references to the real world tend to be cultural or literary, where sex is flirtatious and whimsical, where the only violence is verbal.

Islands are places that encourage introspection and self-discovery: witness Margaret Atwood's *Surfacing* or Marian Engel's *Bear*. They can also contain communities whose existence is threatened from inside or outside: for Canadian examples, see Félix Leclerc's *Le fou de l'île*, Jacques Godbout's *L'île au dragon*, or Hodgins's *Invention of the World*. The private and public significance of life on the two islands will be the theme of the closing part of this comparison.

Poulin's parable seems to focus chiefly on introspection. In line with Falardeau's statement about the verticality of Québec fiction, it is Teddy's destiny and the meaning of his life that most concern us. At first he uses the island merely as a retreat. With Marie's arrival, however, the couple begin to discover the island's unique character—"This place is heaven on earth!" (28) Marie asserts—and they try to live to its rhythms and respect its ecological integrity, agreeing to leave it "exactly as it is" (49). The intrusion of the other characters, however, seems to shrink their *paradis terrestre*; halfway through the book Marie complains: "There's starting to be too many people" (96). Indeed, no island is inviolate, and near the end the Organizer bids Teddy consider the wisdom of Donne's "No man is an island" and join in the group dynamics. But Teddy refuses to reveal his private thoughts; since he will not play, he is first ostracized, then physically expelled, forced into the water and obliged to swim across to the next island, Ile aux Ruaux, uninhabited except for the petrified remains of an old man, a former caretaker.

Even before his expulsion, Teddy has suffered several grave disillusionments. First he discovers that the translations he had been doing for the boss were never published; they had been replaced by ones done by an electronic brain: end of career. Then Marie leaves: end of romance. Finally he learns from the others that although they accept the notion that marginal people may be useful, they consider him not aggressive enough and "outside the margin" (164).

So the novel, like other tales embedded in the main narrative (one of the Hermit of Ile Saint-Barnabé, another of a fight between a cachalot and a giant squid), has an unhappy ending. As far as fiction means anything, what does this tale mean? On a global level it may be a pessimistic commentary on the future of life on an overcrowded planet. On a more local level it may refer, again pessimistically, to the political hopes of the islanded nation of Québec. Ecologically speaking, the message is clear: the islanders do not leave the island exactly as they found it. But I think these social interpretations are less important than a more personal, philosophical one.

The isolated island translator (*island* and *isolated* have the same root) is the writer in the modern world. Teddy is absorbed in his work (the novel contains many examples of the finesse required in translation), but his art is undervalued and his skills prove to be obsolescent. His chief qualities —his meticulousness, his adaptability, and his gentleness (one might say his humanity)—are belittled and rejected. He is betrayed by his lover, his employer, his friends. Growing numbness in his right hand and arm signifies a withdrawal of power and perhaps life. The reader is forced to conclude that, for T. D. B., Donne was probably wrong: we are not "all part of the main"; rather, in Arnold's sad words, "We mortal millions live alone / ... [enisled in] / The unplumbed, salt, estranging sea." Or, to give the thought a contemporary Canadian expression, in Ken Norris's words, "we will only / ever know islands, for we cannot help / but be them" (102).

The conclusion to Cohen's novel is complex but not so distressing. Calvin, Teddy's counterpart and newcomer to the island, is likewise involved in a search for the self, but he is not estranged or expelled; he is finally accepted. At first he feels "like a scientist on a new planet" (16). The island's wildness has overtones of a northern Eden (a common British Columbian theme), and its fertility and freshness make him think of the continent to the east, where he comes from, as "a place that could no longer renew itself ... a vast conglomerate city of doomed smokestacks and concrete" (14). By exposure to this new environment, but even more by the mediation of Laurel, he gradually becomes acclimatized. Laurel's experience precedes his. Six years earlier, under the guidance of Johnny Tulip, she had shaken off the influence of her too rational mapmaker father and has gained some of the intuitive knowledge of island ways possessed by Johnny and his family. Calvin thinks of her as having been "turned wild by this island and ... imparting the same thing to him" (2) in their lovemaking. In fact, her choice of Calvin over Johnny when she discovers she is carrying Calvin's child, and her decision to stay and have the baby on the island consolidate Calvin's integration—as does the fact that he risks his life to save Johnny when C. W. Smith goes on a rampage and tries to shoot the Indian. In the closing pages Laurel anticipates living off the land with Calvin: "In the spring they would explore the coast, live on mussels and clams, make salads of wild peas and plantain" (218). Johnny's blind old mother, who has second sight, predicts a good future for Laurel. She salutes the unvanquished strength of Johnny's spirit. All in all, it is an upbeat ending.

But although it may be much less gloomy than the close of *Les grandes marées*, it is not unconditionally optimistic. The ecological issue is a constant concern throughout the novel. In contrast to Laurel's and Calvin's readiness to adopt island ways, there is a powerful threat of exploitation. "Pretty soon they'll take down the whole island" (66), says Johnny morosely, and his act of protest, blowing up the logging company's caterpillar tractor, is a futile gesture unlikely to stem "the ultimate if narrow triumph of technology over this wild island" (193). C. W. Smith personifies accommodation to the forces of exploitation and destruction. "You'd think it was the end of the world just because we were going to cut down a few trees" (158), he says. His death—he is killed by a bullet from his own rifle—is a minor victory but only a temporary reprieve.

Behind the ecological issue, of course, is the even graver one of the destruction of the Indian way of life. The community, divided into loggers and Indians, teeters on the brink of conflict, and it is the news that, in opening a new road, the loggers have blown up mortuary poles at the old Indian village that sparks the final melee. More than this, Johnny's poor health and drunkenness, his sister Victoria's sickness and suicide, his mother's blindness (which the Vancouver doctors are unable to cure), and Mary Gail's seduction by C. W., all point to decline and degradation. The fact that Laurel is accepted into Johnny Tulip's family almost as a replacement for Victoria is taken as a positive sign, but despite that kinship and her appreciation of the Indian character and gifts—Mary Gail's warmth (she generates heat like Old Gélisol), Johnny's forest skills, his mother's clairvoyance—the future of the Indians looks grim. In his own vision of the future, Johnny sees himself turned into wood. "They wouldn't know whether to bury him or throw him away" (42). So although there is personal fulfillment for some of the characters at the end of *Wooden Hunters*, the progressive note is undercut by skepticism.

Perhaps in the final analysis the main difference between the endings of the two novels is one of emphasis. But emphasis is style, and style is all. One can say that in their conclusions these two books touch on the same

themes and content—violation of the island as sanctuary, growing aggression among island inhabitants, triumph of technology over humanity, a
measure of personal defeat. In the English novel, however, we are concerned about several characters and points of view and are left pondering
the fate of the couple, the family, the community, the island as a place of
human habitation, whereas in the French work we close the book absorbed
in metaphysical speculation about the hero's solitary destiny. The difference in emphasis seems to validate Falardeau's distinction: the French
novel *is* more preoccupied with relations "between man and his destiny
or man and the absolute," while the English novel *is* concerned chiefly with
"man and his milieu or man and society."

What conclusion can one draw after this cursory comparison of two
books, two writers, two types of novel? In *Les grandes marées* the "Author"
speaks of his ambition to write the great novel of America. "The French
novel deals more with ideas," he explains, "while the American novel deals
with action. Now, we are French in America, or Americans of French descent, if you prefer. We in Quebec, then, have the opportunity to write a
novel that will be the product of both the French and the American tendencies" (141). He may be on the right track, but, from present evidence,
the realization of his theory is a thing of the future. For despite the fact
that young Québec writers do seem, like their English-Canadian counterparts, to be assimilating traits from the opposite culture, and despite striking similarities (such as the fictional islands), the two literary traditions
remain as distinct as the regions of the country where the novels are set.
The first conclusion to be drawn, then, is that readers in the United States
must not make the mistake of viewing Canadian literature as univalent.
Canadians are learning to live this difficult and stimulating duality, and
those who study Canadian literature must learn to respect the diversity
too. Second, neither the French nor the English expression of Canadian
reality is exclusive; rather, the two views are complementary, and the
investigation of their complex relations is arduous but rewarding. Earle
Birney's "Pacific Door" comments poetically on the task involved and suggests an alternative to the dichotomy represented by Arnold and Donne:

> Here Spaniards and Vancouver's boatmen scrawled
> the problem that is ours and yours
> that there is no clear strait of Anian
> to lead us easy back to Europe
> that men are isled in ocean or in ice
> and only joined by long endeavour to be joined.... (142)

WORKS CITED

Aquin, Hubert. *Neige Noire.* Montréal: Cercle du Livre de France, 1974. *Hamlet's Twin.* Trans. Sheila Fischman. Toronto: McClelland, 1974.

Arnold, Matthew. "To Marguerite." *Norton Anthology of Poetry.* Ed. Arthur M. Eastman et al. New York: Norton, 1970. 820–21.

Atwood, Margaret. *Surfacing.* Toronto: McClelland, 1972.

Beauchemin, Yves. *Le matou.* Montréal: Québec/Amérique, 1981. *The Alley Cat.* Trans. Sheila Fischman. Toronto: McClelland, 1981.

Birney, Earle. *Selected Poems.* Toronto: Oxford UP, 1966.

Blais, Marie-Claire. *Visions d'Anna.* Montréal: Stanké, 1982. *Anna's World.* Trans. Sheila Fischman. Toronto: Lester and Orpen Dennys, 1984.

Carrier, Roch. *La dame qui avait des chaînes aux chevilles.* Montréal: Stanké, 1981. *Lady with Chains.* Trans. Sheila Fischman. Toronto: Anansi, 1984.

Chauveau, Pierre-Joseph-Olivier. *L'instruction publique au Canada: Précis historique et statistique.* Québec: Augustin Côté, 1876.

Cohen, Matt. *Wooden Hunters.* 1975. Toronto: McClelland, 1984.

Engel, Marian. *Bear.* Toronto: McClelland, 1976.

Falardeau, Jean-Charles. *Notre société et son roman.* Montréal: HMH-Hurtubise, 1967.

Godbout, Jacques. *L'île au dragon.* Paris: Seuil, 1976. *Dragon Island.* Trans. David Ellis. Toronto: Musson, 1978.

Hébert, Anne. *Héloïse.* Paris: Seuil, 1980. *Heloise.* Trans. Sheila Fischman. Toronto: Stoddart, 1982.

———. *Kamouraska.* Paris: Seuil, 1970. *Kamouraska.* Trans. Norman Shapiro. Toronto: Paperjacks, 1974.

Hodgins, Jack. *The Invention of the World.* Toronto: Macmillan, 1976.

Kirby, William. *The Golden Dog.* 1877. New York: American Publishers, n.d.

Langevin, André. *Poussière sur la ville.* Montréal: Cercle du Livre de France, 1953. *Dust over the City.* Trans. John Latrobe and Robert Gottlieb. Toronto: McClelland, 1955.

Laurence, Margaret. *The Diviners.* Toronto: McClelland, 1974.

Leclerc, Félix. *Le fou de l'île.* Paris: Denoël, 1958. *The Madman, the Kite and the Island.* Trans. Philip Stratford. Ottawa: Oberon, 1976.

MacLennan, Hugh. *Two Solitudes.* Toronto: Macmillan, 1945.

Mailhot, Laurent. "Jacques Poulin." *The Oxford Companion to Canadian Literature.* Ed. William Toye. Toronto: Oxford UP, 1983. 675–76.

New, W. H. "Fiction." *Literary History of Canada.* Ed. C. F. Klinck. 2nd ed. Toronto: U of Toronto P, 1976. 233–83.

Norris, Ken. *Islands.* Kingston: Quarry, 1986.

Poulin, Jacques. *Les grandes marées*. Montréal: Leméac, 1978. *Springtides*. Trans. Shelia Fischman. Toronto: Anansi, 1986.

Ross, Sinclair. *As for Me and My House*. 1941. Toronto: McClelland, 1957.

Roy, Gabrielle. *Bonheur d'occasion*. Montréal: Société des Editions Pascal, 1945.

Stratford, Philip. *All the Polarities: Comparative Studies in Contemporary Canadian Novels in French and English*. Toronto: ECW, 1986.

Sutherland, Ronald. *Second Image: Comparative Studies in Québec/Canadian Literature*. Toronto: New, 1971.

Robin McGrath and Penny Petrone

NATIVE CANADIAN LITERATURE

A DEBATE HAS arisen in recent years over the place of native art and literature in Canadian culture. Conservative critics have generally acknowledged the high quality of Indian and Inuit art but have persisted in assigning it to an anthropological or ethnic context, despite the forcible arguments of native artists and specialists in the study of their work that it be included in mainstream collections. Native literature has been even more marginalized, but since writing did not develop indigenously within the native cultures, it has not yet reached the high degree achieved by native art and thus an examination of it in a historical setting can still be useful.

The literature of Canadian natives has its origins in the oral traditions of its seven main cultural areas: Eastern Woodlands, Plains, Plateau, North Pacific Coast, the Western and the Eastern Subarctic, where fifty-three languages derived from eleven basic linguistic groups were spoken, and the Arctic, where six Inuit dialects are in use.

Rooted in and transmitted through storytelling and public ceremony, the oral literature may be classified into three major forms—narrative, secular, and sacred; songs and poems, including chants and prayers; and oratory, ritual and nonsacred. Differing considerably among the various tribes and peoples, the oral literature reflects a rich diversity of culture and history.

Central to the oral tradition was the power of the word, whether spoken, chanted, or sung. It carried the power to make things happen: medicine to heal, plants to grow, animals to be caught, and human beings to enter the spiritual realms. Through this sacred power, the Indians and Inuit sought to shape and control the cosmic forces that governed their lives.

Precontact literature survives in a reduced and modified oral form but is available to readers primarily in the works of the explorers and ethnographers. A staggering collection of Indian folklore, more from some tribes than from others, exists in the journals of, for example, the American Folklore Society, the Royal Society of Canada, and the Canadian Institute; in reprints and bulletins of government agencies such as the Geological Survey of Canada; and in the collections of such early ethnographers as Henry Rowe Schoolcraft, Franz Boas, Marius Barbeau, Diamond Jenness, and Charles Hill-Tout.

Inuit came into prolonged contact with Europeans at a much later date, but there are several ethnographic sources of Inuit songs and stories in this century: the works of Jenness, collected between 1913 and 1918; of Knud Rasmussen, collected in the 1920s; and of Paul Emile Victor, gathered in the 1930s. Jenness took advantage of technology, and the song texts he published can still be heard on tape recordings, but Rasmussen is considered the most sensitive and reliable of the three. Rasmussen, whose mother tongue was Inuktitut, was especially adept at translating poetry.

Although Canada's Inuit did not have a tradition of formal rhetoric, oratorical skill was highly regarded among the Indian people. Orators were trained in dramatic presentation and in the conventional metaphors in which the language of Indian diplomacy and rhetoric was carried out. Each tribe appointed the most eloquent of its members, many of whom rose to the rank of chief on the strength of their ability to deliver official orations at tribal councils and diplomatic negotiations.

The Europeans who first came into contact with the Indians marveled that a people who had neither the wheel nor writing knew the power of the word. They were amazed that the "untrained savage mind" was capable of eloquence. In his *Relation* of 1633, Father Paul Le Jeune praised a Montagnais chief "for a keenness and delicacy of rhetoric that might have come out of the schools of Aristotle or Cicero" (Thwaites 205). In the *New Relation of Gaspesia*, Chrestien Le Clercq, the Recollet priest, declared that the Indians

> are very eloquent and persuasive among those of their own nation, using metaphors and very pleasing circumlocutions in their speeches, which are very eloquent, especially when ... these are pronounced in the councils and the public and general assemblies. (241–42)

During the Anglo-French rivalry for North America, in the seventeenth and eighteenth centuries, outstanding orators such as Capitinal (Montagnais), Kiotseaeton (Mohawk), Jean-Baptiste Atironta (Huron), Tessouat (Algonquin), La Colle (Swampy Cree), and Minavavana (Ojibwa) gave formal orations in the contexts of the fur trade, colonial warfare, and missionary activity. The speeches can be studied both for their historical significance and their literary qualities. After the fall of New France (Treaty of Paris

1763), until shortly after the War of 1812, when their role as military allies ceased, Indian orators like Joseph Brant (Mohawk), Tecumseh (Shawnee), Ocaita (Ottawa), and Grandes Oreilles (Ojibwa), pleading for their very survival, continued the tradition of oratorical excellence.

It is a truism that translation of Indian speeches into French or English presented many obstacles. The Indian predilection for figurative and symbolic language, for allegorical meanings and allusions, contributed in no small degree to the difficulties in rendering exact translation. The eighteenth-century English fur trader Alexander Henry recognized this dilemma and explained, "The Indian manner of speech is so extravagantly figurative that it is only for a very perfect master to follow and comprehend it entirely" (Bain 75, 76).

With the peace that followed the War of 1812 and the failure of Tecumseh's heroic attempts to unite the Indians into a defensive confederacy to resist the large-scale white settlements from the British Isles, missionaries arrived not only to look after the settlers but to Christianize the Indians.

As a result of this program, Indians educated in religious schools began writing in English. The mid-nineteenth century saw, for the first time, literary publication in English—the result largely of the efforts of a coterie of young Ojibwa from southern Ontario, including Peter Jones, George Copway, George Henry, Peter Jacobs, John Sunday, Henry Steinhauer, and Allan Salt. Many Indians took an active part in Methodist missionary work and achieved great fame as preachers or public speakers. Their sermons, often containing themes of conversion and religious experience, were distinguished for their humor and apt illustration. Sunday (1796–1875), one of the most eloquent preachers of his day, delighted his audiences with his droll wit.

Because of the great interest in aboriginal people at the time, personal histories were in demand and autobiography achieved popularity. It was a new form, alien to an oral heritage in which the communal and collective were celebrated. As a result, autobiographical works retained many of the oral features of their preliterate cultures. A unique blend of oral history, tribal beliefs and customs, and personal anecdote, they also clearly reflect their Christian and acculturated influences. The Bible was the chief literary authority in the lives of the converted Indians, and their work is pervaded by deep Christian piety and biblical cadence.

The first Canadian Indian to publish a book in English was Copway (1818–69). *The Life, History, and Travels of Kah-ge-ga-gah-bowh (George Copway)*, published in 1847, was so successful that it went through six editions by the end of the year and was republished in 1850 under the title *Recollections of a Forest Life: Or, The Life and Travels of Kah-ge-ga-gah-bowh or, George Copway*. The autobiography, a blend of tribal history,

ethnography, and personal experience, brought Copway international recognition, and he toured the United States and Europe as a celebrity.

George Henry, or Maungwudaus (1810–?), published a slim volume about
his overseas travel, the first written by a Canadian Indian: *An Account of
the Chippewa Indians, Who Have Been Travelling . . .* (1848). As leader and
chief of an Ojibwa dance troupe during the tour, he was entertained and
honored by royalty and high society alike. The account is interesting because of Henry's reactions to European places, people, and events. "Like
musketoes in America in the summer season, so are the people in this city,
in their numbers, and biting one another to get a living," Henry wrote of
London (3). Although he wrote favorably about French women, Henry, like
Indians two centuries earlier, found bearded men unattractive: "Many of
the gentlemen never shave their faces; this makes them look as if they had
no mouths. Others wear beards only on the upper part of their mouths,
which makes them look as if they had black squirrel's tails sticking on each
side of their mouths" (6).

Journal of the Reverend Peter Jacobs (1848) was the first travel sketch
of Canada published by a Canadian Indian. Jacobs (1805–90) was a keen
observer, and his journal is straightforward and factual. His obituary in the
Daily Times (Orillia, Ontario) on 4 September 1890, stated that he was "at
one time probably the best known Indian on the continent." Wherever he
lectured on the manners and customs of the Indians or preached his sermons at home or abroad, he attracted vast crowds.

Peter Jones (1802–56) was the first native Methodist minister in Canada.
His autobiography, *Life and Journals of Kah-ke-wa-quo-na-by (Rev. Peter
Jones) Wesleyan Minister* (1860), was published posthumously, as was his
*History of the Ojebway Indians, with Especial Reference to Their Conver-
sion to Christianity* (1861). Scores of his letters, sermons, lectures, speeches,
and petitions written in English attest to the vigorous part he played in
the secular and religious life of his time.

Christianized Inuit were also urged to record their life stories by the
early missionaries. Diary keeping was encouraged as a way of ensuring
that these nomadic hunters and gatherers observed the Sabbath as a day
of prayer and reflection; these diaries frequently took the form of autobiographies or were later used in their composition. Lydia Campbell, a
mixed-blood Inuk from Labrador who married a Hudson's Bay Company
cooper, was a fairly typical diary keeper. Campbell was given an exercise
book by the Reverend Arthur C. Waghorn in 1893, when she was seventy-
five years old, and she occasionally took time off from tending her traps
and caring for her husband and motherless grandchildren to document
her early life and her present situation. The diary was originally published
in the Newfoundland *Evening Telegram* in 1894 under the title "Sketches

of Labrador Life." Her daughter Margaret Baikie and her grandniece Elizabeth Goudie later published autobiographies also; the works of the three women provide a picture of life in that area from 1818 to 1972.

From the earliest days of Champlain and Frontenac (governor of New France in the late seventeenth century) to the 1880s, when most Indians were confined to reservations and the breakdown of their traditional tribal structures was complete, a body of literature—petitions, speeches in council and at treaty-signing sessions, letters of protest, memorials, and reports—that might be called "official" arose. The overriding theme is a sense of loss—loss of land, of hunting and fishing rights, of self-sufficiency and dignity, of nationhood. For example, in 1865 Peter Paul lamented that "steamboat make water dirty ... scare 'em fish ... everything noise, bustle, all change—this not Micmac country—Micmac country very quiet, no bustle; their Rivers make gentle murmur; trees sigh like young woman; everything beautiful." In 1896, in a letter to the editor of the *Victoria Daily Colonist*, the Nootka chief Maquinna argued against the outlawing of the potlatch: "The potlatch is not a pagan rite; the first Christians used to have their goods in common ... and now I am astonished that Christians persecute us and put us in jail for doing just as the first Christians" (6).

During treaty-signing sessions, which resembled ancient councils in their drama and ceremonial formality, impressive orators of the late nineteenth century—like Poundmaker (Cree), Crowfoot (Blood), Big Bear (Cree), and Sweet Grass (Cree)—kept alive the tradition of their forebears as they poured forth their embittered eloquence in defense of home and hunting ground, using their ancient formulaic metaphors of sun, hatchet, pipe, and road and their traditional analogies to the natural world.

The last half of the century produced few significant books. One of these, *Origin and Traditional History of the Wyandotts, and Sketches of Other Indian Tribes of North America* (1870), by Peter Dooyentate Clarke, draws upon folk memory to present historical personages and events through a series of vividly dramatized tableaux. Also noteworthy is *Our Caughnawagas in Egypt* (1885), by Louis Jackson, which gives a first-hand account of the famous Nile expedition to the Sudan in 1884–85. Jackson, with a sharp eye for detail, recorded the unusual sights he had observed.

The best-known native writer around the turn of the century was the poet Emily Pauline Johnson (1861–1913), author of *The White Wampum* (1895), *Canadian Born* (1903), and *Flint and Feather* (1912). Johnson also wrote short fiction, notably *Legends of Vancouver* (1911), a collection of short pieces derived from the tales and legends she heard from Joe Capilano, a Squamish chief.

Literary output in the first half of the twentieth century was meager. Lack of interest by publishers as well as a depression and two world wars made publication virtually impossible. The 1960s, however, heralded an outburst of writing in English. Indian and Inuit newspapers and periodicals funded by native organizations or government agencies sprang up across Canada to provide a forum for energy and ideas. Native speakers emerged; Indian oratory once again became a vigorous literary form, and Inuit began developing the rhetorical skills needed to handle large meetings and mass media. Journalistic reports and essays also became popular as a means of disseminating native opinion and information. Whether in speech or in essay, native voices were preeminently political, addressing their persecution, betrayals, and aspirations in explicit terms.

In addition, several books of legends, born from centuries of tradition and published by the natives themselves, also appeared: *Legends of My People, the Great Ojibway*, by the well-known artist Norval Morriseau, and *Son of Raven, Son of Deer*, by the Tseshaht Indian George Clutesi, who, also wrote *Potlatch*, a detailed description of this important traditional rite. Also in this decade, Ethel Brant Monture, a great-great-granddaughter of Joseph Brant, published the biographies of three celebrated Canadian Indians in *Canadian Portraits*. Around the same time *Men of Medeek*, by Walter Wright, as told to Will Robinson, and *Sepass Poems: The Songs of Y-Ail-Mihth*, recorded by Eloise Street in 1911–15, appeared in print.

Because of their geographical isolation, few Inuit had much contact with nonnatives until the 1960s; consequently, there was relatively little Inuit literature in English before that time. Improved transportation and communications and a commitment by the government to promote native language meant that Inuit writers could catch up with their counterparts in the Indian communities. The controversial novel *Harpoon of the Hunter*, by the native bush pilot Markoosie, was a turning point for Inuit literature. Set in the precontact era, *Harpoon of the Hunter* is the story of a disastrous hunt interwoven with a romance based on the fatal-love motif of the old legends. After a series of unfortunate events that result in the deaths of most of the able-bodied men in the camp, the survivors decide to join some people in a nearby camp, but in the last few pages the heroine drowns and the hero commits suicide in despair. The work was critically acclaimed when it was published in English and French and was soon translated into a dozen other languages and published around the world.

For Markoosie, there was considerable irony in his literary success. He wrote the novel in English and then translated it into his own dialect so that it could be published serially in *Inuktitut* magazine; it was later translated back into English for publication by a major press. The success of *Harpoon of the Hunter* convinced government and cultural agencies that the encouragement of writing in the native languages would improve the quality of English-language works by native authors. Funding was consequently made available for the bilingual and trilingual publication of works by native authors. Collections of traditional legends were the most obvious result of this shift in policy. *Eskimo Stories from Povungnituk, Québec*, by Zebedee Nungak and Eugene Arima, *Tales from the Igloo*, edited by the French Oblate missionary Maurice Metayer from the recordings of eight Copper Inuit elders, *How Kabloonat Became*, edited by Mark Kalluak, and *Inuit Legends*, edited by Leonie Kappi, were all published in both the native language and English.

The *Statement of the Government of Canada on Indian Policy*, the controversial white paper that recommended the abolition of special rights for native peoples, sparked a burst of creative activity in the 1970s. A number of Indian political activists published their works: Harold Cardinal, *The Unjust Society*; William Wuttunee, *Ruffled Feathers*; and Harold Adams, *Prison of Grass*. The decade also produced traditional tales and legends retold by tribal elders, such as *Wild Drums*, by Alex Grisdale; *Tales of Nokomis*, by Patronella Johnston; *Tales of the Mohawks*, by Alma Green (Forbidden Voice); and *Medicine Boy and Other Cree Tales*, by Eleanor Brass, who relates legends and stories told to her as a child. Several books of poetry appeared as well: *My Heart Soars*, by the Coast Salish poet Chief Dan George (1899–1981); *Wisdom of Indian Poetry* and *Okanagan Indian*, by Ben Abel; *Indians Don't Cry*, by George Kenny; and *Poems of Rita Joe*, an autobiographical sequence by the Micmac poet Rita Joe. In *Moose Meat and Wild Rice* Basil H. Johnston, humorist and linguist, told entertaining stories about a modern reservation that is outwardly westernized but in spirit very much still Ojibwa.

However, autobiography and its allied forms, based on oral history and frequently written in the as-told-to tradition or with the help of a collaborator, dominated the 1970s. Examples of these works are *Recollections of an Assiniboine Chief* by Dan Kennedy (1877–1973); *Geniesh*, by Jane Willis, a Cree from northern Québec who recalls her childhood and adolescence in Anglican boarding schools; *Voices of the Plains Cree*, by Edward Ahenakew (1885–1961), chronicling the traditions and history of the Plains Cree, as told to Ahenakew by Chief Thunderchild (1849–1927) and as narrated by Ahenakew's fictional character Old Keyam; *First among the Hurons*, the autobiography of Max Gros-Louis, who played a prominent role in the James Bay project; *Buffalo Days and Nights*, the memoirs of Peter Erasmus (1833–1931), the last surviving member of the Palliser Expedition of 1857–60, as told to Henry Thompson in 1920; *My Tribe the Crees*, by Joseph F. Dion, a description of smallpox epidemics and the Riel rebellion; *My People the Bloods*, by Mike Mountain Horse (1888–1964); *Forty Years a Chief*, by George Barker, whose brief narrative is a panoramic sweep of his life told in spartan prose; and *These Mountains Are Our Sacred Places*, by Chief John Snow (Stoney). Most acclaimed is *Half-Breed*, Maria Campbell's autobiographical account of her early years and a starkly realistic portrait of her efforts to survive in a dehumanizing world of poverty, alcohol, drugs, and violence. Campbell's story is a disturbing reminder of the ugliness of the cultural conflict that is part of Canada's social history. But the book ends in victory as Campbell herself finds spiritual freedom through her struggle.

Inuit, too, produced a large number of autobiographical works in the 1970s. Former camp boss Peter Pitseolak, who had long kept a diary, wrote an account of his life and the history of the Cape Dorset area in *People from Our Side*. From Baker Lake came the Reverend Armand Tagoona's *Shadows*; from the Mackenzie Delta, Alice French's *My Name Is Masak*; from a British Columbia prison, *Thrasher: Skid Row Eskimo*, by Anthony Apakark Thrasher; from North Baffin and Hudson's Bay, the anthologies *Stories from Pangnirtung* and *Northern People*, both illustrated by the award-winning artist Germaine Arnaktauyok; and from Ottawa, Minnie Aodla Freeman's *Life among the Qallunaat*. Many shorter autobiographies appeared in magazines and newspapers.

Because of a reluctance to draw attention to themselves as adults, Inuit women who write autobiographies tend to deal only with the early years. The women are still taught that it is unseemly to discuss their accomplishments, although it is quite acceptable to recall the errors of childhood and adolescence. Some writers circumvent this restriction by fictionalizing their experiences, as Minnie Freeman did in her play "Survival in the South," first performed in 1971. Inuit men suffer from no such prohibition and tend to reverse the process, using the adventures of the heroes of old as the structures for their own stories. While Pitseolak obviously sees himself as a Kiviok figure, hot-tempered, virile, impatient, and proud, the writer Nuligak clearly identifies with the humble orphan boy Kaujjarjuk. His work *I, Nuligak* is divided into the three parts essential to the Kaujjarjuk story: the humiliation, the gaining of strength, and the revenge; and although Nuligak does not kill three polar bears at the climax of the story as Kaujjarjuk does, he gets a coveted job on a schooner called the *Polar Bear* and becomes the champion of the young men in his camp.

Since the 1980s there has been a phenomenal burst of creative output. Never before have so many outlets for written expression been available, and native writers are responding in various literary forms. Articulate young poets such as Jeannette Armstrong (Okanagan), Lenore Keeshig-Tobias (Ojibway), Beth Cuthand (Cree), and Annharte (Regina Saulteaux) are publishing in small literary magazines such as *Whetstone*, while established poets, including Daniel David Moses (*Delicate Bodies*), Duke Redbird (*Loveshine and Red Wine*), and Rita Joe (*Song of Eskasoni*), have published collections of their works. Many are experimenting in two and three literary forms to record and interpret their experiences.

Autobiography is still a popular form. Eleanor Brass, in *I Walk in Two Worlds*, tells of her life, from her early years on the File Hills Colony of southern Saskatchewan to her involvement with the Indian Friendship Centres in Regina, Saskatchewan, and Peace River, Alberta. Basil H. Johnston, in *Indian School Days*, remembers his stay during the 1940s at a school run by the Jesuits in the northern Ontario town of Spanish.

Although literature for children did not exist in traditional times, it has become a favorite medium of expression with native writers—probably as a result of publishers' requests. Traditional stories are recast, often from the taped storytelling of tribal elders, and collected in lavishly illustrated books like *Murdo's Story*, as told to the Norway House native Murdo Scribe by his elders. Other writers, including Maria Campbell, Bernelda Wheeler, Jeannette Armstrong, Beatrice Culleton, and Lenore Keeshig-Tobias, are creating their own tales. Campbell's *Little Badger and the Fire Spirit* has been very successful, as has *I Can't have Bannock but the Beaver Has a. Dam*, by Wheeler, or Beatrice Culleton's *Spirit of the White Bison*, in which the bison tells about the decimation of the buffalo.

Most Inuit writers and many Indian/Métis writers publish books for children in their native languages, which are used extensively in northern schools. Some works are in English, however. Norman Ekoomiak has written bilingual children's books, including *Arctic Memories*, and Michael Kusugak has collaborated with the well-known author Robert Munsch on *A Promise Is a Promise*.

A number of young native writers are turning to the short story as the medium for their creativity. For example, Daniel Moses, Gilbert Oskaboose, J. B. Joe, John McLeod, Shirley Bruised-Head, and Jordan Wheeler have used shorter forms ranging from realistic tales to stories of fantasy and allegory to interpret the contemporary life of Canada's natives. Eight native storytellers who attended a Saskatchewan education workshop in 1985 produced a collection of short fiction in *Achimoona* (the Cree word for stories)—a work distinguished by the sensibilities that inspired the authors. Inuit writers like Alootook Ipellie and Markoosie have also been effective in the short story form.

Native writers are beginning to experiment with the novel. Three works of fiction, all by women writers—*In Search of April Raintree*, by Culleton (Manitoba); *Slash*, by Armstrong (British Columbia); and *Honour the Sun*, by Ruby Slipperjack (Ontario)—are powerful indictments of the degradation of Canada's native peoples living in and between two different cultures. *In Search of April Raintree* is the heartbreaking story of two Métis sisters who, after losing both family and heritage, try, against extraordinary odds, to come to grips with their identity. *Slash* traces a young Okanagan Indian's journey from childhood on a reservation through prison and political resistance across North America toward healing and inner peace. *Honour the Sun* is set in an isolated community along the Canadian National Railroad line in northern Ontario. The narrator is a ten-year-old Ojibwa girl called the Owl, whose warm, carefree childhood is shattered when her mother becomes an alcoholic. For the next three years the narrator records her confusion and loneliness as she watches the world around her disintegrate. At boarding school away from the community, the Owl is reassured of a better world through the words her mother taught her. "Honour the Sun, child, just as it comes over the horizon, Honour the Sun, that it may bless you, come another day" (211). Rather than a conventional plot, Slipperjack uses the seasonal cycle to structure the work, in the manner of her ancestors.

Considering the native peoples' love of drama and of performance, the vitality of their theater is not surprising. As part of the resurgence of traditional values, young writers are turning to drama (stage, radio, television) and basing their plots on tribal myth or custom and their search for identity. Representative works include Valerie Dudoward's *Teach Me the Ways of the Sacred Circle*, which is set in Vancouver and focuses on the choice Matthew Jack, the first high school graduate in his family, must make between the Tsimshian way of life and assimilation into the dominant society, and Daniel Moses's *Coyote City*, a ghost story that explores the social pressures native peoples experience when they move to an urban environment.

Tomson Highway, a gifted Cree from Manitoba, has attracted considerable attention. *The Rez Sisters*, the story of seven women from an imaginary reservation on Manitoulin Island who hear of a huge bingo game that is to take place in Toronto, won the Dora Mavor Moore Award for the best new play in 1986–87. His sequel to *The Rez Sisters, Dry Lips Oughta Move to Kapuskasing*, focuses on the reactions of the men when the women decide to form a hockey team. Two other plays, *Aria*, a series of monologues by twenty-two women characters, and *The Sage, the Dancer and the Fool*, in which a young native experiences the city through three elements—his spirit, his mind, and his physical desires—demonstrate Highway's diverse talents.

Inuit drama, which virtually died out with European contact, has experienced a revival under the influence of newly founded Greenlandic and Alaskan theater groups. While few dramatic works have been published, manuscripts circulate among theater groups in Hopedale (Labrador) and Pangnirtunge (Northwest Territories).

Along with the new art forms, traditional stories are being retold to keep alive knowledge of the past. Basil H. Johnston's *Tales the Elders Told* and *Ojibway Ceremonies* both preserve the rich cultural heritage of the Ojibwa people. *Earth Elder Stories*, by Alexander Wolfe, is a collection of the oral traditions of the Saulteaux from Saskatchewan, while *The Birth of Nanabosho*, by Joseph McLellan, revives the legend of the Ojibwa trickster Nanabosho. The Inuit artist Dr. Agnes Nanogak has progressed from illustrating stories collected by non-Inuit to illustrating her own stories. Incidentally, her *More Tales from the Igloo* was translated by her son and daughter-in-law, Billy and Annie Goose.

Native Canadian writing in English is evolving. Young natives, increasingly caught between tradition and mainstream culture, are writing about and interpreting themselves. But once the frictional heat of catharsis is over, they may surmount the walls of self and advance beyond the autobiographical. A few have moved beyond protest and intense indignation to more sophisticated forms of expression. While still looking to their traditional oral literature for direction and inspiration, they are exploring new content. With better education, mastery of the language and the craft, and sense of pride and authority in their spiritual roots, they are asserting their uniqueness within a stronger, more diversified literary tradition.

WORKS CITED

Abel, Ben. *Okanagan Indian.* Cobalt, ON: Highway Book Shop, 1976.

———. *Wisdom of Indian Poetry.* Cobalt, ON: Highway Book Shop, 1976.

Achimoona. Saskatoon: Fifth, 1985.

Adams, Harold. *Prison of Grass: Canada from the Native Point of View.* Toronto: New, 1975.

Ahenakew, Edward. *Voices of the Plains Cree.* Ed. Ruth M. Buck. Toronto: McClelland, 1973.

Armstrong, Jeannette. *Slash.* Penticton, BC: Theytus, 1985.

Arnaktauyok, Germaine, ed. and illus. *Northern People.* Yellowknife: Infonorth, 1977.

———, ed. and illus. *Stories from Pangnirtung.* Edmonton: Hurtig, 1976.

Baikie, Margaret. *Labrador Memories: Reflections at Mulligan.* Labrador: Them Days, n.d.

Bain, James, ed. *Travels and Adventures in Canada and the Indian Territories by Alexander Henry.* Edmonton: Hurtig, 1969.

Barker, George. *Forty Years a Chief.* Winnipeg: Peguis, 1979.

Brass, Eleanor. *I Walk in Two Worlds.* Calgary: Glenbow Museum, 1987.

———. *Medicine Boy and Other Cree Tales.* Calgary: Glenbow Museum, 1978.

Campbell, Lydia. *Sketches of Labrador Life.* Labrador: Them Days, 1980.

Campbell, Maria. *Half-Breed.* Toronto: McClelland, 1973.

———. *Little Badger and the Fire Spirit.* Toronto: McClelland, 1980.

Cardinal, Harold. *The Unjust Society: The Tragedy of Canada's Indians.* Edmonton: Hurtig, 1969.

Clarke, Peter Dooyentate. *Origin and Traditional History of the Wyandotts, and Sketches of Other Indian Tribes of North America: True Traditional Stories of Tecumseh and His League in the Years 1811 and 1812.* Toronto: Hunter, 1870.

Clutesi, George. *Potlatch.* Sidney, BC: Gray, 1969.

———. *Son of Raven, Son of Deer.* Sidney, BC: Gray, 1967, 1975.

Copway, George. *The Life, History, and Travels of Kah-ge-ga-bowh (George Copway), a Young Indian Chief of the Ojebwa Nation.* Albany: Weed, 1847.

Culleton, Beatrice. *In Search of April Raintree.* Winnipeg: Pemmican, 1983.

———. *Spirit of the White Bison.* Winnipeg: Pemmican, 1985.

Dion, Joseph F. *My Tribe the Crees.* Calgary: Glenbow, 1979.

Dudoward, Valerie. *Teach Me the Ways of the Sacred Circle. The Land Called Morning.* Saskatoon: Fifth, 1986.

Ekoomiak, Norman. *Arctic Memories.* Toronto: NC, 1988.

Erasmus, Peter. *Buffalo Days and Nights.* As told to Henry Thompson. Calgary: Glenbow–Alberta Inst., 1976.

Freeman, Minnie Aodla. *Life among the Qallunaat.* Edmonton: Hurtig, 1978.

———. "Survival in the South." *Paper Stays Put: A Collection of Inuit Writing.* Ed. Robin Gedalof. Edmonton: Hurtig, 1980. 101–12.

French, Alice. *My Name Is Masak.* Winnipeg: Peguis, 1977.

George, Chief Dan. *My Heart Soars.* Saanichton, BC: Hancock, 1974.

Goudie, Elizabeth. *Woman of Labrador.* Toronto: Martin, 1973.

Green, Alma. *Tales of the Mohawks.* Toronto: Dent, 1975.

Grisdale, Alex. *Wild Drums: Tales and Legends of the Plains Indians.* As told to Nan Shipley. Winnipeg: Peguis, 1972.

Gros-Louis, Max. *First among the Hurons.* With Marcel Bellier. Trans. from the French by Sheila Fischman. Montréal: Harvest, 1973.

Henry, George. *An Account of the Chippewa Indians, Who Have Been Travelling among the Whites, in the United States, England, Ireland, Scotland, France and Belgium.* Published by the author, Boston, 1848.

Highway, Tomson. *Aria.* Unpublished play, 1987.

———. *Dry Lips Oughta Move to Kapuskasing.* Saskatoon: Fifth, 1989.

———. *The Rez Sisters.* Saskatoon: Fifth, 1988.

———. *The Sage, the Dancer and the Fool.* Unpublished play, 1989.

Jackson, Louis. *Our Caughnawagas in Egypt: A Narrative of What Was Seen and Accomplished by the Contingent of North American Voyageurs Who Led the British Boat Expedition for the Relief of Khartoum up the Cataracts of the Nile.* Montréal: Drysdale, 1885.

Jacobs, Peter. *Journal of the Reverend Peter Jacobs, Indian Wesleyan Missionary from Rice Lake to the Hudson's Bay Territory, and Returning, Commencing May, 1852.* Toronto: Anson Green, 1853.

Johnson, Emily Pauline. *Canadian Born.* Toronto: Morang, 1903.

———. *Flint and Feather.* Toronto: Musson, 1912.

———. *Legends of Vancouver.* Vancouver: privately printed, 1911. Toronto: McClelland, 1961.

———. *The White Wampum.* London: Bodley Head, 1895.

Johnston, Basil H. *Indian School Days.* Toronto: Key Porter, 1988.

———. *Moose Meat and Wild Rice.* Toronto: McClelland, 1978.

———. *Ojibway Ceremonies.* Toronto: McClelland, 1982.

———. *Ojibway Heritage.* Toronto: McClelland, 1976.

———. *Tales the Elders Told: Ojibway Legends.* Toronto: Royal Ontario Museum, 1981.

Johnston, Patronella. *Tales of Nokomis.* Toronto: Musson, 1970.

Jones, Peter. *History of the Ojebway Indians, with Especial Reference to Their Conversion to Christianity.* London: Bennett, 1861.

———. *Life and Journals of Kah-ke-wa-quo-na-by (Rev. Peter Jones) Wesleyan Minister.* Toronto: Anson Green, 1860.

Kalluak, Mark, ed. *How Kabloonat Became and Other Inuit Legends.* Dept. of Education, Government of Canada, 1974.

Kappi, Leonie, ed. *Inuit Legends.* Yellowknife: Dept. of Education, Government of the Northwest Territories, 1977.

Kennedy, Dan. *Recollections of an Assiniboine Chief.* Toronto: McClelland, 1972.

Kenny, George. *Indians Don't Cry.* Toronto: Chimo, 1977.

Le Clercq, Chrestien. *New Relation of Gaspesia, with the Customs and Religion of the Gaspesian Indians (1691).* Trans. and ed. William F. Ganong. Toronto: Champlain Soc. 5, 1910.

Maquinna. *Victorian Daily Colonist* 1 Apr. 1896: 6.

Markoosie. *Harpoon of the Hunter.* Illus. Germaine Arnaktauyok. Montréal: McGill-Queens UP, 1970.

McLellan, Joseph. *The Birth of Nanabosho.* Winnipeg: Pemmican, 1987.

Metayer, Maurice, ed. *Tales from the Igloo.* Illus. by Agnes Nanogak. Edmonton: Hurtig, 1972.

Monture, Ethel Brant. *Canadian Portraits: Brant, Crowfoot, Oronhyatikha: Famous Indians.* Toronto: Clarke, 1960.

Morriseau, Norval. *Legends of My People, the Great Ojibway.* Toronto: Ryerson, 1965.

Moses, Daniel David. *Coyote City.* Stratford: Williams-Wallace, 1990.

———. *Delicate Bodies.* Vancouver: Blewointment, 1978.

Mountain Horse, Mike. *My People the Bloods.* Calgary: Glenbow–Alberta Inst., 1979.

Munsch, Robert, and Michael Kusugak. *A Promise Is a Promise.* Toronto: Annick, 1988.

Nanogak, Agnes. *More Tales from the Igloo.* Trans. Billy Goose and Annie Goose. Edmonton: Hurtig, 1986.

Nuligak. *I, Nuligak.* Ed. and trans. Maurice Metayer. Toronto: Martin, 1972.

Nungak, Zebedee, and Eugene Arima. *Eskimo Stories from Povungnituk, Québec.* Ottawa: National Museums of Canada, 1969.

Peter Paul. Clipping scrapbook 5, of George Patterson. Public Archives of Nova Scotia.

Pitseolak, Peter. *People from Our Side.* With Dorothy Harley Eber. Edmonton: Hurtig, 1975.

Redbird, Duke. *Loveshine and Red Wine.* Cutler, ON: Woodland Studios, 1981.

Rita Joe. *Poems of Rita Joe.* Halifax: Abanaki, 1978.

———. *Song of Eskasoni: More Poems of Rita Joe.* Charlottetown: Ragweed, 1988.

Scribe, Murdo. *Murdo's Story: A Legend from Northern Manitoba.* Winnipeg: Pemmican, 1985.

Sepass Poems: The Songs of Y-Ail-Mihth. Chilliwack, BC: Sepass Trust, 1963.

Slipperjack, Ruby. *Honour the Sun.* Winnipeg: Pemmican, 1987.

Snow, John. *These Mountains Are Our Sacred Places: The Story of the Stoney People.* Toronto: Stevens, 1977.

Statement of the Government of Canada on Indian Policy. Ottawa: Dept. of Indian Affairs and Northern Development, 1969.

Tagoona, Armand. *Shadows.* Ottawa: Oberon, 1975.

Thrasher, Anthony Apakark. *Thrasher: Skid Row Eskimo.* Toronto: Griffin, 1976.

Thwaites, Reuben Gold, ed. *The Jesuit Relations and Allied Documents: Travels and Explorations of the Jesuit Missionaries in New France, 1610–1791.* Vol. 5. New York: Pageant, 1959.

Wheeler, Bernelda. *I Can't Have Bannock but the Beaver Has a Dam.* Winnipeg: Pemmican, 1984.

Whetstone. Native issues. Spring 1985, Spring 1987, Fall 1988. Lethbridge, AB: U of Lethbridge.

Willis, Jane. *Geniesh: An Indian Girlhood.* Toronto: New, 1973.

Wolfe, Alexander. *Earth Elder Stories.* Saskatoon: Fifth, 1988.

Wright, Walter. *Men of Medeek.* As told to Will Robinson. Kitimat, BC: Northern Sentinel, 1962.

Wuttunee, William. *Ruffled Feathers: Indians in Canadian Society.* Calgary: Bell, 1971.

Lorna Irvine and Paula Gilbert Lewis

ALTERING THE PRINCIPLES OF MAPPING: TEACHING CANADIAN AND QUÉBEC LITERATURE OUTSIDE CANADA

> What we are seeing is not just another redrawing of the cultural map—the moving of a few disputed borders, the marking of some more picturesque mountain lakes—but an alteration of the principles of mapping. Something is happening to the way we think about the way we think.
>
> Clifford Geertz, *Local Knowledge*

AT A LATE 1980s meeting devoted to the study of Canadian literature and film, a provocative exchange occurred. An academic from the United States was at the podium, describing the various ways his university and department were enabling students and faculty members to involve themselves in Canadian culture: trips to Canada financed, faculty enrichment programs encouraged, faculty exchanges established, library resources designated for Canadian studies—in short, the general pattern of area studies in United States universities. When he was finished, a member of the audience asked several critical questions. All this is very well, he said, but why are you involved in the study of Canada at all? What does the term *Canadian studies* mean? What are your theoretical grounds?

Each of us has questions about the rationale of categorizing literature. We know that although literature courses have traditionally been designated by the country of origin of authors—a practice currently much less criticized than designations by historical period—packaging cultural products by nationality can encourage holistic readings that often lead to erroneous generalizations. The adjective *Canadian*, like any other adjective pertaining to a nation, becomes problematic when it is meant to give cultural information. For Canada the question is even more complex, since the adjective *Canadian* causes consternation among certain groups for whom the distinctive terms *English-Canadian, anglo-Canadian, French-Canadian, Québécois, Québec,* and even *Acadian* are more accurate and appropriate. In a rapidly changing technological world, it is less and less clear whether national characteristics are inherent or imposed, nor can we ever know to what extent more powerful cultural stereotypes dominate weaker ones.

At the same time, teaching literatures such as Canada's is an important undertaking, particularly to Canadians and Quebecers themselves. Archival research that introduces into any established canon forgotten or little-known writers develops the literary and cultural history of the country. Canadian and Québec literatures have also become important internationally, especially within anglophone and francophone university communities. Teachers in the United States, in British Commonwealth countries, in France, and in many parts of the French-speaking world regularly include on their syllabi fiction, drama, and poetry by such internationally known writers as Margaret Atwood, Marie-Claire Blais, Timothy Findley, Michel Tremblay, Alice Munro, and Anne Hébert. For teachers who are concerned with individual Canadian and Québec writers, or with particular groups of writers from Canada, shared cultural myths often seem apparent in the literatures, and from such shared myths, national codes are hypothesized and sometimes demonstrated. Educating a larger reading public to the various literatures of Canada thus becomes a theoretical as well as a practical undertaking, a blending of cultural and literary issues.

Nationalism and Thematics

One approach to studying Canadian literatures might be termed *thematic.* Although there are inherent problems in demonstrating necessary and sufficient thematic differences among national literatures, and particular problems for Canada because of biculturalism, there are some advantages in using thematic, or partially thematic, methods.

Much of Canada's search for identity has been set up in counterdistinction to thematic patterns perceived as pertaining distinctly to the United States (individual struggle, western frontiers) or as imitative of themes associated with various European literatures (existentialism). To some extent, courses that compare national literary themes focus on connections between culture and literature. Part of this attention, directed toward economic, political, geographical, historical, and linguistic characteristics in

Canada and Québec, not only reflects, but helps construct, Canadian identities. In *The Family Romance*, Eli Mandel reiterates his earlier conviction
that modern Canadian criticism " 'seeks a central role in the development
of national consciousness. It aspires to the attainment of cultural coherence.' " He insists that no one "is likely to dispute the view that the most
cogent and powerful means of describing Canadian culture through its
literary expression has been historically the so-called thematic criticism
of Frye" and goes on to mention several "major critical studies" by scholars
such as John Moss, Margot Northey, and "a host of essays in important
journals" that rely basically on the isolation and categorizing of Canadian
themes (13).

The *Wacousta Syndrome*, by Gaile McGregor, is a comprehensive attempt
to discover, from Canada's literature and art, distinctive cultural themes.
McGregor seeks to develop a national consciousness; to that end she analyzes the Canadian "langscape," collecting, classifying, and interpreting
themes that she isolates in both anglophone and francophone literatures.
Even though the philosophy as well as the content of McGregor's book is
heavily anglicized, it offers sometimes helpful suggestions for course themes
for the teaching of Canadian, and to a much lesser extent Québec, literatures.[1] Influenced by Atwood's controversial *Survival*, McGregor argues that
Canadian literature often reflects the "*interface* between civilization and
the wilderness" (3), an observation that suggests geographical as well as
historical and political borders. Like Atwood, she annotates a Canadian
hostility to nature that results in endurance rather than control. Elsewhere,
she argues that Canadian literature reveals a national concern with "*im-
posing* rather than *deriving* meaning from experience" (54). These general,
somewhat contradictory, observations demonstrate inherent logical problems with many thematic analyses of national literatures, although they
also suggest foci for various kinds of literary courses.

More specifically, because national identity can be most easily described
in opposition to that of other countries, McGregor juxtaposes American
and Canadian themes. Canada's northern "frontier" differs dramatically
from the myth of the American West. McGregor explains that to " 'go beyond' a western frontier . . . is both a commendable achievement in public
terms and an exhilarating experience on a private level. A northern frontier,
in contrast, denotes the *limits of endurance*. It is, in brief, an intangible
but ineradicable line between the 'self' and the 'other,' between what is
and what is not humanly possible" (59). Even though the theoretical bases
for such distinctions are shaky, comparisons like these do generate ideas.
For example, a course in American studies might investigate the mythology
of the Canadian North as it contrasts with that of the American West by
pairing such books as Laura Berton's *I Married the Klondike* and Willa

Cather's *My Ántonia*; Will McCann's *Red Coat* and any Louis L'Amour western; Howard O'Hagan's *Wilderness Man* and Thomas Berger's *Little Big Man*; Michael Ondaatje's *Collected Works of Billy the Kid* and *The Ox-Bow Incident*; Wallace Stegner's *Wolf Willow* and Jim Harrison's *Legends of the Fall*; a Canadian film such as *Please Don't Shoot the Piano Teacher* and any American western.

"Proud humility," "public" rather than "private isolation," "acceptance of process," "survival in the face of natural odds," all combine to suggest to McGregor that the "Canadian symbolic ego" is feminine (155). Indeed, she shows again and again the reversal of sexual roles in Canadian literature—the strength of the female protagonist, the relative weakness of the male. She argues that although Canadian writers tell the patriarchal story, it seldom ends successfully. In the light of United States literature, this observation suggests an idiosyncratic approach to authority that McGregor (like so many other Canadian cultural commentators) sees reflected in Canadian history and in a certain psychological "deference to authority."[2] As Atwood has, she claims that Canadians are fascinated with animal victims; that the heroic, for a Canadian, is often perceived as magical, a way of avoiding active responsibility for feats of bravery or intelligence; that creative activity is frequently imaged as traumatic, almost surrealistic. Accordingly, then, Canadians are so concerned with national identity that their literary works are filled with rituals of naming, catalogs, maps, all efforts to establish "location" (376). Canadians, as the great compromisers, are culturally marked by an avoidance of confrontation. This last observation leads McGregor to a final optimistic argument: that Canada operates in terms of communal rather than individual structures, cooperative strategies that move toward the future.

Some of the themes mentioned by McGregor can be useful pedagogic tools, particularly if they foreground psychological and cultural issues that encourage various critical approaches. Feminist courses on Canadian or Québec women writers being taught in a number of universities in the United States emphasize connections between individual and national psychologies somewhat like those proposed by McGregor. Other courses might compare Québec literature with that of France, or of other postcolonial francophone countries, using a thematic focus such as the pathology of madness. In a course on madness, attention could be placed on approaches stressed at different postcolonial stages, and writers such as Anne Hébert, Roger Lemelin, Marie-Claire Blais, Victor-Lévy Beaulieu, Roch Carrier, and Michel Tremblay for example, could be used effectively to illustrate Québec's idiosyncratic political problems. Another course might concentrate on religious violence, as demonstrated in texts by Hébert, Claire Martin,

Jovette Marchessault, Louky Bersianik, and Carrier, among other contemporary Québécois writers.

Nonetheless, in spite of the imaginative possibilities of thematic courses, a heavy reliance on purely thematic approaches to national literatures has its drawbacks.[3] Summary pronunciations, even of the kind we have listed, often simplify the complexities of the postcolonial mind and shroud the profound cultural problematic that results from Canada's bifurcated position. When national characteristics are generalized, individual differences can be lost and cause–effect patterns obscured. Furthermore, Canada may be unique in rejecting the *either/or* patterns in many nationalistic arguments in favor of more comprehensive *both/and* structures and, because of the important interaction between anglophone and francophone modes of thought, attempting to blend a New World pragmatism with older European approaches. Moreover, in Canada, historical process can be demonstrated (the country is new), and the shifting, not always parallel, stages of cultural maturing made evident.

Indeed, unless thematic approaches are used in sophisticated ways— McGregor's approach often fails—oversimplification can hinder an understanding of particular literatures by encouraging careless thinking: a proclivity to leave out literature and art that do not conform to the category under discussion, the promotion of dangerous cultural stereotypes, and the passive acceptance of so-called national traits. Besides such pitfalls, critics and teachers who rely on thematic categorization are often guilty of circular reasoning. Canadians—and French Canadians as a subset—are first assumed to exhibit certain characteristics that are then discovered in literature and art by the investigating critic. Or, equally circular, repeated themes are linked to Canadian history, geography, politics, and so on, revealing deep-seated reasons for their frequent repetition. Notably, too, nationalistic approaches to literature stress difference rather than similarity. The result is that the United States is usually cast in an opposing, often negative, role. Even worse, within Canada itself, such approaches tend to situate the dual literary and cultural traditions of this dual nation at opposite ends of one national spectrum.

Canada's voice is not monophonic but polyphonic. Describing Canada's symbolic systems by analyzing the complex relationships among history, politics, and language should privilege interpretations that demonstrate alternative perspectives on New World experience. Such an approach— backed by thematic information—can encourage students to recognize connections between art and ideology and acknowledge literature as a process—shifting, altering, constantly re-forming. As in American letters —French and British literatures have a different history—Canadian literary criticism began with a necessary attention to content, to the "most Canadian" work, to standards of "Canadianness."[4] But *Canadian* is an adjective that, in a postcolonial world, bears complex cultural information that should never be standardized even when thematic approaches are used.

From the Margins

Another approach, certainly akin to thematic studies but emphasizing political issues, opens the content and structure of literary canons to postcolonial thinking. Canada's—and, even more so, Québec's—marginal status, a status that obliges constant attention to power relationships, provides some rationale for teaching Canada's literatures from a national perspective. Rick Salutin claims, in *Marginal Notes*, that many Canadians feel themselves "at the edge of something vast, teeming, variegated and contentedly self-absorbed, something that expects to be the object of attention from the outside. We are to it as the margin to a densely printed page" (1). Marginality is a multifaceted issue. Many Canadian and Québec critics, speaking in languages not their own or attempting to think simultaneously in different languages, stress the complex political tensions on the edges of language and literature. Furthermore, Canada's/Québec's particular marginal status results in representations of the New World quite different from those offered by the United States and the Spanish-dominated Mexico. Canada's various cultures and the literatures to which they give rise force boundaries open and help maintain an evolving North America in which monolithic cultural readings can be, if not prevented, at least criticized.

In "Comparative Literature as a Cultural Practice" Mary Louise Pratt argues that scholars (we would add teachers and students) need to be liberated from "petty nationalism." At the same time, Pratt continues, literary critics inevitably "develop elaborate dialogues around questions of national self-understanding, self-criticism, and self-transformation. There is little doubt that such factors shape literary study, with its institutional base in the national literatures" (33). If literature is, to some extent, going to be studied according to its country of origin, teachers should consider how to introduce idiosyncratic, or at least partially distinctive, national questions. For students, demonstrating how nations come to understand their cultural identities, no matter how fictional such understandings are, encourages self-consciousness about their own national prejudices and assumptions. By questioning traditions of realism, teachers can help students see that interpretation is relative, that ideology dominates culture, and that literature both reflects and transforms political issues.

Let us first imagine teaching Canadian literature to students reared on

United States literature, or even teaching Québec literature to American students of French exposed to French "masterpieces." Unlike courses on Canadian literature taught in the United States and to some degree still in Canada, courses on American literature are accepted in the mainstream, as are those on French and English literature. Many historical analyses of American texts exist. Indeed, we now assume American literature to have a past that influences its present, just as France and England have always had. In contrast, Canadian and Québec literatures are still in the process of formation. Acute identity struggles are reflected throughout the literatures. Because Canada often perceives itself and is perceived by others as marginal to the United States and to some extent to England—and because within Canada, Québec sees itself as marginal to France, the United States, and English Canada—it displays a number of postcolonial attitudes to power. Border issues are intense and the imagery of edges, of margins, is pervasive. Canada's New World and bifocal vision refracts imperialist doctrines; tensions between the French and the English, between majority cultures and native and ethnic cultures, between Canada and both mother countries, and between Canada and the United States, immediately raise questions about canons, about literary process and ideology, and about the ways power hierarchies influence literary form and structures. Students learn to investigate the margins between literature and culture by studying literatures (all Third World and neocolonial literatures fall into this category) that are themselves self-conscious about borders.

Marginality increases sensitivity to cultural issues, whereas dominance decreases interest. In the United States, as Pratt argues, "the idea of culture itself needs to be revindicated, against accelerating tendencies in contemporary American public life to trivialize or naturalize culture and to discredit critical knowledge of culture" (34). Such discreditation is a highly sensitive issue in countries whose culture seems threatened by more dominating ones. Because of Canada's proximity to the United States, the trivialization of cultural issues that often marks American discourse threatens Canada's very existence. Americans commonly refer to Canada as simply another of the states of the United States, and to Québec as simply a French anomaly, neither "real" French, Canadian, nor North American, a marginal hybrid. Such approaches illustrate the ways in which dominant ideologies incorporate and alter weaker ones: aggressive incorporation, imperialism. As Pratt also argues, "technological societies and, more important, militarized societies will certainly appear to their makers to 'work' better with a citizenry that lacks" comparative capacities and critical self-awareness (34). If categorizing national characteristics seems presumptuous and arbitrary, ignoring differences valorizes power and reiterates dominance. Ethnocentrism, partially the result of a lack of concern about national differences, encourages cultural blindness and the acceptance of dominant ideologies as universal.

Marginality is, then, a cultural phenomenon that students of all countries should be able to recognize, analyze, and interpret. More specifically, in *Technology and the Canadian Mind*, Arthur Kroker argues that it is Canada's "fate by virtue of historical circumstance and geographical accident to be forever marginal to the 'present-mindedness' of American culture ... and to be incapable of being more than ambivalent on the cultural legacy of our European past" (8). Canada is "in the middle"; caught between a new American technological world and two distinct but interrelated historical pasts (epitomized by England and France), the dual Canadian discourse, even more variegated than Kroker describes, may hypothetically represent a "way of seeking to recover a voice by which to articulate a different historical possibility against the present closure of the technological order" (12). As Kroker aptly remarks, "Canada is, and has always been, the most modern of the new world societies; because the character of its colonialism, of its domination of the land by technologies of communication, and of its imposition of an 'abstract nation' upon a divergent population by a fully technological polity, has made of it a leading expression of technological liberalism in North America" (83). According to Kroker's hypotheses, time and space, in Canada, assume their own New World meanings that evolve from a marginal status and, even more significant, a dichotomous cultural interaction. In Canada and in Québec, peripheralization is unique and therefore an extraordinarily fertile ground for cultural studies and teaching.

Canadian cultures blend the New World and the Old on the periphery. The literatures focus on marginal perspectives, with the distinctly Québec focus perhaps even doubly marginal, postcolonial, and dominated (with signs of increasing health since the 1960s) vis-à-vis its own country and both the francophone and anglophone worlds. Marginality necessarily poses perplexing questions: about realism; about hierarchies of power, almost always from a negative point of view; about cultural relativism; about the shifting boundaries between colonial and postcolonial mindsets; about constructive ways to use technology, while avoiding its excesses; and about relationships between the sexes, between language groups, and between the invaders and the country's native peoples. Thus, around such works as Atwood's *Handmaid's Tale*, Jack Hodgins's *Invention of the World*, Clark Blaise's *Resident Alien, Lunatic Villas* by Marian Engel, Findley's *Not Wanted on the Voyage* and *Telling of Lies*, all the works of Robert Kroetsch, the Canadian stories of Mavis Gallant, Janette Turner Hospital's *Borderline*, Matt Cohen's *Café le Dog*, the novels and short stories of Audrey Thomas, the fictions of Alice Munro, Hubert Aquin, Victor-Lévy Beaulieu, Louis Caron, Jacques Ferron, Tremblay and Carrier, Anne Hébert's *Kamouraska*,

Les enfants du sabbat, and *Les fous de Bassan,* Marie-Claire Blais's *Les nuits de l'underground* and *Visions d'Anna, L'amèr* of Nicole Brossard, Bersianik's *L'Euguélionne,* Antonine Maillet's *Pélagie-la-charrette* and its sequels, *Comme une enfant de la terre* and *La mère des herbes,* by Jovette Marchessault, and the later works of Yolande Villemaire, courses can be structured on such politically oriented topics as postcolonialism or imperialism and literary representations of borders in the New World.

Courses can also be devoted to parodic fiction and drama, as demonstrated in the work of many of these writers. Parody is directed at cultural idiosyncracies among some contemporary English and many French-speaking writers. Québécois writers, in fact, are often brilliantly effective in their attention to the grotesque, sometimes directing their barbs at their "conquerors," at other times at themselves, bitterly recognizing their minority status and attempting to understand themselves in order to exorcise their second-class condition. Because they have little to lose in terms of international power games, Canadians and Quebecers can observe the world with enough objectivity to imagine global perspectives. More powerful countries whose margins are rigid are often blind to cultural tensions outside their own borders.

Other advantages accrue from living on the margins. The Canadian/ Québec imagination tends to be dialogic; multiculturalism pervades the literatures. From a thematic perspective, Atwood and McGregor argue that Canadians associate with victims. And it is true that marginality reflects power from its underside, where action is not heroic but manipulative, where war is not glorious but agonizing, where rugged frontier behavior transmogrifies into a quiet attempt to pacify the wilderness. "Who do you think you are?" asks Alice Munro, questioning the dangers of imperialist thinking. Not caught up in the tug of war, Canadians struggle toward a balanced view. Particularly in the work of Canada's women writers, both French and English, equilibrium, a new perspective, becomes a major literary symbol and structure. Such efforts to deflate rigid thinking and to alter traditional institutions and narratives shed some light on the argument of several Canadian critics that Canada's literatures, since the renaissance of the 1960s, are predominantly concerned with postmodernist issues.

Postmodernism

Although teaching Canadian and Québec literatures is a political act, especially in countries that tend toward imperialistic thinking, it also remains an aesthetic endeavor. These literatures complicate the voices of the New World, serve cautionary roles in the hegemony of the West, promote cultural multiplicity often because of their dual heritage, use irony to situate violence, and attempt to balance technology and history, the new and the old. It is for these reasons that teachers, critics, and students have been encouraged to investigate the ways in which Canadian writers engage in literary postmodernism.

Such investigations can become the focus of various courses. For example, students and teachers might trace the ways in which recent fiction exposes the disintegrating plots that have dominated past narratives. Two of these—the imperialist narrative and the patriarchal narrative—are of particular interest in postcolonial cultures, largely because both comment on the vicissitudes of power. Clearly, shifting power relationships loosen borders; one of the results of less rigid boundaries is the opening up of new space. In Canadian and Québec literatures, that new space, quite dramatically, has often been filled by female narratives and female points of view. As a balance to the exploration of masculine space—whether in political or personal terms—Canadian and Québec literatures suggest different readings of history and of landscape: of culture in general. Because women writers have been privileged in contemporary Canada, they have been crucial in forming the metaphors and structures of anglophone and francophone Canadian literatures.

Apart from focusing on women novelists, short story writers, poets, and dramatists, teachers interested in thematic, political, and literary studies might devote a course to the relationship between fathers and sons. Contemporary male writers such as Cohen, Ondaatje, Clark Blaise, Kroetsch, Yves Thériault, Gérard Bessette, Jacques Godbout, and Tremblay illustrate the crises that dominate father-son stories. The same course could consider the attempts of these and other writers to situate the feminine in their work. For example, Findley, in *The Telling of Lies*, Matt Cohen, in *Nadine*, and Tremblay, in *Albertine, en cinq temps*, have chosen a female narrator or dramatic character, consistently staying within the terms of her vision and acknowledging the legitimacy of her story. Other male writers coopt their female characters, overpowering them and even sometimes eliminating them.

Canadian and especially Québec literatures have produced many experimental texts. Indeed, Québec feminist writers, like French theoreticians and postmodern writers, have attempted to deconstruct society by boldly tampering with literary forms, by entering the spheres of language, by exploding space, language, and form from within, by emptying out images, narratives, characters, and words, by creating new space. In *Gynesis*, a study of modernity and the intersections between French and American thought, Alice Jardine makes these literary strategies abundantly clear, emphasizing, in her analysis, the sharp differences between an American "pragmatic" approach to interpretation, which tends to increase images, narrative, characters, and words, and the French attempt to "empty out" (235). Canada has the opportunity to combine these approaches. What both Canadian and Québec writers can and do do—from a feminist consciousness and with a constant awareness of their marginality—is to attack cultural paradigms that have been responsible for imperialist doctrines, paradigms that dominate Western culture as they have so much of the world. While anglophone Canadian writers have traditionally not experimented with literary form and structure, particularly in comparison with contemporary Québec writers, many writers—women, especially, along with their French/Québec counterparts—are introducing female space into a patriarchal North America, contradicting, inverting, and recasting in postmodern ways the more usual narrative and locale of the father.

A number of writers come to mind as being germane. For example, the experimental feminist writers of Québec, such as Nicole Brossard, Madeleine Gagnon, and France Théoret, and the more radical of the poets—Michel Beaulieu, André Roy, Paul Chamerland, Lucien Francoeur, Gatien Lapointe, Claude Beausoleil, and Yolande Villemaire—might be compared with such anglophone feminist writers as Audrey Thomas, Marian Engel, Alice Munro, Joy Kogawa or poets like Daphne Marlatt, Robert Kroetsch, Erin Moure, George Bowering, or Michael Ondaatje. Students in the United States would benefit from investigating the connections between female space and a male-created and dominated technocracy, between Western and Eastern philosophies, and between a masculine and a feminine aesthetic. Like other postcolonial literatures, those of Canada reflect self-conscious searches for voice, communal structures rather than individualistic ones, the conservation of nature rather than its conquest, and a conglomeration of spatial metaphors—not simply thematic concerns but conspicuously psychological, political, and aesthetic ones. Canadian and Québec literatures thus become excellent, perhaps unique, departure points for the study of postmodernism and alterity, offering students the opportunity to increase the range of literary texts at their disposal, as well as giving them new ways of reading.

Teachers ought to encourage students to learn about other cultures and other perspectives. By escaping the rigid boundaries of the self, students may discover ways of understanding national borders. The relinquishing of "mastery," as teachers and students learn to do when studying the marginal literatures of modernity, has many political implications. When traditional notions of time and space break down, the artificial separation between male (patriarchal) chronology and female (maternal) space can evolve into a unity of culture and nature. The effort is apparent in many works of Canadian/Québec literature. The powerful countries should invent new kinds of subjectivity, and the developing voices of marginal countries help them to do so. In fact, Canadian and Québec writing offers a balance to an American literature in which, as Jardine argues, "belief in the total freedom of the self—beyond adversity—goes to the very core of American ideology and its traditions" (235). If European, and particularly French, writers are participating in an extreme emptying out and decentering of the images of patriarchal discourse—images to which American writers have clung—somewhere in the middle, perhaps at two points along the spectrum, exist the literatures of Canada, acknowledging both extremes but offering another dual perspective.

Canadian and Québec writers frequently pose questions about psychological and physical boundaries, and about nationality and the role of literature in the establishment and perpetuation of cultural myths. They address them in drama (especially in some of the experimental collective drama of Québec), in long documentary poems, in fantasies like Bersianik's *L'Euguélionne* and Robert Kroetsch's *Studhorse Man*, and in film, another rich source of comparative study. Even courses that trace communal patterns in Canadian and Québec literatures of the nineteenth and twentieth centuries, influenced by Northrop Frye's often quoted reference to garrison mentalities, can demonstrate that, as the individual blends into the community, the community moves beyond national boundaries into international contexts.

Lost people, as Atwood well knows, need maps of the territory, the marking of Geertz's "picturesque mountain lakes." And literature is a map. But principles of mapping change. New configurations emerge. We have suggested ways of approaching the study and teaching of Canadian/Québec literatures, ways that can be useful in both Canadian and non-Canadian contexts. Postcolonial literature in general, and the peculiarly dual literatures of Canada in particular, offer a wealth of primary texts, and a variety of theoretical issues, for the development of curricula that reflect more accurately than do traditional canons the shifting boundaries of the world.

NOTES

[1]Literary criticism in Québec is heavily influenced by and focused on modern French theory, and has moved far away from the thematic studies prevalent in the early 1960s and 1970s. Works such as Sainte-Marie-Eleuthère's *La mère dans le roman canadien-français* or Paulette Collet's *L'hiver dans le roman canadien-français* have been replaced by works like André Belleau's *Le romancier fictif* and Pierre Hébert's *Le temps et la forme.*

[2]*Deference to Authority* is the title of Edgar Friedenberg's study of the Canadian

character; in it he argues that Canadian passivity (even smugness) results from a persistent colonial acceptance of authority. Alice Jardine's discussion, in *Gynesis*, of the differences between a monarchy and a democracy, between Protestantism and Catholicism—related as they are to psychological and philosophical cultural stances—adds complicated but relevant perspectives to the issue of deference, particularly in a bifurcated country like Canada.

[3]An "antithematic" emphasis in Canadian criticism was stated by Barry Cameron and Michael Dixon in "Mandatory Subversive Manifesto" and has been developed by such critics as Paul Stuewe, B. W. Powe, and W. J. Keith, who explains why he cannot write an essay devoted to the family in Canadian literature: "Above all, there is a disturbing sense of the deterministic and the stereotypical pervading the whole enterprise. Why should writers of different age, gender, ethnic origin, social position, religious affiliation, etc., etc., portray 'the family' (or anything else, for that matter) in a similar way just because they show up on census-returns or passport-statistics as belonging to the same nation?" (322).

[4]We are indebted here to Nina Baym, who, in "Melodramas of Beset Manhood," writes of United States literature:

> The earliest American literary critics began to talk about the "most American" work rather than the "best" work because they knew no way to find out the best other than by comparing American with British writing. Such a criticism struck them as both unfair and unpatriotic. We had thrown off the political shackles of England; it would not do for us to be servile in our literature. Until a tradition of American literature developed its own inherent forms, the early critic looked for a standard of Americanness rather than a standard of excellence. Inevitably, perhaps, it came to seem that the quality of "Americanness," whatever it might be, *constituted* literary excellence for American authors. (65)

WORKS CITED

Atwood, Margaret. *The Handmaid's Tale.* New York: Ballantine, 1986.

———. *Survival: A Thematic Guide to Canadian Literature.* Toronto: Anansi, 1972.

Baym, Nina. "Melodramas of Beset Manhood." *The New Feminist Criticisms.* Ed. Elaine Showalter. New York: Pantheon, 1985. 63–80.

Belleau, André. *Le romancier fictif: Essai sur la représentation de l'écrivain dans le roman québécois.* Sillery: PU du Québec, 1980.

Bersianik, Louky. *L'Euguélionne.* Montréal: La Presse, 1976. *The Euguélionne.* Trans. Gerry Denis, Alison Hewitt, Donna Murray, Martha O'Brien. Victoria: Porcépic, 1981.

Berton, Laura Beatrice. *I Married the Klondike.* Toronto: McClelland, 1954.

Blais, Marie-Claire. *Les nuits de l'Underground.* Montréal: Stanké, 1968. *Nights in the Underground.* Trans. Ray Ellenwood. Toronto: General, 1978.

———. *Visions d'Anna.* Montréal: Stanké, 1982. *Anna's World.* Trans. Sheila Fischman. Toronto: Lester and Orpen Dennys, 1985.

Blaise, Clark. *Resident Alien.* Markham, ON: Penguin, 1986.

Brossard, Nicole. *L'amèr: Ou, le chapitre effrité.* Montréal: Quinze, 1977. *These Our Mothers: Or, The Disintegrating Chapter.* Trans. Barbara Godard. Toronto: Coach, 1983.

Cameron, Barry, and Michael Dixon. "Mandatory Subversive Manifesto: Canadian Criticism vs. Literary Criticism." *Studies in Canadian Literature* 2 (1977): 137–45.

Cohen, Matt. *Café Le Dog.* Markham, ON: Penguin, 1985.

———. *Nadine.* Markham, ON: Penguin, 1986.

Collett, Paulette. *L'hiver dans le roman canadien-français.* Québec: PU Laval, 1965.

Eleuthère, Sainte-Marie. *La mère dans le roman canadien-français.* Québec: PU Laval, 1964.

Engel, Marian. *Lunatic Villas.* Toronto: McClelland, 1981.

Findley, Timothy. *Not Wanted on the Voyage.* Markham, ON: Penguin, 1984.

———. *The Telling of Lies.* Markham, ON: Penguin, 1986.

Friedenberg, Edgar. *Deference to Authority: The Case of Canada.* New York: Sharpe, 1980.

Gallant, Mavis. *Home Truths.* Toronto: Macmillan, 1981.

Geertz, Clifford. *Local Knowledge: Further Essays in Interpretive Anthropology.* New York: Basic, 1983.

Hébert, Anne. *Les enfants du sabbat.* Paris: Seuil, 1975. *Children of the Black Sabbath.* Trans. Carol Dunlap-Hébert. Don Mills, ON: Musson, 1977.

———. *Les fous de Bassan.* Paris: Seuil, 1982. *In the Shadow of the Wind.* Trans. Sheila Fischman. Toronto: General, 1984.

———. *Kamouraska.* Paris: Seuil, 1970. *Kamouraska.* Trans. Norman Shapiro. Toronto: General, 1982.

Hébert, Pierre. *Le temps et la forme: Essai de modèle et lecture de trois récits québécois.* Sherbrooke: Naaman, 1983.

Hodgins, Jack. *The Invention of the World.* Toronto: Macmillan, 1977.

Hospital, Janette Turner. *Borderline.* Toronto: McClelland, 1985.

Jardine, Alice. *Gynesis: Configurations of Woman and Modernity.* Ithaca: Cornell UP, 1985.

Keith, W. J. " 'To Hell with the Family!' An Open Letter to *The New Quarterly*." *New Quarterly* 7 (1987): 320–24.

Kroetsch, Robert. *The Studhorse Man.* Toronto: Macmillan, 1969.

Kroker, Arthur. *Technology and the Canadian Mind.* Montréal: New World, 1984.

Maillet, Antonine. *Pélagie-la-charrette.* Montréal: Leméac; Paris: Grasset, 1979. *Pélagie.* Trans. Philip Stratford. Toronto: General, 1983.

Mandel, Eli. *The Family Romance.* Winnipeg: Turnstone, 1986.

Marchessault, Jovette. *Comme une enfant de la terre: Le crachat salaire.* Montréal: Leméac, 1975.

———. *La mère des herbes.* Montréal: Quinze, 1980.

McCann, Will. *Red Coat.* Ontario: Paperjacks, 1981.

McGregor, Gaile. *The Wacousta Syndrome: Explorations in the Canadian Langscape.* Toronto: U of Toronto P, 1985.

O'Hagan, Howard. *Wilderness Man.* Vancouver: Talonbooks, 1958.

Ondaatje, Michael. *The Collected Works of Billy the Kid: The Left-Handed Poems.* Toronto: Anansi, 1970.

Powe, B. W. *A Climate Charged: Essays on Canadian Writers.* Oakville: Mosaic, 1984.

Pratt, Mary Louise. "Comparative Literature as a Cultural Practice." *Profession 86.* New York: MLA, 1986. 33–35.

Salutin, Rick. *Marginal Notes: Challenges to the Mainstream.* Toronto: Lester and Orpen Dennys, 1984.

Stegner, Wallace. *Wolf Willow.* Toronto: Macmillan, 1955.

Stuewe, Paul. *Clearing the Ground: English-Canadian Literature after Survival.* Toronto: Proper Tales, 1984.

Tremblay, Michel. *Albertine, en cinq temps.* Montréal: Leméac, 1984.

Robert Kroetsch

READING ACROSS THE BORDER

1.

CANADIAN LITERATURE IS the autobiography of a culture that insists it will not tell its story. It is the autobiography of a culture that locates itself against the security of all direct arrivals at self-knowledge by elaborate stratagems of border, of periphery, of the distanced center.

2.

The Canadian draws a boundary, then proves its existence by crossing it. I am not American, the Canadian says. Hello, America, the Canadian says, here I am, I am your kin, love me.

3.

Here I am. But where is here? asks that wily sage Northrop Frye. The Canadian sensibility, he says, "is less perplexed by the question 'Who am I?' than by some such riddle as 'Where is here?'" (220).

4.

Canadian writing is not a writing *at* the border; in fact, it has a distrust, often, of that kind of writing. Rather, it is a writing *of* the border, the creation of a line that endlessly confounds itself into the conundrum (the riddle) of the other.

5.

A borderline case. How does one read into a literature that insists on writing itself outward, *away*?

6.

George Bowering writes the fundamental Canadian long poem in *Kerrisdale Elegies* by reacting, almost line by line, to Rilke's *Duino Elegies*. Bowering cannot read German. He likes the uncertainty of translations. He likes the inadequacy of translations. He doesn't especially like Rilke or Europe. I am not Rilke, Bowering says, and then he posits his own middle age, his location in a residential area in Vancouver, against all that Rilke spoke. Bowering insists on the Atlantic as a vast difference. And then he proceeds to make his poem out of that oceanic border. Out of his willful crossing of that oceanic border.

7.

Notions of "other" are radically active in the Canadian psyche and the embodiment and illumination of that psyche: CanLit. That a boundary also connects what it would separate is part of the predicament.

Michael Ondaatje, in a poem (much of it a prose poem) as radical as *The Collected Works of Billy the Kid*, cannot address the Canadian experience at all until he enters solely into the other of the American folk hero whose realization he can only doubt.

8.

Canadian writing is, from its inception (see, for instance, Haliburton's Sam Slick stories), a shadowed writing. Not overshadowed. Shadowed, rather, in its deliberate employment of concealment as a strategy, shadowed secondly in the sense of being secretly followed—at least in its own imagination. The story Canadian writing tells itself includes a slightly paranoid sense of being "followed," an unease that breeds in turn a curious insistence on innocence. "I didn't do it," the child says in school, before the accusation is made, recognizing or sensing the presence of a disapproving authority.

9.

"For which I am not responsible," the voice says, in parenthesis, in Margaret Atwood's poem "You May Wonder." That marvelous poem at once lures us into a reading and instructs us in how to read. The reading act in the Canadian poem is problematic in its versions of tradition and convention and code. The boundaries that allow and direct the reading are both posited and refused. To put it another way, the contract is negotiated in the process of reading.

"You May Wonder" begins:

> You may wonder why I'm not describing the landscape for you.
> This island with its complement of scrubby trees, picturesque
> bedrock, ample weather and sunsets, lavish white sand beaches
> and so on. (For which I am not responsible.) There are travel
> brochures that do this better, and in addition they contain
> several very shiny illustrations so real you can almost touch the
> ennui of actually being here....

10.

The title of Atwood's poem announces and conceals the uncertainty and the necessity of an I–you relationship. I can speak myself only by speaking *to* you. But further, I can only speak myself by speaking "you." Indeed, beyond that, I may be speaking to myself by addressing you: "You may wonder why I'm not describing the landscape to you." I may wonder why I'm not describing the landscape to myself.

And "may," too, is problematic, suggesting mere possibility, not realization, suggesting present or future, not any consolation of past or completion.

11.

You may wonder. Canadian writing loves the disguise of cliché. You've heard this expression before, you've used it yourself. This is a negotiable reading.

This is an invitation to that edge of surprise where we delay, extend the idea of surprise against its own moment, into the problematics of time. The Canadian lyric is tempted by narrative, distracted by the discursive.

12.

Narrative becomes a boundary of the lyric, asserting itself as anecdote, as an uncertain historical trace, as myth. But narrative runs the risk of action, of making something happen.

We must always approach but never achieve the moment of resolution.

Or of revolution. Delay is everything. The narrative impulse encounters the boundary of reflection, of meditation, of a baffling elegiac remembrance of what was about to happen. Shadowed, we are shadowed: we are in Canada a people followed in stealth by the future, and that shadowing tempts us into immobility.

13.

Canadian writing is a postcolonial writing that comes close to cherishing that center it could not reject by revolution and now as a matter of principle will not accept. That governing principle insists that Canadian writing locate itself as periphery, the exciting periphery of a defined and stuffy and self-satisfied center that is not always locatable, that may not even exist at times, that may, worse yet, at times be exactly where the periphery is. But the narrative of empire that is behind all this was a powerful and "real" narrative, and to speak oneself free of that narrative takes strategies of a dangerous and desperate sort.

Does the center function as source or other? In either case, the periphery lives with the abiding risk of annihilation.

14.

The endless task of the Canadian writer is to invent a place in the place of Canadian geography. "In the place of," here, becomes the dislocating pun, the pun that riddles Canadian writing.

Landscape is a question of appalling weight in Canadian writing, partly because there is in Canada so much landscape, with no accepted tradition, no code, if you will, for its being read. Or perhaps, because of that, there is no landscape in Canada, no way to translate "scrubby trees, picturesque / bedrock, ample weather and sunsets" into landscape.

15.

What, in this version of the New World, happened to Mother Nature?

The "elements" in Atwood's poem are a failed or even maliciously distorted translation of a preceding text, a mistranslation that willfully confounds its European predecessor.

CanLit is the materialization of nature's unreadability.

16.

Canadian writing proceeds by a kind of parody defined in Linda Hutcheon's *Theory of Parody*: "Like Genette, I see parody as a formal or structural

relation between two texts. In Bakhtin's terms, it is a form of textual dialogism" (22).

In calling to mind the figure of Bakhtin, Hutcheon reminds us not only
of the dialogic exchange but of the carnivalization of what would seem to
be the prior text by the one that would seem to follow.

17.

"I see parody," Hutcheon writes, "as operating as a method of inscribing
continuity while permitting critical distance. It can, indeed, function as a
conservative force in both retaining and mocking other aesthetic forms"
(20).

Hutcheon describes, discourses on, the inevitable double text that is part
of Canadian writing. Every text seems to announce its incompleteness, its
desire for completion—in other texts.

That process of doubling, of distancing, of desiring, quite possibly finds
its fullest exposition in the novels of Hubert Aquin.

Hubert Aquin, writing in French, wrote down the basic paradox of all
Canadian writing. The nameless hero of *Prochain épisode*, with his many
possible names, with his madness and his sanity, with his compulsion to
talk and his wish not to be understood, reveals himself in his hiding.

18.

No wonder, then, that Canadians long so eagerly to read what they so
fervently believe cannot be written. The namelessness is the name, but
must be written even to be nameless—but cannot remain nameless if
written.

19.

No wonder, then, that Canadian writers, confronting half a continent, like
to imagine islands. Aquin's writing prisoner, in *Prochain épisode*, is briefly
secure and free on the island that is Montréal. Atwood, in her novels
Surfacing and *Bodily Harm*, has her artist figures find definition when
confronted with the literal boundaries of islands. The small town, in many
Canadian novels, by a process of metonymy, becomes island.

20.

In Sinclair Ross's classic Canadian novel *As For Me and My House* the small
town of Horizon becomes a parody of the center; the horizon itself, on a

great sheet of prairie, becomes boundary. The nameless woman inside those confining circles must slowly and painfully write herself across her horizons; and, finally, as reader of the text that she has so compulsively written, she must go in pursuit of her own scattering of words.

WORKS CITED

Aquin, Hubert. *Prochain épisode.* Montréal: Cercle du Livre de France, 1965. *Prochain Episode.* Trans. Penny Williams. Toronto: McClelland, 1967.

Atwood, Margaret. *Bodily Harm.* New York: Simon, 1982.

———. *Surfacing.* Toronto: McClelland, 1972.

———. "You May Wonder." *The Contemporary Canadian Poem Anthology.* Ed. George Bowering. Toronto: Coach, 1983. 14.

Bowering, George. *Kerrisdale Elegies.* Toronto: Coach House, 1984.

Frye, Northrop. *The Bush Garden: Essays on the Canadian Imagination.* Toronto: Anansi, 1971.

Haliburton, Thomas C. *The Clockmaker.* 1836. Toronto: McClelland, 1958.

Hutcheon, Linda. *A Theory of Parody.* New York: Methuen, 1985.

Ondaatje, Michael. *The Collected Works of Billy the Kid: The Left-Handed Poems.* Toronto: Anansi, 1970.

Ross, Sinclair. *As for Me and My House.* 1941. Toronto: McClelland, 1989.

André J. Senécal

QUÉBEC LITERATURE:
A BRIEF BIBLIOGRAPHIC GUIDE

THIS BRIEF SELECTION of works dealing with Québec literature is organized into the sections Research and Reference Guides; Literary Criticism, focusing on Québec literature and the cultural climate in general, with subsections of fiction, poetry, and plays; Periodicals; and Dictionaries. Works are arranged alphabetically within each section. Full bibliographic data are provided for all titles reviewed. For the availability of a title, the reader may consult Biblio-Informatica, *Les livres canadiens disponible de langue française* (Montréal: Bibliodata, 1987–).

Research and Reference Guides

Cantin, Pierre, Normand Harrington, and Jean-Paul Hudon. *Bibliographie de la critique de la littérature québécoise dans les revues des XIXe et XXe siècles.* Ottawa: Centre de recherche en civilisation canadienne-française, Université d'Ottawa, 1979.

Cantin, Pierre, and René Dionne, eds. *Bibliographie de la critique de la littérature québécoise et canadienne-française dans les revues canadiennes (1974–78).* Ottawa: PU d'Ottawa, 1988.

The second volume continues Cantin, Harrington, and Hudon. It is the first installment of an ambitious project that seeks to isolate all references to French-Canadian literature, however trivial some might be, published in Canadian periodicals from their appearance in the 1820s to the 1980s. The project will include a revised and augmented edition of the first volume published by Cantin, Harrington, and Hudon. The work is arranged in three parts, although almost all of the data have been placed under the heading "Author." Copious indexes are included.

Fortin, Marcel, Yves Lamonde, and François Ricard. *Guide de la littérature québécoise.* Montréal: Boréal, 1988.
The guide contains a selection of books on literature and allied fields: reference works, general works, titles on specific genres. Reliable annotations make Fortin a useful source, and an index offers access to topics.

Gauvin, Lise, and Laurent Mailhot, eds. *Guide culturel du Québec.* Montréal: Boréal, 1982.
A selection of books and articles on language and literature and the fine and the performing arts is the focus of this volume. The cultural compendium is supplemented by cursory treatment of geography, history, political science, sociology, economics, psychology, and philosophy. The work contains well-informed sections on anglophone and allophone cultures, and useful details on institutional resources and the media. The annotations are short, and there is an index.

Lemire, Maurice, ed. *Dictionnaire des oeuvres littéraires du Québec.* 5 vols. Montréal: Fides, 1980–88.
The work of Lemire and his research team offers the most comprehensive critical and bibliographical tool available on the literature of Québec written in French. Each volume bears upon a definite period (Des origines à 1900; 1900–1939; 1940–1959; 1960–1969; 1970–1975) and contains a general introduction, a chronological table of literary and historical events with an exhaustive bibliography of the critical works consulted. Entries are arranged alphabetically by literary works published during the period considered. Each signed article on a given work includes a summary and an analysis of the work, a complete bibliography of its different editions, and the most salient book reviews and articles on the work and the author. The *Dictionnaire* has become the essential reference source in the field. Unfortunately, it does not include works published after 1975. For a more extensive inventory of the critical reception of Québec literature, consult the bibliographical project of Cantin, Dionne, et al.

Senécal, André. *A Reader's Guide to Québec Studies.* Québec: Gouvernement du Québec, 1988.
This bibliography identifies over 1,100 important titles published in book form on reference material and key subjects: art and architecture, cinema, ethnology, geography, history, language, literature (creative works and criticism), music, politics, and sociology. It also offers a selection of major periodicals currently published on these topics. The work was compiled for English-speaking users and contains both French and English titles. Indexes and a directory of publishers are included.

Literary Criticism

General Essays

Bouchard, René, ed. *Culture populaire et littératures au Québec.* Stanford French and Italian Studies 19. Saratoga: Anma Libri, 1980.
Essays on nationalism, religion, lexicography and the major literary genres are included in this work.

Bourassa, André-Gilles. *Surrealism and Québec Literature.* Trans. Mark Czarnecki, from 2nd ed., rev. Toronto: U of Toronto P, 1984.
Bourassa's chronological study traces and discusses the influence of surrealism on all genres, with references to the visual arts. Bourassa underscores the special way in which surrealism defined itself in Québec as well as the role that Québec authors played at the international level. A bibliography, chronology, and index are included.

Lamonde, Yves, and Esther Trépanier. *L'avènement de la modernité au Québec.* Québec: Institut Québécois de Recherche sur la Culture, 1986.
These ten essays on the emergence of modernism in literature, dance, music, painting, the sciences, the social sciences, and the media are studied from postmodern perspectives that posit a rupture with the recent past. The first half of the century is seen as a pivotal time of transition that offers an essential grounding for an interpretation of literature since the 1960s.

Moisan, Clément. *Comparaison et raison.* Montréal: HMH-Hurtubise, 1987.
Moisan, along with Ronald Sutherland, is one of the few Canadian writers who cast a critical glance at the separate evolution, literary and cultural, of Canada's two dominant linguistic communities. The fourteen essays of this book, written between 1968 and 1984, offer a philosophical as well as a rhetorical and ideological context to establish a comparison between French-Canadian and English-Canadian literatures. Some of the essays are examples of the various methodologies Moisan has refined as a result of his research on the modes of existence of literary traditions.

Nepveu, Pierre. *L'écologie du réel.* Montréal: Boréal, 1988.
This series of brilliant essays explores the new, postmodern context of literary creation, and its Québec manifestation in particular. Nepveu defines a new Baroque that lends itself to an intermingling of modes and tropes, that evolves under the signs of irony and the burlesque. His broad introspection (the author is a renowned novelist and poet) has its origin in the early age of Québec literature. The analysis of the works of such writers as Emile Nelligan, Octave Crémazie, and Hector de Saint-Denys Garneau serves to elucidate the contemporary consciousness.

Pelletier, Jacques, ed. *L'avant-garde culturelle et littéraire des années 1970 au Québec.* Montréal: U du Québec à Montréal, Department d'Etudes Littéraires, 1986.

In a series of uneven appraisals, the manifestations of the avant-garde in literature, the plastic and the performing arts, and the social sciences are examined.

Essays on the Novel

Belleau, André. *Le romancier fictif.* Sillery: PU du Québec, 1980.

In his semiotic study on the sociocultural context of literary creation and the relationship between society and the fictional form, Belleau analyzes works by Gabrielle Roy, Gérard Bessette, Jacques Godbout, and others in which the narrator is the main character. Bibliography and index are provided.

Cagnon, Maurice. *The French Novel of Québec.* Boston: Twayne, 1986.

A general introduction to the genre and major novelists. The work discusses individual works in cursory fashion, and references to the sociocultural context are often uninformed. Despite these shortcomings, the volume is unique in its appraisal of the Québec novel from its beginnings until the mid-1980s. The bibliography includes information on novels that have been translated into English.

Stratford, Philip. *All the Polarities: Comparative Studies in Contemporary Canadian Novels in French and English.* Toronto: ECW, 1986.

The author pairs French- and English-speaking authors to analyze their themes and styles: Hugh MacLennan and Gabrielle Roy; Margaret Laurence and Anne Hébert; Marie-Claire Blais and Alice Munro; Robert Kroetsch and Roch Carrier; Hubert Aquin and Margaret Atwood. The work is a well-informed discussion on the similarities and differences between the two literatures.

Whitefield, Agnès. *Le je(u) illocutoire: Forme et contestation dans le nouveau roman québécois.* Québec: PU Laval, 1987.

The work, an analysis of Réjean Ducharme's *L'avalé des avalés*, Anne Hébert's *Kamouraska*, Gérard Bessette's *L'incubation*, Gilbert Laroque's *Serge d'entre les morts*, and Hubert Aquin's *Prochain épisode*, discusses the significance of the passage from the third-person to the first-person narrative in Québec prose.

Essays on Poetry

Moisan, Clément. *A Poetry of Frontiers: Comparative Essays on Québécois and Canadian Poetry.* Trans. Linda Webber. Victoria: Porcépic, 1983.

The work provides a comparison of pairs of poets (Anne Hébert and Patricia K. Page, Rina Lasnier and Margaret Avison, Irving Layton and Gaston Miron, Michèle Lalonde and Margaret Atwood, and others) that underlines, through an analysis of dominant themes and images, the complementary and contrary points between the two literatures. Bibliography and index are included.

Nepveu, Pierre. *Les mots à l'écoute: Poésie et silence chez Fernand Ouellette, Gaston Miron et Paul-Marie Lapointe.* Québec: PU Laval, 1979.
    In his analysis of three poets of the Hexagon generation whom Nepveu identifies as representatives of major tendencies of the Québec literary imagination of the 1950s and 1960s, the critic interprets poetic discourse as a criticism of history and subjectivity that brings about an interrogation on identity and integration of the self.

Essays on the Theater

Godin, Jean-Cléo, and Laurent Mailhot. *Le théâtre québécois II: Nouveaux auteurs, autres spectacles.* Montréal: HMH-Hurtubise, 1980.
    This introduction to the productions of the 1970s comments on several types of performances and major authors: Barbeau, Garneau, Michel Tremblay. The volume contain bibliographies.

Lavoie, Pierre. *Pour suivre le théâtre au Québec.* Québec: Institut Québécois de Recherche sur la Culture, 1985.
    The work reviews a large and varied body of evidence (books, articles, audiovisuals, theses, archival materials) on the contemporary Québec theater, along with a proposal for increased financing and documentation. It contains an important bibliography.

Weiss, Jonathan. *French-Canadian Theatre.* Boston: Twayne, 1986.
    This broad chronological introduction to Québec dramatic literature, with an informed selection of major playwrights, discusses individual plays in a balanced and well-informed manner. The author seriously underplays the contribution of woman playwrights, however.

Periodicals

To keep abreast of the current production, one will gain a general overview from *Livre d'ici*, the French-language counterpart to *Quill and Quire*. The trade publication features news of the Québec publishing world. The section Nouveautés announces new releases, while the pull-out section Forthcoming Books/Livres à paraître offers information on books about to be released. These listings are provided by the National Library of Canada through CIP: The Canadian Cataloguing in Publications Program.

While *Livre d'ici* provides an overview of new titles, it offers the bare bibliographical skeleton of the beast. To obtain current information on the world of literary creation and criticism, the reader can turn to *Lettres québécoises*, a journalistic magazine, or to *Voix et images*, the only serious journal devoted exclusively to the criticism of Québec literature. Each issue of the latter contains a dossier on one major author (interview, essays, bibliography), essays on other writers or topics, and substantial book reviews.

To gain access to current periodical literature, the searcher can consult *Point de repère*, Québec's *Reader's Guide to Periodical Literature*. Issued bimonthly, it continues *RADAR* and *PERIODEX*. Author, title, and subject access to major Québec periodicals and other selected periodicals of the francophone world is provided.

Journalistic reviews of creative works and of monographs on Québec literature and culture are found in *Lettres québécoises*.

Dictionaries

A word must be said about the French, found between quotation marks and otherwise, that permeates the novels of Roch Carrier and Jacques Godbout, the plays of Michel Tremblay and Marie Laberge, the poetry of Gaston Miron, and countless other writers—a lexicography quite different from the varieties across the ocean. The reader will not often find the new words in the *Robert* or *Larousse*. At present, the best reference work is the *Glossaire* of the Société du Parler Français au Canada.

Belisle, Louis-Alexandre. *Dictionnaire nord-américain de la langue française.* Rev. ed. Montréal: Beauchemin, 1979.

The volume contains a representative but not exhaustive list of words that are used in Québec but are nonexistent in prescribed metropolitan French. Often incorrect in its linguistic attributions (especially Canadianisms, Anglicisms) and erratic in its orthographic code for assimilated Anglicisms and local pronunciations, it should not be used as an authority on usage or pronunciation. The *Bélisle* is more inclusive and more up-to-date than the *Glossaire* but far less reliable.

Pichette, Jean-Pierre. *Le guide raisonné des jurons: Langue, littérature, histoire et dictionnaire des jurons.* Montréal: Quinze, 1980.

To account for the richness of the Québec vocabulary and the often crucial shade of meaning or emotional range conveyed by swear words (a vital variable often sacrificed by English-Canadian translators), the reader can turn to Pichette.

Robinson, Sinclair, and Donald Smith. *Practical Handbook of Québec and Acadian French.* 1973. Rev. and expanded ed. Toronto: Anansi, 1984.

This list, arranged by topic, of common words and expressions with their English translation and equivalent in normative French, is difficult to use as a reference work precisely because of its topical organization. Also included are a section on Acadian French and chapters on grammar and pronunciation.

Société du parler français au Canada. *Glossaire du parler français au Canada. Contenant: 1. les mots et locutions en usage dans le parler de la province de Québec et qui ne sont pas admis dans le français d'école; 2. la définition de leurs différents sens, avec des exemples; 3. des notes sur leur provenance; 4. la prononciation des mots étudiés.* Québec: L'Action sociale, 1930. Québec: PU Laval, 1968.

Words are arranged alphabetically. Each entry contains a definition and notes on the word's origins and pronunciation, and there is a bibliography.

Arnold E. Davidson

ENGLISH-CANADIAN LITERATURE: A BRIEF BIBLIOGRAPHIC GUIDE

WHAT FOLLOWS IS a highly selective listing. For the most part and in the interest of brevity, I have not included works of a more specialized nature that, in effect, are already annotated in the individual essays contained in this volume, nor have I included studies of individual authors, for these can readily be found in the annual MLA bibliographies as well as in the books and bibliographies here noted.

Research and Reference Guides

The Canadian Encyclopedia. 3 vols. Rev. ed. Edmonton: Hurtig, 1988.

This is an indispensable reference work covering Canadian topics and Canadians from Sir John Joseph Caldwell Abbott or Maud Elizabeth Seymour Abbott to David Zeisberger and Janusz Zurakowski. Subsequent revisions are promised.

Davey, Frank. *From There to Here: A Guide to English-Canadian Literature since 1960.* Erin, ON: Porcépic, 1974.

In this volume Davey provides concise interpretive assessments of the literary accomplishment of some sixty contemporary writers, and as an added bonus George Bowering provides a similar entry on Davey. Each entry includes a primary and brief secondary bibliography.

Dictionary of Canadian Biography. 11 vols. to date. Toronto: U of Toronto P, 1966–.

Modeled, as its title suggests, on the British *Dictionary of National Biography* and arranged alphabetically and chronologically (according to the éntrant's year of death), the twelve volumes of the first series will cover Canadians who died between the beginning of the tenth century and the beginning of the twentieth and, in the process, the work will provide a comprehensive survey of Canadian history. A second series of volumes will then cover, decade by decade, those who died in the twentieth century.

Fee, Margery, and Ruth Cawker, eds. *Canadian Fiction: An Annotated Bibliography.* Toronto: Martin, 1976.
    Fee and Cawker include, alphabetically, "authors who had at least one work in print during 1973 or 1974." Under each author's name is a chronological listing of his or her published works, and most works listed are followed by a brief synopsis. Some critical studies are listed for the most important writers, and some of these are also summarized. The volume includes an extensive annotated listing of secondary sources.

Gnarowski, Michael. *A Concise Bibliography of English-Canadian Literature.* Rev. ed. Toronto: McClelland, 1978.
    Much information is packed into some 150 pages. The works of individual authors are arranged chronologically and according to genre. Most works are followed by a listing of significant reviews. Biographical and bibliographic studies of particular authors are noted, and a listing of selected critical studies is also provided.

Hoy, Helen. *Modern English-Canadian Prose: A Guide to Information Sources.* Detroit: Gale, 1983.
    This bibliography includes reference sources, literary histories, criticism and theory, secondary bibliographies, book reviews of major works, locations of uncollected stories, and libraries holding manuscript materials. In addition, sections on individual writers begin with a brief biographical summary followed by listings of their works and criticism on these works.

Lecker, Robert, and Jack David, eds. *The Annotated Bibliography of Canada's Major Authors.* Toronto: ECW, 1979–.
    This ongoing series covers both French-Canadian and English-Canadian authors of the nineteenth and twentieth centuries. Some volumes are devoted to poetry and some to prose writers. Each volume contains extensive annotated bibliographies of works by and on several authors. Particularly useful are the assessments of the available criticism on individual authors.

Lecker, Robert, Jack David, and Ellen Quigley, eds. *Canadian Writers and Their Works.* Toronto: ECW, 1983–.
    Another ongoing series, this one assesses the "development of Canadian fiction and poetry over the last two centuries." Ten volumes are projected

for poetry and ten for fiction. In each volume, five writers are covered by "discrete critical essays" that are, in effect, condensed versions of Twayne books.

New, W. H., ed. *Dictionary of Literary Biography: Canadian Writers.* Detroit: Gale, 1986–.

In this ongoing series, two volumes entitled *Canadian Writers since 1960* (*DLB* vols. 53, 60) and one of two volumes called *Canadian Writers, 1920–1959* (*DLB* vol. 68) have already been published. Each volume contains signed biocritical essays on the individual writers covered as well as author portraits and other illustrations (such as manuscript pages, book jackets, or important places) and primary and secondary bibliographies. Each volume also provides an extensive supplementary reading list.

Stevens, Peter. *Modern English-Canadian Poetry: A Guide to Information Sources.* Detroit: Gale, 1978.

This bibliography includes reference works, literary histories, general and critical studies, and major poetry anthologies. In addition, there are bibliographical listings of primary works by individual poets writing from 1900 to 1977 (as well as brief biographical sketches of each poet), and a selected list of criticism on individual authors, groups of authors, movements, and other literary phenomena.

Toye, William, ed. *The Oxford Companion to Canadian Literature.* Toronto: Oxford UP, 1983.

Individual entries by major Canadian critics cover a wide range of overlapping subjects (such as "Inuit Literature," "Science Fiction and Fantasy in English and French" and "Biographies and Memoirs in English") as well as single authors or works. Useful cross-references at the end of most entries point the reader to other pertinent sections in the book.

Histories and Literary Histories

Keith, W. J. *Canadian Literature in English.* London and New York: Longman, 1985.

The author early praises James Reaney's brief poem "To the Avon River above Stratford, Canada": "before / I drank coffee or tea / I drank you / With my cupped hands / And you did not taste English to me." Focusing on the historical development of different genres in English Canada, Keith is especially concerned with the "taste" of all this literature—the ways in which it is influenced by but is not British or American. The discussions of writers and their works are always perceptive, and the concluding "Individual Authors" appendix provides useful brief biographies, bibliographies, and annotated criticism.

Klinck, Carl F., ed. *Literary History of Canada.* 3 vols. 2nd ed. Toronto: U of Toronto P, 1976.
An exhaustive survey of Canadian literature from the beginnings to the mid-1970s. Volume 4, edited by W. H. New and published in 1990, massively updates the work.

McNaught, Kenneth. *The Pelican History of Canada.* Harmondsworth, Eng.: Penguin, 1969.
A readily available and often revised history of Canada, this one-volume paperback is essentially a synopsis, in readable narrative form, of more specialized and scholarly accounts of Canadian history.

New, W. H. *A History of Canadian Literature.* London: Macmillan, 1989.
Beginning with Indian and Inuit cultures, texts, and myths and ending with the encoding (of myth, history, gender, etc.) experiments of the 1960s, 1970s, and 1980s, this is a comprehensive and critically astute guide to the literatures of Canada. Particularly useful for the reader seeking a panoramic overview is the sixty-page chronological table.

Literary Criticism

Atwood, Margaret. *Survival: A Thematic Guide to Canadian Literature.* Toronto: Anansi, 1972.
The subtitle flaunts the "T" word, which much subsequent Canadian criticism has decried. But Atwood is Atwood. Her highly selective and obviously idiosyncratic *Guide* is pervaded by her intelligence and wit and, as such, is eminently readable.

Craig, Terrence. *Racial Attitudes in English-Canadian Fiction, 1905–1980.* Waterloo, ON: Wilfrid Laurier UP, 1987.
Operating from a sophisticated definition of *racism* that moves beyond biologism to include religious, linguistic, and cultural attributes, this study analyzes shifting racist and xenophobic attitudes exhibited in and/or portrayed by English-Canadian writers.

Davey, Frank. *Surviving the Paraphrase.* Winnipeg: Turnstone, 1983.
This collection of essays provided one of the first full-length repudiations of thematic criticism as a method and, implicitly, an ideology.

Frye, Northrop. *The Bush Garden: Essays on the Canadian Imagination.* Toronto: Anansi, 1971.

Along with *Survival, The Bush Garden* is one of the seminal works of thematic criticism. This study brings together many of Frye's essays originally published in the annual "Letters in Canada" section of the *University of Toronto Quarterly* between 1950 and 1959. Most famous is his discussion of the liberation of postcolonial Canadian writing from what he terms the earlier predominant "garrison mentality."

Godard, Barbara, ed. *Gynocritics/Gynocritiques: Feminist Approaches to Canadian and Quebec Women Writers.* Toronto: ECW, 1987.
The eighteen essays here printed (originally delivered at the Dialogue Conference held at York University in 1981) represent a wide range of feminisms highlighting both similarities and differences between Canadian and Québec perspectives. The collection is bilingual (essays in English are preceded by abstracts in French and vice versa) and includes a 115-page comprehensive "Bibliography of Feminist Criticism in Canada and Quebec."

Howells, Coral Ann. *Private and Fictional Worlds: Canadian Women Novelists of the 1970s and 1980s.* London and New York: Methuen, 1987.
In this volume, which is itself a tribute to Canadian literature's emerging international status, an Australian scholar living and teaching in England sets out "to answer the question repeatedly asked outside of Canada about Canadian fiction: 'Why are there so many good Canadian women writers?'" and in the process also writes perceptively on eleven of those writers. The book includes brief but useful biographies for each of the authors considered.

Hutcheon, Linda. *The Canadian Postmodern: A Study of Contemporary English-Canadian Fiction.* Toronto: Oxford UP, 1988.
That "the postmodern 'different,'" Hutcheon observes, "is starting to replace the humanist 'universal' as a prime cultural value ... is good news for Canadians who are not of Anglo or French origin." It is good news, too, for Canada, which is neither the United States, England, nor France. Starting with Canada as different and with the differences that pervade Canada, Hutcheon traces the play of differences in much recent Canadian fiction and defines thereby a Canadian postmodernism at odds with the conventional judgment that Canadian novels are traditionally realistic.

Irvine, Lorna. *Sub/Version.* Toronto: ECW, 1986.
Drawing partly on Dennis Lee's study of authorship in what he terms "colonial space" and even more on feminist investigations into the problematics of writing in patriarchal space (colonial space being but a version of this larger realm), Irvine shows that English Canada's major contemporary women novelists, like their Québec sisters, practice *l'écriture féminine* and must be read accordingly. This she does by astute attention

to the subversions perpetrated through these writers' covertly layered texts.

Jones, D. G. *Butterfly on Rock: A Study of Themes and Images in Canadian Literature.* Toronto: U of Toronto P, 1970.

Borrowing substantially from Frye's "garrison mentality" thesis and contrasting the different claims of wilderness and culture postulated by some three generations of Canadian writers, Jones modestly concludes that these authors "have arrived at the first days of creation ... of finding words for the obscure features of our own identity," and, in the process, have "been engaged in a more profound and ... original exploration of life than is frequently assumed."

King, Thomas, Cheryl Calver, and Helen Hoy, eds. *The Native in Literature: Canadian and Comparative Perspectives.* Toronto: ECW, 1987.

The twelve essays in this volume are arranged into three categories: background studies, studies of how particular white authors make use of native material, and studies of native narratives. That last grouping especially serves "to break down the traditional assumption that a discussion of the Native in literature means simply an examination of how the presence of the Native has influenced white literature."

Kroetsch, Robert. *The Lovely Treachery of Words: Essays Selected and New.* Toronto: Oxford UP, 1989.

These delightfully idiosyncratic essays are both personal musings by one of Canada's most interesting and experimental writers and intellectual assessments by one of the country's shrewdest critics. On topics diversely Canadian, they range from "The Fear of Women in Prairie Fiction: An Erotics of Space" to "For Play and Entrance: The Contemporary Canadian Long Poem."

MacLulich, T. D. *Between Europe and America: The Canadian Tradition in Fiction.* Toronto: ECW, 1988.

Contradicting the usual view that a coherent "tradition" of Canadian fiction arose only recently, MacLulich argues that the "first full flowering of the Canadian novel" occurred in the 1920s. This study asks the question of why and how a Canadian tradition emerged, especially in relationship to European cultural developments and North American geopolitics, and, essentially thematic, sees Canadian fiction emphasizing a (non-American) "value of community" and "traditional religious and ethical perspectives" supported by a "formal conservatism."

Marshall, Tom. *Harsh and Lovely Land: The Major Canadian Poets and the Making of a Canadian Tradition.* Vancouver: U of British Columbia P, 1979.

The tradition traced here is an English-Canadian one, which Marshall sees as falling into, roughly, four stages: first, the "dear bad poets" of the nineteenth century; then the T. S. Eliot–influenced early modernists; next, more specifically Canadian modernists; and, finally, a culminating "fourth stage, the explosion of innumerable new talents in the heady 1960s." That Marshall's study is now somewhat dated is one tribute to his fourth stage and the ongoing vitality of poetry in Canada.

McGregor, Gaile. *The Wacousta Syndrome: Explorations in the Canadian Langscape.* Toronto: U of Toronto P, 1985.

Neothematic criticism for an unthematic time, *The Wacousta Syndrome* exhibits this approach's besetting sins (selective readings and oversimplified generalizations) as well as its chief virtue (an intriguing mapping of new national territory, such as the relationship between Canadian literature and the visual arts).

Moss, John. *Sex and Violence in the Canadian Novel: The Ancestral Present.* Toronto: McClelland, 1977.

Canada's answer to Leslie Fiedler's *Love and Death in the American Novel*, this not always reliable thematic study argues in lively fashion that Canadian literature is distinguished by its "affinity for sex and violence, particularly as they relate to divers matters of identity."

Neuman, Shirley, and Smaro Kamboureli, eds. *A Mazing Space: Writing Canadian Women Writing.* Edmonton: Longspoon-NeWest, 1986.

Deriving from the 1983 conference Women and Words/Les Femmes et les Mots, this impressive collection brings together a number of critics and theorists who address issues of Canadian literature and feminism with sophistication, insight, and often brilliance. Many essays are substantially influenced by French feminist theory or, more generally, poststructuralism and psychoanalysis.

New, W. H. *Dreams of Speech and Violence: The Art of the Short Story in Canada and New Zealand.* Toronto: U of Toronto P, 1987.

New seems to ask the question of how two societies that have "committed themselves historically to evolutionary or orderly development" can be both "riddled with violence" and hospitable to the creative tumult necessary for the production of the best fiction. New's comparative approach to the sociology of Canadian aesthetic production perceptively addresses the history of the short story in Canada (and New Zealand).

Petrone, Penny, ed. *First People, First Voices.* Toronto: U of Toronto P, 1983.

A collection of writing and speeches by Canadian Indians from the 1630s to 1980s, this volume marks a beginning in what should be the ongoing process of reprinting earlier native Canadian literatures. Many of the selections have power today, including the words of a Micmac chief (whose name is not recorded) who, in 1676, asked Chrestien Le Clercq, rhetorically: "For if France, as thou sayest, is a little terrestrial paradise, art thou sensible to leave it?"

Usmiani, Renate. *Second Stage: The Alternative Theatre Movement in Canada.* Vancouver: U of British Columbia P, 1983.

Focusing on both English-Canadian and Québec experimental theaters of the 1970s, *Second Stage* argues that "the alternative theatre movement has produced one of the most exciting phenomena ever to appear on the cultural scene of this country." The book provides a fascinating (if selective) overview of Canada's most innovative theater companies and the works they produced.

Periodicals

Well over two hundred Canadian periodicals (popular magazines as well as academic journals) are listed, along with subscription information, in the annual *Canadian Magazines for Everybody*, distributed by the Canadian Periodical Publishers' Association, 2 Stewart Street, Toronto, ON M5V 1H6 Canada (phone: 416 362-2546). Major traditional literary journals include *Canadian Literature, Canadian Poetry, Essays on Canadian Writing,* and *Studies in Canadian Literature.* Somewhat more experimental criticism can be found in *Line: A Journal of Contemporary Writing and Its Modernist Sources, Open Letter, Tessera,* and *Signature: A Journal of Theory and Canadian Literature.* The Annual Bibliography issues of the *Journal of Commonwealth Literature* and the Summer "Letters in Canada" issues of the *University of Toronto Quarterly* (highly selective overviews of the literature and scholarship produced during the previous year) are also useful. Finally, *Books in Canada* and *Quill and Quire* provide ongoing assessments of the current literary scene, while *Canadian Literature Index* and *Canadian Periodical Index* provide bibliographic coverage.

Ordering Canadian Books

Obtaining books and book information from Canada can be difficult. However, the annual *Canadian Studies* catalog, printed and distributed by several trade associations, offers considerable assistance. The catalog can be ordered from the Association of Canadian Publishers, 260 King St. West, Toronto, ON M5A 1K3 Canada, or Canadian Book Publishers' Council, 45 Charles Street East, 7th floor, Toronto, ON M4Y 1S2 Canada. This interdisciplinary list includes current offerings from many Canadian presses and has sections titled "Suggestions for Ordering Books from Canada" and "Sources for Canadian Books." Any of the suggested sources will mail books, as will many bookstores (when in Canada, find a good bookstore, meet the owner or manager, reach a mutually advantageous arrangement). I began ordering books years ago on that basis from Longhouse Book Shop (497 Bloor St. West, Toronto, ON M5S 1Y2 Canada; phone 416 921-9995) and have always found this establishment to be most helpful. Incidentally, Longhouse is listed in the *Canadian Studies* catalog, which notes that it has over 25,000 Canadian titles in stock and will accept Visa and Mastercard orders.

Canadian Studies in the United States

The American Council for Québec Studies publishes *Québec Studies*. For memberships and subscriptions, contact Professor Jane Moss, Department of Modern Languages, Colby College, Waterville, ME 04901. The Association for Canadian Studies in the United States (One Dupont Circle, Suite 620, Washington, DC 20036) publishes *The American Review of Canadian Studies* as well as a newsletter and sponsors a biennial Canadian studies conference.

CONTRIBUTORS

BARRY CAMERON is professor of English at the University of New Brunswick. He has published books on John Metcalf and Clark Blaise, edited *Studies in Canadian Literature*, and written many articles and reviews on Canadian poetry, fiction, and criticism.

ARNOLD E. DAVIDSON is research professor of Canadian studies at Duke University. He is the author of *Mordecai Richler*, coeditor of *The Art of Margaret Atwood*, and has written books on Joseph Conrad and Jean Rhys. He has published some seventy articles, mainly on Canadian literature, in journals in Canada, Britain, France, Japan, and the United States.

BARBARA GODARD is associate professor of English and women's studies at York University. She is author of *The Listening Eye: Audrey Thomas, Her Life and Work* (forthcoming), editor of *Gynocritics/Gynocritiques: Feminist Approaches to Canadian and Quebec Women Writers*, and founding editor of the feminist critical collective *Tessera*. She has written on English-Canadian, Québécoise, and native Canadian writers and feminist critical theory and has translated into English works by Antonine Maillet, Yolande Villemaire, Louky Bersianik, and Nicole Brossard.

TERRY GOLDIE, associate professor of English at York University, has published widely on Canadian, Australian, New Zealand, African, and West Indian literatures. He is a contributing editor of *Books in Canada* and reviews theater regularly for radio, newspapers, and magazines. His most recent work is *Fear and Temptation: The Image of the Indigene in Canadian, Australian, and New Zealand Literatures.*

KAREN GOULD is director of women's studies and professor of French at Bowling Green State University. She is the author of *Claude Simon's Mythic Muse* and *Writing in the Feminine: Feminism and Experimental Writing in Quebec*, is coeditor of *Orion Blinded: Essays on Claude Simon*, and has published widely on Québec women writers and feminist theory. She is also editor of the interdisciplinary journal *Québec Studies*.

MARY JEAN GREEN is professor of French at Dartmouth College, where she has also chaired the Women's Studies Program. Her books on French literature include *Louis Guilloux: An Artisan of Language* and *Fiction in the Historical Present: French Writers and the Thirties*. Past editor of *Québec Studies*, she has written extensively on Québec fiction and is working on a book on Québec women writers.

DAVID M. HAYNE is emeritus professor of French at the University of Toronto and a fellow of the Royal Society of Canada. He has published more than a hundred books, articles, and book reviews on the literature of Québec.

LINDA HUTCHEON is professor of English and comparative literature at the University of Toronto. She has written extensively on Canadian fiction, and has chapters in the *Literary History of Canada* and the *Canadian Encyclopedia*. Her books include *Narcissistic Narrative: The Metafictional Paradox, Formalism and the Freudian Aesthetic, A Theory of Parody, A Poetics of Postmodernism*, and *The Canadian Postmodern: A Study of Contemporary English-Canadian Fiction*.

PATRICK IMBERT is professor of French at the University of Ottawa. He has published two books, *Sémiotique et description balzacienne* and *Roman québécois contemporain et clichés*, as well as numerous articles in *Semiotica, Littérature, The Canadian Review of Comparative Literature*, and other journals.

LORNA IRVINE is associate professor of English and American studies at George Mason University. She is the author of *Sub/Version* and guest-edited an issue of the *American Review of Canadian Studies* devoted to women in Canada. She has published many articles on Canadian writers and is working on a book on modernity and Canadian fiction.

D. G. JONES's many volumes of poetry include *Under the Thunder the Flowers Light Up the Earth*, which won the Governor General's Award. He is the author of *Butterfly on Rock: A Study of Themes and Images in Canadian Literature*, a translator of Québec poetry, and founding editor of the bilingual poetry journal *Ellipse*. He teaches in the *Département de lettres et communications* at the University of Sherbrooke.

W. J. KEITH is professor of English at University College, University of Toronto. He is the author of numerous books and articles on British and Canadian literature, including *Canadian Literature in English*. From 1976 until 1985 he edited the *University of Toronto Quarterly*, and was elected a fellow of the Royal Society of Canada in 1979.

ANNETTE KOLODNY, dean of the faculty of humanities and professor of English at the University of Arizona, is author of the award-winning studies *Lay of the Land* and *The Land before Her*, as well as numerous articles on women writers and feminist theory. A collection of her essays, *Dancing through the Minefield*, is to be published by Indiana University Press.

ROBERT KROETSCH is a poet, novelist, and critic. His novel *The Studhorse Man* won the Governor General's Award. He was a founding editor of the postmodern journal *boundary 2* and is professor of English and writer in residence at the University of Manitoba. Many of his books are discussed extensively in various essays in this volume.

CAMILLE LA BOSSIÈRE teaches British, Canadian, and United States literature at the University of Ottawa. Author of *Joseph Conrad and the Science of Unknowing* and *The Dark Age of Enlightenment: An Essay on Québec Literature*, he has edited *On Eighteenth-Century Literature* and *Translation in Canadian Literature*. His study of Montaigne, Carlyle, Emerson, Melville, and Conrad, *The Conflict of Convictions*, is scheduled to appear under the imprint of Bucknell University Press.

PAULA GILBERT LEWIS is professor of French and dean of the College of Arts and Sciences, George Mason University. She is the author of *The Aesthetics of Stéphane Mallarmé in Relation to His Public* and *The Literary Vision of Gabrielle Roy: An Analysis of Her Works*, and the editor of *Traditionalism, Nationalism, and Feminism: Women Writers of Québec*.

ROBIN MCGRATH is assistant professor of English at the University of Alberta. Her publications include *Paper Stays Put: A Collection of Inuit Writing* and *Canadian Inuit Literature: The Development of a Tradition*.

JANE MOSS is professor of modern foreign languages at Colby College. She has published numerous articles and reviews on Québec theater and fiction in *The American Review of Canadian Studies, Québec Studies, Canadian Literature, The French Review, Modern Language Studies, Women and Performance*, and *The Journal of Canadian Culture.* She is especially interested in feminist theater and, in addition to her work on Québec, has published on French women's theater in *Signs.*

SHIRLEY NEUMAN is professor of English at the University of Alberta and founding editor of Longspoon Press and NeWest Press. Co-editor of *A Mazing Space: Writing Canadian Women Writing*, she is the author of numerous books and articles on Canadian, English, and United States literature, and is working on a book on the novels of Gertrude Stein.

W. H. NEW is professor of English at the University of British Columbia and editor of the critical quarterly *Canadian Literature.* His published works include *Articulating West, Malcolm Lowry, Canadian Short Fiction, Dreams of Speech and Violence: The Art of the Short Story in Canada and New Zealand*, and *A History of Canadian Literature.*

PENNY PETRONE, professor of English education at Lakehead University, is the author of *First People, First Voices* and *Northern Voices.* She is working on a critical book on Canadian Indian literature for Oxford University Press.

ANDRÉ J. SENÉCAL is associate professor of French and director of Québec studies at the University of Vermont. He has written *A Reader's Guide to Québec Studies*, a multidisciplinary bibliography, as well as bibliographies on Québec government publications. He is also the author of numerous articles on Québec fiction and is writing a book on Anne Hébert.

PHILIP STRATFORD, who teaches English at the University of Montréal, is a well-known commentator on and translator of Québec literature. His comparison of Canadian novels in French and English, *All the Polarities: Comparative Studies in Contemporary Canadian Novels in French and English*, won the Gabrielle Roy Prize for criticism in 1987, and his translation of *Un Second Souffle*, by Diane Hébert, won a 1988 Governor General's Award.

INDEX